The Rodeo and Hollywood

THE RODEO AND HOLLYWOOD

Rodeo Cowboys on Screen and Western Actors in the Arena

Jim Ryan

McFarland & Company, Inc., Publishers
Jefferson, North Carolina, and London

The present work is a reprint of the illustrated case bound edition of The Rodeo and Hollywood: Rodeo Cowboys on Screen and Western Actors in the Arena, *first published in 2006 by McFarland.*

LIBRARY OF CONGRESS CATALOGUING-IN-PUBLICATION DATA

Ryan, Jim, 1939–
The rodeo and Hollywood : rodeo cowboys on screen and Western actors in the arena / Jim Ryan.
  p.   cm.
Includes bibliographical references and index.

ISBN 978-0-7864-7523-0
softcover : acid free paper ∞

1. Western films — United States — History and criticism.
2. Rodeo performers — United States — Biography.
I. Title.
PN1995.9.W4R93   2013   791.43'6278 — dc22   2006015606

BRITISH LIBRARY CATALOGUING DATA ARE AVAILABLE

© 2006 Jim Ryan. All rights reserved

No part of this book may be reproduced or transmitted in any form or by any means, electronic or mechanical, including photocopying or recording, or by any information storage and retrieval system, without permission in writing from the publisher.

On the cover: Rex Allen (1955 San Antonio rodeo souvenir program cover).

Manufactured in the United States of America

*McFarland & Company, Inc., Publishers
Box 611, Jefferson, North Carolina 28640
www.mcfarlandpub.com*

To my wife Romella,
the wind beneath my wings, who assisted
and supported my efforts with love.

To my children and grandchildren
with the hope that they will understand a bit
of how things were, "when I was a boy."

To my late friend Clint Brown,
who taught me that a true fan
gives as well as receives.

Acknowledgments

The author expresses his thanks to librarians and historians nationwide whose replies to correspondence, responses to telephone inquiries and assistance during in-person visits provided pieces of the story.

Special thanks to Gerald F. Vaughn, whose 1976 *Rodeo News* article "Rodeoing Back Then — Movie Cowboys' Love Affair with Rodeo" broke ground on the subject.

A heap of Western gratitude to the next generation's Meegen and Michael McClure, and Quenten and Lana VanEgeren for their endless patience as computer mentors.

My first rodeo was very special. I must thank childhood friend Steve Dunlap, who sparked the interest; Mr. and Mrs. Glen Gray, and son Doug, who made it possible; Mom and Dad, who consented to a boy's dream; Walter Dill and Mary (Bonzagni) Dill, who made it happen; and Gene Autry, who more than lived up to a boy's expectations.

The following archives, libraries, museums, historical societies and photo shops were also very helpful: Albuquerque Public Library, Albuquerque, New Mexico; American Heritage Center, University of Wyoming, Laramie, Wyoming; Ardmore Public Library, Ardmore, Oklahoma; Arizona State Library, Phoenix, Arizona; Boston Public Library, Boston, Massachusetts; Buffalo Bill Historical Center, Cody, Wyoming; Burt County Museum, Tekamah, Nebraska; California Rodeo Museum, Salinas, California; California State Library, Sacramento, California; Camp Pendleton Library, Pendleton, California; Canon City Public Library, Canon City, Colorado; Canyon County Historical Society Museum and Archives, Nampa, Idaho; Carbon County Historical Society, Red Lodge, Montana; Casey Tibbs Foundation, Fort Pierre, South Dakota; Center for American History, The University of Texas-Austin, Texas; Center for the Study of the Western Experience, Oklahoma City, Oklahoma; Central Arkansas Library System, Little Rock, Arkansas; Cheyenne Frontier Days Old West Museum, Cheyenne, Wyoming (Christina Bird, Robert D. Grant); Country Music Foundation Library and Media Center, Nashville, Tennessee; Denver Public Library, Denver, Colorado; Douglas County Historical Society Library/Archives Center, Omaha, Nebraska; Dublin Public Library, Dublin, Texas; Dublin Rodeo Heritage Museum, Dublin, Texas; Eddie Brandt's Saturday Matinee, North Hollywood, California; Fort Worth Public Library, Fort Worth, Texas; The Gene Autry Oklahoma Historical Museum, Gene Autry, Oklahoma; Hill Memorial Library, Louisiana State University, Baton Rouge, Louisiana; Houston Metropolitan Research Center, Houston Public Library, Houston, Texas; Idaho State Historical Society, Boise, Idaho; Idol Rashid Memorial Library, Fort Madison, Iowa; Illinois State Historical Library, Springfield, Illinois; Jerry Ohlinger's Movie Material Store, New York, New York; Kansas Sports Hall of Fame, Abilene, Kansas; Kansas State Historical Society Center,

Topeka, Kansas; Klamath County Library, Klamath Falls, Oregon; Lancaster Historical Society, Lancaster, Wisconsin; Los Angeles Public Library, Los Angeles, California; Louisiana State Library, Baton Rouge, Louisiana; Louisville Public Library, Louisville, Kentucky; Marland Estate Museum, 101 Ranch Room, Ponca City, Oklahoma; Memphis Shelby County Library, Memphis, Tennessee; Minneapolis Public Library, Minneapolis, Minnesota; Mohave County Historical Society, Kingman, Arizona; Montana State Historical Society Library, Helena, Montana; National Cowgirl Museum and Hall of Fame, Fort Worth, Texas; Nelson Museum, Cheyenne, Wyoming; Nevada Historical Society, Reno, Nevada; Nevada State Library, Carson City, Nevada; North Platte Public Library, North Platte, Nebraska; Oklahoma Historical Society, Oklahoma City, Oklahoma; Old Greer County Museum, Mangum, Oklahoma; Old Town Museum, Elk City, Oklahoma; Oregon State Library, Salem, Oregon; Palm Springs Historical Society, Palm Springs, California; Pendleton Public Library Special Collections, Pendleton, Oregon; Pikes Peak Library District, Colorado Springs, Colorado; Porter Henderson Library, Angelo State University, San Angelo, Texas; Professional Rodeo Cowboys Association-Media, Colorado Springs, Colorado; ProRodeo Hall of Fame, Colorado Springs, Colorado; Pueblo Public Library, Pueblo, Colorado; Rodeo Historical Society, Oklahoma City, Oklahoma; St. Joseph Public Library, St. Joseph, Missouri; Sharlot Hall Museum, Prescott, Arizona; State Historical Society of Iowa, Des Moines, Iowa; State Historical Society of Missouri, Columbia, Missouri; State Historical Society of Wisconsin — Archives Division, Madison, Wisconsin; Stephen Sally, New York, New York; Stewart's Photography, Colorado Springs, Colorado; Switzerland County Public Library, Vevay, Indiana; Texas Department of Corrections, Huntsville, Texas; Texas Sports Hall of Fame, Waco, Texas; Tom Mix Museum, Dewey, Oklahoma; Tucson Rodeo Parade Museum, Tucson, Arizona; University of Nevada Las Vegas Library, Las Vegas, Nevada; University of Oregon Library, Eugene, Oregon; University of Texas at Arlington Library, Arlington, Texas; The Vernon Daily Record, Vernon, Texas; Waco-McLennan County Library, Waco, Texas; Warren Air Force Base, Cheyenne, Wyoming; Washington State Library, Olympia, Washington; "The Western Horseman," Colorado Springs, Colorado; Wyoming Division of Cultural Resources, Cheyenne, Wyoming; Wyoming Historical Society, Cheyenne, Wyoming.

I also thank these rodeos for their contributions and assistance: Arkansas State Fair, Livestock Show and Rodeo, Little Rock, Arkansas; Nebraskaland Days/Buffalo Bill Rodeo, North Platte, Nebraska; Pikes Peak or Bust Rodeo, Colorado Springs, Colorado; River City Roundup/Ak-Sar-Ben Rodeo, Omaha, Nebraska; Snake River Stampede, Nampa, Idaho; Southeastern Livestock Exposition Rodeo, Montgomery, Alabama; Tri-State Rodeo, Fort Madison, Iowa (Larry Roberts).

These individuals also deserve a special mention: Lee Aaker; Anna Lee Mills Aldred; Rex Allen, Jr.; Dale L. Ames, "Galaxy Patrol"; Michael Ansara; Frank Bogert; Peter Breck; Rachel Bascom Broad; Peter Brown; Polly Mills Burson; Kenny Call; Harry Carey, Jr.; Bill Catching; Cecil and Wayne Cornish; Johnny Crawford; Ivan Cury; Marge Earlywine; Richard and Eleanor Eaton; Larry Floyd, for Willie Phelps; Shirley Flynn; Robert Fontana; Jack French; Audrey O'Brien Griffin; Cynthia Brown Hale; Ty Hardin; Kelo Henderson; Patricia Hildebrand; Carolyn Colborn Holden; Robert Horton; Whitey Hughes; Will Hutchins; Dick Jones; Janet Keith; Jon Locke; Al Mann; Boyd Magers; Cleo Weisel Meek; Jan Merlin; Montie Montana, Jr.; Bruce Moore; Jean and Gary Orr; Corky Randall; Dale Robertson; Kevin Ryan; Nancy Kelley Sheppard; Lee Silliman; Wayne Spencer; Mary Ann Mayfield Stephen; Sharon Tarr; Buck Taylor; Jerry Ann Portwood Taylor; Clint Walker; Jim Willett; and Gloria Winters.

Contents

Acknowledgments	vii
A Note on Institutional Names	x
Introduction	1
I Rodeo Personalities with a Hollywood Connection	7
II Individual Movie and Television Actors Performing at Rodeos	101
III Television Casts Performing at Rodeos	227
IV Rodeo-Related Films	311
Appendix A — Golden Age Rodeo Personalities	343
Appendix B — 25 Rodeos Presenting Western Stars	357
Appendix C — 11 Special Rodeos	363
References	387
Index	393

A Note on Institutional Names

The names of some halls of fame have changed over time. Many inductions mentioned took place under previous designations. This volume uses the names interchangeably.

The National Cowboy and Western Heritage Museum, Oklahoma City, Oklahoma, was previously called the National Cowboy Hall of Fame. A Rodeo Hall and a Hall of Great Western Performers are located within the museum. For brevity, this institution is referred to as the National Cowboy Museum.

The National Cowgirl Museum and Hall of Fame, Fort Worth, Texas, was previously called the National Cowgirl Hall of Fame and was, at one time, located in Hereford, Texas. The museum continues to feature a hall of fame.

The Santa Clarita, California, Western Walk of Fame was previously called the Newhall Western Walk of Fame. The newer designation emphasizes the county rather than the city. The Western Walk of Fame remains in the same location.

Introduction

Rodeo's earliest ancestors are cowboy boasting and informal contests at the end of roundups and open-range cattle drives. Gradually, these cowboy contests became part of community celebrations. At first, rodeos were confined mostly to the West and Midwest, but they moved eastward as promoters sensed their growing potential to draw a paying audience. By the 1920s, Madison Square Garden presented rodeo.

Parallel to the development of rodeo's contests, Wild West shows, which emphasized exhibitions, enjoyed popularity. Perhaps the quintessential Wild West entertainer was "Buffalo Bill" Cody, whose true-life exploits were many but who gained his widespread fame as the hero of dime novels. According to author Bill Russell, the public came as much to see Buffalo Bill as to see the historical recreations in his widely imitated show.

About the time of World War I, rodeo gained ascendancy over the Wild West show, but the spirit of Buffalo Bill lived on through celebrities' appearances in the rodeo arena. As the years went by and the world of entertainment changed, the "cowboy" stars of movies and television were more and more frequent guests at rodeos around the country. In turn, actual rodeo stars began appearing on screens both large and small.

Hollywood celebrities fit quite naturally into the rodeo lineup. To fill the time between events and relieve the tension of competition, entertainment has been a part of rodeo almost from the time that it became a spectator sport. Acts over the years included axe throwing, whip cracking, horseshoe pitching, tumbling, archery, horseback football and a variety of trained animal and musical acts. U.S. presidents, sports stars and such diverse entertainers as Harpo Marx, Arthur Godfrey, *Star Trek*'s "Mr. Spock," clown Emmett Kelly, Jr., Elvis Presley and Lassie have lent their celebrity to rodeos.

The appearance at rodeos of movie and TV Western stars, from the 1930s into the 1970s, generated a negative response from some rodeo purists. Organizers hoped that a star's popularity would draw a sufficient crowd to meet expenses. There was resentment that contestants were not the stars of their sport. Contesting rodeo cowboys, paying an entry fee to risk injury, failure and lack of prize money, often looked down upon entertainers who performed 30 minutes or less in relative safety for substantial pay.

Yet, the lot of rodeo-headlining Western stars was not entirely carefree. Occasionally, a star was cheated out of his paycheck. Juggling film and rodeo commitments could lead to transportation nightmares. However uncomfortable outdoor rodeo weather, the show must go on. Merely threatening weather often reduced gate receipts. A star who broke attendance records at one rodeo might face sparse crowds at the next. The indoor "tanbark" mix of dirt, other materials and animal droppings could affect the voice and health of those exposed over time. A star wished for the timely arrival of his horse and back-up musicians. If dependent upon local support, he could only hope that short rehearsal time would produce an adequate performance. Action acts had a high risk of injury; failure-prone sound systems could impair any act; and riders shared concern that blaring bands, popping flashbulbs and audience noise would agitate their mounts. Indoor sub-surfaces were often slippery. Finally, the presence of mean-tempered rodeo roughstock sometimes led to the unexpected. Suffering from a cough, dodging roughstock and scraping mud or excrement from his expensive boots, a star might wonder if rodeo engagements were worth *any* fee.

On the positive side, the excitement created by popular Western stars made new fans for rodeo. Stars also lifted the spirits of untold numbers of disabled and disadvantaged persons, especially youngsters. Rodeos, during the heyday of Western films and TV shows, were as much a part of the cowboy phenomenon as stick horses, cap pistols and Saturday matinees.

In July of 1995, this author surveyed for the last time Boston Garden's parquet floor and rafters strung with championship sports banners. Except for our tour group, the arena was deserted, yielding as Boston's major indoor event venue to the new Fleet Center. The familiar Garden confines recalled hours spent at the circus, ice shows, sporting events, concerts and college graduation. Predominant among the flood of pleasant memories were the 1949 and 1950 World's Championship rodeos. Vivid impressions endure of the grand entry, rodeo events, trick riders and clowns. Most unforgettable to a ten-year-old was the thrill of seeing Gene Autry and Champion.

Schooling and military assignments separated me from rodeo until the last of the movie and TV cowboy stars were relinquishing the rodeo spotlight to country music singers. In the mid–1970s, I revived a boyhood interest in movie and TV Westerns as a hobby. At the 1980 Western Heritage Award ceremonies in Oklahoma City, Gene Autry's wife, Ina, introduced me to Gene. Thirty years after my rodeos, Gene recalled fond memories of his rodeo years. I've been fortunate to meet other Western star rodeo performers, as well as rodeo personalities, some of whom have a Hollywood connection.

In the late 1990s, when I was employed by the ProRodeo Hall of Fame, I learned more about the now-past era when favorite Western stars appeared at rodeos. Tapping sources across the country for pieces of the story has been a rewarding experience.

This book provides career profiles of both actors and rodeo cowboys who crossed over between acting and cowboying from the late 1930s to the 1970s. It also covers films with rodeo themes and characters.

The first section, "Rodeo Personalities with a Hollywood Connection," provides biographies of those whose work in rodeo or Wild West shows led to work in film and television. Some of these men and women remained principally rodeo or Wild West performers; others became better known for their work in Hollywood.

The second section, "Individual Movie and Television Actors Performing at Rodeos," profiles actors whose work in Western films or television series led to individual appearances at rodeos and Wild West shows. These actors usually appeared alone, rather than with their co-stars, and often they appeared in character; for example, Michael Ansara performed at rodeos in the costume of his Indian character, Cochise, from the television series *Broken Arrow*.

Television actors who appeared in America's best-known and longest-running television Westerns often made rodeo appearances in the company of one or more other cast members. For example, Lorne Greene and Dan Blocker of Bonanza usually appeared together. On the other hand, Pernell Roberts and Michael Landon usually appeared solo. Because their careers were so intertwined, it is difficult to cover the rodeo appearances of any of these actors individually, and for that reason the book includes a third section, "Television Casts Performing at Rodeos." In this section the reader will find profiles of the careers and rodeo appearances of the casts of eighteen long-running television series. Regardless of whether the actors in this section usually appeared solo or with other cast members, all are covered within the entry for their particular show.

A reader looking for information on a particular actor should begin with the index, which will refer the reader to the proper section of text.

The fourth section covers rodeo-related films. Following that section are appendices covering Golden Age rodeo personalities; 25 rodeos presenting Western stars; and 11 special rodeos.

William F. "Buffalo Bill" Cody, with Wild West Show tepees in background, c. 1913 (courtesy Buffalo Bill Historical Center, Cody, WY. P.69.1543).

"He who has brought the romance of America to young America has not lived in vain…"
— Buffalo Bill

I

Rodeo Personalities with a Hollywood Connection

ART ACORD (1890–1931) Art Acord spent his early years in Indian Territory (Oklahoma) and in Utah. As a teen, he learned horsemanship, cattle handling and manly conflict resolution on ranches. By his early twenties, he had performed in the Dick Stanley–Bud Atkinson Wild West Show and had won rodeo trophies. With Hoot Gibson, Art performed stunts and wrote stories for the growing silent movie industry. He worked rodeos, Wild West Shows and ranches on a seasonal basis. Grange B. McKinney's book *Art Acord and the Movies* best documents Art's rodeo accomplishments, information on which is scanty.

For the 1912 Klamath Falls (Oregon) Round Up, Art and another cowboy traveled hundreds of miles of ranches, Indian reservations and open country to test-ride over 100 horses, selecting about 20 as contest-worthy. At the rodeo, Art won the bucking horse contest's $250 prize money on Cyclone, and exhibited fancy riding skills. Bulldogging, he held a steer with his teeth, hands in the air. At Pendleton's 1912 Roundup, he placed third in bronc riding, won the bulldogging event, and competed in the maverick race, Roman standing race and drunken ride.

Around 1912, Art got film parts in addition to stunt work. He starred as Buck Parvin in filmed versions of Charles Van Loan's *Saturday Evening Post* stories. Seriously injured, he recovered. In 1916, he competed at the New York Stampede. A day later, he helped judge Yakima Canutt's wager ride on "Fox." In 1917, he co-starred with Theda Bara in *Cleopatra*. About this time, his marriage ended in divorce, and his life began to be controlled by alcohol.

He was discharged from World War I Army service in 1919. Following a Wild West tour, he signed for a Universal film series. His 18-chapter serial *The Moon Riders* was applauded. Following a group of two-reel films and some historical serials, he starred in more than a dozen hard-riding, action-packed Universal Blue Streak Westerns, considered among the best from the 1920s. These films made Art a top Universal cowboy star, and he was honored with a star on Hollywood's Walk of Fame.

Art's personality was a mix of admirable qualities and volatility aggravated by alcohol. He was generous to old rodeo pals, and rescued an actress from a dangerous oil well fire scene. He was known for real-life fistfights, some with other Western stars. On more than one occasion, the studio dismissed him for drinking. When a second marriage failed and his contract was not renewed, his behavior precluded his hiring by any but the lowest budget independent studios. In the late 1920s, Art's alcoholism, physical aggressiveness

Lobby card for Art Acord's film *Loco Luck* (1927) (courtesy Eddie Brandt's).

and shady activities led to brushes with the law. His film career ended with the silent film age. He died in Mexico under mysterious circumstances.

PRAIRIE LILY ALLEN (c. 1888–1951)   Born in Tennessee, Lily Allen moved to Chicago. Riding broncs for Dubrock's Wild West and Indian Show, she wore a mask to conceal her identity from her parents. She worked on a motion picture in Chicago. She also rode in circus concerts and rodeos. At the 1916 New York Stampede, she won the title of champion cowgirl bronc rider; she was among the best in the country. For a time, she was married to a rodeo contestant and movie player, William "Slim" Allen.

JERRY AMBLER (1912–1958)   Jerry Ambler was born at Minburn, Alberta, on his parent's farm-ranch. As a youngster, he drove a 12-head team, broke wild horses and wrote a school composition on his desire to ride broncs. At age 16, he tested rodeo-bound wild horses, and he won day money riding broncs in adult competition. He was wiry at less than 140 pounds. By 1935 he had won saddle bronc, steer riding and all-around cowboy championships. At Calgary, he was champion twice in saddle bronc riding and three times in bull riding. He often flew to rodeos. In late 1941, he piloted Gene Autry to Klamath Falls to purchase rodeo stock. In the 1940s, he won three saddle bronc riding championships at

Boston Garden. At Portland, Oregon, he placed in the 1943 finals in all five events en route to winning that rodeo's all-around cowboy honors.

During World War II, he operated a dairy and commuted to a Portland shipyard. Returning to rodeo, he won the IRA and RCA saddle bronc world championships in 1946. He received a $1,000 award from Selznick International Studios, promoting their film *Duel in the Sun*. In 1947, he was IRA world champion saddle bronc rider, placing third in the RCA's standings. In 1948, he was Pendleton's saddle bronc riding champion. In Burbank, California, he and Wag Blessing operated the Pickwick Café, a hangout for cowboys who alternated rodeo and movie work. Jerry endorsed Camel cigarettes, Ambler and Blessing Western shirts and Jerry Ambler spurs by P.M. Kelly. His films included *The Boy from Indiana* (1950) and *Beyond the Purple Hills* (1950). Jerry died in an automobile accident. He is an inductee of the Rodeo Hall at the National Cowboy Museum.

BOB BAKER (1910–75)   Born in Forest City, Iowa, Stanley Leland Weed moved west with his family at age 14. He worked on cattle ranches, acquiring the nickname "Tumble." Working as a dude ranch guide, he rode broncs and bulls, and roped calves at rodeos. Serving in the U.S. Army Cavalry at Fort Bliss, Texas, he learned to play the guitar, and he sang for pay on El Paso radio. Discharged in 1934, he was a guide at the Grand Canyon and competed at more rodeos. The following year, he worked at Chicago's radio station WLS, but subsequently returned to the Grand Canyon.

Under the name Bob Baker, he starred in a series of 12 Universal musical Western films from 1937 to 1939, acquiring his own Pinto mount, Apache. Among his greatest assets as a Western star were his cowboy appearance, riding ability and singing. He did most of his own film stunts, but his acting lacked polish. The studio stopped promoting his stardom. From late 1939 through 1940, he made six Universal "trio Westerns" with Johnny Mack Brown and Fuzzy Knight.

Following a brief second tour of military service (1940–41), he served Flagstaff, Arizona, as a law enforcement officer, returning to Hollywood periodically until 1944 for small parts, stunt work and doubling on a few films. He sold Apache to Montie Montana and resumed his police officer duties for about a decade. He operated saddle shops in Arizona until health problems forced his retirement. He died of cancer at Prescott, Arizona.

Western film star Bob Baker.

TILLIE BALDWIN (1888–1958)   Born in Norway, Tillie Baldwin came to America at age 14, never having seen a bucking horse. A hairdresser in New York, she visited a movie set where Will Rogers let her ride a horse. She joined the 101 Ranch Wild West Show for a season. Following a winter with Bison pictures in California, she alternated Wild West Shows and rodeos. Without hobbled stirrups, she won cowgirl bronc riding at a Los Angeles rodeo. At Pendleton in 1912 and elsewhere, she won both trick riding and bronc riding. Adding bulldogging to her skills, she toured fairs with a Wild West act. Later, she managed Fred Stone's ranch. She is an inductee of the Rodeo Hall at the National Cowboy Museum.

BUZZ BARTON (1913–80) William Andrew Lamoreaux was born in Gallatin, Missouri, on his parents' farm and later moved to Newhall, California. He acquired riding and roping skills early, reportedly performing at rodeos as a trick rider while a pre-teen. The freckle-faced lad came under the tutelage of Andy Jauregui, who outfitted him in name-inscribed chaps, boots and a Western hat. Using his motion picture contacts, Andy was instrumental in getting him into the movies. From about age 12, he was doubling juveniles and women. During the years 1926–27, he appeared in films for Rayart studios, supporting Western star and friend Jack Perrin. His name was shortened to Billy Lamarr. In the spring of 1927, F.B.O. Studios changed his name to Buzz Barton and starred him in a silent Western film series (1927–29), with titles emphasizing his juvenile, red-haired persona (e.g., *The Boy Rider*, *The Little Buckaroo*, *The Fightin' Redhead*, *The Bantam Cowboy*, *Rough Ridin' Red* and *The Freckled Rascal*). These action-laden films showcased Buzz's genuine riding and roping skills.

Youthful Western star Buzz Barton (courtesy Eddie Brandt's).

The silent film era, however, was giving way to "talkies." In the 1930s, Buzz supported stars Yakima Canutt, Rex Bell and Wally Wales. He appeared in RKO's *Powdersmoke Range* (1935) and with circuses in the East. During this period, he competed in rodeos, where he is reported to have won individual rodeo championships in bronc riding and steer wrestling. With Buck Jones and Red Ryder, he endorsed Daisy air rifles. Following World War II Naval service, he worked on ranches. In 1956, he reportedly returned to California and served the film industry as a horse wrangler.

TEXAS ROSE BASCOM (c. 1922–93) Born in Mississippi, Rose Flynt was raised in Columbia, Missouri, and married bull rider Weldon Bascom. Initially self-taught to trick rope, she performed at rodeos across the country. She eventually painted her clothing, boots and ropes with fluorescent colors, adding fringes for visual impact. Under black lights, her regalia displayed glowing colors in motion. "Most photogenic" in her Los Angeles modeling class, Rose, in a white buckskin costume, was hired by the U.S.O. For several months, she toured military hospital wards, performing up to 34 shows a day. She roped at the Hollywood Canteen and at Leo Carrillo's rodeos. She performed on early TV and in the film *The Time, the Place, and the Girl* (1946). In *Smokey River Serenade* (1947), she twirls her rope in a talent contest. She entertained overseas military personnel with Tex Ritter, Johnny Grant and Bob Hope. In the early 1950s, she joined Bill Elliott's rodeos and stage shows. She performed with film stars in the "Western Hall of Fame" (a live event) and roped on a daytime TV show with Leo Carrillo and Harry Morgan. She had a role in *The Lawless Rider* (1954), directed by Yakima Canutt, did theater shows with Western actor Tom London and performed with Rex Allen. Rose was inducted into the National Cowgirl Hall of Fame.

SAMMY BAUGH (1914–) Earning his nickname, "Slingin' Sam," as a baseball third baseman, Sammy Baugh gained fame as a football quarterback. He led Texas Christian

Texas Rose Bascom (top, center) in a scene from the film *The Time, the Place, and the Girl* (Warner Bros., 1946) (courtesy Rachel Bascom Broad).

University to victory in the first Sugar Bowl and earned All-American honors. He was also a calf roper on the university rodeo team. His Washington Redskins won two world championships and four division titles during his 16-season Hall of Fame professional career. He starred in Republic Studios' 12-chapter Western serial *King of the Texas Rangers* (1941), but decided against further moviemaking. While playing professional football, he roped at rodeos. Retired to his Double Mountain Ranch in Texas, he coached football and rodeo at Hardin-Simmons University. For many years, he was a top amateur roper in his West Texas home area.

FLOYD BAZE (c. 1935–) Floyd Baze competed at rodeos for more than 20 years, primarily in saddle bronc riding and steer wrestling. He was a stuntman first on TV series such as *Stoney Burke* and doubled for Neville Brand on TV's *Laredo*. In films, he doubled Lee Marvin in *Monte Walsh* (1970) and William Holden in *The Wild Rovers* (1971), among others. On weekends and between pictures, he competed at rodeos. He and his son Larry doubled for Robert Preston and Steve McQueen, father and son characters, in *Junior Bonner* (1972).

BERTHA BLANCETT (1883–1979) Bertha Blancett was born in Cleveland, Ohio, and moved to Colorado. She competed, without stirrup hobbles, in cowgirl bronc riding

Sammy Baugh (right) in a scene from Republic Pictures' serial *King of the Texas Rangers* (1941). Other players are Kermit Maynard (left) and Duncan Renaldo (seated) (courtesy of Eddie Brandt's).

at Cheyenne in 1904 and 1905. She then joined Wild West Shows. She and her husband Dell did stunts for two years with the Bison Moving Picture Company. Dell was killed in World War I. At Pendleton, Bertha won the women's relay race three years in succession and twice won the bronc riding. She performed exhibitions and Roman riding at rodeos and Wild West shows for years. She became a Yosemite National Park guide, and then a rodeo pickup person. Bertha is an inductee at the Rodeo Hall of the National Cowboy Museum.

FAYE BLESSING (1920–99) Faye Johnson was born at Craig, Colorado. When she was in her mid-teens, her mother passed away and the family moved to Burbank, California. With a carload of wild horses, her father established the Lazy 3 Ranch and Riding Academy, and provided animals for motion pictures. Faye was inspired by the rodeo trick riding of Vern and Myrtle Goodrich. Following high school, she and two brothers rode and roped in California. Throughout the 1940s and well into the 1950s, she trick-rode at rodeos across the country. For seven years she performed at Madison Square Garden and Boston Garden. In 1944, she married rodeo contestant Wag Blessing, 1947 world champion bull rider and a movie stuntman. Faye doubled for Rhonda Fleming and Ginger Rogers, and for Betty Hutton as Texas Guinan in *Incendiary Blonde* (1945). Her long blonde hair personified the golden age of rodeo. Astride her caramel tan and white spotted horse with a

Trick rider Faye Blessing at the Colorado State Fair Rodeo in the late 1940s (courtesy Doubleday Collection, Wyoming Division of Cultural Resources, Cheyenne. Neg. #401).

natural black eye, she performed at rodeos with outstanding contract acts, contestants and Western star headliners. She publicized rodeos, rode in the quadrille and, when at Boston, raced at Rockingham Park. She endorsed Western clothing, saddles and Stetson hats featuring a "Faye Blessing crease." She worked on war bond drives. Two of her later performances were in Mexico City and at the Chicago Amphitheater. Faye was inducted into the National Cowgirl Hall of Fame.

MAY BOSS (c. 1930–) May Boss trick rode at rodeos, including Cheyenne, the Los Angeles Coliseum, Madison Square Garden and Boston Garden. A six-decade stuntwoman, she instructed Mamie Van Doren for her part in *Born Reckless* (1958) and stunted for Westerns from *Fort Dobbs* (1958) through *Wild Wild West* (1999).

Buff Brady, Jr., at the 1956 Boston Garden rodeo (courtesy Richard and Eleanor Eaton. Used with permission).

TILLIE AND ED BOWMAN Tillie and Ed Bowman both were ranch-raised and participated in rodeos. In the Los Angeles area, Ed contributed to Western movies for Bison films. He also traveled with the 101 Ranch Wild West Show. In the late teens, he returned to Hollywood, working with several Western stars. In 1921, Ed and Tillie were married and both worked in motion pictures. She began as a trick roper and later turned to bronc riding. The couple worked rodeos, Wild West Shows and circuses.

BUFF BRADY, JR. (1918– 2004) William Albert Brady, Jr., was the son of Big Buffalo Brady, rodeo competitor and performer, and contributor to early 1920s Western films. From age 16 through 1938, Buff, Jr., trick-rode and roped at the Ellensburg (Washington) Rodeo, where his dad and stepmother had performed since 1928. Buff, Jr., entertained at Prescott in 1940 and at Las Vegas Helldorado Days in 1941. In 1942, he was with Gene Autry's Flying A Ranch Rodeo and at the World's Championship Rodeo at New York, Boston and Buffalo. Throughout the 1940s,

Buff was a "regular" at rodeos, often appearing with his wife Ruby and teaming with Ray Berwick and Susie. In 1948, he made one of eight appearances at Los Angeles' Sheriff's Rodeo.

Everett Colborn endorsed Buff, Jr., as "the greatest rodeo act ever presented in anybody's arena." Employing colorful Western dress and beautiful mounts, Buff combined acrobatics with trick riding and roping. He roped moving horses and riders from horseback, on foot, on his back, standing on his head or while turning somersaults. He tap danced to the tune "Pony Boy, Pony Boy" while fancy roping. His riding included vaults, trick and fancy maneuvers and "going under the horse's belly."

Buff and friend Rex Rossi worked in both rodeo and Hollywood. At Republic Studios, he appeared in a serial and in Roy Rogers' *The Golden Stallion* (1949). He was also in Rex Allen's *The Rodeo King and the Senorita* (1951). He doubled Roy on episodes of TV's *The Roy Rogers Show*. For nine weeks in mid–1952, he performed with Tex Ritter's London show, "Texas." At 1955 rodeos, he sported long hair he had grown for his role as an Indian in the movie *The Indian Fighter*, performing his riding stunts in a horseback fight scene with star Kirk Douglas. He continued to appear at rodeos, but found more work in films and on Western TV series. He displays horsemanship skills as one of Burl Ives' mean-spirited sons in *The Big Country* (1958). He doubled Stewart Granger and Fess Parker, among others. He was also in *Silverado* (1985). Buff, Jr., is an inductee of the Rodeo Hall at the National Cowboy Museum.

Former rodeo rider X Brands in costume and make-up as "Pahoo," his role on TV's *Yancy Derringer*.

X BRANDS (1927–2000) X Brands (X was his true middle name) competed at rodeos primarily as a bareback rider. His first film was *The Wild One* (1954), and he doubled Bill Williams on TV's *The Adventures of Kit Carson*. He was the Indian sidekick on TV's *Yancy Derringer*.

CRAIG BRANHAM An All-American track and field athlete in college, Craig Branham is a team roper who has modeled and has appeared in TV commercials. His Westerns as stuntman and actor include TV's *Dallas* and *Crazy Horse* (1996).

TROY BROWN A former bull rider, Troy Brown has been a stuntman since 1989. His credits include *The Quick and the Dead* (1995), *Wild Wild West* (1999) and numerous non–Westerns. He has served as a stunt coordinator.

RENO BROWNE (1924–91) Josephine Ruth Clarke was born on a ranch near Reno, Nevada, where she learned to rope steers, twirl a lariat and trick ride. She pursued piano and dancing while attending private schools, and won trophies at rodeos and horse shows. In Hollywood from 1942, she studied drama and appeared on stage, aspiring to use her musical and dancing talents. Instead, Monogram Studios put her in Westerns. Her movie mount, Major, was her palomino stallion, Ora Plaza. Queen of the 1945 Reno Rodeo, she rode in later grand entries as a former queen, in 1947 (winning

Rodeo queen turned Western leading lady Reno Browne.

"best parade horse"), 1950 and 1956. Billed as Reno Blair in her first film, she shortly became Reno Browne. Between 1946 and 1950, she rode as leading lady to Jimmy Wakely, Johnny Mack Brown and Whip Wilson. Attractive and petite, Reno had an extensive Western wardrobe, a radio program and a comic book. In 1947, she toured Europe and was presented at the Court of St. James. Her rodeos included Las Vegas' Helldorado Days parades in 1947 and 1948. At the 1949 Klamath Basin Round-Up, she was billed as "Queen of the Westerns." She and Major appeared at theaters and rode in the kids' parade. She autographed photos on Main Street, rode in grand entries and appeared twice at the Cal-One nightclub. As queen of the 1952 Rodeo of the Stars, she was made an honorary member of Palm Springs' Mounted Police. A pilot and aircraft owner, Reno flew Civil Air Patrol missions. A tap, ballroom and ballet dancer, she was a swimmer, a skater, a markswoman and an archer. She composed the song "My Palomino and I" and designed many of her own fashions. Retired from Hollywood, she and one-time husband Lash LaRue operated a Reno motor court in the early 1960s. She traveled widely. In the 1980s, she was a guest at Western film festivals. Reno succumbed to cancer.

A.H. "HIPPY" BURMEISTER (1894–1985)   A former champion rodeo bronc rider, "Hippy" Burmeister served from 1915 to 1923 as a Western movie stunt rider with major cowboy stars.

FRED BURNS (1878–1955)   Born at Fort Keough, Montana, Fred Burns learned his cowboy skills on the ranch and range. He rode bucking horses for Buffalo Bill's Wild West

Fred Burns (right) supports Tex Ritter (second from right) and Arkansas Slim Andrews (center, rear) as other cowboys look on in this scene from *Ridin' the Cherokee Trail* (Monogram, 1941) (courtesy Eddie Brandt's).

Show, was once billed as "Lasso King of the World" and competed in early cowboy contests. Both Fred and his younger brother **Robert "Bob" Burns (c. 1881–1957)** began film careers in the early teens, at times appearing together. Each enjoyed limited starring Western roles in the silent era, and then compiled many credits in supporting Western parts in the 1930s and '40s. Fred was familiar to Western fans as a sheriff. Bob traveled in the early 1940s with Gene Autry's Flying A Ranch Rodeo. Fred made films until the mid–1940s. Bob worked into the early 1950s. Bob's son, Forrest Burns, was also a Western supporting player.

POLLY MILLS BURSON (1919–2006) Pauline Shelton was born on a ranch at Ontario, Oregon, to a riding and rodeo family and took the name of her steer wrestler stepfather, Johnny Drayer. Her mother, Norma, was "sweetheart of the powder puff derbies." Polly traveled to fairs and rodeos with her parents; she was bucked off her first calf before an audience at age nine and won her first race at age 12 when her horse ran away with her. She trick-rode at a few rodeos and won Salinas' last (1938) trick-riding competition. She married rodeo contestant George Mills and eased his transition to rodeo clown. She tied for the trophy cup and title "World Champion Cowgirl" at Cheyenne's 1939 ladies relay race. As Polly focused on trick riding, a 1941 newspaper exclaimed, "She is as graceful as a ballet dancer when she springs to the ground and leaps back into the saddle on her running mount. One of the best-dressed women in rodeo and one of the most attractive, Polly Mills' act is spectacular."

She performed at New York City and Boston through 1944, when she and George divorced. Of her riding practice, she said, "You have to keep working on your tricks all the

Polly Mills Burson doing a Cossack drag (courtesy Doubleday Collection, Wyoming Division of Cultural Resources, Cheyenne. Neg. #206).

Polly Mills Burson executing a hippodrome stand at the Nimes, France, coliseum during a 1956 European tour.

time. There's no such thing as perfecting them. Each show is different in one way or another, and you have good days and bad days, just as in anything else."

With her 1945 marriage to Wayne Burson, movie stuntman and rodeo contestant, Polly turned her attention to Hollywood. She trick-rode mostly at California rodeos. Stuntwoman Babe DeFreest, known from rodeos and races, encouraged her. Polly, doubling, staged a struggle on a cliff, culminating in a 25-foot fall for the serial *The Purple Monster Strikes* (1945), earning her Screen Actors Guild card. She rode for several actresses, including Dale Evans, in Westerns and serials, but wisely pushed to perform other stunts. *The Perils of Pauline* (1947) provided variety, including a transfer from a running horse to a train. Polly's daring extended to fights, falls, water stunts, driving a wagon team, car scenes, stair tumbles, even swordplay. Versatility led to steady employment, as she doubled leading ladies, including Kim Novak in *Vertigo* (1958). She also doubled smaller men and boys, and played film parts. Called "Aunt Polly" by co-workers, she helped actresses with their riding skills. Between films, she performed at rodeos, served as a jockey and coached women in trick riding.

Following the end of her marriage, Polly trick-rode at overseas Wild West Shows, and then returned to movie stunting. She doubled Kim Darby in *True Grit* (1969), Barbara Stanwyck on TV's *The Big Valley* and Linda Cristal on *The High Chaparral*. On Universal's *Earthquake* (1974), during a trial run of a scene where a dam bursts, she was trapped against a house, receiving the full force of the rushing water and the debris it carried. Her knee and shoulder injured, she retired after 27 years of stunt work. She was a founder in 1967 of the United Stuntwomen's Association and earned life membership. She was the first woman inducted into the Hollywood Stuntmen's Hall of Fame. Polly received a Golden Boot Award and was inducted into the National Cowgirl Hall of Fame.

WAYNE BURSON (1920–97) Wayne Burson competed at California rodeos in saddle bronc riding, steer and bull riding, and steer wrestling into the late 1940s. He began movie stunt work, had parts in Western serials and doubled stars Henry Fonda, Glenn Ford, Ronald Reagan and Jimmy Wakely. For the Lone Ranger TV series, he helped train the horses Silver and Scout, and doubled for Jay Silverheels as Tonto. He left films in the early 1960s.

BILL BURTON (1945–) A Professional Rodeo Cowboys Association rodeo contestant in the 1960s and '70s, Bill Burton moved from roughstock riding events to steer wrestling and team roping. A movie stuntman, he made a number of Western films and TV shows, including some with his horse Custer, who was trained to jump or fall on cue. He then moved into other stunts: motorcycles, fire scenes and jumping a vehicle into the ocean. In the 1970s, he won CBS-TV's stuntman contest two of the first three years. He became a stunt coordinator and second unit director.

HAL BURTON A rodeo team roper, Hal Burton doubled Michael Landon on TV's *Bonanza* and *Little House on the Prairie*. He served as stunt coordinator on the latter show. He later accumulated movie credits, including *Rustler's Rhapsody* (1985), *Tombstone* (1993), *Rough Riders* (1997), *Wild Wild West* (1999) and *Hidalgo* (2004).

KENNY CALL (1944–) Born in Oklahoma City and raised in a rodeo-rich family environment, Kenny Call began roping and tying calves at age eight. He acted in high school

World champion steer roper and actor Kenny Call (courtesy Kenny Call).

plays. By age 21, he was competing in PRCA steer roping, calf roping and team roping. In the Army, he experienced the modern pentathlon.

Returning to rodeo, he qualified for the steer roping national finals nine times in a 12-year span (1972–83). In 1974, he was runner-up to the steer-roping champion. He was the Prairie Circuit's steer roping champion in 1976 and runner-up in 1977. He finished the 1978 season in second place in the world standings. In the sixth round of the Laramie steer-roping finals, a steer kicked him between the eyes. Groggy from the impact, he persevered to complete his tie in the lengthy time of 124.71 seconds, leaving him in fourth place. In the final four rounds, he came from behind to win the world championship.

Encouraged by Ben Johnson, Kenny attended acting school and modeled while working a Texas cattle ranch and competing at rodeos. In 1982, at Cheyenne, he set an arena record time for steer roping. He joined the Screen Actors Guild and moved to Newhall, California. In addition to bit parts, stunts and TV commercials, he won a role in *Cattle Annie and Little Britches* (1978). He competed only at selected rodeos. His Western film work includes *The Legend of the Lone Ranger* (1981), *Silverado* (1985) and *Lonesome Dove* (1989). He was also in the TV movies *Wild Times* (1980) and *Bonanza: Under Attack* (1995). Retired from competition in 1990, Kenny, a lifetime PRCA member, participates in celebrity ropings for charity. As an actor and in rodeo, he felt that his greatest gain was in friendships made.

YAKIMA CANUTT (1895–1986)   Enos Edward Canutt was born on a ranch near Colfax, Washington, to a family of Scotch-Irish, Dutch-German ancestry. His nickname later suggested that he was part Indian. As a pre-teen, he was riding broncs at a nearby ranch that provided bucking stock for the local fair. In his 1979 autobiography *Stunt Man*, he stated, "[B]y the time I was fourteen I could mount a wild bronc with the same assurance that I had when mounting a well-broken horse." At the 1911 Colfax fair, he was willing to try an exhibition ride for a $50 purse, but his father objected. By riding local broncs, he earned his dad's okay to compete at the next fall's fair, where he won his first bronc-riding contest.

Enos left home, and returned to rodeo in the fall of 1914. At Pendleton, he acquired his nickname, "Yakima," when lumped with other contestants from that town. Picked up by rodeo announcers, the new handle stuck. He began bulldogging and briefly tried bull riding. At Pendleton, Yak was second in bronc riding in 1915, and saddle bronc champion in 1917, 1919 and 1923. He placed second for the second time in 1920. Bulldogging champion at Pendleton in 1920 and 1921, he was awarded the Police Gazette belt buckle as all-around champion in 1917, 1919, 1920 and 1923. In 1923, he won the first leg of the Roosevelt Trophy for most combined points accumulated at Cheyenne and Pendleton. That year, at

Yakima Canutt (center) with fellow bronc riding finalists Lee Caldwell (left) and Jackson Sundown (right) at the 1915 Pendleton Round-Up. Yak took second that year (photograph by Bus Howdyshell, used with permission of Matt Johnson. Obtained from the ProRodeo Hall of Fame, Colorado Springs, CO).

Madison Square Garden, he won bulldogging and took second in bronc riding. At Fort Worth, Yak was first in bronc riding three consecutive years (1921–23).

A large part of Yak's rodeo reputation derived from his rides of two famous bucking horses, Fox and Tipperary. The first horse underwent confusing name changes. Author Theodora Goebel called Fox Yak's "destiny horse." In at least five documented rides (not all contest rides) over a period of years, he bested the big Canadian sorrel three times. Some say it was five out of seven. At the 1919 Sheepshead Bay rodeo, Fox bucked off a man a day for ten straight days. Yak won a bet that he would ride Fox, spurring fully through each jump. In 1917 at Medicine Hat, Saskatchewan, he rode Fox again to qualify for the finals. On the same horse in the finals, he was disqualified for losing a stirrup. At Calgary in 1919, it was proposed that Yak substitute (according to practice of the time) for an injured rider who had drawn Fox. Going into the finals in first place with prizes of $1,000 cash and a silver-mounted saddle, he reportedly was not initially interested. When stories circulated that he was avoiding Fox, according to author Fred Kennedy, Yak relented. Thus began, in Kennedy's words, "one of the greatest exhibitions of bronc riding and horse motion ever seen up to this day." Staying with the horse for eight jumps, Yak's spur tangled in the horse's mane. He was bucked off and hung up until the heel of his boot separated. The crowd applauded horse and rider. Having failed in a proxy ride on his old nemesis, Yak, fighting pain, then rode I.B. Dam to win the saddle bronc crown. Pendleton organizers bought Fox, and Yak won Pendleton in 1923 on the horse, now called No Name.

The second horse, even more indelibly linked with Yak, was Tipperary, named for the World War I song that became its theme song. Offered for exhibition rides for a purse, Tipperary bucked off or disqualified more than 80 prospective riders. In 1920, at Belle Fourche, South Dakota, Yak attempted an exhibition ride on Tipperary for a $500 purse. Mounting the snubbed horse, he made the first recognized qualified ride on Tipperary. Supporters claimed that the rain-muddied arena hampered the horse's bucking. In 1921, Belle Fourche invited Yak and another notable bronc rider to participate in a ride-off on Black Diamond and Tipperary, bucking from a chute. Yak's two rides were successful. His opponent's were not. Yak insured a place in rodeo history by conquering Tipperary for the second time. Tipperary partisans claimed that film examined later confirmed eyewitness statements that Yak had momentarily lost a stirrup on the judges' blind side. Nonetheless, he again won the $500, was credited with the only official qualified rides on Tipperary and later was awarded a gold "Tipperary Medal."

At a 1919 rodeo at Los Angeles, Yak met former competitor Ben Corbett, who introduced him to Tom Mix. Yak got some movie work, but returned to some of his greatest rodeo triumphs. A newsreel of the Roosevelt Trophy presentation in Los Angeles caught the attention of independent film producer Ben Wilson. Yak then starred in 1924's *Ridin' Mad* and other silent action Westerns. Doing his own hard-riding stunts, Yak was quite believable as a cowboy star. At rodeos, he was the "Broadway Cowboy," while his movie billing was "America's Champion Cowboy."

Competing in bronc riding and bulldogging, Yakima Canutt won all-around cowboy honors at Colorado Springs' first rodeo in 1922 (photographer unknown. Photograph courtesy of ProRodeo Hall of Fame, Colorado Springs, CO).

Yakima Canutt, movie cowboy hero, c. 1920s (courtesy Eddie Brandt's).

Yak's exploits added to rodeo legend. Spectators recalled him waving his hat with his free hand (to show that he had not pulled leather) and tossing it in the air when completing a ride, and his flying dismounts, intended to fool the horse into thinking it had thrown its rider. Along a rodeo parade route, he rode his horse in and out of saloons. Once, his parade horse became his draw in the bucking chute. Buddies tricked him into a damaging bar fight on the eve of his short-lived marriage to rodeo competitor Kitty Wilkes. In 1918, on Navy furlough, he contested in uniform at Pendleton, only to lose his title when bucked off just short of a qualified ride. He admitted waving to the admiring crowd a jump too soon. In 1922 at Colorado Springs, he bulldogged a bucking horse to rescue a cowboy hung up in the stirrup, knocking himself out in the process. He regained consciousness to win the bulldogging event. After victory toasts from his all-around cowboy trophy cup, he reportedly fired his pistol atop Pike's Peak. Established as a film star, but tardy for a charity exhibition rodeo, he mounted a horse with short stirrups. Following a glowing introduction, he was soundly bucked to the ground.

By the late 1920s, Yak was still a capable rodeo hand, but several factors slowed his film career. His contract with Ben Wilson expired. As talkies came in, his voice was not suitable for leading roles, and transition to sound was slower for outdoor filming. The Depression also limited opportunities. In the early 1930s, he made a rodeo tour, and then went to work for Nat Levine's Mascot Pictures. Married to Audrea, his lifelong mate, he was determined to be a professional stunt man. Stunts were an established part of motion pictures; however, Yak was a pioneer in meticulous planning of stunts and in devising complex action sequences to minimize hazard to man and animals. It was not unusual for Yak to double the star, as he did Harry Carey in *The Devil Horse* (1932), and play a featured role in the same film.

Beginning in 1933, Yak collaborated on John Wayne's Monogram series, forging a friendship. Wayne benefited from Yak's skill at choreographing screen fistfights and adopted some of Yak's walk and carriage. In fall of 1934, Yak represented the movie industry at the Sydney Royal Agricultural show in Australia. By 1936, Mascot had merged into Republic Studios, where action film technicians produced the finest quality B-Westerns. Yak helped develop the riding skills of radio singer Gene Autry, and doubled for numerous Western stars. A stagecoach stunt, first executed in 1937, became the showcase of Yak's career and of John Ford's *Stagecoach* (1939). For MGM's *Gone with the Wind* (1939), Yak devised stunts, doubled Clark Gable and acted in a small role. Republic offered Yak increased responsibility and films with larger budgets.

Yakima Canutt, Western movie villain, c. 1930s.

Involved in planning stunts, Yak's physical talents were still in demand. In years of rodeoing, he had avoided serious injury. Maintaining movie fantasy, however, began to take a toll. In a 1940 bronc-riding scene, a horse's fall caused the saddle horn to puncture Yak's abdomen. Later that year, he directed action for *Dark Command* (1940), devising a stunt of driving a buckboard over a cliff into water, another thrilling sequence that added to his reputation. In a 1941 leap from a coach, Yak broke both legs. Injuries convinced him to phase out his physical stunt work.

On the Republic film *Dakota* (1945), Yak achieved his second unit directing ambition, and went on to renown in this field. Keeping a hand in Westerns, he also worked for Walt Disney and MGM Studios. From the 1953 medieval adventures *Ivanhoe* and *Knights of the Round Table*, to the jungle of *Mogambo* (1953), to the historical spectaculars *Spartacus* (1960), *El Cid* (1961) and *Khartoum* (1966) and the war drama *Where Eagles Dare* (1967), he proved his mettle with some of filmdom's top directors. Perhaps his greatest achievement was directing, without serious injury, the chariot race scenes in *Ben-Hur* (1959).

In 1966, Yak received a special Academy Award acknowledging his contribution to film safety. He was inducted into the Pendleton Round Up Hall of Fame. He received a Western Heritage Award at the National Cowboy Hall of Fame and, with Tipperary, was inducted into that institution's Rodeo Hall, which displays a pair of Yak's chaps. In August 1984, he received a Golden Boot Award from his Western film peers. At a Belle Fourche ceremony in 1985, he received a bronze statue honoring his first Tipperary ride. That year, his star was dedicated on Hollywood's Walk of Fame. Yak was also inducted into the Hollywood Stuntmen's Hall of Fame. In 1986, as he prepared for the Texas Sesquicentennial at Fort Worth, site of past rodeo triumphs, health problems culminated in his death. In 1997, a Yakima Canutt Museum opened in his hometown. Yak's sons, Tap and Joe, both became stuntmen.

TOMMY COATS (1900–54)   A rodeo bronc and bull rider, Tommy Coats performed movie stunts, doubled actors and acted as one of the posse or outlaw gang during the period 1933 to 1951. He also coached Betty Hutton for *Incendiary Blonde* (1945) and was an animal handler.

DON COLEMAN (1898–1985)   Lloyd Donald Coleman was born on a ranch near Sheridan, Wyoming. He ran cattle, hauled hay and enjoyed participating in local rodeos, for which he practiced on his neighbors' bucking horses. He broke horses for a large ranch and for sale to the government at Fort Keough, Montana. At Miles City's 1913 Round Up, he placed second in bareback riding. After World War I Army service, he returned to rodeo. In 1921, he rode Whisper in the finals to win the bronc riding championship at South Dakota's Interior Rodeo. That same year, at the Bozeman (Montana) Stampede, he rode Sky Rocket to win the bronc riding championship over a field that included Yakima Canutt and other top riders. He was a bulldogging contender at the Pendleton Round Up.

While co-producing the Cody Stampede in 1922, Coleman was engaged as a model. Mrs. Harry Payne Whitney (Gertrude Vanderbilt), internationally known sculptress, had been commissioned to produce an equestrian bronze portraying William F. (Buffalo Bill) Cody as a guide, scout and frontiersman. Coleman (aided by his brother George) spent about a year in New York City on salary modeling Buffalo Bill. For authenticity, a horse and Col. Cody's clothing and equipment were shipped from Wyoming. Weighing three tons and standing over 12 feet tall, "The Scout," finished in the spring, was shipped west by railroad and unveiled July 4, 1924, in Cody, Wyoming.

While in New York, Coleman worked as an advertising model and contested at the 1923 Madison Square Garden rodeo. A chance meeting with Rudolph Valentino resulted in a role in the 1924 film *The Sainted Devil*. Early in 1925, Coleman relocated to Hollywood, where he worked at a movie ranch. Aided by a friend, rodeo contestant Tom Grimes, Coleman was ramrod for a group of cowboys breaking 1,200 horses at Yuma, Arizona, for the film *Beau Geste* (1926). He then secured bit parts at various film studios and had parts in two-reel Universal films with Ben Corbett and Pee Wee Holmes. He appeared in *The Lost Trail* (1926) with Al Hoxie, and *The Bugle Call* (1927) with Jackie Coogan. Producer-actor Leo Maloney changed his first name from Lloyd to Don.

Don appeared in two 1927 Pathe Westerns, supporting Maloney. Pathe signed him to a five-year contract to make one film a year, all produced and directed by Maloney, with Ben Corbett as sidekick. His first starring picture was *Boss of Rustler's Roost* (1928). *The Bronc Stomper* (1928) is a rodeo-related film. One movie horse was Ghost. Don's final starring feature was *.45 Calibre War* in 1929. Conversion to sound films, the Depression and the untimely death of his mentor, Leo Maloney, ended his starring film career. He appeared in Western character roles into the sound era. Settling in 1932 on the Mill Iron Ranch near Willits, California, he raised quarter horses and Hereford cattle. For several years, he helped organize the Willits Frontier Days Fourth of July celebration. In 1976, he was a Western film festival guest at Los Angeles. He was a lifetime member of the Rodeo Cowboy's Association.

Rodeo contestant and Western film star Don Coleman, c. late 1920s (courtesy Eddie Brandt's).

Young Clay O'Brien (later Cooper) in costume for his role in the ABC-TV series *The Cowboys* (1974) (courtesy Eddie Brandt's).

CLAY O'BRIEN COOPER (1961–)   Clay O'Brien Cooper grew up in Sylmar, California. Exposed to jackpot team ropings at his stepfather's arena, he began roping at age six. Responsibility and a strong work ethic were ingrained at an early age. Prerequisites to roping included twice-daily livestock care and success in school. His idols were team ropers, and he dreamed of being a champion. When he was about nine, his riding and roping qualified him for a role in John Wayne's film *The Cowboys* (1972). He appeared in additional Western movies and on TV, and then returned to roping. Clay roped in junior rodeos as a teen. When his mother and stepfather separated, he left high school at the start of his senior year.

To focus totally on roping, he moved to Gilbert, Arizona. Using some of his acting money, he rented a mobile home and a horse shelter, and roped in his practice pen. He competed in jackpot and amateur ropings, and qualified for the College National Finals Rodeo. He turned professional. Having gone by his stepfather's name, O'Brien, he added his natural father's name, Cooper, out of respect for both men. In the winter of 1985, he formed a partnership with Jake Barnes. Sharing a goal of world championship performance, he and Jake became neighbors so they could practice together, roping from 60 to 100 steers per ten-hour day. Clay's technique derived from combining bits from the many fine ropers he had observed over the years. Seeking consistency, he worked first on the fundamentals, and then added speed. He acquired a top roping horse. Also a steer wrestler and calf roper, he was competitive in all-around rankings. From 1985 through 1989, and in 1992 and 1994, he and Jake won team roping world championships. As of this writing, Clay is still qualifying for the National Finals. He and Jake, contesting separately, were 1997 inductees into the ProRodeo Hall of Fame.

TEX COOPER (1877–1951)

Raised on a Texas ranch, Tex Cooper moved to Indian Territory (Oklahoma) in 1891. He performed with Buffalo Bill at the 1893 Columbian Exhibition in Chicago. In 1907, he helped the Miller Brothers organize the 101 Ranch Wild West Show and remained with the ranch for 25 years. Working with Tom Mix, among others, he rose to the positions of chief of cowboys and ringmaster. He played Buffalo Bill at rodeos. He was a character actor in dozens of B Western films from 1935 to 1951.

BEN CORBETT (1892–1961)

A native of Hudson, Illinois, Ben Corbett was by his late teens competing in riding events at rodeos in the Northwest, including the Pendleton Round Up. He was a noted bulldogger, Pony Express relay rider and Roman rider. At Pendleton in 1913 he won the three-day standing race on Friday, but lost overall to Hoot Gibson. In 1915, he placed second to Sid Seale in that event. He was also

Tex Cooper, rodeo performer and Western character actor (courtesy Stephen Sally).

accomplished at fancy roping. Around 1915, while still participating in rodeos, Ben entered motion pictures as a stuntman for Bison under Thomas Ince. In 1919, he got Yakima Canutt stunt work on Jack Hoxie's silent serial *Lightning Bryce*. In World War I, Ben served in the "Powder River, Let 'er Buck" unit led by rodeo rider Lee Caldwell.

From silents into the sound era, from the 1910s into the 1950s, Ben worked in movies, mostly Westerns, for a variety of studios. Never rising above co-star or sidekick rank and often relegated to bit character player or stuntman, he had many credits and great longevity in support of cowboy heroes. While working in films, he contested at rodeos until at least the mid–1920s. The following describes his participation in the 1923 Prescott (Arizona) Frontier Days, "Ben Corbett made a spectacular show in the bulldogging when ... he got a big steer down in short order. The pretty part of his stunt was the high dive he made for the horns. The steer came down with such a thud and in such a cloud of dust that for several moments the spectators in the stands wondered just what was bulldogger and which part was steer."

He also competed at Salinas in 1925. Highlights of Ben's film career include a 1919–20 "Tempest Cody" series, a mid–1920s series of shorts with Pee Wee Holmes, "Bud 'n Ben" Westerns (1933–34) and a 1938–39 series as Tim McCoy's sidekick Magpie.

Rodeo contestant and Western film player Ben Corbett (courtesy Eddie Brandt's).

Alex Cord as the Ringo Kid in 20th Century–Fox's 1966 remake of *Stagecoach*.

ALEX CORD (1931–)

Alex Cord's initial interest was in racehorses, thoughts of which sustained him through a bout with polio. He later rode bareback broncs and bulls at rodeos, including those of Col. Jim Eskew. He tried trick riding with Rex Rossi, and then rodeoed in the West. He studied drama in New York and appeared in stage productions for ten years, including in London. He worked with horses for five years on a California ranch. On TV, he was in episodes of *Laramie* and *Gunsmoke* and was a continuing cast member on *Airwolf*. His Western films include *Stagecoach* (1966), *A Minute to Pray, A Second to Die* (1968) and *Grayeagle*

(1976). Interested in all types of riding, he rides on the celebrity rodeo circuit. Alex received the Buffalo Bill Award and a Golden Boot.

EVERETT CREACH (1933–94)   Everett Creach, a high school rodeo competitor, began as a stuntman by doubling young Roddy McDowall in the 1940s *Flicka* movies. He worked on John Wayne films and many more into the 1990s. He served as a stunt coordinator and acted on TV series.

WORTH CROUCH (1915–43)   Texas-born Worth Crouch was a former rodeo man turned stuntman. Making the World War II morale film *We've Never Been Licked* (Universal, 1943), he was killed when a caisson on which he was riding overturned.

BABE DEFREEST (1907–86)   Thelma "Babe" DeFreest was a stuntwoman and bit actress of the 1930s and 1940s. In Republic action films, she doubled Linda Stirling and other leading ladies, and she oriented Polly Mills Burson to that profession. Like Polly, Babe had been a rodeo racer.

DANNY DENT (1944–74)   Danny Dent competed as a rodeo steer wrestler, was a trick rider and rodeo clown, and had a Brahma bull contract act. He trained and worked with animals for movies and television, including a mountain lion for *The Wild Rovers* (1971) and various animals on TV's *Lancer*, *Kung Fu* and *Little House on the Prairie*.

JOHN DODDS (1948–2005)   Born in Alberta, bull rider John Dodds won the Canadian championship four times, and qualified for the National Finals Rodeo three times in the 1970s. As a movie wrangler and stuntman-double, he worked with stars Kirk Douglas, Lee Marvin and Charles Bronson. He contributed to such Western films as *Buffalo Bill and the Indians* (1976), *Legends of the Fall* (1994), *Last of the Dogmen* (1995) and *Shanghai Noon* (2000). He was involved in TV's *Monte Walsh* (2003) and in several episodes of the series *Lonesome Dove*.

ROSS DOLLARHIDE (1921–77)   Ross Dollarhide, born in Burns, Oregon, was a World War II Navy pilot. Entering his first rodeo in 1945, he was a multi-event entrant. He won saddle bronc riding at the Cow Palace in 1948 and 1949, and won 1949 bareback and saddle bronc riding at Mandan, North Dakota. He was champion all-around cowboy three consecutive years at Oregon's Chief Joseph Days Rodeo, and set a Cow Palace record in steer wrestling. In 1953, he was all-around champion at the Cow Palace. He received a trophy for winning all-around cowboy honors at seven rodeos. That year, he was world champion steer wrestler. In 1954, he was team roping champion at Redding and top money winner at Salinas. As a stuntman, he appeared in dozens of movies and a Chrysler commercial. Making a film in Flagstaff, Arizona, he was trampled by a horse. He got to his feet and was thought to be uninjured. A hotel maid found him dead in his room the following day. He was inducted into the National Cowboy Museum's Rodeo Hall of Fame.

MILDRED DOUGLAS (1895–1983)   Born in Philadelphia, Mildred Douglas rode horses while attending Connecticut boarding school. She performed for the 101 Ranch Wild West Show. At rodeos, she rode broncs and steers. Twice, she was world champion woman bronc rider. In 1916 at Kansas City, she took second place in a trick-riding contest that she had entered just to provide the minimum number of contestants. In the winter of 1916, she was a Western film extra. At Cheyenne in 1917, she substituted as a relay racer. In 1931, Mildred married Pat Chrisman, Tom Mix's business manager and horse trainer. She was in films with Tom, and she and Pat worked in the Sells-Floto Circus. She later became a nurse. She was inducted into the Cowgirl Hall of Fame.

BUFF DOUTHITT (c. 1925–) Buff Douthitt was champion calf roper at Ellensburg in 1947 and at Boston Garden in 1955. In 1954, at Detroit, he set an indoor rodeo world's record for steer wrestling. For about 20 years, he presented a slack rope-walking act. He served Western films first as a wrangler, and then played the mayor in European TV's *Lucky Luke*. He is an inductee at the Rodeo Hall of the National Cowboy Museum.

TROY ELLERMAN (1963–) Troy Ellerman grew up in a rodeo family, trick rode at age six and performed in the family rodeo act at age nine. He competed in bull riding at the college and circuit levels. He served as Paul Hogan's stunt double in *Lightning Jack* (1994) and has worked in other film and TV ventures. A practicing attorney, he was named PRCA Commissioner in December 2004.

H.P. EVETTS World champion team roper in 1974, H.P. Evetts qualified for the National Finals Rodeo in seven additional seasons. He worked as a movie stuntman and bit actor from the 1970s into the 1990s. His credits include *Comes a Horseman* (1978), *The Villain* (1979), *Dances with Wolves* (1990) and *Wyatt Earp* (1994).

SAMMY FANCHER (1933–) Sammy Fancher was born at Kingman, Arizona, into a rodeo family. She lived on a cattle ranch and traveled the circuit with her father, a multi-event competitor. Riding at age two, she soon had three horses, becoming an accomplished roper and barrel racer. She partnered with her father and other team ropers in RCA competition. Competing in calf roping against men in practice and jackpots, she did well. She demonstrated her calf roping skill between rodeo events. Until 1968, when rules banned her, she hazed for steer wrestlers. She qualified for the barrel racing world finals during the 1960s, finishing as world champion in 1965. With black hair, a dark complexion and brown eyes, befitting her part–Indian heritage, she attractively represented her sport. With Rex Allen, Slim Pickens and others, she advertised Tony Lama boots. She conducted barrel racing clinics and trained barrel racing horses for sale. Elected president of the Girls' Rodeo Association (GRA) in 1975, she supported equal prize money for barrel racers, a reality in the 1990s. In 1957, Sammy, with Rex Allen and rodeo cowboys, won a role in Walt Disney's *The Horse of the West*. In the 1967 movie *In Cold Blood*, she played the mother of one of the murderers. She became a Hollywood stuntwoman, doubling Jane Fonda in *Comes a Horseman* (1978), and contributing to at least a dozen other motion pictures into the 1990s.

RICHARD FARNSWORTH (1920–2000) A third generation Californian, Richard Farnsworth was born in the Los Angeles area. He rode and developed an affinity for horses from about age ten. Dropping out of school, he worked at a polo stable. One day, studio officials sought horses and riders for a film. When he determined that daily pay for movie work equaled his weekly stable wage, he signed to ride and wrangle horses, beginning a lifetime association with Hollywood. An early film was the Marx Brothers' *A Day at the Races* (1937). Dick found $25 a day and $10 extra for going over steeplechase hurdles good pay for the times. Initially, he worked as a riding extra, did horseback falls and got shot with bullets or arrows, feeling that his slight, wiry build adapted well to this rough-and-tumble life. Making a living as a stuntman wasn't easy. Established stuntmen resisted horsemen expanding their role to include fistfights and other stunts. When a rare opportunity arose, one had to prove willing and capable regardless of how dangerous the stunt, or be out of a job. Gradually, he progressed to professional stunt person.

A few weeks might pass between movie assignments. From 1938 for about ten years, Dick joined fellow movie horsemen contesting at rodeos during filming breaks, beginning as an amateur bull and bareback bronc rider. He later gave up bull riding and wrestled the light steers of the time. He, Slim Pickens and Ben Johnson were movie stuntmen and rodeo contestants in the early 1940s. He saw rodeos as recreation and a chance for added income. In later years, he emphasized his enjoyment of his time in rodeo. With pride, he retained his CTA button and held a PRCA Gold Card.

Dick had some success as a bareback bronc rider at rodeos. In 1944, he placed second at Clovis and competed at Madison Square Garden. At Preston, Idaho, in 1945, he won at his first night rodeo. The same year, at Bishop, he split third place both days. In 1946 at Escondido, he was third at a rodeo that featured Wayne Burson and Carol Henry. In 1947, at Gilmore Stadium, Los Angeles, he won prize money of $148. He was able to wrap up movie stunt work to compete at the Del Mar rodeo with Boyd Stockman, Walt LaRue, Rocky Shahan and Wayne Burson. He contested in Oregon, Nevada, Colorado and Chicago.

In 1946, Dick got significant work on *Red River*, doubling and advising Montgomery Clift, who had not been a Western actor. That year, he married and settled in Hollywood. About two years later, he gave up rodeo to concentrate on increasing stunt work and his family. For the movies, he wrecked wagons, fell from horses, staged fights, transferred from horses to stagecoaches and trains, and was a skilled archer. He approached with confidence the often-dangerous stunts he attempted, but was among early stuntmen who addressed safety concerns. As a horseman, he was fortunate that his prime stunting years coincided with heavy emphasis on Western films. In non–Westerns, he was a competent broadswordsman and saber handler. In his behind-the-scenes Hollywood career, he contributed to nearly 300 films and TV shows. He doubled stars Roy Rogers, Charlton Heston, Henry Fonda, Kirk Douglas, Jimmy Wakely and more. On TV, he doubled Guy Madison on *Wild Bill Hickok* and Guy Williams on *Zorro*.

Good-looking and in fine physical condition, Dick excelled at action scenes, but was camera-shy and uncomfortable speaking any but the briefest dialogue. He was satisfied with his stuntman's living and lacked any aspiration to become an actor. He had roles with minimal dialogue in Western films from 1969 to 1977. In 1977, he was offered a role with significant dialogue in *Comes a Horseman*. Though apprehensive, Dick went ahead with the project. His character, "Dodger," was a cowboy oldtimer with the wisdom of experience. Approaching senior status, Dick found that moviemakers and audiences responded positively to his natural screen presence. He was a genuine cowboy type who, not surprisingly, was believable playing a cowboy. For this role, he won the National Film Critics Award and received an Academy Award nomination as Best Supporting Actor.

In 1980, Richard played John Coble in *Tom Horn*, starring Steve McQueen. Years earlier, Steve had fired him from his TV show *Wanted: Dead or Alive* over a minor disagreement. Then, at age 60, Richard played the title character in *The Grey Fox*, a Canadian film relating the true exploits of a gentleman train robber, Bill Minor. Richard as a young man had read about Minor. The same age as the character when the film events transpired,

Richard bore some physical resemblance to him, exemplified a similar kindly demeanor, and identified with him. His ease in, and enthusiasm for, the role resulted in a film masterpiece, earning the Canadian Film Institute's Oscar equivalent, the Genie, as Best Foreign Actor, and additional awards and nominations. Richard deemed *The Grey Fox* his best and favorite film. He disclaimed acting ability, stating that he was lucky to land roles that fit his personality. He credited movie success to his horsemanship.

With pal Wilford Brimley, Richard appeared in the baseball film *The Natural* (1984) and on the TV series *The Boys of Twilight* (1992). With friend Ben Johnson he was in the TV movie *Wild Horses* (1985). *Anne of Green Gables* (1985) demonstrated his preference for family fare. Gradually, he slowed movie commitments, keeping his rodeo attachments and raising racehorses. He settled on a ranch in

Former rodeo cowboy and movie stuntman Richard Farnsworth in ***The Grey Fox*** (United Artists Classics, 1983).

Lincoln County, New Mexico. In 1998, he left semi-retirement to star in *The Straight Story*, the simple tale of an Iowa man traveling the roadside by tractor to visit his ailing, estranged brother in Wisconsin. Theatrical release was limited, but Richard's marvelous performance, in his late seventies, as Alvin Straight earned him nominations for a 2000 Academy Award and Golden Globe as Best Actor. He received an Independent Spirit Award.

Both father and son Richard Hill (a stuntman known as Diamond) were part of the film *Paint Your Wagon* (1969). Diamond doubled for his father in *The Grey Fox*. Richard died at home after battling cancer. His late-in-life efforts left a film legacy for all to enjoy into the future.

Richard's honors included the Golden Boot Award and the Buffalo Bill Award. In 1991, at Las Vegas, he was named ProRodeo Citizen of the Year. That year, the National Cowboy Hall of Fame presented him a Western Heritage Award for narrating the documentary film *The Man They Called Will James*. In 1997, he was inducted into the Hall of Great Western Performers at the National Cowboy Hall of Fame. His saddle plaque was placed in the Santa Clarita, California, Western Walk of Fame. Visitors to Los Angeles' Autry Museum of Western Heritage can see a bareback rigging and a Madison Square Garden armband from Richard's rodeo days and hear him narrate an audio-visual presentation.

EVELYN FINLEY (1916–89) Evelyn Finley, born in Douglas, Arizona, was raised on dairy ranches in Arizona and New Mexico. She had her own horse at age nine. At school,

Lobby card featuring Evelyn Finley as leading lady to Johnny Mack Brown in *The Sheriff of Medicine Bow* (Monogram, 1948).

she participated in plays, instrumental music and sports. A rider and stand-in for the New Mexico filming of *The Texas Rangers* (1936) and *The Light That Failed* (1937), Evelyn decided in 1940 to try Hollywood. She was first cast as Tex Ritter's leading lady in *Arizona Frontier* (1940). In her movie career, Evelyn acted in Westerns and doubled for some of Hollywood's top actresses. Ray "Crash" Corrigan once stated that her riding made the cowboy heroes look bad by comparison. For her final leading lady role, she was billed as Eve Anderson in the 12-chapter Columbia serial *Perils of the Wilderness* (1956).

On TV, she worked with Gene Autry, Roy Rogers and the Lone Ranger. From the early 1940s, in addition to movie work, she kept active with horses. With a Mark Smith–trained act, "Educated Horses and Beautiful Girls," she played San Francisco in the fall of 1941. She performed as a trick rider at Leo Carrillo rodeos and with a circus. Based on her movie doubling, Gene Autry signed her to trick ride at his rodeos. At Glenn Randall's stables in the late '60s, Evelyn worked first as secretary, and then learned classical and circus dressage. As an assistant to the Randalls, she trained and exhibited a liberty act for Circus Vargas, and worked on other Randall horse projects. Her final film was *Silverado* (1985). Evelyn passed away of heart failure at Big Bear, California.

LARRY FINLEY (1921–77) Beginning at age 14, Larry Finley, born in Benton, Missouri, participated in local rodeos. By 16, he had ridden a bronc at Prescott. He won his first buckle in 1939. He and brother Frank competed at Gene Autry's eastern rodeos in 1942 and at Los Angeles in 1946. In 1947, he was champion all-around cowboy at Phoenix and RCA world champion bareback rider. In 1948 at Madison Square Garden, three Finley brothers competed. In 1949, he was saddle bronc and bareback champion at Midland, Texas, and Ogden, Utah. Thrown by a horse that year, he broke his back. In 1950, he was bareback champion at Boston Garden for the second time. In 1951, he was first in saddle bronc riding at Reno and bareback champion at Caldwell. At Joseph, Oregon, he rode the horse that had earlier broken his back, and won the saddle bronc average. In 1957, he taught trick riding skills to John Wayne's 18-year-old son Pat, who helped Larry secure the role of an outlaw in *The Young Land* (1959). He rodeoed less after that, working as a stuntman and actor on TV shows, including *Gunsmoke*, and in over 50 movies such as *The Man Who Shot Liberty Valance* (1962), *The Cowboys* (1972), *The Culpepper Cattle Company* (1972) and *The Man Who Loved Cat Dancing* (1973). Despite his filmmaking, Larry never abandoned rodeo. Casey Tibbs presented him a trophy for bronc riding over five decades.

SAM GARRETT (1892–1989)   Oklahoma-born Sam Garrett, Pendleton's 1914 all-around cowboy champion, was famed as a trick roper at Wild West Shows, rodeos and circuses. His reputation included trick roping championships at Cheyenne. He roped with Will Rogers in London and before four U.S. presidents. His films included two in 1931 with Wally Wales and Buzz Barton, and the serial *The Vigilantes Are Coming* (1936). Sam roped in Johnny Mack Brown's *Law of the Range* (1941), was a roping instructor for *I Dood It* (1943), played Will Rogers in *The Dolly Sisters* (1945) and roped again in *The Harvey Girls* (1946). He led youth roping contests at Los Angeles' Sheriff's Rodeos. In 1948, his loop around the sheriff and Western leading lady Phyllis Coates publicized that rodeo. In 1967, he returned to Pendleton as parade grand marshal. He is an inductee of the Rodeo Hall at the National Cowboy Museum.

JERRY GATLIN (1933–)   Jerry Gatlin entered professional rodeo in 1953 as a saddle bronc and bareback rider. He was 1956 champion all-around cowboy of the Colorado Cowboy's Association. He began in films as an extra and riding double on *Gunman's Walk* (1958). As a movie stuntman and coordinator, he was involved in more than 70 films, many of them Westerns. He doubled Earl Holliman and worked on several John Wayne films. He also trained movie horses.

HOOT GIBSON (1892–1962)   Edmund Richard Gibson was born at Tekamah, Nebraska, the only one of six major early Western stars born west of the Mississippi. He joined his mother, storekeeper-father and siblings in hometown plays. He learned early to ride and rope. His first mount was reportedly a burro, succeeded by a horse named Tom, so loved that when the horse died, Hoot kept its ears under his pillow. Hoot was stabbed with a hatpin for one of many instances of teasing girls. Prior to age ten, he and a friend twice a day herded milk cows from pasture to milking barns and back for 50 cents per month per head.

At age 15 in California, where his mother had relocated for her health, he made deliveries for the Owl Drug Company, a possible origin for his nickname "Hoot." On his own, Hoot rounded up and broke wild horses, and punched cattle in Nevada, Colorado and Wyoming. One source states that he began his show business career with the Robbins Brothers Wild West and Rodeo Show of Glenrock, Wyoming. He and Art Acord eventually joined the Dick Stanley–Bud Atkinson Wild West Show. He tried out bucking horses, and then was a bronc rider and bulldogger. Returning from Australia to California, Hoot was wrangler, extra and stuntman for a movie production company off and on for several years, working with D.W. Griffith, Tom Mix and Harry Carey.

At the 1912 Pendleton (Oregon) Round Up, 21 years old and outfitted in worn jeans, chaps and saddle, Hoot won the standing race and accumulated enough points in other events to win champion all-around cowboy honors, gaining national attention. He returned to movie stunt work, even donning women's clothing to double female stars. Returning to Pendleton in 1913, he defeated Ben Corbett to win the cowboy standing race. Harry Carey helped Hoot get roles in his Universal Westerns. In 1916, Hoot rode broncs at Sheepshead Bay, New York. By 1917, Hoot's one-time roommate John Ford directed Hoot and Harry Carey in several films. Of Hoot's tank corps service during World War I, his hometown newspaper wrote, "If Edmund proves as nervy and daring in the tank as he does in pulling off thrilling stunts in the movies, no Huns will get by his machine." Hoot, however, stayed Stateside. Resuming his film career, he soon starred in a series of short Universal films. In *One Law for All* (1920), a film that Congress requested to stress American citizenship, Hoot represented the typical, wholesome American young man. His first full-length starring feature was *Action* (1921).

Hoot donated trophy cups for calf-tying champions at Prescott's rodeos. In 1924, he drove a four-abreast chariot team to defeat Ben Corbett at Pendleton. His crew filmed scenes for his movie *Let 'Er Buck* (1925). From 1927 until *The Concentratin' Kid* (1930), his final Universal film, he headed his own company, Jewel Productions. For about five years (1925–30), he was a top Hollywood star and the idol of many an American youth. On-screen, he wore ordinary cowboy clothing and seldom wore a gun belt, although he produced a gun when he needed one. His character often experienced misfortune, but retained a sense of humor.

Hoot Gibson, silent Western film star, c. 1920s (courtesy Eddie Brandt's).

In all, Hoot made over 90 shorts and over 70 feature films in his long association with Universal. After starring at Tex Austin's 1928 Chicago Rodeo and filming scenes there for *King of the Rodeo* (1929), he returned to Hollywood in a private railroad car attached to the Gold Coast Limited. He endorsed a booklet for youngsters, "Rope-Spinning with the Hoot Gibson Rodeo Rope." Uncertainty over applying sound technology to outdoor films led to non-renewal of his contract. Unfortunately, a lavish lifestyle had consumed Hoot's fine salary. His years as a big-time movie star came to a close. Within a few months, he was hit hard by the financial crash, loss of his film contract, divorce and the death of friend Art Acord.

Hoot was briefly married to film star Sally Eilers. In 1931, he returned to Nebraska for a week-long theater engagement with the Hoot Gibson Rangers. At a Rough and Ready youth rodeo, he awarded a pony to a young contest winner. At the theater, hometown well-wishers serenaded him and paid him tribute. From 1931 to 1933, he resumed making Westerns for Allied, where production values and distribution were not what he was accustomed to. Enjoying polo and auto racing, he also indulged his love of flying. He won the 1931 National Air Races, and competed in 1933 at Los Angeles against Ken Maynard. His plane crashed during the race, and he was hospitalized for fractured vertebrae and broken ribs.

About 1930, Hoot traded a home at Big Bear Lake for an interest in a Saugus, California, ranch, where a rodeo tradition had already begun. With Skeeter Bill Robbins as foreman, the Golden State Ranch held annual Hoot Gibson Ranch Rodeos, which continued after he relinquished interest in the property. Hoot said that the rodeos began as a novelty for movie stars. Accommodating about 19,000 spectators, the rodeos were first-class events. Celebrities often attended, and Edward Bohlin created trophy buckles. At the 1933 rodeo, Montie Montana, Mabel Strickland, Paris Williams and Jack Knapp performed. Glenn Strange was chute boss, and Skeeter Bill Robbins directed the arena.

In October 1932, Hoot flew to present a rodeo twice daily for 16 days at Dallas' State Fair of Texas. Skeeter Bill Robbins was arena master. After performances, he met with children, including those from St. Joseph's Orphanage. Awarding model plane trophies, he posed for photos in front of his private plane at the fair's aviation exhibit. In 1934, Col. Johnson introduced him to an ovation at Madison Square Garden. At the 1936 Chicago Stadium rodeo, Hoot appeared on a WLS Western radio show and rode in the grand entry.

From 1935 to 1936, Hoot made a half-dozen films for Diversion and two for RKO, *Powdersmoke Range* and *The Last Outlaw*, both starring Harry Carey. In 1937, he made only the 12-chapter Republic serial *The Painted Stallion*. From mid–1937 until 1943, he made no films, but appeared in circus Wild West concerts. By 1940, he performed rope tricks backed by a band in a stage show. Near Wilkes-Barre, Pennsylvania, he hired Dorothy Dunstan, a young singer-yodeler-guitar player. Later, Dorothy toured northeast states with Hoot. From 1940 into 1942, Hoot headlined some Jim Eskew eastern rodeos. He and Dorothy married in July of 1942 at Las Vegas.

In the early 1940s, Hoot Gibson Rodeos were produced in California cities. Hoot employed Abe Lefton, Andy Jauregui, Tex Cooper, Polly Drayer (later Polly Mills Burson), Homer Holcomb, Betty Miles, Faye Johnson, George Mills, Montie Montana, Slim Pickens, Rex Rossi, Don Reynolds, Don Stewart and Alice Van. Dorothy rode in the grand entry, sang the National Anthem and entertained. In May 1943, Hoot's Los Angeles Coliseum rodeo set a one-day attendance record. He was disappointed the next year when Roy Rogers was chosen to star. The times were changing. In 1943, Hoot and rodeo announcer Abe Lefton briefly operated "The Painted Post" beer bar-dance hall in North

Hoot Gibson, special guest at the 1958 Houston Livestock Show Rodeo, grants a young fan's autograph request (Harold Israel photograph courtesy Houston Metropolitan Research Center, Houston Public Library, Houston. Press #1175).

Hollywood. Hoot returned to the screen in 1943 in a "Trail Blazers" series for Monogram, co-starring with Ken Maynard and/or Bob Steele. In 1944, after ten low-budget films, the series (and Hoot's career as a cowboy film star, in decline for some years) was finished.

After retiring from films, Hoot at various times operated a dude ranch, had a TV program, promoted real estate and was a greeter at Las Vegas hotel-casinos. He had a role in *The Marshal's Daughter* (1953) and a bit in *The Horse Soldiers* (1959). Among his rodeo appearances were Truth or Consequences, New Mexico (1945), Helldorado Days, Las Vegas (1946) and the California Rodeo at Salinas (1949). He was featured in the 1953 Palm Springs rodeo parade. In 1954, he was special guest at the Riverside (California) Sheriff's Rodeo. Headliner Hugh "Wyatt Earp" O'Brian introduced and paid tribute to Hoot, guest at the 1958 Houston rodeo. The opening of Caldwell, Idaho's, Night Rodeo included Hoot's sixty-sixth birthday party. Robert Horton was the headliner, Western stars Rex Bell, "Big Boy" Williams and Bob Steele were on hand, and Mrs. Gibson sang in tribute. That same year, Hoot was at Lewiston, Idaho's, rodeo. At Pendleton, he displayed his 1912 all-around championship saddle, now exhibited at the National Cowboy and Western Heritage Museum. Hoot made a final cameo screen appearance in *Ocean's 11* (1960), set in Las Vegas where he lived his final ten years.

Following a lengthy cancer battle, he died. Eddie Dean sang at the service and Western stars attended. Hoot was inducted into Omaha's Ak-Sar-Ben Western Hall of Fame and the National Cowboy Hall of Fame.

MICKEY GILBERT   Mickey Gilbert, a rodeo veteran, doubled for Lee Majors on *The Fall Guy*. A stuntman and bit actor in many Western and action films, he became a stunt coordinator and second unit director. He contributed to *Rooster Cogburn* (1975), *The Old Gringo* (1989), *Young Guns II* (1990), *City Slickers II* (1994) and *The Horse Whisperer* (1998). Two sons became stuntmen.

THURKEL "TURK" GREENOUGH (1905–95)   Turk Greenough, Montana-born saddle bronc rider, was the first American to win the big rodeos: Calgary, Cheyenne (three times), Pendleton and Salinas. He rode some of the toughest horses of his era. The saga of Turk's rodeo family is recounted in the documentary film *Take Willy With 'Ya: The Ridin' Greenoughs and the Golden Age of Rodeo* (1989). Turk's sisters, Alice and Marge, Wild West and rodeo riders, were inducted into the Cowgirl Hall of Fame. Later family generations

Turk Greenough riding the saddle bronc Top Hat (courtesy Doubleday Collection, Wyoming Division of Cultural Resources, Cheyenne. Neg. #379).

Turk Greenough dressed as film double for Tex Ritter (courtesy Carbon County Historical Society, Red Lodge, MT).

also made their mark in rodeo. From 1930 to 1948, Turk was a stuntman and a movie extra, doubling such actors as Tex Ritter, Randolph Scott, Bruce Cabot and others. He worked with Gene Autry, Roy Rogers and John Wayne, contributing to such films as *Gone with the Wind* (1939), *Duel in the Sun* (1946) and *Angel and the Badman* (1947). Turk and his sisters are inducted at the Rodeo Hall of the National Cowboy Museum.

DONNA HALL (1929–2002) Growing up around rodeo and movie making, Donna Hall made her mark in both fields. Her father was a rodeo contestant, jockey and movie stuntman who doubled silent female stars. On one of two stunt jobs as a youngster, Donna rode a Thoroughbred out of the starting gate and around a track. Following high school, she raced horses at Caliente and other tracks, and trick-rode at California rodeos, Madison Square Garden and Boston Garden. She worked 300 head of movie horses for Hollywood livestock supplier Clarence "Fat" Jones. Mentored by Polly Mills Burson, she became a movie stuntwoman, often working on Westerns. Her stunts included transfers to trains, stagecoaches and wagons. She mastered jumps between teams of horses and transfer from a Roman team to wagon seats. She did saddle falls and bulldogs. Donna doubled for Doris Day in *Calamity Jane* (1953), Barbara Stanwyck in *The Violent Men* (1955), Jane Fonda in *Cat Ballou* (1965) and many others. Doubling for Carolyn Jones and Debbie Reynolds in

Rodeo trick rider–movie stuntwoman Donna Hall practices her routine prior to the 1957 Los Angeles Sheriff's Rodeo held at the Coliseum (Rothschild photograph courtesy Herald Examiner Collection, Los Angeles Public Library. HE-001–516).

How the West Was Won (1963), she drove four- and six-up covered wagons, participated in a 1,500-head buffalo stampede and rode a raft wrecked in the Rogue River. She did stunts for Gail Davis' TV Western series *Annie Oakley* (1953–56), including the show's opening scene, standing on a running horse and firing at a hand-held playing card. A founding member of the Stuntwoman's Association, Donna received the Golden Boot Award.

EDITH HAPPY (CONNELLY) (1925–99) Young Edith alternated time with her father in her home area of Boston and her mother in California, riding horses on both coasts and learning trick riding in the West. Married in 1945 to bulldogger Don Happy, she trick-rode at rodeos across the country, including Madison Square Garden and Boston Garden, for more than two decades. Crediting her success to her horses, she practiced with them daily and cared for them immediately following a performance. Her full-sleeve blouses were often hand-designed and sewn with sequins. Her trademark was leaning out far over her horse's head while doing a Hippodrome stand. For a while, Edith and Don lived near, and worked rodeos with, Andy Jauregui. Alice Broberg, of *Hoofs and Horns*, wrote, "Edith Happy can keep her pretty nose in the books as rodeo secretary and slip out in a few minutes to do her unequalled hippodrome, drag and one-foot stand with feminine charm and daring speed." Both Edith and Don did movie stunts. She doubled leading ladies in films from *Loaded Pistols* (1949) to *The Last Sunset* (1961).

Edith Happy (Connelly), trick rider, rodeo secretary and Hollywood stuntwoman, pictured with her horse Lady, at the Lewiston, Idaho, rodeo, c. 1947 (*Lewiston [ID] Tribune* photograph, used with permission. Obtained from PRCA–Media, Colorado Springs, CO).

She drove four-, six- and eight-horse wagon hitches. For *Westward the Women* (1952), she drove wagons, herded horses and acted as a muleskinner. In *The FBI Story* (1959), she and Sharon Lucas staged a fight scene. She also worked on *Cimarron* (1961) and on TV's *Have Gun, Will Travel*. Her children, Clifford and Bonnie, became movie stunt people. Later husband Lex Connelly was killed in a 1984 light plane crash. Edith has been inducted into the Rodeo Hall at the National Cowboy Museum and the ProRodeo Hall of Fame.

BILL HART   Bill Hart competed at rodeos, and then played "Red," rodeo cowboy on the *Stoney Burke* TV series. An actor-stuntman, he was on episodes of many TV series, including *Gunsmoke*, and doubled Glenn Ford on TV's *Cade's County*. His film work included such Westerns as *Santee* (1973) and *Young Guns* (1988).

NEAL HART (1879–1949)

Born in New York, Neal Hart served as a cowboy and law officer in Wyoming. Performing with the 101 Ranch Wild West Show about 1914 brought him to moviemaking with Universal's John Ford–Harry Carey unit. He got featured parts, and then his first starring role in 1917. By 1919, he wrote, produced and/or directed many of his own films, eventually becoming popular as "America's Pal." While filming rodeo scenes for a 1927 serial in Rawlins, Wyoming, he donated a horseshoe-shaped gold ring with jewels for presentation to the rodeo's top winner. From the 1930s to the late 1940s, Neal played supporting roles.

CHUCK HAYWARD (1920–98)

A horseman at an early age, Chuck Hayward competed at rodeos, primarily as a saddle bronc rider, following World War II Merchant Marine service. From stable work, he progressed to motion pictures, including more than 20 films with John Wayne. He doubled Clint Eastwood, Steve McQueen

Neal Hart, silent Western film star.

and Richard Widmark. He had roles and bits in feature films such as *The Big Country* (1958), and in Western TV series.

BUDDY HEATON (1929–)   An Oklahoma rodeo bronc rider from 1938, and clown-bullfighter, Buddy Heaton was known for his trained buffalo, Clyde, and an assortment of performing animals. An Arab rider in *Desert Sands* (1955) and a rodeo clown in *Bus Stop* (1956), he was also seen in episodes of Western TV series.

THE HENDRICKS FAMILY   At rodeos, the Hendrickses presented stunt riding and trained horse acts, including Roman jumping, a car jump and a dancing horse. Lee and Byron doubled on films such as *Gallant Bess* (1947) and *Rodeo King and the Senorita* (1951). They showed the horse Gallant Bess at rodeos.

"BUZZ" HENRY (1931–71)   Reportedly a juvenile trick rider and roper at regional rodeos, Robert "Buzz" Henry had appeared, by age 12, in over 50 films, including Westerns. He starred in *Buzzy Rides the Range* (1940) and *Buzzy and the Phantom Pinto* (1941). He had a tumbling act in vaudeville. Offered a circus job, he elected instead to ride bareback broncs at rodeos. At a 1945 Gilmore Stadium rodeo, he exhibited his jumping horse, Golden Pat. He served as stunt double, bit player and stunt coordinator for movies for over 25 years.

CAROL HENRY (1918–87)   A rodeo steer wrestler, Carol Henry doubled many of Hollywood's B-Western heroes and played bit parts from the early 1940s to 1965. In late 1942, while doubling Russell Hayden on a Columbia production, he was injured when a stagecoach upset. He doubled Richard Martin as sidekick Chito in RKO's post-war Tim Holt Western series and appeared in Western TV series.

CHUCK HENSON (1931–)   Descended from the famed Greenough family, Chuck Henson competed before becoming a rodeo clown-bullfighter. Clown of the Year in 1977, he was inducted into the ProRodeo Hall of Fame. He became a movie stuntman, contributing to TV Westerns and such films as *Tom Horn* (1980). Often he drove a stagecoach or a runaway team, or worked with livestock.

ROBERT HINKLE   A former rodeo competitor, Robert Hinkle acted on episodes of such TV Westerns as *Wagon Train*, *Gunsmoke*, *Wyatt Earp* and *Tombstone Territory*, and as the rodeo announcer in *Hud* (1963). As a film producer, he won a special Academy Award in 1956. He promoted the careers of Marty Robbins and Chill Wills. He has directed and written for the screen. In the 1980s, he worked in marketing for Flying U Rodeos.

HOMER HOLCOMB (1896–1971)   Rodeo clown Homer Holcomb had roles in the Harry Sherman productions *Stick to Your Guns* (1941) with Hopalong Cassidy and *American Empire* (1942). Arena injuries forced him into early retirement. He is inducted into the Rodeo Hall at the National Cowboy Museum and the ProRodeo Hall of Fame.

CHRIS HOWELL   A former rodeo hand, Chris Howell began working as a stuntman in 1972 and became an actor and a stunt coordinator on a variety of films, including some Westerns. His son is actor C. Thomas Howell.

Young Western star Buzz Henry (courtesy of Eddie Brandt's).

Silent Western film star Jack Hoxie in an advertisement for *Ridin' Thunder*, Universal, 1925 (courtesy Eddie Brandt).

JACK HOXIE (c. 1888–1965) Born in Indian Territory (Oklahoma), Jack Hoxie worked as a teen cowboy and bronc buster. He competed at rodeos as a bronc rider and bulldogger, and performed with Dick Stanley's Wild West Show. Between 1911 and 1915, he rotated among rodeos, Wild West shows and films. He won a bulldogging championship at Bakersfield, California, and was named national riding champion. Throughout most of the 1920s, his horsemanship and ability to handle action made him a popular star of silent Westerns. He performed at circuses and Wild West Shows from the 1930s into the 1950s.

FRED HUMES (c. 1896–1971) Fred Humes was born in Pennsylvania. His riding and roping skills, first exercised as a teen on the rodeo–Wild West circuit, earned him a berth in Hollywood. Following World War I Army service, he supported Universal films, some with Hoot Gibson, in bit roles and as a stuntman.

Star of silent Westerns Fred Humes.

Shortly, he starred in 1920s silent Westerns. With the advent of sound films, he returned to stunting and character roles until 1935. He later worked in Alaska's energy industry.

ANDY JAUREGUI (1903–90) Near Santa Paula, California, Leandro (Andy) Jauregui was born into a large Basque family descended from the Pyrenees Mountain region separating France and Spain. Andy's name was mispronounced and misspelled throughout his rodeo career. Andy's father diversified, raising mainly cattle, with some sheep and goats, and moved to Ventura County, ideal for grazing and riding. Growing up with a special closeness to horses, Andy had his own mount and rode the three miles to school. An accomplished hand by age 13, Andy, with his dad's approval, left school to help an older brother run the ranch. He concentrated early on his life's work: riding, roping and managing livestock. For recreation, he roped calves and rode bucking horses. He first rode before an audience at a shoestring rodeo organized by black bronc rider Jesse Stahl (Calgary's 1919 bareback champion). The next year, still in his mid-teens, Andy entered his first "real" rodeo, at Santa Barbara, as a saddle bronc rider. Wearing batwing angora chaps, he won the $15 prize money by audience applause. At about age 17, he left home to rodeo, mostly competing on broncs, steers and bulls.

While on the rodeo circuit, Andy courted and married Camille, his lifetime partner and mother of their four daughters. He worked for Clarence "Fat" Jones' Newhall stable, furnishing livestock and wagons for movies. He became a stuntman in silent and early sound era Westerns, working with the top film cowboys of the day. When not filming, he rodeoed. He mentored young Buzz Barton. As he frequented the pay window, the attraction of rodeo prevailed over film work. For unwanted movie jobs, he recommended his brother Ed, who adopted stunting as his life's occupation, often driving teams of horses. Ed drove a chariot team in *Ben-Hur* and for ten years he doubled Lorne Greene on *Bonanza*.

In 1928, the Jauregui family moved to a several-thousand-acre ranch in Placerita Canyon. Leased from an oil company, the J-Spear Ranch (after both men's names) initially was part of the Jauregui-Jones partnership, which ended in 1933 when the movie stable moved to North Hollywood. Andy bought the cattle herd and the ranch, a frequent Western film location and camping area for rodeo families. He trained horses, including Rowdy, an outstanding calf-roping horse of his time. His light handling of horses led to friendship with Will Rogers, who purchased polo ponies and roping horses as well as roping stock.

After about ten years, Andy ceased riding bucking stock to become a premier roper of the 1930s. In 1931, he was rodeo's world champion steer roper. At Salinas, he won roping events three different years, and for two consecutive years won two roping events. He competed at Prescott, Salinas and Madison Square Garden. In 1934 he was world champion team roper. In 1935, he broke the calf-roping record at Pendleton. He won the calf-roping event at Cheyenne in 1938. His last big victory was the calf-roping championship at Phoenix in 1941, but he roped and won through the 1940s. He still roped occasionally in 1964.

Andy enlarged his herd and acquired bucking stock. The primary stock contractor in California, he produced rodeos for over 30 years, up to 35 rodeos a year. He often served as arena director or judge. He supported the Palm Springs rodeo for more than 20 years and the Los Angeles Sheriff's Rodeo for 18 years. He held rodeos in Nevada, Utah and Oregon. In Arizona, he produced rodeos at Yuma for 26 years and at Prescott for 13 years. The *Rodeo Sports News* reported that he had produced more rodeos in 1966 than any other stock contractor. A personal favorite bronc was Cheyenne, saved from the slaughterhouse to be named, after 20 years in the arena, as the top winning bareback horse. Esteemed horses retired to his pastures.

Andy eventually became the senior active rodeo stock contractor. In 1967, he sold his rodeo company. One of the rodeo community's most respected citizens, he stayed on additional years to ease the transition. A bronze sculpture received at Casey Tibbs' 1973 Cowboy Reunion cited Andy's 50-year contribution to rodeo. Casey noted his habit of carrying cowboy entry fees. Among Hollywood's Western stars, Andy shared friendships with Harry Carey, William S. Hart and Joel McCrea, whose favorite horse, Ribbon, Andy broke and trained. Notable was his lack of prejudice regarding race, national origin or disability in his selection of associates. Andy was honored with a saddle on Newhall's Western Walk of Fame. He was inducted into the Rodeo Hall at the National Cowboy Museum and into the ProRodeo Hall of Fame. The Autry Museum in Los Angeles displays a pair of his chaps.

BEN JOHNSON (1918–96) Benjamin Franklin Johnson, Jr., "Son," was born at Foraker, Oklahoma, and raised near Pawhuska, an area known for champion ropers. His father, three-time 1920s Cheyenne steer roping champion Ben, Sr., was foreman of the 75,000-acre Chapman Barnard Ranch and manager of his own ranch. Ben, Jr., learned early to ride and herd horses, and to rope and herd cattle. Beginning school, he had a pony for transportation and quickly progressed to full-size horses. By age eight, he was roping anything in sight. Biographer J.P.S. Brown relates that Ben at age 13 worked as a full-time cowboy for a year, having sole responsibility for a remote cow camp. He completed most of his high school years while competing at the few local rodeos his resources allowed.

In the early 1940s, Ben provided horses for Howard Hughes' film *The Outlaw* (1943). He accompanied horses first to location in Arizona, and then to Hollywood. When his quick reaction saved a favorite Hughes horse from injury, Ben became a friend of the producer. The difference between his Hollywood paycheck and his cowboy wages convinced him to stay. He married Carol, daughter of movie stable operator Clarence "Fat" Jones. He won a buckle for rodeo calf roping in 1941. Endorsed by Gary Cooper for membership in the Screen Actors Guild, he worked as a riding extra, stuntman and double for Western stars. Movie income allowed him to rope at rodeos and jackpots, mostly in California. In 1948, he worked on two John Ford–directed Westerns, *3 Godfathers* and *Fort Apache*, both starring John Wayne. On the latter film, he doubled John Agar. His quick-thinking, courageous response to a potentially disastrous stunt accident earned him the director's gratitude and a profitable contract.

Ben starred as a cowboy roper in *Mighty Joe Young* (1949). That same year, he had a supporting role in John Ford's cavalry film *She Wore a Yellow Ribbon*. Star John Wayne gave one of his finest performances in a story with many memorable characters. Yet, exiting theater audiences buzzed about the handsome young Sgt. Tyree whose riding, often with Indians in pursuit, set a new standard. Ben stated that he would rather ride 100 miles on horseback than speak one line of dialogue, and Mr. Ford endured Ben's repeated reference to "all them words." However, under Ford's direction, Ben's explanation of the meaning of an Indian arrow and his line, "That ain't in my department, sir," made a positive impression. He also gained rodeo notice, setting a short-lived arena calf roping record at Pendleton.

Ben and Harry Carey, Jr., starred in John Ford's *Wagonmaster* (1950), and the men remained lifelong friends. In his book *Company of Heroes*, Carey praises Ben's riding. Ben was prominent in John Ford's *Rio Grande*, notable for its music and a Roman-riding

Ben Johnson, 1953 world champion team roper, as Sgt. Tyree in the John Ford–directed film *She Wore a Yellow Ribbon* (Argosy/RKO, 1949).

sequence. He credited Western stars George O'Brien and John Wayne with teaching him about moviemaking. His sense of humor and horsemanship made him a respected member of John Ford's stock company, but misunderstanding led to Ford banishing him from his films for more than ten years. He had a featured role in *Fort Defiance* (1951) and starred in *Wild Stallion* (1952).

After his father passed away in the fall of 1952, Ben pursued rodeo roping full-time. At year's end, he was rodeo's 1953 world champion team roper. Winning a buckle, but failing to show a profit, he concluded that movie work provided the more steady income. Yet, he often stated that his proudest achievement was his rodeo championship. That same year, Paramount released George Stevens' classic Western *Shane*, in which Ben played a badman redeemed at the film's finish.

At rodeos, he was sometimes referred to as Ben "Movie" Johnson, but he occasionally suffered the same indignities as other competitors. At a charity rodeo in Victorville, his horse reared in the chute, threw him and broke his ribs. At Fort Worth, following an especially glowing introduction, Ben's loop completely missed his first calf. Team roping at Tucson, Ben threw his loop and was leaning out of the saddle. The loop missed, the horse anticipated a catch and Ben was knocked to the ground. The rope caught his leg, dragging him about 100 feet before releasing. He was left dusty and with more soreness than he let on. Once it was known that he was unhurt, peers ribbed him about the "Hollywood stunt." Beginning in 1954, an annual Ben Johnson Memorial Steer Roping was held at Pawhuska, Oklahoma, in honor of Ben, Sr. Participating in 1960, Ben's horse fell with him during a practice session. With several injured ribs, Ben was forced to sit out that year's competition.

Ben continued to make movies and TV shows, mostly Westerns. Following a guest role on *Have Gun, Will Travel*, a rodeo announcer commented, "He died a horrible death last night on TV, but he is sure roping good today." In the early 1960s, he had a recurring role as the one-armed "Sleeve" on the Western TV series *The Monroes*. In 1964, John Ford cast him in *Cheyenne Autumn*, and in 1969 he was in Sam Peckinpah's *The Wild Bunch*. Interspersed among his "big picture" credits were projects geared toward family audiences. Due to the script's profane dialogue, he at first turned down a role in *The Last Picture Show*. When John Ford asked him as a favor to take the part, Ben reached a compromise whereby he cleaned up his dialogue. His portrayal of Sam the Lion won him the 1971 Oscar for Best Supporting Actor and other awards.

Ben worked in additional John Wayne films and several made-for-TV films and mini-series. Beginning in the 1970s, he was in many non–Westerns. Twice he returned to his rodeo roots, playing a shady stock contractor in *Junior Bonner* (1972) and an aging ex-rodeo hand in *My Heroes Have Always Been Cowboys* (1991). He starred in the 1993 TV film *Bonanza: The Return*, and in 1994 he was a cowboy baseball team owner in *Angels in the Outfield*. Making films until his passing in 1996, and working for some of the finest directors, modest Ben attributed his success to playing Ben Johnson better than anyone else.

Ben helped young rodeo competitors and assisted the transition of several rodeo personalities to the movie business. He proudly watched his nephew, John Miller, win world team roping championships in 1970 and 1971, and place in the top ten in four additional years. John worked in movies and joined his uncle as an inductee at the ProRodeo Hall of Fame. Ben's investments made him a wealthy man. He served as a ProRodeo Hall of Fame trustee at its inception in 1979 and headed the Hall's 1985 fundraising drive. In 1988, he was roasted during the National Finals Rodeo in Las Vegas, and signed a Jimmy Don Cox lithograph to benefit the Hall of Fame. He participated in events at the National Cowboy Hall of Fame. Ben was consistently friendly to fans. By holding a series of pro-celebrity rodeos, he raised money for children's charities. For these efforts, Roper Western wear called him "Champion of Children."

In 1974, Ben was honored by the Oklahoma legislature. He received the Buffalo Bill Award at North Platte, Nebraska. In 1982, he was inducted into the Hall of Great Western Performers at the National Cowboy Hall of Fame. His portrait, with Slim Pickens, was unveiled the following year. He was among the first recipients of the Golden Boot Award and received a star on Hollywood's Walk of Fame. When Ben died suddenly of a heart attack in Mesa, Arizona, the world lost a humanitarian, a Western star who spent over 50 years making films and a cowboy who was true to his values. Louis L'Amour accurately described him as "the epitome of the cowboy and the Western man." A Ben Johnson Memorial Award was established by the Rodeo Historical Society.

BRAD JOHNSON (1959–) A steer wrestler and roper since college, Tucson native Brad Johnson appeared in advertisements. He was cast in TV's 1987 series *Force III*, the big screen's *Always* (1989) and the TV films *Rough Riders* (1997), *Soldier of Fortune* (1998) and *Crossfire Trail* (2000).

C.L. JOHNSON (1964–99) A rodeo bull rider, C.L. Johnson began performing stunts on *Dances with Wolves* (1990). In addition to TV work and commercials, he performed stunts for *Last of the Mohicans* (1992) and other films. He was inducted into the Hollywood Stuntmen's Hall of Fame.

JOHN JORDAN (c. 1900–69) John Jordan was born in Chicago, Illinois. Exposed to the West as a youngster, he later herded cattle on an Arizona ranch. Bringing bucking stock to Flagstaff's Fourth of July rodeo, he came away with saddle bronc prize money and a pair of chaps. He worked in movies with Tom Mix and Hoot Gibson. He was one of 20 top riders picked to enter Chicago's 1933 World's Fair rodeo, went to Tex Austin's 1934 London rodeo and was Calgary's 1937 North American bronc riding champion. Still riding, by 1938 he began to announce rodeos. His quiet, conversational delivery was laced with interest, information and humor. Late in 1945, a home fall from a colt resulted in a fractured skull that left residual nerve damage. He recovered and resumed announcing in mid–1949. The Jordans made their home in Chandler, Arizona. In 1955, friend Carl Dossey was killed protecting his son from a runaway team in the hometown parade. The sudden loss so affected John that he retired from announcing. He passed away from a heart attack.

TRACY KEEHN-DASHNAW (1960–) Tracy Keehn-Dashnaw, once a rodeo performer, began work as a stuntwoman in 1984. Her credits include *¡Three Amigos!* (1986). She has doubled for Kim Basinger and Melanie Griffith.

ALLEN KELLER (1943–) An Olathe, Colorado, cowboy and All-American college wrestler, Allen Keller was a ranked steer wrestler and steer roper from the mid–1960s to the mid–'70s. He was 1972 world champion steer roper. A hunting friendship with director Sam Peckinpah led to movie work, primarily in Westerns, as a wrangler, stuntman, double and bit player. His films included *Heaven's Gate* (1980) and *Pale Rider* (1985). He furnished horses, saddles, wagons and other equipment for films.

Jay Kirby, rodeo cowboy and Hopalong Cassidy film sidekick (courtesy of Stephen Sally).

JAY KIRBY (1920–64)   Jay Kirby entered rodeos part time. While attending UCLA, he was selected to play "Johnny" or "Breezy Travers" in six Hopalong Cassidy films in 1942 and 1943. Following World War II military service, he was in another dozen or so Westerns and serials. He appeared in a Tim Holt film and in a number of TV Western series until early 1957.

JACK KNAPP   At four feet, six inches, Jack "Pee Wee" Knapp made an exhibition bull ride at Madison Square Garden in 1927. From 1944 through 1951, he often served as the third rodeo clown or performed an act of acrobatic roping and comedy bullfighting with his wife Bobbie. He was known for last-minute dives through a trap door just ahead of a charging bull. He appeared in *King of the Rodeo* (1929) with Hoot Gibson.

MEL LAMBERT (1920–99)   Mel Lambert was raised on Oregon's Chiloquin Indian Reservation. At age 16, he tried all rodeo events and learned to pilot a friend's plane. Later, he flew his own plane to rodeos. He first specialized in bareback bronc riding and trick roping. In 1938, he quit rodeo riding to become a rodeo announcer. He trick-roped between jobs and to entertain young hospital patients. He sometimes doubled as rodeo bookkeeper. His rodeos included Salinas, the New Mexico State Fair, Pendleton, the All-Indian National Finals and the National Finals Rodeo. Mel was often reminded about his embarrassing rodeo introduction of Western star Dale Robertson as "Dale Evans." Each man gained a story to tell. An occasional movie stuntman and actor, his credits include *The Great Sioux Uprising* (1953), *The Great American Cowboy* (1973), *One Flew Over the Cuckoo's Nest* (1975) and *Three Warriors* (1977). With Rex Allen and Slim Pickens, he endorsed Tony Lama boots. A U.S. Navy veteran, his sideline was selling automobiles and, later, aircraft. Selected as the Rodeo Historical Society's 1979 Man of the Year, he was inducted into the Hollywood Stuntmen's Hall of Fame, the ProRodeo Hall of Fame and the Rodeo Hall of the National Cowboy Museum.

WALT LARUE (c. 1921–) Born in Canada, Walt LaRue entered bareback bronc and bull riding at rodeos, including Madison Square Garden. Between 1944 and 1949, he averaged about 25 rodeos per year. From the 1940s into the '90s, he was a stunt double for Roy Rogers, Harry Carey, Jr., and others, and did bit acting parts in movies. He was a Western singer, artist and creator of cowboy cartoons.

RICK LEFEVOUR (1955–) A rodeo and Wild West Show performer, Rick Lefevour began work as a movie stuntman in 1981. In addition to many films, he worked on TV's *The Fall Guy*.

GARY LEFFEW (1944–) A seven-time National Finals Rodeo qualifier between 1966 and 1976, Gary Leffew was world champion bull rider in 1970. Stressing positive thinking, he conducted bull-riding schools. He appeared in over 100 commercials, had a rodeo scene in Clint Eastwood's *Pink Cadillac* (1989) and contributed to other films. He was inducted into the ProRodeo Hall of Fame.

ABE LEFTON (1910–58) Born Abe Leifkowitz in Angel's Camp, California, Abe later simplified his name. He worked with horses, was a bronc rider and a rodeo clown. First announcing through a pasteboard megaphone, he gradually became one of the finest announcers of his time. He described action, kept audiences informed about contestants and made humorous quips. His pleasing voice maintained crowd interest, moved the rodeo along and forestalled panic in dangerous situations. When a jumping Brahma bull broke a rail separating the arena from spectator seats, building crowd anxiety, Abe calmly remarked, "The man who knocked his wife over in getting away from the bull can come back now. It is perfectly safe." With clown Homer Holcomb, he perfected verbal exchange between announcer and clown. He made the first live radio broadcast of Houston's rodeo. He announced major rodeos from the late 1920s into the 1950s, including Madison Square Garden, Boston Garden and the Los Angeles Sheriff's Rodeo. He was a regular announcer for the Hoot Gibson and Gene Autry rodeos. He announced for 25 years at Salinas. Abe was in two Gene Autry films, *Melody Trail* (1935) and *The Old Corral* (1936). In 1943, he and Hoot Gibson operated the Painted Post nightclub in North Hollywood. At his 1946 marriage on the *Bride and Groom* radio program, bridesmaids included trick riders Tad Lucas, Polly Mills Burson and Faye Blessing. Gene Autry was best man. Once challenged by wild horse race contestants to try the event, he left his booth and acquitted himself quite well. Beginning in the late 1940s, health problems forced him to cut back engagements. He died from Parkinson's disease at Newhall, California. He is an inductee of the Rodeo Hall at the National Cowboy Museum.

TERRY LEONARD (1940–)   Terry Leonard, a PRCA rodeo cowboy and team roping champion at the 1995 Prescott rodeo, participated in Olympic decathlon events and played Canadian professional football. From the 1960s, he was a movie stuntman, contributing to several John Wayne films, Western TV series and *Raiders of the Lost Ark* (1981). A stunt coordinator and a second unit (action) director, he was inducted into the Stuntmen's Hall of Fame.

FRED LERNER (1935–)   Rodeo cowboy Fred Lerner began work as a stuntman-actor in 1959, becoming a stunt coordinator and second unit director. He worked on such Westerns as *Butch Cassidy and the Sundance Kid* (1969), *Soldier Blue* (1970) and *Little Big Man* (1971) and on episodes of Western TV series, including *Rawhide*, *Kung Fu* and *Gunsmoke*. Most of his films and TV shows were of the non–Western, action variety.

PETE LOGAN (1915–93)   Pete Logan was born in Junction, Illinois. Working in radio, he responded to a 1944 advertisement for a rodeo announcer. He read a book about rodeo, and then announced his first rodeo at Belle Fourche. He told an interviewer, "I had never seen a rodeo before." He kept his radio job while becoming an RCA announcer. Pete's rodeo-announcing career spanned four decades and was estimated at 30,000 announcing hours. He worked for the Autry/Colborn World's Championship Rodeo organization for ten years. At the mike at San Antonio for more than 30 years, he received a belt buckle in 1983 honoring his five hundredth performance. He pioneered televising rodeo, broadcasting Gene Autry's World's Championship Rodeo on the Dumont network to the East Coast and Midwest. In 1955, he announced the first coast-to-coast rodeo telecast from San Antonio on NBC-TV. With Cy Taillon, he announced the first National Finals Rodeo in 1959. Eight times he was chosen for rodeo's most prestigious event. He appeared as a rodeo announcer in three films: *The Misfits* (1961), *Run Appaloosa Run* (1969) and *Junior Bonner* (1972). He was also in *Hang Your Hat on the Wind* (1969) and on episodes of TV's *Daniel Boone* and *Gunsmoke*. He advertised Justin Boots. After retirement from rodeo, he had a syndicated radio program, *Grass Roots Gold*. He passed away in Townsend, Montana, after a long illness. He had been made an honorary Texas Ranger, and was inducted into the Rodeo Hall of the National Cowboy Museum and the ProRodeo Hall of Fame.

SHIRLEY and SHARON LUCAS   The Lucas sisters, Shirley and Sharon, were born and raised in Bartlesville, Oklahoma. It was said that when they were youngsters, they rode to school standing upright on an old farm horse. For a time, they practiced tricks just for fun, but their father's death in 1945 forced them to take life more seriously. They moved to California in 1946 and practiced until they became expert riders. Shirley, the older of the two, was a blonde. Sharon was a brunette. They often dressed alike. For a while, their mother managed the act and accompanied her daughters on the road. Their trailer served as home and office, and the horses were hauled behind. While the sisters were adept at trick roping, trick riding was their preferred specialty. At times, both young ladies performed on the same horse. Early in their careers, they practiced at the Pickwick Arena under Polly Mills Burson's supervision. They trick-rode in the Grantland Rice movie short *Sport Lite*, *Colliers* magazine featured them in a photo essay and they authored an article on trick riding for *The Western Horseman*. Sometimes they performed solo. The California-based ladies doubled and acted in such films as *Hellfire* (1949) and *A Woman of Distinction* (1950). Sharon worked in *Son of Paleface* (1952) and *The Rare Breed* (1966). Shirley was in *Annie Get Your Gun* (1950) and *Texas Carnival* (1951). Both sisters had roles in MGM's *Westward the Women* (1952) and in a *Cisco Kid* TV episode.

CHRIS LYBBERT (1954–) Chris Lybbert grew up on a farm in Coyote, California. With a rope in his hand as soon as he could walk, he roped hay bales and buckets, and tethered calves to practice tying. His father, a former PRCA calf roper, supported the boy's interest. Chris entered his first youth rodeo at about age eight. Too small for high school football, he competed in rodeos. He had a late growth spurt of six or seven inches in height and about 50 pounds in weight. Having grown too big for roughstock riding, he roped calves and wrestled steers. He roped every day while attending Cal Poly on scholarship, and he was 1977 inter-collegiate calf-roping champion.

As a professional calf roper and steer wrestler, Chris qualified for the 1979 and 1980 National Finals Rodeos in both events. In 1981, for the second consecutive year, he won the Finals' calf-roping average. In 1982, he was world champion all-around cowboy. Chris gave his horses at least 75 percent of the credit and acknowledged his traveling partner, mentors and family. In 1986, he was world champion calf roper and runner-up in the all-around standings. Chris qualified for the National Finals nine times in calf roping and five times in steer wrestling.

In 1987, while competing at Denver's National Western Rodeo, Chris was scouted for a movie role as Hopalong Cassidy in *The Great Bar 20*. Chris lacked acting experience, but looked the part of a cowboy hero and certainly could ride. The project was presented as a

World champion all-around cowboy Chris Lybbert in advertisement for the film *The Great Bar 20*, never released under that title.

tribute to old Westerns, with mild language and avoidance of sex scenes, but he feared an "R" rating for violence. He wore a white hat and rode a palomino heeling horse borrowed from a rodeo team roper. The film's villain taught Chris gun-handling techniques. Following two weeks of rehearsals, five weeks of filming began at Nevada locations. The cast included two veterans of TV Westerns, Clu Gulager and Will Hutchins (as a rodeo announcer). Legal problems kept the film unavailable until 1999 when a modified and retitled version was released directly to home video. Poorly done, it was just as poorly received. Perhaps Chris was 40 years too late to become a movie cowboy hero. He is inducted into the Rodeo Hall of the National Cowboy Museum and the Pro Rodeo Hall of Fame.

CLIFF LYONS (1902–74)   Cliff Lyons was raised on a farm in Madison, South Dakota. When his veterinarian father passed away in 1921, Cliff joined an uncle contesting at rodeos and forming a short-lived Wild West Show. By 1926, he followed Yakima Canutt from rodeo to movie stunting. Beginning with silent films, the friends sometimes worked together, staging fistfights, horseback chases and wagon crashes. As "Tex" Lyons, he starred in a series of silent Westerns and doubled in action scenes for Western stars. He doubled for Gene Autry in his first starring feature, *Tumbling Tumbleweeds*, and for Tom Mix in his final film, the serial, *The Miracle Rider*, both in 1935.

Stuntman Cliff was reliable and fearless. Not a swimmer, he strapped on a life belt and accepted water stunts. For the film *Jesse James* (1939), he jumped a horse 75 feet from a cliff into water for Tyrone Power, and then repeated the stunt for Henry Fonda. He became a regular crew member on John Ford–directed productions and those starring John Wayne. He then advanced to stunt coordinator and second unit director. Stuntman Chuck Roberson, in his book *The Fall Guy*, describes experiences on location under the supervision of Cliff, nicknamed "Mother" for his strictness.

Dedicating *3 Godfathers* (1949) to the late Harry Carey, John Ford showed Cliff in silhouette mounted on the star's horse. Playing Trooper Cliff in *She Wore a Yellow Ribbon* (1949) and a sheriff in *Wagonmaster* (1950), Cliff directed the second unit on both. He had other parts. He coordinated battle scenes involving multiple, near-simultaneous horse falls for *The Alamo* (1960), *The Comancheros* (1961) and *Major Dundee* (1965). He was a director of the Screen Actors Guild.

Cliff Lyons, rodeo rider, stuntman, stunt coordinator and actor, dressed for a role (courtesy Stephen Sally).

HARRY MADSEN   Since the 1970s, Harry Madsen, a former rodeo contestant, has been a stuntman, stunt coordinator and pyrotechnic expert working out of the East. He is most likely to do fire stunts, falls, car chases and crashes.

LARRY MAHAN (1943–)   One of rodeo's most famous names was born on a farm in Salem, Oregon. Larry Mahan rode the calves he pushed for ropers and entered youth rodeos. He won multiple titles at Arizona's state high school rodeo. Turning professional in 1963,

Program cover for a Larry Mahan rodeo held in conjunction with Spokane, Washington's EXPO in 1974.

he qualified for the 1964 National Finals Rodeo. He was 1965 world champion bull rider. In 1966, contesting in saddle bronc, bareback and bull riding, he became the first rodeo cowboy to exceed $50,000 in prize winnings and won the first of five consecutive all-around cowboy championships. Nicknamed "Bull," he frequently piloted his Comanche aircraft to rodeos. In 1973, he won a sixth all-around cowboy title, a record (tied in 1979) that stood for 25 years. Larry qualified for 12 consecutive National Finals Rodeos.

Larry exemplifies the businessman-cowboy. He has instructed through rodeo schools, a book and videos. He promotes his own lines of Western fashion. He is seen in print advertisements and in several films, including *J.W. Coop* (1972), *The Honkers* (1972), *Mackintosh and TJ* (1976) and *Good Old Boys* (1995). *The Great American Cowboy* (1973), by Keith Merill, arguably the finest rodeo film ever made, features the competition between Larry and Phil Lyne for the 1972 All-Around Cowboy championship. Narrated by Joel McCrea, the film earned a 1973 Academy Award as Best Feature-Length Documentary. At one time, Larry sang at rodeos, fairs and nightclubs. He has appeared on various TV shows and as a TV rodeo commentator. He raises cattle and horses, has mastered aspects of horsemanship and participates in rodeo and charitable functions. Larry is an inductee of the Rodeo Hall at the National Cowboy Museum and of the ProRodeo Hall of Fame.

AL MANN (c. 1903–2002) Al Mann, a native of Wyoming, competed in rodeos in the early 1920s. When a movie company came to the area, he allowed himself to be roped off his horse for the film. His wife Irene was a trick rider. Al went on to become a rodeo contract and circus performer, specializing in jumping horses. While in New York, he doubled Ken Maynard on the film *Janice Meredith* (1925).

WILLIAM BENNET MARKLEY, JR. (1913–86) Bill Markley rodeoed as a steer wrestler and worked as a clown-bullfighter for 16 years, assisting younger clowns, including Slim Pickens. He was a stuntman in the 1950s, doubling for Chill Wills.

KEN MAYNARD (1895–1973) Ken Maynard was born at Vevay, Indiana, and shortly moved to Columbus. The young daredevil reportedly crashed a bicycle-powered biplane and accepted a circus' challenge to ride a steer. Neighbors recalled that he practiced trick riding in vacant lots and gave public performances of his skills. He left home in his teens, honing his roping and trick riding skills with Wild West Shows and circuses. Following World War I engineer service, he headlined Ringling Brothers Circus Wild West Show.

Reports of Ken winning rodeo championships are probably exaggerated. A spectator at 1929's Pendleton Round-Up, he made no mention of contesting earlier, stating, "I played in Pendleton eight or nine years ago when I was with the circus." He may have competed at some rodeos. About the title "world champion trick rider," Ken told a reporter in 1929, "I won the world's championship in several places, but darned if I know now whether I really was world's champion. There were three of us fellows who could all ride about equally well and we always tried to keep apart... The other two, I think, were world's champions, too. Of course, though, each of us think that we're just a little bit better than the other." Spurious attribution of championships notwithstanding, Ken's riding proficiency among cinema cowboy stars was unquestioned.

Inspired by Buck Jones, Ken made motion picture contacts, resulting in minor screen parts in 1923. His riding as Paul Revere in *Janice Meredith* (1925) demonstrated his potential as a Western star. With his palomino horse Tarzan, Ken joined Tom Mix, Hoot Gibson

Ken Maynard and Tarzan at the 1941 Fort Worth, Texas, rodeo (courtesy *Fort Worth Star-Telegram* Photograph Collection. University of Texas at Arlington Libraries, Arlington. AR 4062–73–38).

and Buck Jones, as a hard-riding, top-tier Western action star. His films featured his riding skills and contributions by Tarzan. Madison Square Garden's 1927 World Series Rodeo program featured a pictorial spread on Ken. In the late 1920s, Madison Square Garden's champion cowboys were awarded Ken Maynard Trophies.

Until the end of the 1920s, Ken enjoyed the lifestyle of a silent film superstar. He had a Hollywood mansion, cars, motorcycles, a boat and his own airplane. He traveled to Europe and Latin America. A multi-talented individual, he contributed ideas and writing to his films. Making the transition to sound pictures, he sang and accompanied himself in several later films. Credited as the first of the singing cowboys, he recorded Western songs; a songbook was published under his name. In 1934, Gene Autry and Smiley Burnette were introduced in his films *In Old Santa Fe* and *Mystery Mountain*.

In the 1930s, Ken made Westerns at a number of different studios at varied budgets. He worked hard and was sensitive to the image he projected, but he had a weakness for alcohol, was abrasive to work with and often failed to stay within budget. These traits caused more than one studio to drop him. In 1936, Ken lost a sizable investment when his Wild West Show failed. By the later 1930s, his films were fewer and made at lower-budget studios. He toured with circuses.

In 1941, Ken headlined major rodeos at Fort Worth, Chicago and San Francisco. His rodeo act featured sharpshooting and a successor to the original Tarzan that had died the previous year. In early 1943, Ken starred at a rodeo he and Jute Smith produced at Los Angeles' Gilmore Stadium. He began a Monogram series of six Trail Blazer films with old pal Hoot Gibson. Although past their prime, the stars were still capable of entertaining fans. Ken's final starring Western was *Harmony Trail* in 1944. Throughout the 1940s, he made theater and circus appearances. He starred at the California Rodeo at Salinas in 1952 and at Sacramento's Days of '49 Rodeo in 1954. From May through October of 1955, he appeared at a dozen or so Bob Estes' rodeos, touring Louisiana, Oklahoma and Texas.

Ken lived out his retirement years in reduced circumstances and relative obscurity, estranged from his brother Kermit. In 1962, he attended the funeral of old compadre Hoot Gibson. Bertha, his wife of 28 years, died in 1968. That year, the Rodeo Sports News carried Lysle Greenman's sale offer of Ken's silver-trimmed Bohlin saddle for $1,750. Kermit passed away in January 1970. One of the most memorable Western film stars of the 1920s and 1930s, he died of stomach cancer at the Motion Picture Home.

KERMIT MAYNARD (1897–1971) Kermit Roosevelt Maynard was born in Vevay, Indiana. He developed his horsemanship skills early in life, and was active in sports. Urged by brother Ken, Kermit moved to Hollywood as a movie stuntman. As "Tex" Maynard, he starred in a series of silent Westerns (1927–28), gaining experience but minimal pay. He returned to stunting in support of brother Ken and other Western stars, and some acting. At a location ranch to film jousting scenes for Will Rogers' film *A Connecticut Yankee in King Arthur's Court* (1930), Kermit spotted a blue-gray horse in the corral. He rode the four-year-old, steady-gaited horse in the film, bought him for $90 and named him Rocky. After finishing second in 1931, Kermit won the California Rodeo's 1933 trick and fancy riding championship on Rocky.

From 1934 to 1937, Kermit starred in a series of 18 outdoor adventures for Ambassador, with Rocky as his principal steed. These films, with Western, Northwest Mounted Police or lumberman stories, had above-average supporting casts and action. Adequate as an actor and a superior horseman, Kermit did not achieve lasting stardom, but returned to stunting

Kermit Maynard, Salinas' 1933 trick riding champion, Western film star, stuntman and supporting player (courtesy of Eddie Brandt's).

and character parts. From the 1940s, he was a familiar face in Western films and TV series. For more than 20 years, Rocky lived in retirement on Kermit's small North Hollywood ranch.

Stunting in Canada on *Northwest Stampede* (1947), Kermit and Polly Mills Burson were trampled by horses rushing from a corral. Protecting Polly with his body, he incurred head and back injuries that required hospital treatment. Discontinuing stunt work in the late 1950s, he retired from the screen in the early 1960s. In later years, he was a representative of the Screen Extras Guild, played golf and coached youth sports.

ROY MCADAMS   At age 19, Roy McAdams was reserve world champion bullfighter of the American Junior Rodeo Association. He rode professionally for several years. Rodeo skills helped him get his first stunt and acting jobs. He worked on TV's *Dallas*, the miniseries *Lonesome Dove* and in movies, including *Silverado* (1985). He has written for the screen.

FRANK MCCARROLL (1892–1954)   Minnesota-born Frank McCarroll worked on ranches, did some boxing and wrestling, and contested in Wyoming rodeos. In the mid–1920s, he won steer wrestling championships at New York City and Chicago rodeos. Beginning in the 1930s, he worked as a movie stuntman, double and actor for 20 years, mostly in B-Westerns. His craggy face often represented one of the villain gang.

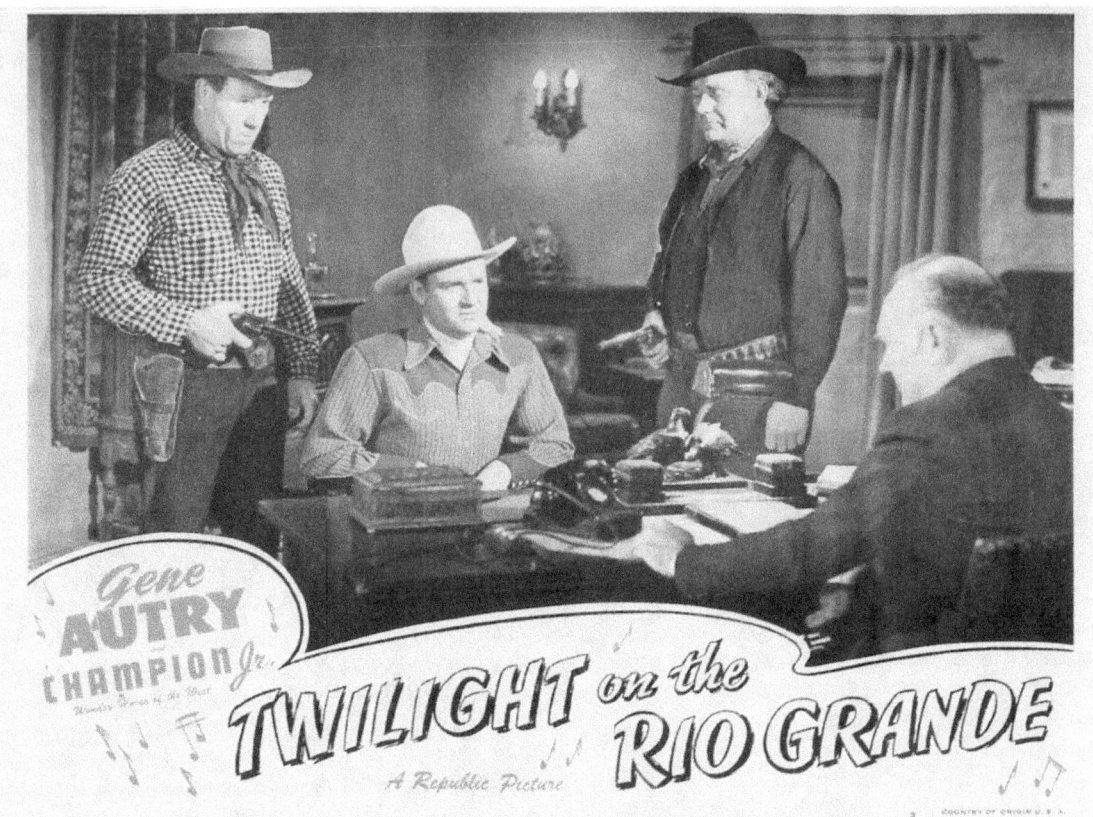

Former rodeo contestant Frank McCarroll (left) and Tex Terry (right) are heavies covering Gene Autry in this lobby card scene from *Twilight on the Rio Grande* (Republic, 1947), (© 2004 Autry Qualified Interest Trust and The Autry Foundation, provided courtesy Gene Autry Entertainment).

WILEY MCCRAY (c. 1916–77)   Wiley McCray began riding rodeo bulls and broncs in 1931. He became a rodeo clown in 1938, generally specializing as a barrel man and adding laughter to the arena. He was the first clown inducted into Omaha's Ak-Sar-Ben Western Hall of Fame. He admitted to "five or so" movies, including *The Honkers* (1972) with friend Slim Pickens.

MIKE MCGAUGHY   Mike McGaughy, a professional movie stuntman, actor and stunt coordinator from 1970, is a PRCA roper of long standing. His films include Westerns, as well as other action-oriented movies. He coordinated stunts for *The Legend of the Lone Ranger* (1981), *¡Three Amigos!* (1986) and *8 Seconds* (1994), and the TV movies *Bonanza: The Return* and *Bonanza: Under Attack*. He won the "Most Spectacular Stunt Sequence" award for the mini-series *North and South*. He has appeared in commercials and participated in celebrity roping-cutting events for charity.

VERA MCGINNIS (1892–1990)   An early cowgirl trick rider and relay racer, Vera McGinnis won championships in both events at Tex Austin's London rodeo in 1926. She toured Europe and Asia, and worked as a film stuntwoman and actress. In 1934, she was seriously injured in a racehorse fall. She was inducted into the Rodeo Hall of the National Cowboy Museum.

GENE MCLAUGHLIN (1929–)   Gene McLaughlin was born in Chester, Pennsylvania. His father, a trick roper and rodeo rider, taught older brother Don to trick rope as a toddler. Gene, two years younger, learned mostly by watching. The boys first performed at the Million Dollar Pier in Atlantic City when Gene was three years old. Beginning in 1934 and continuing for 14 years, Gene and Don roped at Madison Square Garden's rodeo. They

Gene McLaughlin, trick roper (Gene McLaughlin personal photograph, obtained from PRCA–Media, Colorado Springs, CO. Used with permission).

witnessed the 1936 Boston Garden walkout and joined the Cowboys Turtle Association. They performed at many rodeos until the brother trick roping act ended in the late 1940s. From high school age, both contested in calf roping. Don won world championships as a calf roper five times and as a steer roper three times, ranking in the top ten for one or both of his events for most of his career. He passed away in 1994. Gene continued trick roping solo, returned to Madison Square Garden as a calf roper, taught lariat roping at a dance studio and operated a stable in Dallas. In a 1966 trick roping contest at Oklahoma City, Gene was runner-up to Jim Eskew, Jr. At Palm Springs' 1967 rodeo, he performed his trick roping act on ice skates. He began in 1963 as a movie stunt double and bit player. His film work included six years on TV's *Bonanza* and involvement in individual episodes of *The Big Valley*, *Gunsmoke* and *Code Red*. He played Will Rogers in the TV movie *Ziegfeld: The Man and His Women* (1978). With his son Cliff, he participated in *Gambler II* (1983), starring Kenny Rogers. He coached Johnny Crawford in trick roping and loaned Johnny his roping horse for competitions. His many film credits include *Urban Cowboy* (1980). He coached Keith Carradine in roping for his role in Broadway's *The Will Rogers Follies*. Gene continues to enter senior rodeos and exhibit his trick roping.

JIMMY MEDEARIS   Jimmy Medearis, a top rodeo trick rider, became a movie wrangler and has handled movie livestock all over the world. He was head wrangler on *Stir Crazy* (1980).

TOM MIX (1880–1940)   Born at Mix Run, Pennsylvania, Tom Mix learned to ride as a young man. Buffalo Bill's Wild West Show and stories inspired him to become a Western star. At Col. Zach Mulhall's Oklahoma ranch, he prepared for Wild West Shows at the St. Louis World's Fair in 1904 and at Madison Square Garden in 1905. He reportedly roomed with friend Will Rogers on the road. He joined the Miller Brothers' 101 Ranch, meeting Bill Pickett and developing roping and trick riding skills. In 1907 he toured with their Wild West Show, billed as "Champion All-Around Cowboy." He also entered rodeos.

At the 1909 Alaska-Yukon-Pacific Exhibition in Seattle, Tom (with Cheyenne Bill's Wild West and Congress of Rough Riders) displayed roping skills. In addition, promotions promised, "Pony Express by Tom Mix, champion pony express rider of the world." One report stated,

> The pony express riding by Tom Mix won instant favor. He gave a great exhibition of the horsemanship that made the pony express of the American frontier world renowned in the old days. Leaping from a running horse with his mail pouch, Mix seized a waiting pony by the mane and saddle pommel and was off hanging by the horse's side for a long distance before climbing into the saddle.

When a rival show opened nearby, Cheyenne Bill's show added wild steer events. One report read,

> Tom Mix, broncho buster and pony express rider, is giving a great exhibition of roping, tying, and riding wild range cattle. Mix will do stunts this afternoon and tonight that will make even old-time Westerners sit up and take notice. There is plenty of excitement from the time the steers are chased into the arena until they are finally subdued and ridden by Mix and his brother broncho busters.

Making movies in the area of Canon City, Colorado, in 1909, Tom was champion of the Royal Gorge Rodeo. With the Selig film company, he developed his screen persona and contributed details to his films. He appeared with Col. Mulhall's Wild West Show at the 1910 Appalachian Exposition at Knoxville, Tennessee. In March 1912, Tom accompanied Guy Weadick to Calgary to obtain backing for a Stampede, a mission finalized in Mr. Weadick's subsequent meetings.

At the annual Prescott Frontier Days Rodeo in the summer of 1913, Mr. and Mrs. Tom Mix led the grand entry. Tom entered a number of events. In the trick and fancy roping event, "Tom Mix, who exhibited a number of stunts not quite so elaborate [as the winner] was awarded second money." A reporter commented,

> Mr. Mix is also skilled, and was contented to receive the second prize, which he well earned. This feature provided the drawing card of the day, and has never before been equaled in this section in the variety of the stunts both men so cleverly executed.

Tom also contested in bronco busting. In the bulldogging event,

> Tom Mix had the misfortune to have his steer interfered with by another coming on the track, when he was compelled to postpone the attack to throw it to the ground, several watchers giving the loss of time at least 5 seconds. Mix made the most beautiful leap from the saddle of the day, after the field was clear, and made the time of 18.5 seconds. His feat was given a deserved ovation.

The potato race was engaged by two four-man mounted teams, one captained by Tom. Each man, armed with a sharpened lath, tried to spear potatoes out of a box 100 yards from his home goal, and carry them to his side's box. Tom's team won first prize. Tom participated in the horseback tug of war and in the wild horse race. He placed second out of two contestants in the trick-riding event, reports stating, "Mix was decidedly outclassed, although he is a wonderfully daring and skilled horseman." In the finale of the day, Tom entered the steer-riding event. The outcome as reported:

> None of the riders remained on top for more than six jumps, and most of them fell overboard before they got to going. Tom Mix, however, managed to sail to the best advantage...

Mrs. Mix placed second in the cowgirl race, and, overall, Tom collected $99 in prize money.

At the Northern Arizona Fair Rodeo in the fall of 1913, Tom led the parade, served as director and judge, and won the relay race. Event #1 was entitled, "Range pastimes— Tom Mix and his Fox Film Company." Tom returned to Prescott in later years. In 1915, at a Los Angeles rodeo, Tom was an outrider on Tony in a race between two four-horse chuckwagons. The teams collided, crashing the wagons, and spilling Tom and Tony in the process. Tony was unhurt, but Tom was injured.

With the progressive Fox studio, Tom's daring action and flamboyant manner made him the right man at the right time to dominate Westerns in the "Roaring Twenties." The influence of Tom Mix and his horse Tony on future Western films is undeniable. Tom in the mid–1920s made a personal appearance tour, visited Europe and called on the president of the United States. The late 1920s saw additional films, but the end of the decade brought the Depression, the onset of sound films and Tom's departure from Fox. He made a handful of sound Westerns for F.B.O., and then toured with a circus. In response to popular demand, he returned to Hollywood to make additional sound films for Universal from 1931 to 1933. During this period, he appeared with William S. Hart and Tim McCoy at a Hoot Gibson rodeo in California.

Tom left Hollywood again to tour with a circus, soon obtaining ownership. In early

Tom Mix and Tony.

1934, he visited Fort Worth's opening rodeo performance. Later that year, he volunteered to appear at the Texas Prison Rodeo. His final film was the Mascot serial *The Miracle Rider* (1935). His circus enjoyed some success, but eventually folded. In 1936, Tom was in the press box at Tucson's La Fiesta de los Vaqueros rodeo. He won a chariot race with Buck Jones at a 1938 Newhall, California, rodeo. In early 1940, he appeared at the Palm Springs rodeo, and then was killed in an Arizona automobile accident on October 12. At the Madison Square Garden rodeo, in progress, headliner Gene Autry paid tribute to Tom's rodeo contributions.

Tom was inducted into the National Cowboy Hall of Fame's Hall of Great Western Performers, and he was honored with a Golden Boot Founders Award.

MONTIE MONTANA (1910–98) Montie Montana was born Owen Harlan Mickel, the youngest of five children, in North Dakota, but moved early with his family to Wolf Point, Montana, which he claimed as his hometown. In 1916, he saw his first rodeo, organized by his dad for a local celebration. A rope spinner's performance excited his enthusiasm to develop his own competence. During a power outage at a local theater, Montie's impromptu rope trick performance on stage was his first before an audience. Roping outside the theater and train depot brought donations in his hat to buy an occasional movie ticket. His dad sold horses during Miles City's rodeo, where Montie secured his first job over the 1925 Fourth of July holiday. Standing on a horse behind his dad, Montie roped for the duration of the rodeo parade. For $5 a day, he spun his rope at the rodeo.

Montie went along when his parents sold their house and took to the road. His dad gave illustrated talks on the West, and Montie trick-roped. As he drove the family's live-in vehicles, he got to know much of the country. Financial receipts were spotty, but the family kept going. In 1926 at Livingston, Montana, Montie earned $100 for three days of rodeo trick roping. In his mid-teens, he acquired a retired circus pinto of about the same age, beginning a lifetime association with pintos, most of which were publicly called Rex. At Miles City, he was awarded a hat as the best-dressed parade cowboy. His parents augmented his outfit with decorations so Montie, like his idol Tom Mix, could present a flashy appearance. In later years, Montie and his troupe wore beautiful costumes. His parents, who formed a whip act, had a sense of show business and encouraged their son. For a time, the family traveled with a circus. In 1928, Montie entertained, with his dad, at the Pendleton Roundup. In 1929, they were briefly part of Buck Jones' Wild West Show. They were billed as "The Montana Cowboys." When an announcer, forgetting his name, introduced him as "Montie from Montana," the young roper became Montie Montana. Montie roped at Madison Square Garden's rodeo with his parents' whip and boomerang act.

Settling in California in 1930, Montie roped at Hoot Gibson's Saugus rodeo and for radio broadcasts before live studio audiences. He worked fairs and rodeos, mostly in the Los Angeles area. In 1933, he married Louise. Montie's early association with Hollywood included teaching 40 young women to spin ropes for the Shirley Temple film *Stand Up and Cheer* (1934). He starred with former rodeo hands Yakima Canutt and Ben Corbett in the Western *Circle of Death* (1934). At the Wolf Point rodeo in 1935, Montie trick-roped and trick-rode. Louise gradually began to play a bigger role, trick-riding and being part of Montie's roping catches. In 1936, Montie added pinto liberty horses to his act. Hiring trick ropers and riders, he coordinated and furnished rodeo contract acts. By 1938, he joined rodeo's new Cowboys' Turtle Association. That year, he introduced son Montie, Jr., who soon joined the family act. Montie and family entertained at rodeos throughout the western United States and Canada.

Montie Montana (on Sheik).

Aside from Will Rogers, Montie was probably the best-known and most popular in his field. He was described as showman-wise and colorful. His smile, personality and humorous patter exuded an enthusiastic, carefree spirit that evoked audience rapport. His polished act earned praise for its professionalism, speed, class and showmanship. Outside the arena, he was known for warm friendliness. Away from the public eye, he practiced his riding-roping maneuvers and trained his horses, always developing younger horses for the future. During World War II, he worked on a farm and performed for servicemen. He contributed to some films. In 1944, daughter Linda was born, becoming part of advertisements as a toddler. By 1949, she joined the family act. The "Montie Montana Family" performed at rodeos into the late 1960s. In the early 1970s, when Montie and Louise divorced, father and son continued to perform.

In 1945, Montie began a 20-year relationship with Weber's Bread that brought him and a stagecoach to schools, where he talked and entertained. Personal contact with thousands of schoolchildren (as well as advertising) made Montie even more recognizable. Publicity was one of Montie's strengths. At rodeo locations, newspapers commonly pictured him riding Rex into a business or public building. On Weber Bread tours, rodeo clowns Slim Pickens or Jess Kell often drove the stage. A radio program, *Weber's All-Star Western Theater*, featured Montie and The Riders of the Purple Sage.

In the later 1940s, Montie appeared in the film *Sitting Pretty* and he played a sheriff in *Down Dakota Way* (1949) with Roy Rogers. He rode in President Truman's inaugural parade. For the film *The Story of Will Rogers* (1952), he doubled star Will Rogers, Jr.'s, horse-catch roping and lent technical support. At President Eisenhower's 1953 inaugural parade, he was

Montie Montana, spinning a lariat loop from atop his horse, entertains patients outside the Fort Carson Army Hospital during the 1957 Pikes Peak or Bust Rodeo. He also toured wards with his horse (courtesy Pikes Peak Library District Local History Collection, Colorado Springs, CO. Stewarts #1853).

Montie Montana in New Mexico's Rodeo de Santa Fe parade in 1997, Montie's last performing season.

photographed roping (with permission) the newly elected chief executive. Montie obtained roles in, or provided behind-the-scenes advice for, Western TV series. He trick-rode and doubled and/or appeared in John Ford films. While at a 1971 Madison Square Garden rodeo, Montie took his horse to the top of the Empire State Building.

In his later years, Montie could look back upon service to charitable causes involving youth, hospitals, senior citizens and military servicepersons. He was Honorary Mayor of Northridge, California, for ten years and Chief of Staff for the Los Angeles County Sheriff's Posse for 27 years. He performed at the Dodge National Circuit Finals Rodeo in 1987 and at the opening of the 1993 National Finals Rodeo in Las Vegas. Wolf Point, Montana, saluted his fiftieth year in show business, with many celebrities paying tribute. He was inducted into rodeo halls of fame at Pendleton, Salinas and Colorado Springs.

In 1989, Montie was inducted into the Rodeo Hall of the National Cowboy Museum. He received a Golden Boot Award and was honored in Newhall's Walk of Western Stars. In 1993, he completed 60 consecutive years of appearances in the Tournament of Roses Parade, and he published his autobiography, *Not Without My Horse*. The ProRodeo Hall of Fame inducted him in 1994. In 1997, he was honored guest and grand marshal at the fortieth anniversary of the Brawley, California, Cattle Call Rodeo. The PRCA's senior performing contract entertainer at age 86, he performed at Pendleton, Ellensburg and Santa Fe rodeos. He was proud of his record of fulfilling performance commitments. Montie passed away following a series of strokes.

BENNIE MOORE (1952–) A former rodeo cowboy, Bennie Moore became a stuntman. He prefers horse stunts but has worked primarily in non–Western TV and films since the 1970s.

DENNIS MOTES Dennis Motes, with his brother as partner, was 1977's world champion team roper. He qualified for the National Finals Rodeo nine times. He was a wrangler for *Heaven's Gate* (1980) and *Far and Away* (1992). He has worked as a stuntman and he contributed to the TV series, *Paradise*.

PAT NORTH OMMERT (c. 1930–) Pat North was a child rodeo star as part of her mother's dancing horse act. She debuted as a trick rider at age 16. She raced in Tijuana's Powder Puff Derby, and trick-rode at Los Angeles' Coliseum, Madison Square Garden and many other rodeos. She served as a movie extra, once doubled Anne Baxter and appeared in *A Star Is Born* (1954).

Pat North Ommert was adept at trick riding as shown in this 1959 photo of her one-foot flyaway, and at Roman riding (Ken Frey photograph for Pat North Ommert's personal publicity folio. Used with permission of Pat North Ommert).

GEORGE ORRISON (1929–2001)   A Los Angeles rodeo cowboy, George Orrison performed stunts on TV's *Laramie* and *Laredo*. He doubled Lee Marvin in *Cat Ballou* (1965) and appeared in many Clint Eastwood films.

CHUCK PARKISON (1918–88)   Born at Rapid City, South Dakota, Chuck Parkison rode bareback horses and bulls as a teen, and served rodeos as a bucking chute supervisor. While working at California's Douglas Aircraft in the early war years, he assisted with saddle club rodeos. Upon discharge from Army ordnance service, he substituted for an ill rodeo announcer, stopped competing, and then announced full-time. Providing information on rodeo contestants, describing action, introducing celebrities and playing straight man for clowns, he felt was the greatest announcing challenge in sports. He announced the nation's largest indoor rodeo at Houston for 24 years and the largest outdoor rodeo at Cheyenne for 26 years. He announced at Madison Square Garden, Boston Garden and the Texas State Fair Rodeo, in addition to many others. Six times, he announced the National Finals Rodeo. When the lights went out at an Idaho night performance, he led the crowd in 30 minutes of singing.

He was the first celebrity endorser for Tony Lama boots and promoted Tem-Tex clothing. He appeared in three rodeo films, *Bronco Buster* and *The Lusty Men*, both in 1952, and *The Honkers* (1972), as well as in TV's *Stoney Burke* and *Wide Country*. For TV, he was in an episode of *Screen Director's Playhouse* with Casey Tibbs and on *Dallas*. In 1976, his eldest son Cappy, a Hollywood stuntman, was killed in a movie location accident.

Chuck continued to announce many of the nation's major rodeos. He died of a heart attack between performances at Cheyenne. Singer Johnny Western participated in an arena memorial service. Chuck was honored in 1970 as ProRodeo's Man of the Year. He was inducted into the Ak-Sar-Ben Western Hall of Fame and the ProRodeo Hall of Fame.

PAT PAUL   Pat Paul was a rodeo trick rider. She appeared with Tex Ritter's 1952 London show "Texas" and contributed to such films as *The Story of Will Rogers* (1952).

SLIM PICKENS (1919–83)   Louis Burton Lindley, Jr., was born at Kingsburg, California. To circumvent his father's opposition to his rodeo riding, he competed under aliases, one of which, "Slim Pickens," stuck. At age 16, he left home to rodeo, entering all riding events and steer wrestling. Prize money was not abundant. Jobs included horse trainer, oil field roughneck, mountain guide, dairyman and ranch worker. For a $5 fee, he substituted as a rodeo clown and began on-the-job training. He fought bulls and competed until World War II Army Air Corps service. Medically discharged in early 1944, he soon returned to rodeo action. Clown Homer Holcomb once said that Slim was "too good to quit rodeo and not good enough to stay with it." A rodeo promoter thought Slim was a natural clown because he looked so funny riding a bronc. His face, he was told, was funny enough that he didn't need clown makeup. When injuries forced Homer's retirement, Slim added Homer's bookings to his own.

Slim was tall for clowning, yet quick on his feet. He said his size made a good target for the bulls. Distinctive in his toreador outfit and cape, he stated that a bullfighter could make his job as dangerous as he wished. He was never one to avoid risk, to save a downed rider or to thrill an audience. His early act included his mule Judy. He Roman-rode with mounts of divergent size, did take-offs on trick riding and donned a Lone Ranger–style mask to race

In a series of 11 films, including *Red River Shore* (Republic, 1953), Slim Pickens (right) was sidekick to singing cowboy Rex Allen (center). Douglas Fowley is on left.

Judy against a cowpony in the "garbage derby." He burlesqued the bulldogging and roping events. Playing Dr. I. Cutem Up and undertaker Digger O'Dell, he announced that he could give both first and last aid to contestants. His clowning earned rave reviews and more job offers.

In March 1949, Slim married Maggie, whom he met at the Modesto rodeo. In August, fire destroyed their cabin home in California. The show went on. That fall, traveling between Texas and Oregon rodeos, Slim had car problems that delayed him until the rodeo closed, resulting in lost wages. To focus on clowning, he limited his contesting to steer wrestling, from which he acquired a "trick knee" that went out every so often. With mobility and speed impaired, he took on a more stationary bullfighting style. Relying on know-how and his cape to guide bulls around him, he remained at the top of his field.

In 1945, he made $25 working on the film *Smoky*. He gained a part in *Rocky Mountain* (1950). From 1952 through 1954, he was sidekick to singing cowboy Rex Allen in 11 Republic films. The two were friends for life. Other films included several for Republic and some for Walt Disney Studios including *The Great Locomotive Chase*.

During the 1954 rodeo season and beyond, Slim clowned and fought bulls, but sometimes entertained. Hollywood fame made him more popular than ever. He rode into the arena on his trained horse at a dead run, using an A-frame saddle with no cinch. Reaching the center of the arena, the horse lowered its head and stopped suddenly. Slim, with saddle, flew over the horse's head. He got up, took a bow and proceeded to cue his high-schooled horse through a series of tricks, including blanket stealing and a drunken act. At Eugene, Oregon, in 1955, he appeared first in a floppy black hat and cowboy clothes. He switched to the character of Davy's brother "Half Crockett" and, finally, to his matador outfit. He appeared at theaters showing his films. An advertisement in the 1956 *Rodeo Sports News Annual* called him "The Sagebrush 'Valentino' of the Silver Screen" and "The Beau Brummell of All Rodeo Clowns."

In *The Big Country* (1958), Slim's Appaloosa Dear John, a trained bucking horse, played wily Old Thunder, Gregory Peck's nemesis. Allowing no one else to ride his horse, Slim doubled the star in some riding and falling scenes. As time went on, Slim at 200 pounds was not so slim. A regular cast member on several TV series, he was a guest on others and was in TV movies. In 1959 at Camdenton's J Bar H Rodeo, he shared star billing with Casey Tibbs and Tex Wiliams. He clowned into the early 1960s, stating that rodeo let him meet the public and motivated him to get his weight down — and that he just plain liked it. About rodeo, he later said, "I've found out there's some pretty smart people around who ain't never been on a gentle horse yet."

The "Roving Romeo of the Rodeo Circuit," Slim was involved in incidents that became part of rodeo's legend. Having hocked his boots to help pay entry fees at an early Prescott rodeo, he walked about in his stocking feet confident that prize winnings would allow him to redeem the boots. At Clovis in 1947, he followed a bull over the fence onto the track, distracting the animal from bystanders until it could be restrained. In 1949, when a Toppenish pick-up man fell under a rampaging bull, Slim ran in and directed the bull away from the fallen rider, who suffered only minor injuries. In 1951, when the Cow Palace initiated a new bareback wild horse race, Slim set the example for reluctant cowboys. On a movie set, he steered a bull away from an unaware Yakima Canutt.

Slim picked up his share of arena injuries. He rode at Dublin with his collarbone in a cast. Shortly, he fell from a saddle bronc and was stepped on, breaking ribs. In 1947, a bull nicked him at San Francisco. In 1951 at Fort Worth, a bull knocked him, still limping from an earlier injury, over the rail. He struck his head on a concrete wall and was bruised. An early tally of injuries showed two broken legs, two skull fractures, two cracked elbows, feet broken three times and multiple broken ribs. A Calgary newspaper reported in 1954, "[T]he bull riding event ... almost spelled disaster for veteran clown Slim Pickens... The bull's horn ripped his clothing to shreds and grazed his body. For a moment it was thought he had been gored, but after recovering his wind, Pickens was soon back in action although he admitted later that it was the closest shave he had experienced in years of fighting ... bulls." At Edmonton in 1956, he was kicked in the head by a bareback bronc, incurring a slight concussion and 18 stitches. In 1957 at Stockton, a bull's kick to his face resulted in 30 stitches and ousted him from the rodeo. In the early 1960s at Medicine Hat, Alberta, a bull ran over his spine, leading to his retirement from rodeo clowning.

As a character actor, Slim played memorable roles in films such as *One-Eyed Jacks* (1961), *Blazing Saddles* (1974), *Tom Horn* (1980) and *Honeysuckle Rose* (1980). He drove the stage in the remake of *Stagecoach* (1966) and in *The Ballad of Cable Hogue* (1970). As a rodeo clown in *The Honkers* (1972), he sang his composition, "I'm a Rodeo Cowboy." Some were comedy parts, but he was also convincing as a villain. *Dr. Strangelove* (1964) jump-started his movie career just about the time that rodeo injuries were taking their toll. Replacing injured Peter Sellers, he was cast as B-52 pilot, Major T.J. (King) Kong, shown riding an atomic bomb to earth. He quipped that Peter Sellers' ankle was the best break he ever had. Film offers were more frequent, more lucrative and more varied.

Slim and Don Collier accepted Salinas' 1962 award for their TV Western *The Outlaws*. In 1966 at Cheyenne Frontier Days, Slim presented Wyoming's governor with a commemorative carbine. He and his family attended the 1967 Palm Springs Rodeo. He advertised Tony Lama boots, Gross Tailor, Tem-Tex jeans, Panhandle Slim and Bailey Hats.

In 1973, he was a guest at Prescott, where he had clowned and ridden bulls 33 years earlier. Film commitments cut his visit short.

In 1975, he narrated a 60-minute TV documentary entitled *Rodeo — A Matter of Style*. At private social gatherings, he recited numerous songs and poems. Rex Allen, Jr., recalled that he first heard lyrics to the song "When the Work's All Done Next Fall" when Slim recited them at the Allen household. In 1979, Slim recorded recitations for Blue Canyon Records.

At North Platte, Nebraska, Slim received the Buffalo Bill Award. He was named 1974 Rodeo Man of the Year. He was a trustee of the ProRodeo Hall of Fame. In 1982, he was inducted into the Hall of Great Western Performers at the National Cowboy Hall of Fame. Slim appeared to be recovering from surgery for removal of a small brain tumor; however, he died of pneumonia in 1983.

BILL PICKETT (1870–1932)

Bill Pickett, born one of 13 children of former slaves, was raised in Travis County, Texas. As a youngster, he watched cow dogs subdue steers by biting their lips. He and his brothers broke wild stock for a living. One day in the 1880s, Bill leaped from his horse, grasped a recalcitrant steer and imitated the cow dog by biting the animal's lip, gaining the steer's compliance. Repeating this practice in an arena act, Bill, "The Dusky Demon," well under six feet in height and weighing about 155 pounds, won renown as the first bulldogger–steer wrestler. Others followed his lead.

Bill worked with Tom Mix at the 101 Ranch and joined the Wild West

Bill Pickett, credited with originating the event of bulldogging or steer wrestling, starred in the film *The Bull-Dogger* (Norman Film Company, 1923). (North Fort Worth Historical Society photograph, used with permission. Obtained from PRCA–Media, Colorado Springs, CO.)

Show. His tours included Cheyenne Frontier Days. At Madison Square Garden, with Will Rogers, he helped retrieve a runaway steer from the stands. He visited Canada and Europe. In 1908, to satisfy his boss' bet, he rode into a hostile Mexican bullring to prevail, despite injuries, over a fighting bull.

Retired in 1917, Bill returned to the 101 Ranch, where he had worked behind the scenes filming movies. He appeared in two short films, including *The Crimson Skull* (1924). *The Bull-Dogger* (1923), displaying his cowboy skills, is in the Library of Congress. Working to liquidate the ranch's stock in 1932, he was kicked in the head by an unruly horse and died of the injury. He is buried on the 101 Ranch's Cowboy Hill. His boss Zack Miller released a poem, "Old Bill Is Dead." Bill was inducted into the Rodeo Hall at the National Cowboy Museum and the ProRodeo Hall of Fame. A statue of Bill bulldogging is displayed at the Cowtown Coliseum in Fort Worth. A black rodeo series is named for him.

WILBUR PLAUGHER (1922–) Rodeo competitor and clown Wilbur Plaugher appeared in two Disney films, *The Horse with the Flying Tail* (1960) and *Run Appaloosa Run* (1969). He was also in two episodes of TV's *Daniel Boone*, and in Gospel Films' *More Than a Champion* (1980). He was inducted into the ProRodeo Hall of Fame.

DAN POORE Dan Poore rodeoed with Rex Allen in Willcox, Arizona. He won calf roping at several rodeos and was 1951 IRA world champion steer wrestler. Encouraged by Ben Johnson, he did movie stunts and bit roles in early 1950s Westerns.

JERRY ANN PORTWOOD (TAYLOR) (1930–) Born in Seymour, Texas, Jerry Ann Portwood was raised on a ranch and, by age six, was riding in stock shows. In 1945, she

Wilbur Plaugher, rodeo competitor, rodeo clown and film player, confronts a Brahma bull at the Pikes Peak or Bust Rodeo. Jimmy Schumacher is the clown in the barrel (courtesy Pikes Peak Library District Local History Collection, Colorado Springs, CO. Stewarts #1241).

was an official "ranch girl" at Madison Square Garden and Boston Garden. The 15-year-old drum majorette and school newspaper editor was the youngest to be invited. Dressed in Western clothing, the ranch girls traveled about a city promoting the rodeo. In the arena, they were introduced prior to the grand entry. The cities, the rodeo and the headline star, Roy Rogers, impressed her. Inspired by top trick riders, she became one. Developing her skills on her palomino, Mazie, she trick-rode at major rodeos. In 1948, she returned as a trick rider to Madison Square Garden, where Gene Autry was the star. Among her New York publicity chores, she delivered steaks, purportedly from cattle used in the film *Red River*, to radio disc jockeys. Known for style and color, as well as her riding skill, she chose rodeo because she enjoyed riding and rodeo people.

Rex Allen became a family friend. She invested in a wardrobe of 60 costumes, seldom repeating an outfit at a rodeo. Her white Cadillac convertible with plaid top hauled a coordinated horse trailer.

In 1952, Jerry Ann trick-rode twice a day for more than two months in London with Tex Ritter's Wild West–type production, "Texas." Briefly a Hollywood stunt rider, her films included *The Boy from Oklahoma* with Will Rogers, Jr., but she preferred live performances. In the mid–1950s, she returned to cutting competition, winning the first National Cutting Horse Association Tournament of Champions in Weatherford, Texas. She placed in that event's top six for five years, competing until 1970. She was inducted into the National Cowgirl Hall of Fame in part because she "typifies a colorful, involved spirit of living significant to the American cowgirl."

Steve Raines, rodeo rider and actor in films and TV's *Rawhide* (courtesy Stephen Sally).

JIM PRATT (c. 1956–) Jim Pratt was saddle bronc champion at the 1976 College National Finals Rodeo and on the 1981 Sierra Circuit. His bronc riding ability led to movie stunt work, primarily horse stunts. His Western projects to date include *Dances with Wolves* (1990), *Back to the Future Part III* (1990), *City Slickers* (1991), *Conagher* (1991) and the TV projects *Tallmen*, *Lonesome Dove*, *Far and Away* and *Young Riders*.

STEVE RAINES (c. 1916–96) Steve Raines' rodeo career included a successful 1940 ride at Prescott of Sky Bomb, a bronc unridden that season. He began work as a stuntman and actor in Western films in 1947, and doubled Alan Ladd's riding in *Shane* (1953). His role in *Cattle Empire* (1958) led to the part of drover Jim Quince in TV's *Rawhide*. In 1960 and 1961, he joined the *Rawhide* cast as a guest at the U.S. Marines' Camp Pendleton Rodeo.

GLENN RANDALL (1908–92) Glenn H. Randall was born at Melbeta, Nebraska. Ranch-raised near Gering, he had a special way with horses. Inspired by rodeo and circus acts, he trained family horses to lie down and sit up. At age nine, he sold one of his trained animals to a circus. Following high school graduation, Glenn rodeoed, riding bulls and bareback broncs. At Cheyenne Frontier Days, he was a rodeo clown. He broke horses and mules for the Army's Fort Robinson remount station. In Wyoming, he trained horses, including Thoroughbred trotters and pacers. He worked 250 horses for Tim McCoy's Wild West Show.

Glenn trained Thoroughbred racehorses in California in the early 1940s. With World War II looming and racing's immediate future questionable, he got permission to operate his own training stable on the premises. In 1941, he met movie cowboy Roy Rogers through Nebraska natives Art and Ace Hudkins, who operated a motion picture rental stable. The Hudkins leased the golden palomino Trigger for Roy's films. In 1941, Roy hired Glenn as Trigger's trainer, commencing a relationship based on mutual respect and friendship. Glenn urged Roy to purchase Trigger so as to have his own horse for personal appearances. The $2,500 price strained Roy's finances, but Glenn negotiated payments over time. A grateful Roy steered the livestock business for his films to the Hudkins. Glenn stabled Roy's horses at his home, developing a close relationship and maintaining a daily training regimen. He quickly taught Trigger more than 30 tricks on cues transferred to Roy, and developed special tricks for films. Trigger's fame as "The Smartest Horse in the Movies" built Glenn's reputation.

For Roy's road appearances, Glenn transported and cared for the horses, insuring peak performance. Combined with a visit to his parents, Glenn presented Trigger in a free show in connection with Minatare, Nebraska's, 1947 Days of '49 Rodeo. For 24 years, traveling to major cities and overseas, he handled Trigger and other horses for Roy, including Trigger, Jr., and Dale Evans' Buttermilk. Roy received priority for his services, but Glenn expanded his Hollywood horse training assignments. Training and renting horses for the movies, Glenn was known for special talent, good business sense and dependability.

Beginning in 1948, Glenn and family developed contract acts to present at rodeos, including an eight-palomino liberty horse act, "The Roy Rogers Liberty Horses." Roy approved the act's debut at Los Angeles' All-Palomino Horse Show and incorporated it into the Los Angeles Sheriff's Rodeo and his Roy Rogers Rodeo. Glenn soon added Trigger, Jr., and the Red Pony (from the 1949 film) to his act, which performed, often independently of Roy, for a decade at North American rodeos, with Circus Vargas and on national TV. Glenn's wife Lynn assisted in training, drove a large horse transporter and, dressed in evening clothes, presented an arena act, "Rhythm on Wheels." Pulling her in a buggy, her black horse Top Hat executed a series of dance steps until a group of pigeons landed on its back. Son Corky could put the Liberty Horses and Trigger, Jr., through their paces. With horses Comet and Zephyr, he and his wife Joan had an arena act called "Hoofbeat Harmony." Corky provided horses and coordinated livestock for many films.

In Rome in 1958, Glenn trained more than 60 horses for the chariot race choreographed by Yakima Canutt for MGM's Academy Award–winning film *Ben-Hur*. He

Glenn Randall on Dale Evans' horse Buttermilk (Glenn Randall photograph courtesy Corky Randall. Used with permission).

overcame a language barrier, imparting English commands to horses, many of which were Lipizzaners from Yugoslavia. Seeing the potential for entertaining North American audiences with a scaled-down recreation of the race, he purchased two matched teams of four horses each, one team white and the other dappled. He and son Glenn, Jr., devised a "Ben-Hur chariot race" to thrill fans at rodeos, fairs and horse shows. Dressed as ancient Romans in caped costumes and helmets, Glenn, Sr., as Ben-Hur, manned a white and gold chariot driven by the white team, while Glenn, Jr., as the villainous Messala drove a purple and gold chariot pulled by the dappled team. For effect, the horses were taught to snort, rear and paw. Upon introduction, the two chariots charged into the arena, spraying dirt as they executed turns. Pulling abreast, they raced at top speed for three laps. Glenn, Sr., overtook his son's early lead. Near the finish, in a carefully staged spill, Glenn, Jr., pressed a lever, causing his chariot to separate from its tow frame and bounce high. Leaping to the tow frame, he catapulted through the air and tumbled to the ground. Glenn, Jr., subsequently became a Hollywood stuntman and stunt coordinator.

Glenn's philosophy that horses respond best to a soft voice and kindness led to a system of reward and withholding of reward. In the 1960s, he trained and furnished animals, and provided rolling stock to movie studios. When the production of Westerns diminished, these assets were auctioned, and Glenn confined his activities to training and instruction. Beginning in the late 1970s, Glenn performed basic training for the Black Stallion films, turning the final touches over to his sons Corky and Glenn, Jr. Glenn was still training horses when he passed away.

Glenn trained Rex Allen's Koko, Casey Tibbs' Midnight and Gene Autry's TV Champion. From steeds of Western stars in the 1940s and 1950s, through animal actors of the late 1970s and early 1980s, his trainees contributed to many movies. He entertained thousands at personal appearances across the country and overseas. He twice won the American Humane Society's Patsy Award, and he received a Golden Boot Award. He was inducted into the Ak-Sar-Ben and ProRodeo Halls of Fame, and into the Rodeo Hall of the National Cowboy Museum.

LARRY RANDLES (c. 1943–92)   A professional rodeo cowboy from 1963, Larry Randles rode bulls as well as bareback and saddle broncs. Friend Casey Tibbs got him started in rodeo and in movies. He worked on *Born to Buck*, on TV's *Gunsmoke* and in several Western features, including *The Cowboys* (1972), *The Mountain Men* (1980), *Pale Rider* (1985), *Silverado* (1985) and *¡Three Amigos!* (1986).

FLORENCE HUGHES RANDOLPH (1898–1971)   At age 14, Florence left riding mules on a small Augusta, Georgia, family plantation, to join a Wild West show. She competed at rodeos in trick riding and ladies bronc riding. In 1919, she defeated male contestants to win the Roman race at Calgary. She contested at many big city rodeos, winning ladies bronc riding in 1926 at Philadelphia. A riding double for the movies, she also produced rodeos and Wild West concerts for circuses. Florence is an inductee of the Rodeo Hall at the National Cowboy Museum.

DENNIS REINERS (1937–)   Dennis Reiners qualified for the National Finals Rodeo several times and was 1970 world champion saddle bronc rider, the first rodeo world champion from Minnesota. He was inducted into the ProRodeo Hall of Fame. In *J.W. Coop* (1972), Dennis played "Hot Pistol Billy."

DON KAY "LITTLE BROWN JUG" REYNOLDS (c. 1939–) The son of Fess Reynolds, a three-decade rodeo competitor, clown, trick rider and presenter of contract animal acts, Don Reynolds had early experiences with animals. Fess, trainer of unusual animals for films and rodeo, recalled doing ranch chores on horseback while carrying Don in a pillowcase. Don estimated that he was riding solo by age two. He had his own trick riding and roping act at age five. Nicknamed "Little Brown Jug," or "Jug," he usually worked solo. His act included swinging off and back on the saddle, standing on a Shetland pony while spinning two ropes and Roman riding. He Roman-jumped a pair of palominos over obstacles and a miniature auto. He also roped on the ground. He used Highbrow, a white pony, and a brown called Stranger. Don's cowboy skills and showmanship pleased crowds. In his first year, he was out of action for about two months when he and his pony were knocked over by a stray female rider. By 1949, he had made over 200 rodeo performances, including Pendleton, Fort Worth, Las Vegas and the Los Angeles Coliseum.

On the rodeo circuit, Roy Rogers recommended that Don try Hollywood. Don stunt-doubled child stars, and appeared in films with Western stars Roy, Eddie Dean, Gene Autry and Charles Starrett. He played Little Beaver in four Red Ryder color films released by Eagle-Lion in 1949. He was also in *The Red Pony* (1949) and *The Painted Hills* (1951). For a time at rodeos, he was billed as "Little Beaver," accompanied on at least one occasion by

Don Kay Reynolds (right) as Little Beaver and Jim Bannon in a publicity still from Eagle-Lion's 1949 Red Ryder film series.

Jim Bannon ("Red Ryder"). Later, he took over some of his father's rodeo contract acts and trained an assortment of animals. In 1954, he traveled with a pet mountain lion cub, Hippo. He frequently shared the arena with others who worked in Hollywood. Fans of Western films and rodeo fondly remember Don Kay Reynolds.

MAX REYNOLDS A rodeo contract performer, Max Reynolds more recently appeared with the Great American Wild West Show as Buffalo Bill. In the TV movie *Buffalo Girls* (1995), he doubled Peter Coyote in his role as Buffalo Bill.

"Skeeter Bill" Robbins (courtesy Stephen Sally).

"SKEETER BILL" ROBBINS (1887–1933) "Skeeter Bill" was born Roy Raymond Robbins at Box Elder Park, Wyoming. Ranch-raised, he spent his life around horses. As a young man, he entered local rodeos, winning his first bronc-riding championship at Laramie in 1907. Tall and thin, Roy stood out in a crowd. His friendly smile and slow speech led to natural humor. Some say Roy's nickname "Skeeter Bill" was transferred from his lookalike brother Bill. Others have it that a smaller-sized Wild West cowboy, in joking retaliation, carved "Skeeter" in Robbins' saddle. Whatever the origin, Robbins kept the name throughout his professional career.

"Skeeter Bill" was a contestant, contract performer and promoter of rodeos. He married Canadian-born Dorothy Morrell, a top cowgirl, whom he met at a rodeo. He was a bronc rider and a bulldogger and was handy with a rope. He was a wild horse race contestant and a steer roper. In later years, he mostly entered California rodeos. Traveling to a London rodeo in 1924, he discussed his poetry with Rudyard Kipling. Promoting rodeos, he typically included a cowboy dance, expecting one or the other to show a profit.

As did Yakima Canutt, Skeeter Bill once rode the bronc Pancho Villa in a ride brokered by silent screen star Douglas Fairbanks. The resulting attention got Bill a film role in which he was eaten by rats while confined in a dungeon. Established in Hollywood by 1929, he supported Hoot Gibson in 28 films. As foreman of Hoot's Newhall-Saugus ranch in the early 1930s, he supervised preparations and directed arena activities for rodeos. He bought most of Hoot's bucking stock, which he contracted to rodeos. In 1933, Skeeter Bill was killed in an automobile accident.

GERALD ROBERTS (1920–2004)   Gerald Roberts was born into a Kansas rodeo family. At ages 13 and 14, he rode for a Wild West Show. Rodeoing at age 15, he found early winnings scanty. Competing in all three riding events, he won his first trophy saddle, as all-around cowboy, in 1938 and his first bull-riding buckle at Cheyenne in 1939. He was 1942 world champion all-around cowboy. From 1945 through 1955, he finished in bull riding's top five eight times. In the all-around cowboy category, he won a second world championship and placed among the top ten four additional years. In 1946 at Madison Square Garden, his leg and ankle were broken so seriously that doctors considered amputation. Following surgery, he healed and resumed winning championships, including bull riding at Madison Square Garden and saddle bronc riding at Cheyenne. In 1950, he was North American all-around champion at Calgary. He won his last trophy saddle in saddle bronc riding at Miami's 1960 Orange Bowl Rodeo.

For several years, Gerald did movie stunts for Glenn Ford, George Montgomery and others. His films included *Jubal* (1956), *Born Reckless* (1958) and *Westbound* (1959). A wayward bull curtailed his 1957 plan for a weekly Rodeorama at Burbank's Pickwick Arena. He declined a job on TV's *Rawhide* to take part in the Brussels World's Fair rodeo. In 1967, he bought Ace Hudkins' movie stable. Plaiting bull ropes beginning in 1958 led to Chap-Parel, Inc., offering chaps, bronc reins and gear bags. He was inducted into the Kansas Sports and ProRodeo Halls of Fame, and into the Rodeo Hall at the National Cowboy Museum.

Gerald Roberts contests in saddle bronc riding at the 1955 Pikes Peak or Bust Rodeo (courtesy Pikes Peak Library, District Local History Collection, Colorado Springs, CO Stewarts # 1184).

REX ROSSI (1919–)   Rex Rossi was born at a Kentucky rodeo to a family of itinerant circus and rodeo performers. He started trick roping at a rodeo when he was four years old, and spent most of his life as a contract roper and rider with rodeos and circus Wild West Shows. Tom Mix influenced his coming to Hollywood, and the two remained friends. Rex doubled Western film star Bob Steele from 1938 and for about 15 years after that. The two were lifelong friends. He contributed to over 300 films as a movie cowboy double, but time and again returned to live audiences. In 1943 and 1944, he worked rodeos, including several headlined by Hoot Gibson or Leo Carrillo. In 1946, he appeared with Gene Autry's Flying A Ranch Rodeo and toured eastern cities with Jim Eskew's rodeo, starring Roy Rogers. From 1947 through 1949, he worked with Eskew, including a 1948 tour with "Wild Bill" Elliott. His act expanded from trick roping to riding, including a "Flying Quarter Horse" Roman riding and jumping team.

Rodeo performer and Hollywood stunt double Rex Rossi at the 1956 Boston Garden rodeo (courtesy Richard and Eleanor Eaton. Used with permission).

In 1950 and 1951, Rex's act played Madison Square Garden and Boston Garden. By the mid–1950s, he was traveling in a trailer about ten months of the year. During this period he supported Cisco Kid rodeo appearances. In 1956, he performed at the Los Angeles Sheriff's Rodeo. He was injured in 1958 when going "under the horse's belly." At one point in 1959, Rex, with his wife and partner Wanda, had performed at more than 50 rodeos without lost time due to injury. Rex was on the program at Fort Worth's 1961 rodeo. He placed third at a fancy roping contest in 1966. In 1969, at the Dixie

National Rodeo, he was seriously bruised when his leg hit the wall as he executed a series of cartwheels and somersaults. With one foot caught in a stirrup, he was dragged a short distance. In the mid–1970s, he was still performing. He is inductee of the Hollywood Stuntmen's Hall of Fame.

SANDY SANDERS (1919–2005)   For his rodeo contract act, Sandy Sanders rode a golden palomino, Sunlight, and, later, a horse named Cherokee. He participated in the 1944 Texas Rodeo at the Montreal Forum and in the 1950 Reno Rodeo parade. He worked in Gene Autry and Roy Rogers TV shows, and in Gene's Columbia features. He doubled Clayton Moore on *The Lone Ranger*, and lent his talents to several Western films and TV series. He also trained horses.

WALTER SCOTT (c. 1940–)   A former rodeo cowboy, and a movie stuntman from the early 1960s, Walter Scott worked with John Wayne, Clint Eastwood and Steve McQueen. He doubled James Caan in *Comes a Horseman* (1978). He worked on *Heaven's Gate* (1980), *Silverado* (1985), *Far and Away* (1992), *Bad Girls* (1994) and *Ruby Jean and Joe* (1996).

ROCKY SHAHAN (c. 1925–81)   Once a rodeo contestant, Robert "Rocky" Shahan contributed to Westerns in the 1940s and 1950s. From 1959 to 1965, he played Joe Scarlett on TV's *Rawhide*. With other *Rawhide* cast members, he was at Camp Pendleton's Marine Corps Rodeos in 1960 and 1961.

Sandy Sanders, rodeo and film performer, in the film *Cow Town* (Columbia, 1950) (Columbia Pictures photograph by Van Pelt, courtesy Eddie Brandt's).

Rawhide (CBS-TV) cast, with Rocky Shahan at right. Foreground left, Clint Eastwood; center, Eric Fleming (courtesy Jerry Ohlinger's).

BILLY SHANNON (1935–81) A rodeo cowboy, Billy Shannon became a stunt double and bit player, working on Westerns and other films between 1957 and 1978, including the TV series *High Chaparral* and *Cade's County*.

JIM SHEPPARD (1937–77) An Oregon-born former rodeo cowboy, Jim Sheppard doubled for Audie Murphy and worked on other Western and non–Western films, as well as episodes of several Western TV series. Doubling Jason Robards, Jr., on the film *Comes a Horseman* (1978), Jim, according to script, fell from his horse and, with his foot caught in the stirrup, was dragged along the ground. Noise on the set caused the horse to bolt. Jim was tossed around, struck his head on a hard object and was killed.

DEAN SMITH (1932–) Born in Texas, young Dean Smith rode broncs and roped calves at local rodeos, dreaming of becoming a rodeo champion. Encouraged by his high school coach, he joined sports in his junior year, excelling at track and football. An honor student at the University of Texas, Austin, he played on two Southwest Conference championship football teams and on a Cotton Bowl championship squad. Undefeated as a freshman in the 100-yard dash, he was conference champion in 1952, 1954 and 1955. His three 440-yard relay championship teams twice set a world record. As a sophomore, he was a 400-meter relay gold medal winner at the Helsinki Olympics. Following Army service, Dean signed with the National Football League's Los Angeles Rams. A 165-pound wide receiver, he was speedy, but one of the NFL's smallest. When traded, he returned to Texas. There, his grandmother urged him to pursue his dreams in Hollywood. James Garner

Athlete, actor and stuntman Dean Smith.

referred him to Dale Robertson. Dean doubled Dale on TV's *Tales of Wells Fargo* and coordinated stunts for *Iron Horse*.

On John Wayne's *The Alamo* (1960), Dean acted as one of Jim Bowie's troops and doubled Frankie Avalon. He made a scissors jump over a horse and took a man to the ground, a stunt not previously executed. Dean earned stunt work on John Ford's last four Westerns and became a regular in John Wayne films. In *McLintock!* (1963), he executed a jump through a plate glass window for Maureen O'Hara. He doubled in several Paul Newman and Robert Redford films. Some of his most memorable scenes were as an outlaw. He contributed to numerous TV Westerns and starred in the film *Seven Alone* (1975). His talents enhanced *Maverick* (1994). An honorary member of the Professional Rodeo Cowboys Association, he has participated in charity riding events. In 2002 and 2004, he hosted celebrity rodeos to fight cancer. He has been inducted into the Hollywood Stuntmen's Hall of Fame, the Longhorn Hall of Honor at the University of Texas and the Texas Sports Hall of Fame. He received a Golden Boot Award.

DON STEWART (c. 1932–86) Don Stewart was performing at rodeos around the country as a juvenile trick rider and roper at age five or six. In the early 1940s, his California rodeos included those headlined by Leo Carrillo and Hoot Gibson. He appeared in three B-Western films in 1943–44.

Young rodeo and movie performer Don Stewart (right) with Western star Tom Keene in *Where Trails End* (Monogram, 1942) (courtesy Eddie Brandt's).

Boyd Stockman (right) takes a swing in this scene from the Johnny Mack Brown film *Gun Talk* (Monogram, 1947) with Zon Murray (center).

BOYD STOCKMAN (1916–98) At rodeos, Boyd Stockman competed in calf roping, team roping and steer wrestling. By the mid–1940s into the 1960s, he was a versatile stuntman-actor, primarily in Westerns. He kept rodeoing in the Western region and placed high in IRA rankings for team ropers.

J.W. STOKER (1927–) A Tom Mix Wild West Show inspired J.W. Stoker to trick ride and rope. At age ten, he worked a summer with the Clyde Miller show. For about ten years, he and his sisters performed at Midwest rodeos. Enhancing his solo act with fluorescent black lighting, he sometimes teamed with other performers. In 1980, he doubled for actor Sam Bottoms in *Bronco Billy*, and he has contributed to other film projects. In 1985 and 1986, he was rodeo's top specialty act. More recently, he trick-ropes with the Great American Wild West Show. He was inducted into the Rodeo Hall of the National Cowboy Museum.

MABEL STRICKLAND (1897–1976) Mabel Strickland, raised in Walla Walla, Washington, competed in relay racing, steer riding, bronc riding, trick riding and steer roping. In the winter of 1917 in Los Angeles, she worked in films as a riding double. She trick-rode at the 1921 Reno Rodeo. At the 1934 California Rodeo at Salinas, she won the cowgirl relay race and placed in the ladies free-for-all race. She was in Western films in the 1930s. Mabel is an inductee of the Rodeo Hall of the National Cowboy Museum.

J.W. Stoker jumps through a loop on horseback. (J.W. Stoker personal photograph, used with permission. Obtained from PRCA–Media).

Leonard Stroud (left), with Tom Mix (center) and Ralph R. Doubleday (right), rodeo photographer (courtesy Doubleday Collection, Wyoming Division of Cultural Resources, Cheyenne. Neg. #283).

LEONARD STROUD (1893–1961) Born at Markstown, Texas, Leonard Stroud left home as a boy to join a circus, and later trick-rode in the Wild West portion of Ringling Brothers circus. From 1914, he contested in multiple rodeo events. In 1918, he won four events at Sheepshead Bay and bronc riding at Cheyenne. Will Rogers tutored him in roping. A daring innovator in trick riding, he was considered the best of his time. He appeared in films and doubled for Western stars in the 1920s and '30s. Leonard is inducted into the Rodeo Hall of the National Cowboy Museum.

JOHN TATUM (c. 1944–94) John Tatum was a rodeo bullfighter-clown for 16 years between the early 1960s and 1980, when he retired from rodeo after suffering a broken neck. In the early 1980s, he made commercials. He secured a small part in the TV mini-series *The Blue and the Grey*, and then found a demand in films for riding his trained falling horse. He also worked on *Calamity Jane* (1984) and *Silverado* (1985).

CASEY TIBBS (1929–90) The youngest of ten children, Casey Duane Tibbs grew up on his parents' sod and log homestead near Fort Pierre, South Dakota. From boyhood, he worked with horses in one capacity or another, and aimed to be the best bronc rider in the world. He became rodeo's youngest saddle bronc world champion in 1949. In 1950, he won

Rodeo headliner Casey Tibbs, astride Midnight, greets a fan along the 1955 Pikes Peak or Bust Rodeo parade route (Stewarts photograph. Used with permission).

Calgary's North American titles in both saddle bronc and bareback riding for the second consecutive year, and he was saddle bronc champion at Pendleton. At age 22, he became rodeo's first world champion triple-crown winner: saddle bronc, bareback bronc and all-around cowboy. Between 1949 and 1959, he won a total of nine RCA world championships, six in saddle bronc riding, two as all-around cowboy and one in bareback riding.

Known for playing tricks on peers and for a preference for the color purple, Casey rode broncs with a style that was likened to dancing with a partner. He drew attention to his sport like no rodeo cowboy before or since. Inspired youth followed him into rodeo, and promising rookies were measured against his standard. To this day, his name is probably rodeo's best-remembered. Some say he might have gained more rodeo honors had he not answered the lure of Hollywood. Others say he might have made more of a mark in entertainment if he had left rodeo. In 1951, he appeared briefly in Universal's *Bronco Buster* at Cheyenne and followed the crew back to Hollywood. He appeared in several films and TV shows, and contributed stunt work and technical advice to others. In the thick of rodeo competition, he could not be tied down with conflicting movie work. Studios objected to rodeo's danger and wanted him to put on weight. With a trained horse, Midnight, he was a headline attraction at some rodeos.

Casey wrote, produced and appeared in the documentary *Born to Buck* (1966). Narrated by Henry Fonda and Rex Allen, the film records a 120-mile Dakota wild horse roundup accomplished by Casey and friends. To prove his theory that bucking horses are a product

Contestant and headline performer Casey Tibbs puts his high-schooled horse, Midnight, through a routine at the 1955 Pikes Peak or Bust Rodeo (courtesy Pikes Peak Library District Local History Collection, Colorado Springs, CO. Stewarts #1176).

of breeding, Casey assembled retired rodeo broncs and selected outlaw horses on the open range of South Dakota. Left to nature for years, the herd grew to about 400 head, exceeding government allowances. Forced to make a roundup, Casey decided to film it. The drive encountered obstacles before arriving at a rodeo arena, where the horses were tested before a crowd at auction. The National Cowboy Hall of Fame recognized the film.

Casey made TV pilots and was considered for others, but a series never materialized. His uncompromising dealings with executives may have cost him greater Hollywood exposure, but he excelled at making friends. In 1989, he received a Golden Boot Award. Casey served on the RCA's board of directors and promoted the idea of a National Finals Rodeo. He was inducted into the Ak-Sar-Ben and ProRodeo Halls of Fame, and into the Rodeo Hall at the National Cowboy Museum. In August of 1989, the ProRodeo Hall of Fame unveiled a larger than life-sized outdoor bronze of Casey astride Necktie. Friends commissioned "The Champ," inside which sculptor Edd Hayes placed a bronze heart inscribed, "Ride, Cowboy, Ride." Present for the unveiling festivities, Casey later died of cancer at his home. Singer Charlie Daniels said Casey was "as West as the sunset, and cowboy to the core."

Advertisement for Casey Tibbs' documentary film *Born to Buck* (1966) (courtesy of Eddie Brandt's).

R.L. TOLBERT (1940–) Colorado-born R.L. Tolbert rode saddle broncs and wrestled steers at rodeos from the early 1960s. A Tucson movie extra, he moved to California and worked with horse trainer Glenn Randall. As he became a stuntman and worked his way up to stunt coordinator, rodeo became occasional. He placed first in steer wrestling at a 1998 Inglewood, California, rodeo. His Western films include *Heaven's Gate* (1980), *Silverado* (1985) *Pale Rider* (1985), *The Quick and the Dead* (1987) and *Far and Away* (1992). His talents may be seen on such TV projects as *The Sacketts*, *Rodeo Girl*, *Little House on the Prairie* and *The Yellow Rose*. A regular stunt double for Sam Elliott, R.L. coordinated stunts for *Conagher* (1991).

RUDY UGLAND Former rodeo man Rudy Ugland has done movie stunts and has had film roles. Managing one of the largest livestock contracting operations, he has served as head wrangler on films from *Lawman* (1971) to *The Hi Lo Country* (1998).

THE VALKYRIES Young horsewoman Sydney Hall persuaded her Palm Springs parents to acquire six Roman-trained white horses. Soon, she and two other young women were practicing an arena act. Their name, "The Valkyries," derived from the Norse legend

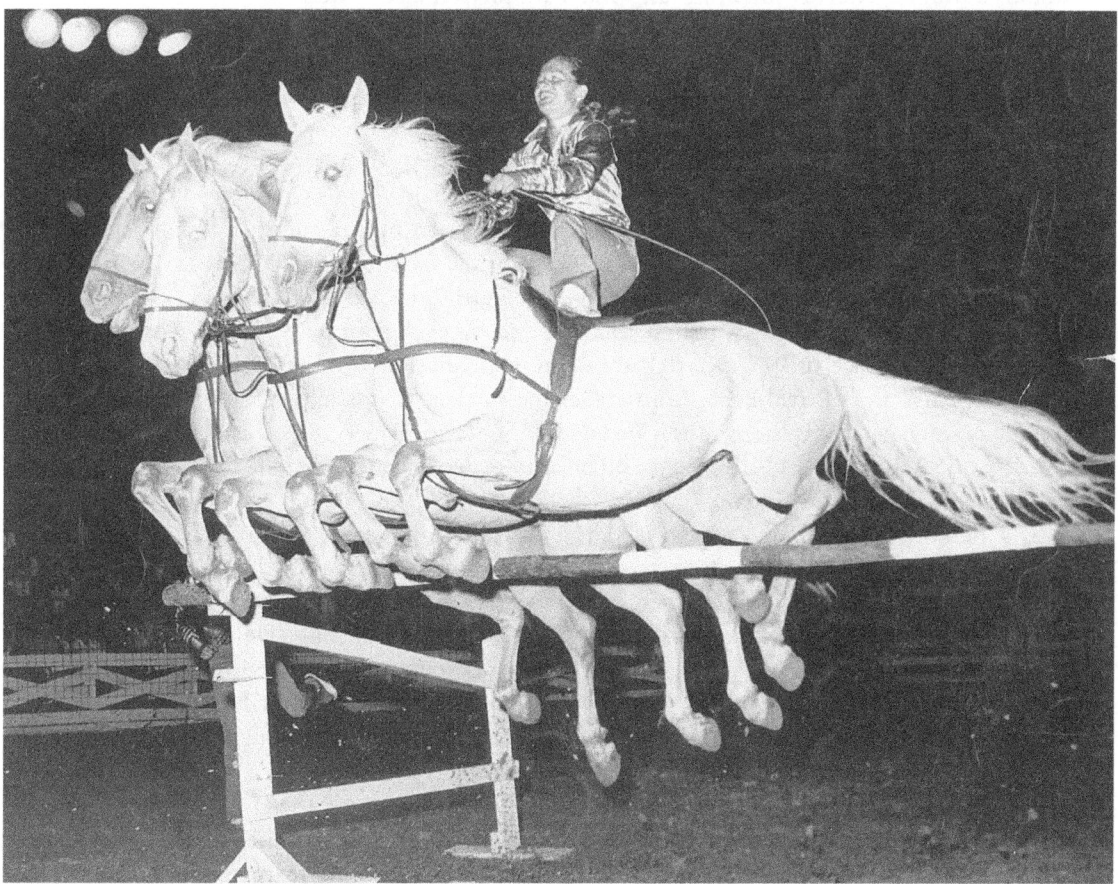

Audrey O'Brien Griffin, of the Flying Valkyries, Roman-jumps three of the troupe's white horses over an obstacle at Beaumont, Texas, 1956 (Robert C. McDonald photograph for Audrey O'Brien Griffin's personal publicity folio. Used with permission of Audrey O'Brien Griffin).

of goddesses on flying white horses who carried dying soldiers to Valhalla. The act included the "six-up": one woman Roman-riding two horses while driving two pair of horses in front in a figure-eight pattern in and out of barrels. The women also Roman-rode three or four horses abreast over hurdles. In the "crossfire jump," one woman on three horses raced in one direction and executed a jump over a hurdle simultaneously with another rider going in the opposite direction. For their Roman riding, the young women flexed their knees and wore tennis shoes, placing their feet at a slight angle, with toes crossing the horses' pad-protected backbones. Performers had to unload and load, exercise, rehearse and groom the horses daily.

In the 1950s, they traveled to rodeos, fairs and horse shows across the United States and Canada. They first performed at Los Angeles' 1950 Sheriff's Rodeo. They entertained with Gene Autry at Boston Garden in 1951 and 1957. They appeared in the Roy Rogers film *Heart of the Rockies* (1951) and in *Bronco Buster* (1952). They played Madison Square Garden in 1953 and the Texas Prison Rodeo in 1955. One woman attracted as a Valkyrie rider was Audrey O'Brien. A rider from age 11, she also rode calves and bareback broncs, roped, rode Roman-style and jumped horses. At age 19, she joined the Valkyries for two years, going to the 1958 Brussels World's Fair. She continues to ride. Mary June Johnson, Lolly Roberts, Mary Stetler, Donna Still and Ida Volquartsen also rode.

ALICE VAN (SPRINGSTEEN)   Alice (original name VanderVeen) learned trick riding from her sisters. At age 12, she debuted at a Coliseum show celebrating Los Angeles' 150th anniversary. She trick-rode at the 1931 La Fiesta celebration and at Victor McLaglen's riding club. Her first rodeo was at Hoot Gibson's ranch at Saugus, California. In 1932, she performed trick and Roman riding at the Second Annual World's Congress of Rough Riders and Rodeo in Los Angeles, and in the Olympic opening ceremonies. She mastered 41 trick riding maneuvers. At Tex Austin's 1933 World's Championship Cowboy Contest in Los Angeles, Alice won dual championships: Cowgirl Trick and Fancy Rider, and Cowgirl Relay Rider. At Salinas, she was first in trick and fancy riding in 1934 and won the half-mile free-for-all race in 1937. Invited by the queen, she was the first American woman to appear at Australia's Royal Easter Show. Despite broken ribs, she completed her nine performances. That same year, she trick-rode at the Reno Rodeo. She performed at rodeos throughout California and the West, and at 1945 rodeos headlined by Roy Rogers at Madison Square Garden and Boston Garden.

When only 15 years old, Alice raced as a jockey at top tracks, winning the Powder Puff Derby at Agua Caliente in Mexico. In 1938, she became only the third woman certified as an official Thoroughbred conditioner. Her movie stunt career began with *In Old Kentucky* (1935). She doubled many actresses, including former roommate Dale Evans. She also stunted for Gail Davis as "Annie Oakley." She was married 28 years to Western movie producer-director R.G. "Bud" Springsteen. Alice received a Golden Boot Award. Upon induction into the National Cowgirl Hall of Fame, she was cited as "a fearless horsewoman."

JACK O. WATT (BRAD KING) (1918–91)   Jack Watt won the Western States rodeo championship and the Nevada state amateur rodeo championship in the late 1930s. As Brad King, he portrayed Johnny Nelson in five 1941 Hopalong Cassidy features. He was a guest at that year's Reno Rodeo. Following World War II service as an Army Air Corps pilot, he made more films. He starred in *Trouble at Melody Mesa* (1944), composed a number of Western songs and had his own TV show.

Left to right are Jack O. Watt (Brad King) and William (Hopalong Cassidy) Boyd, Eleanor Stewart and J. Farrell MacDonald in *Riders of the Timberline* (Paramount, 1941) (courtesy Jerry Ohlinger's).

TED WELLS (1899–1948) Born in Midland, Texas, Ted Wells grew up on a Montana ranch, learning cowboy skills that led him to rodeo trick riding. Becoming a Universal Western star in 1927, he made films through the silent era and into the early sound period. In the late 1930s into the '40s, he had supporting roles and served as stunt double for William "Hopalong Cassidy" Boyd.

GEORGE WILBUR (1942–) George Wilbur entered the movie stunt field in 1967 after contesting at rodeos. He worked on films with John Wayne and Clint Eastwood, in addition to numerous other films. He was affiliated with the Western TV series *The Monroes*.

BILL WILLIAMS (1921–64) Colorado-born Bill Williams became a movie stuntman and continued contesting at rodeos. In 1947 and 1948, he was a regional saddle bronc riding and all-around champion. In 1949, he joined the RCA.

Silent western star Ted Wells.

In 1952 at Cheyenne, he contested and doubled in rodeo scenes for actor John Lund in Universal's *Bronco Buster*. He contributed to *Gunfight at the OK Corral* (1957). He took falling stunt horses to the 1958 Brussels World's Fair Wild West Show. Eventually, he focused solely on movie stunting. In 1964, working near Gallop, New Mexico, on the movie *The Hallelujah Trail*, he was tragically killed when he misjudged a leap from a wagon before it plunged into a gully.

GUINN "BIG BOY" WILLIAMS (c. 1899–1962) Born on a ranch in Decatur, Texas, Guinn Williams learned to ride and rope as a youngster. He excelled in sports at Decatur Military Academy and studied law at North Texas State College. Upon discharge from commissioned Army service during World War I, he left home to pursue professional baseball. Disappointed, he rode and roped at rodeos. As "Tex Williams," he stunt-rode and played bit roles in motion pictures. In 1919, the six-foot-two, 205-pound Guinn appeared in a Will Rogers comedy film. The humorist's designation "big boy" became his nickname. Between films, he contested at rodeos. In 1921, he wrote and starred in the first of several silent Westerns for various independent producers. He participated in the 1925 Pendleton Roundup. He kept busy in other film genres and in Western supporting roles. He was Roy Rogers' sidekick, "Teddy Bear," in two 1944 films. He supported Randolph Scott, Errol Flynn and Ken Curtis. The final two of his 100-plus films starred John Wayne. Guinn was a celebrity guest at the 1945 Helldorado Days. During Chicago's 1948 rodeo, he was at a theater premiere of *Station West*. He joined Rex Bell and Bob Steele honoring Hoot Gibson's birthday at the 1958 Caldwell (Idaho) Night Rodeo. He was featured in two Western TV series, *My Friend Flicka* and *Circus Boy*, and he had filmed a new series pilot at the time of his death from uremic poisoning.

Rodeo rider turned Western actor Guinn "Big Boy" Williams (courtesy Eddie Brandt's).

PARIS WILLIAMS An advertisement for the 1932 Reno Pony Express Days Rodeo listed Paris Williams among such notables as Jack Dempsey, Rex Bell, Bob Steele, Mabel Strickland and Bonnie Grey, an indication of her status as a distinguished trick rider. In 1934, she placed second to Alice Van in the women's trick and fancy riding contest at Salinas. She was also a movie stuntwoman and the mother of stuntman Jack Williams.

JAY WILSEY (1896–1961) Born in Missouri, Jay Wilsey seasoned his cowboy skills, including trick riding, with Wild West Shows and rodeos. Following stunting and bit parts, he starred in 1924 Westerns as *Buffalo Bill, Jr*. He was featured in two serials in the 1930s, but settled into Western supporting roles and stunting for Charles Starrett. He retired from films in 1941.

ANDY WOMACK (1907–92)   A building contractor before becoming a rodeo clown, Andy Womack returned to that business. In the arena, he was known for mule and monkey sidekicks. Among his films were *Bus Stop* (1956) and *Stay Away Joe* (1968). He was inducted into the ProRodeo Hall of Fame.

HANK WORDEN (c. 1899–1990)   Hank Worden was born in Iowa and raised on a Montana ranch. He attended college, and then became a rodeo contestant. Competing at Madison Square Garden's rodeo circa 1930, he responded to an audition for the musical play *Green Grow the Lilacs*. He earned a role, sharing an apartment with fellow cast member Tex Ritter. He provided comic relief in Tex's films (1937–39), and supported other Western stars. He was a guide and guest ranch wrangler in Arizona. Later, he became a highly recognizable character actor. He was "Old Mose" in *The Searchers* (1956).

Hank Worden (right, at piano) in *Sundown on the Prairie* (Monogram, 1939) with (left to right) Horace Murphy, Tex Ritter and Dorothy Fay (Mrs. Tex Ritter) (courtesy Eddie Brandt's).

WEN WRIGHT (1916–54)   Wen Wright was a rodeo contestant, and he worked as a Hollywood stunt double and bit actor from 1938 to 1950. He doubled for William Boyd in *Silver on the Sage* (1939). Doubling Bob Wills on a Western film, he broke his leg and shoulder when a stagecoach overturned.

WALTER WYATT (1940–86)   Steer wrestling champion at Salinas in 1961 and at Pendleton in 1966, Walter Wyatt qualified three times for the National Finals Rodeo and, in 1971, was Sierra Circuit champion. He began as a full-time movie stuntman with three John Wayne films. Other Westerns included *Little Big Man* (1971), *Blazing Saddles* (1974), *Tom Horn* (1980) and *Silverado* (1985). He contributed to the Western TV series *Lancer* (1968) and *The Quest* (1976).

II

Individual Movie and Television Actors Performing at Rodeos

NICK ADAMS (1931–68) Nick Adams, "Johnny Yuma" of ABC-TV's Western series *The Rebel* (1959–62), appeared at 1962's U.S. Marine Rodeo at Camp Pendleton, California.

REX ALLEN (1920–99) Rex Elvie Allen, named for Western star Rex Bell, was born in Willcox, Arizona. Early years were spent on the family homestead at Mud Springs Canyon, 40 miles northwest of Willcox. The remote, primitive setting of Rex's boyhood helped develop his ranching skills and marksmanship, but created hardship. He slept in the corner of a one-room cabin. The family's water source was a quarter-mile distant, the mail drop eight miles away and medical care all but non-existent. By age nine, he had lost an infant sister to "summer complaint," an older brother to rattlesnake bite and his mother to blood poisoning. Caring relations and his music teacher encouraged him to overcome these tragedies. When the family moved closer to town, his father's trucking business left Rex to handle farm chores.

Nick Adams as ABC-TV's *The Rebel* (courtesy Jerry Ohlinger's).

Rex credited his dad with giving him both a moral upbringing and an interest in music. Aided by a $4 Sears, Roebuck guitar and instruction booklet, acquired at about age 11, he accompanied his dad's fiddle at dances. He sang for coins outside the barbershop and theater. A pleasing baritone voice with a three-octave range led to his radio debut at age 13. He sang in the school glee club, with church choirs, and at lodges and benefits. His musical interest and talent overcame a condition of crossed eyes that defied correction despite generous efforts of a local service group. He drew inspiration from his guitar-playing cousin, Cactus Mack, who ventured to Hollywood with another cousin, Glenn Strange. At age 16, Rex won a vocal contest.

Rex graduated from high school, worked construction with his dad and landed a Saturday job on Phoenix radio. Singing for free at a Trenton, New Jersey, radio station, he sold his pictures for ten cents each, and met expenses by dish washing and by running a hydraulic press on a mill's midnight shift. After working at a San Diego aircraft factory, he returned to Trenton as a paid radio singer. With the Sleepy Hollow Gang, he first played fiddle, and then sang harmony, on Philadelphia radio. He sang and did odd jobs at a nearby park featuring music stars on summer weekends. Visiting performers Lulu Belle and Scotty recommended that Rex audition for the National Barn Dance on Chicago's WLS. He joined in March 1945. In Chicago, he had his eyes corrected, met his wife, and worked regional fairs and theaters. He secured a Mercury recording contract and appeared on television. In 1949, he had a CBS radio show with the Sons of the Pioneers. He composed his radio theme, "Arizona Waltz."

In 1949, he signed with Republic Studios as a singing cowboy. Glenn Randall purchased Koko, a horse too spirited for Dale Evans. Rex recognized the distinctive beauty of Koko's dark chocolate coat, set off by a white mane and tail. From *The Arizona Cowboy* (1950) through 1954, he starred in 19 Republic Westerns, supported by the Randall-trained Koko, "The Miracle Horse of the Movies," in all but the first film. Buddy Ebsen and Slim Pickens were his most frequent sidekicks. The close of the B-Western era shortened Rex's career as a cinema cowboy hero.

In 1957, Rex starred in 39 episodes of *Frontier Doctor*, a highly rated syndicated TV series. To prepare for the show, he observed at a hospital and studied medical history so as not to exceed the period's knowledge.

Rex Allen comic books were published from 1951 through 1958. He recorded the hit songs "Crying in the Chapel," "Streets of Laredo" and "Don't Go Near the Indians." He also narrated nature and Western-oriented Walt Disney films and TV programs, the General Electric Carousel of Progress and the children's film *Charlotte's Web* (1973). An endorser of Western clothing and Tony Lama boots, his voice was heard on Purina Dog Chow and other TV commercials. He made additional family-oriented films and many personal appearances. Honored with a star on Hollywood's Walk of Fame, he was also inducted into the Hall of Great Western Performers at the National Cowboy Hall of Fame and into the Western Music Association Hall of Fame. He received a Golden Boot Award. The Rex Allen Museum opened in 1989 in Willcox, Arizona, featuring an outdoor statue of Rex and Koko.

Rex Allen on the Rodeo Trail

Growing up around rodeo, Rex was familiar with rodeo cowboys of his youth. During and immediately following his high school years, he entered local amateur rodeos with schoolmate Dan Poore, sometimes borrowing money for entry fees. He rode saddle broncs, bareback broncs and steers. He also roped calves and wrestled steers. Winning $5 now and then made it seem worthwhile. At age 19, he broke his leg at a rodeo. He rode his first and last Brahma bull at Tucson. Later, Rex joked that he set four records in bull riding: he was bucked the highest, stayed up the longest, came down the hardest and raised the most dust. His experience gave him a special affinity for rodeos and rodeo people. He, in turn, was welcomed at rodeos.

More than any individual Western performer, Rex was a rodeo entertainer. In 1952, while his starring films were being released, he was on parade at Las Vegas' Helldorado Days and headlining Los Angeles' Sheriff's Rodeo. In 1953, he played longer stands in San Antonio and Nampa. He scheduled rodeos into the mid–1970s. He decided against forming his own rodeo because he was in demand by many rodeo producers. Western TV shows provided variety in rodeo guest stars, but Rex seemed to be the hero cowboy most satisfying to both rodeo audiences and sponsoring committees. Many cities invited him back because his talent and friendliness were ideally suited to rodeo. He promoted rodeos and made himself accessible to fans. These factors, plus his extraordinary singing voice, contributed to longevity and multiple appearances on the rodeo circuit. He hoped for an occasional break to go fishing. In Spokane one year, he got a bigger thrill: a ride in an Air Force jet.

Rex submitted to innumerable interviews, rode in countless rodeo parades, signed autographs and handed out photos to large groups of youngsters. He appeared at breakfasts, luncheons, dinners and banquets. He met people at public functions and at private homes, and spoke at service club meetings. Wherever he went, he was likely to sing. He sponsored coloring and essay contests to generate young people's interest in rodeos. Winners received hats, boots, outfits or autographed photos, and might attend a special dinner with Rex. He crowned numerous rodeo queens, and in Albuquerque one year he helped interview 20 queen candidates. He posed for pictures with Army enlistees, champion calves and cutting horses, twirling clubs and mayors. In a rodeo arena, he gave away the bride in a horseback wedding ceremony. He was photographed as the "Frontier Doctor" writing a prescription to encourage state fair attendance.

Rex arrived by special train, publicized the soapbox derby and dedicated a boys' ranch. In Nampa in 1953, he met a two-year-old boy who shared his name. The two visited on Rex's succeeding rodeo dates until the boy had become a young man of 25. In 1955, when his leg was in a cast from a snow sport accident, and in 1959 when he was wearing a heavy

Rex Allen and Koko in the 1958 Pikes Peak or Bust Rodeo parade (courtesy Pikes Peak Library District Local History Collection, Colorado Springs, CO. Stewarts #2147).

Rex Allen (with the musical group the Frontiersmen) holds a youngster as part of his act at a night performance of the 1958 Pikes Peak or Bust Rodeo (courtesy Pikes Peak Library District Local History Collection, Colorado Springs, CO. Stewarts #2078).

back brace and limping from a horseback mishap, Rex's rodeo shows went on. Rex served as arena director for a day at the national roping finals in 1960. In 1966, at Camdenton's J-Bar-H Rodeo, he filled in for an ailing rodeo announcer. He traveled from a performance with the Omaha Symphony Orchestra to entertain at a special Coeur d'Alene, Idaho, rodeo for the 1967 World Boy Scout Jamboree.

When it came to visiting hospitals and institutions, Rex took a back seat to no one. At Casper, Wyoming, in 1955, a five-year-old boy attending the Kid's Day rodeo matinee felt the first pangs of appendicitis. Just as the scared boy was about to be wheeled in for surgery, Rex caught up to lend encouragement. At Houston, he donned a hospital mask and gown to visit a burn victim. At North Platte's St. Mary's Hospital, he signed autographs for patients, visitors, nuns, expectant fathers and soon-to-be-born babies. The next day, he visited three more facilities.

On his visits, Rex answered questions and posed for group photos. He held songfests for audiences of nine or 90. He visited the very young, as well as seniors, without neglecting the caretakers. To appear at the Home on the Range for Boys rodeo gathering at Sentinel Butte, North Dakota, with Casey Tibbs, he commuted from a California rodeo in a chartered Cessna. While performing at San Angelo's rodeo, Rex and rodeo cowboy Harry Tompkins visited the Boys Ranch of West Texas. He autographed boys' hats and left his signed hat for the ranch. He accepted a certificate of Boys Ranch citizenship, but had to

Rex Allen, accompanied by accordion player Hi Busse of the Frontiersmen, plays the fiddle during his spot as featured performer at the 1958 Pikes Peak or Bust Rodeo (courtesy Pikes Peak Library District Local History Collection, Colorado Springs, CO. Stewarts #2072).

leave before a large cherry cobbler inscribed "Hi Rex" was served. He once said, "I'll never turn my back on a child if I can help it." He noted that visiting the needy "makes up for me not being able to go to church when I'm on the road." He earned keys to cities in 43 states, honorary law enforcement badges and many tokens of appreciation.

In early years, downtown theaters often played one of Rex's films. He entered the arena at a fast pace on Koko, engaged in a little patter, and then put Koko through his repertoire of tricks. Koko greeted the crowd by waving a foreleg, reared and demonstrated a kissing face. He answered questions yes or no with an appropriate movement of his head, knelt to say his prayers and bowed to the crowd's applause. Rex played his guitar and yodeled as he sang Western songs. One song might be a rousing hand-clapping number, encouraging audience participation. He varied his program from one performance to another, favoring such songs as "Old Folks at Home," "Highways Are Happy Ways," "Lazy River," "Tumbling Tumbleweeds" or a tune with a local tie-in. He appealed to the younger set by performing the "Rodeo Twist," complete with gyrations. He often played a hoedown number on his fiddle, made humorous comments and, in early years, fired blanks from his six-shooter.

Early in his rodeo career, Rex did a number, "That Little Boy of Mine," that required the participation of a young boy. The youngster might be a local boy, the son of a rodeo cowboy or one of his own. The boy walked across the arena under a spotlight as Rex sang, often ending in his arms. He commented that the boy looked just like his own, and sometimes it was. Years later, he related, "I haven't done that little boy thing in ten years, but people still request that I do it so their little boys can see it." Another crowd-pleaser was his singing of "Red River Valley," as a small herd of longhorns was driven around the arena. He rode Koko slowly around the arena perimeter, taking time to shake youngsters' hands and placing a straw hat on the head of a lucky boy or girl. After exiting, he signed autographs.

Rex credited his act's success to his horse Koko. The full impact of Koko's coloring was not apparent in black and white films, so rodeo fans had an advantage. Koko usually was transported, in an average year more than 40,000 miles, in a luxury stock trailer especially designed for his comfort and safety. By 1962, Rex was still touring with Koko; however, more than one Koko, Jr., had been trained to fill in as needed. Rex reported that it took at least a solid year of training, and continual sharpening, to prepare a horse for the rodeo act. In February 1962 at Houston, Koko celebrated his twentieth birthday with a cake. About this time, controversy developed. Having a few Koko lookalikes for rodeo work, Rex sold a horse to a Texas buyer as a gift to his wife. Fans feared that the original Koko was sold. Then, Rex posed with "old" Koko, explaining that he had sold another horse. A Koko, Jr., carried on most rodeo work. The original Koko was retired to pasture in 1964. Upon his death in 1968, his remains were interred in a Willcox park.

Rex performed at rodeos most frequently with the Men of the West or other musical back-up groups. He sometimes shared the rodeo spotlight with Slim Pickens, Montie Montana, Pedro Gonzalez-Gonzalez or other stars. At San Angelo in 1962, his father, for the first time, joined the act, fiddling a hoedown to Rex's guitar accompaniment. Father and son visited the family's Coke County homestead.

Wherever Rex went on the rodeo road, much was made of his "pretty" wardrobe, with outfits that stood out regardless of the arena's size. His luggage held about 30 matching outfits, fancy boots and a pearl-gray ten-gallon hat. He had suits, shirts and giveaway straw hats. His shirts, about which he said, "All are wild," tended to be brightly colored and heavy on jewels and fringes. His fashions earned him the title, "The Most Colorful Star of the Entertainment World" and attracted the desired attention. He joked with audiences about his clothing, referring to himself as a "Hollywood cowboy" and to his outfit as "this monkey suit," or a "seersucker suit, sold by Sears and bought by a sucker." He told audiences he wore simple Levis and a blue shirt when working on the home ranch. A musician's comment that he wore ragged underwear beneath his expensive costume prompted Rex, in mock retaliation, to fire blanks from his six-shooter. Two aspects

II. Individual Movie and Television Actors at Rodeos

Rex Allen and Koko perform at Houston's 1962 Fat Stock Show Rodeo (courtesy Houston Metropolitan Research Center, Houston Public Library, Houston. Press #1175).

of his dress went generally unnoticed. Returning to his hotel room on the day of his National Barn Dance acceptance, he noticed that his socks didn't match. He continued the practice of unmatched socks. Although time on the road caused him to miss important family events, he kept family with him by wearing a tie clip displaying each child's likeness and name.

Rex collected revolvers, and in his early years he shared his six-shooters with youngsters. In 1968, he joined the nation in mourning the assassinations of Dr. Martin Luther King, Jr., and Senator Robert F. Kennedy. Visiting historic sites in Springfield, Illinois, he recalled the assassinations of Abraham Lincoln and President John F. Kennedy. Mindful of the violent passings, he vowed to hang up his six-shooters, explaining, "I'd rather be remembered for a song that I sang than for being fast on the draw. I won't flaunt guns in front of kids."

Known in the movies as "The Arizona Cowboy," Rex at rodeos, was most often called "Mr. Cowboy" or "The Voice of the West." He earned favorable reviews for his rodeo performances:

> Cowboy star Rex Allen proved again that he is Southwest Idaho's favorite Western actor and singer by bringing down the house last night with his performance and personality [Nampa, Idaho, 1955].
>
> Rex Allen, hailed as the top name in filmdom's western world, again was a crowd pleaser. Allen's songs, fiddling, tricks, and patter brought enthusiastic response from the capacity audience which occupied even the standing room.... Allen's warmth went out to the audience and brought them to their feet yelling for more [Pueblo, Colorado, 1957].
>
> Rex Allen just seems to have a way of getting to folks and making himself as friendly as the neighbor down the road.... Rex brought Western neighborliness into the arena with him and the crowd loved it. Not as a star, but as a friend and neighbor... Spotlighted in darkness he began talking with the home folks, then brought a hushed stillness over the huge arena as he sang one of the more popular Western ballads, "Streets of Laredo" [Lewiston, Idaho, 1957].
>
> Allen's voice, speaking and singing, his ability to put over a song, but above all his personality, have made him a favorite.... He also knows how to tell a joke and is an excellent story teller [Ponca City, Oklahoma, 1966].

Rex stated, "Rodeo is my favorite. It's my favorite sport, and I'm more geared for rodeo." He noted that he knew about every rodeo man in the business by his first name. In a simpler outfit than the one he wore in the spotlight, he liked swapping stories behind the chutes. He said, "The crowd at a rodeo is alive and excited and a pleasure to have as an audience," and "There's just nothing like an audience reaction — which you get right now. I think you work a lot better." He observed, "I like to get back to 'my people'—country people, westerners, the cowhands behind the chutes at a rodeo."

Rex liked to point out the relative safety of singing at rodeos versus his earlier contesting. At Mandan, North Dakota, in 1953, just as he was riding into the arena, Koko spooked, threw his head back suddenly and slammed Rex in the face; at his next engagement, Rex sported a black eye. In 1971, his fifth year as star of Edmonton's Canadian Western Stock Show, Rex was extended a formal salute. Upon his introduction, garbed in a silver-threaded red jacket and waving his white hat, he galloped his steed across the arena. Confronted by a photographer's flash, the horse stopped and Rex didn't. For the first time in his career as a rodeo entertainer, he was dumped on the arena surface. Uninjured, he proceeded with his musical act, after which the mayor presented him a key to the city and other gifts. Interviewed, Rex said, "I have always figured it would [happen] one day. I always wondered where it would be. I guess the horse decided Edmonton was the best place."

In the late 1950s, Rex regularly donated a trophy saddle to the runner-up in the RCA's all-around cowboy rankings. In 1957, he attended the RCA Convention in Denver and helped the RCA president resolve a conflict between the RCA and the American Guild of

Variety Artists (AGVA) over union alignment of rodeo entertainers. In 1961, he entertained at the RCA convention. For a time, he served as trustee for the National Cowboy Hall of Fame. In 1979, he entertained at the ProRodeo Hall of Fame's opening gala.

As Rex was winding down his rodeo appearances, son Rex, Jr., was becoming a star in his own right. Born in 1947 in Chicago, Rex, Jr., often accompanied his dad on the rodeo circuit and eventually followed in his musical footsteps. He sang at Rex Allen Days at age five. As he grew up, he rode bulls and performed as a rodeo clown. He joined the 1960s folk music movement, served in the U.S. Army in the latter part of that decade, and then had a number of hit recordings in the contemporary country style. In 1982, his album "The Singing Cowboy Rex Allen, Jr." showcased his hit single, "Last of the Silver Screen Cowboys," on which both his dad and Roy Rogers collaborated. In the 1970s and '80s, as country artists succeeded Western stars at rodeos, Rex, Jr., bridged both worlds. He performed at such rodeo cities as Casper, Colorado Springs (twice), Fort Worth, Montgomery, Waco, Nampa and San Antonio (with Rex, Sr.). Like his dad, he visited and performed at hospitals and senior citizen centers. The state of Arizona adopted his 1982 composition "Arizona" as an official state song. Rex, Jr., has been prominent in Nashville's country music television.

In 1951, Rex, Sr.'s, home community of Willcox, Arizona, initiated a Rex Allen Days celebration and rodeo, ongoing as of this writing. Rex was inducted into Omaha's Ak-Sar-Ben Western Hall of Fame in 1964. Rodeo producers named Rex 1967's "Rodeo Man of the Year," the first entertainer so named. Rex, a dues-paying member for more than 20 years, was made a Professional Rodeo Cowboys Association life member in 1971. In 1984, he was

Advertisement for Rex Allen, Jr., appearance at the 1975 Pikes Peak or Bust Rodeo.

parade grand marshal for the Pikes Peak or Bust Rodeo, which awarded him a Spencer Penrose buckle. In 1985, he received the Buffalo Bill Award at North Platte, Nebraska. He was an original inductee into the Pikes Peak or Bust Rodeo Hall of Fame.

TOD ANDREWS (c. 1921–72)   Tod Andrews, chosen to play the title role in *The Gray Ghost*, studied the true-life "Gray Ghost of the Shenandoah Valley," Major John Singleton Mosby. Mosby led Confederate guerrillas operating behind Union lines during the Civil War. At a time of mounting civil rights unrest, networks and sponsors were sensitive about launching a show with a Confederate hero. Released by CBS in syndication, the show enjoyed high ratings in such diverse regions as Boston and Seattle.

Tod Andrews, TV's "Gray Ghost" (courtesy Jerry Ohlinger's).

"The Gray Ghost" on the Rodeo Trail

Tod Andrews' first rodeo was in 1958 at Montgomery, Alabama, once capital of the Confederacy, where some senior residents recalled the historical figure. Officials and 200 fans, many youngsters, met their first rodeo star upon his airport arrival. His act consisted of a "salute to the 'Old South,'" accompanied musically by the Robert E. Lee High School Band, outfitted in Confederate regalia. At one performance, the aerial mike cord broke, forcing the star to the bandstand in order to be heard. A reporter called the incident an act of "Yankee sabotage." Tod's traditional ride around the perimeter to shake hands with youngsters was well-received. Generating "tremendous audience response," he drew capacity crowds totaling over 40,000 spectators. This successful rodeo appearance gave promise; however, no additional rodeos were discovered.

MICHAEL ANSARA (1922–)   Michael Ansara, born in Syria of Lebanese heritage, came to the United States at an early age. After ten years in Massachusetts, his family moved to California. He left Los Angeles City College for stage preparation at Pasadena Playhouse. Following World War II Army Medical Corps service, he appeared in stage productions and landed film parts. On the 1956 TV series *Broken Arrow*, he played Cochise. The show stressed Cochise's heroic dignity and his bond of trust with Tom Jeffords (John Lupton). The series portrayed Native Americans in a favorable light and presented positively the possibility of reconciliation between the races. Michael lent the role a humanity and nobility, with which audiences, including young viewers, could identify. In a later series, *Law of the Plainsman*, he played Harvard-educated Native American Sam Buckheart, a Deputy U.S. Marshal, dealing similarly with prejudice.

Michael Ansara, Cochise of TV's *Broken Arrow*.

"Cochise" and "Sam Buckheart" on the Rodeo Trail

Michael Ansara entertained at North American rodeos. He endured whatever discomfort his costume, including wig, created and stepped off his arriving flight as Cochise, a colorful and impressive sight that often became a front-page newspaper photo. At Lawton, Oklahoma, a crowd of 350, including the mayor and 20 Comanche Indians, greeted him at the airport. His rodeo act included recitation of Indian lore. At Fort Smith's 1958 Arkansas-Oklahoma Rodeo, he signed autographs, posed for photographs with youngsters and visited children in hospitals. In 1960, with Eddy Arnold, he appeared for seven days at Houston's Fat Stock Show Rodeo. By this time, he was starring as Sam Buckheart. Fans viewing Michael's somewhat rare rodeo performances were fortunate indeed.

Gene Autry at the Aquatennial Rodeo, Minneapolis, Minnesota, July 1940 (obtained from Doubleday Collection, Wyoming Division of Cultural Resources, Cheyenne, Neg. #286 © 2004 Autry Qualified Interest Trust and The Autry Foundation, provided courtesy Gene Autry Entertainment).

GENE AUTRY (1907–98) Orvon Gene Autry was born September 29, 1907, at Tioga, Texas. By age five, he was singing in his preacher grandfather's church choir, and at age 12 he bought his first guitar from Sears, Roebuck. He rode horses and did typical rural chores. Moving near Ravia, Oklahoma, he completed school, worked at a movie theater and sang for three months with a traveling medicine show. As relief telegraph operator for the Frisco line at Chelsea, Oklahoma, he strummed his guitar and sang. Both telegraph customer Will Rogers and a New York music company recommended that he gain radio experience. With an unpaid spot on Tulsa station KVOO, he became "Oklahoma's Yodeling Cowboy." Singing when he could at civic gatherings, he returned to the railroad. On a 1929 New York visit, he landed a recording contract with a Sears, Roebuck label. From 1931 to 1934, he sang on Sears' Chicago radio station, WLS, including "The National Barn Dance." The Sears catalog offered his records, songbooks and guitar. In 1932, he married Ina Mae Spivey. Midwest personal appearances included the 1933 Chicago World's Fair. His recording "That Silver-Haired Daddy of Mine," co-composed with Johnny Long, earned the first gold record for sales.

Gene and WLS co-star Smiley Burnette appeared briefly with Ken Maynard in a feature film and in a serial, and then starred in the serial *Phantom Empire* (1935), which combined Western and science fiction elements with music. The singing cowboy concept was a success. Despite initial awkwardness, Gene, with Smiley as sidekick, made 51 feature films for Republic Pictures, from *Tumbling Tumbleweeds* (1935) to *Bells of Capistrano* (1942). He periodically disputed contract issues with the studio, but his pictures placed him, from 1940 through 1942, among Hollywood's top ten. Beginning in 1940, he starred in weekly *Melody Ranch* radio programs for Wrigley Gum. He promoted his films with personal appearances, and benefited from the sale of records and merchandise. He also wrote and published songs.

In July 1942, he enlisted in the Army Air Corps, serving for three years during World War II. Broadcasting an Air Corps radio program, he mostly boosted morale. A private pilot in civilian life, he trained in larger aircraft and flew C-47 missions for the Air Transport Command in the United States and in the China-Burma-India Theater, earning a flight officer's commission.

Upon discharge, Gene resumed his radio program and completed four more Republic films. Securing his release, he formed his own production company, making 31 Columbia films, from *The Last Roundup* (1947) to *Last of the Pony Riders* (1953). He scored seasonal

Fans greet Gene Autry upon his airport arrival for the debut performance of his Flying A Ranch Rodeo, February 1942 (obtained from Houston Metropolitan Research Center, Houston Public Library, Houston. Press #4447. © 2004 Autry Qualified Interest Trust and The Autry Foundation, provided courtesy Gene Autry Entertainment).

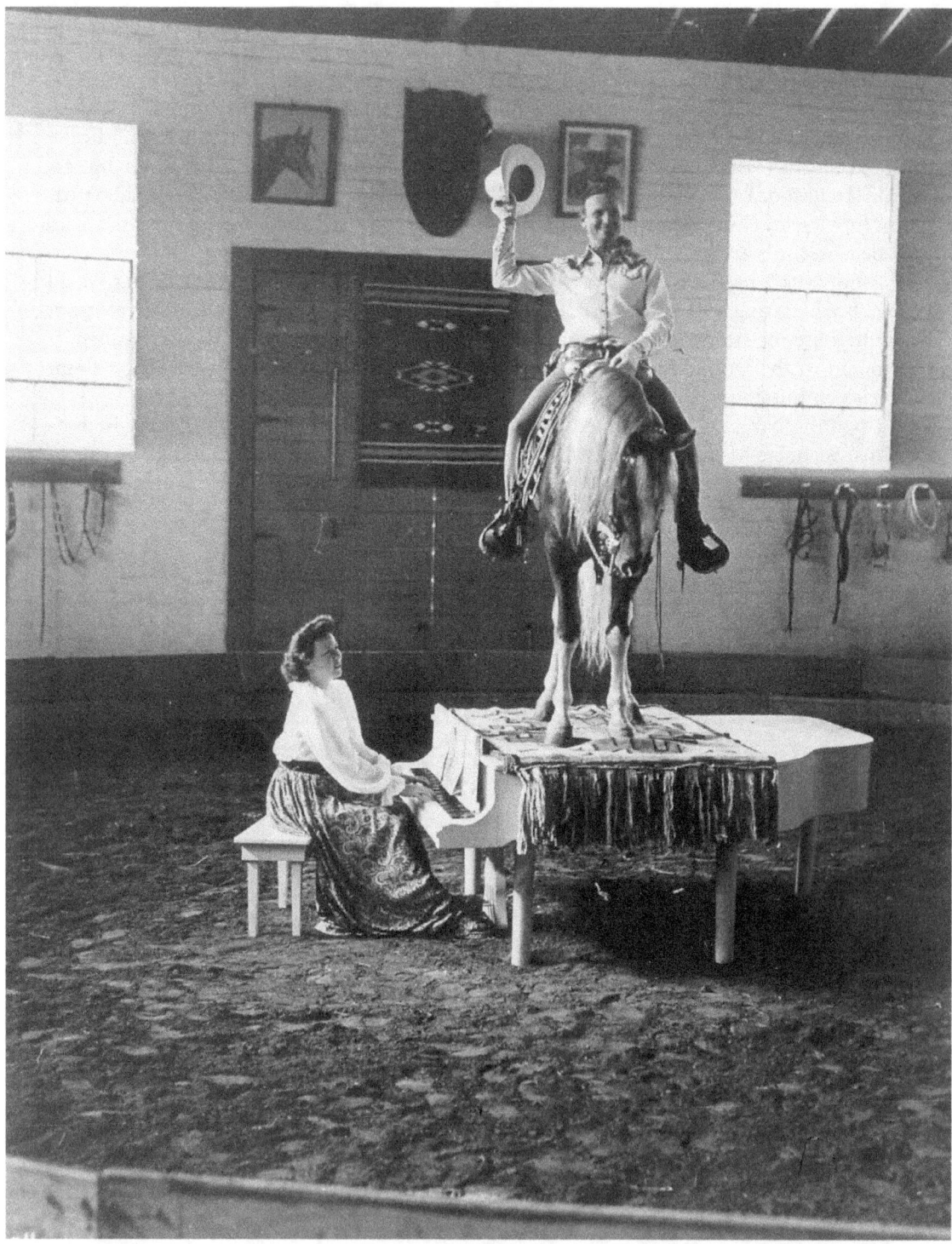

Mrs. Ina Autry is at the keyboard while Gene and Champion pose atop the piano at Gene's home training facility. He is practicing a routine introduced in 1946 at rodeo arenas, with horse trainer Johnny Agee simulating play (photograph obtained from Eddie Brandt's. © 2004 Autry Qualified Interest Trust and The Autry Foundation, provided courtesy Gene Autry Entertainment).

Gene Autry presented Tony Whitecloud's Jemez Pueblo Indian dancers at rodeos and in his film *Apache Country* (Columbia, 1952) (obtained from Eddie Brandt's, © 2004 Autry Qualified Interest Trust and The Autry Foundation, provided courtesy Gene Autry Entertainment).

recording hits with "Rudolph the Red-Nosed Reindeer" and other songs. Original half-hour episodes of *The Gene Autry Show* were telecast from mid–1950 to October 1955, most with Pat Buttram as his sidekick. His Flying A Productions produced additional TV series: *The Range Rider, Annie Oakley, Buffalo Bill, Jr.* and *The Adventures of Champion*. The *Melody Ranch* radio program continued until 1956, and Gene Autry comic books sold well. In 1953, he bought the Placeritas (Monogram) Ranch and used it for TV filming. He toured with rodeos and stage shows, earning five stars on Hollywood's Walk of Fame, one each for films, radio, television, recording and personal appearances.

By the late 1950s, public tastes were changing and Gene at middle age had prepared for a clean break from performing. Through wise investments, he owned radio and TV stations and hotels. Awarded the Major League California Angels franchise in 1966, former semi-pro baseball player Gene settled into the role of businessman and team owner. He was a long-standing board member of the National Cowboy Hall of Fame. His wife of 48 years, Ina, passed away in May of 1980. The following year, he married Jackie, whom he had known as a banker. In the late 1980s, he and Pat Buttram introduced his films on The Nashville Network's *Melody Ranch Theater*. In 1988, The Autry Western Heritage Museum opened in Los Angeles, providing exhibits of Western history and Hollywood cowboys. Gene passed away on October 2, 1998. He was inducted into the National Cowboy Hall of Fame and the Country Music Hall of Fame.

Gene Autry on the Rodeo Trail

Gene Autry may have appeared at rodeos as a WLS radio personality in the early 1930s. Once he moved to Hollywood, he frequented Los Angeles–area rodeos. In July 1939, at the New York World's Fair Wild West Show and Rodeo, Ruth Mix crowned him King of the Cowboys. That fall, he reportedly stepped from the stands and sang at Madison Square Garden's rodeo. His national popularity was revealed in January 1940: In Washington, D.C. to visit a newspaper carrying his comic strip and attend President Roosevelt's March of Dimes Birthday Ball, he was nearly caught in a crush of more than 1,000 fans at a downtown March of Dimes stand.

Gene's San Fernando Valley home, Melody Ranch, built in 1940, had a two-story indoor horse training facility directly off the living room, prompting columnist Erskine Johnson's comment, "Gene Autry lives in the same house with horses." He and Champion practiced their rodeo routines under spotlights and to a machine amplifying arena noise. A system of flushing water sanitized and deodorized the facility. In spring 1940, Eastern arena managers experimented with Gene as a rodeo star. His appearances with JE Ranch Rodeos at Pittsburgh and Philadelphia proved to be an attendance draw. At Pittsburgh, Johnny Agee signed as Gene's horse trainer. That summer, at the Minneapolis Aquatennial Championship Rodeo, Gene presented Champion's tricks, sang and jumped Champ through a flaming hoop. In an interview, he promoted rodeo, explaining entry fees and citing prize money as the only source of contestant income.

Gene's tight Hollywood filming schedule made it difficult to transport Champion to Madison Square Garden's fall rodeo opening. Planning and adaptation by TWA and Gene's horse handlers resulted in Champ becoming the first horse to fly coast-to-coast. A special ramp allowed access to Champ's stable at the plane's rear. A swinging harness eased the shock of possible turbulence. The two-day flight included off-loading Champ at a half-dozen TWA-served cities, providing publicity for Gene and the airline. At the last stop, Washington, D.C., Champ, attempting to re-board, lost his footing climbing the rain-slick ramp, scratching his foreleg and neck on the rail. With a rubber mat, he gained traction and boarded the plane for New York's LaGuardia Field, where a busload of cowboys and a band greeted the history-making flight. Gene took part in New York City's rodeo parade to City Hall, an outdoor show and ward visits at Bellevue Hospital, and a Garden matinee for disabled and underprivileged children, setting an attendance record of 500,000 spectators. Following Boston Garden's rodeo, he performed for no salary at a Toronto rodeo benefiting Canadian Relief for London air raid victims.

While fulfilling Eastern rodeo dates in 1941, Gene planned his own rodeo. Aided by associates, he spent considerable money and energy to acquire rodeo stock. With rodeo manager Eddie Allen, he purchased Joe Greer's Lancaster, Wisconsin, stock. That summer, rodeo veterans Hardy Murphy and Lonnie Rooney helped Gene purchase the 1,200-acre "old Berwyn Ranch," nine miles north of Ardmore, Oklahoma. Barns for the Flying A Ranch headquarters were constructed of native rock. Rooney was named ranch manager. At Madison Square Garden, Gene put a pair of trained palominos, Robin Hood and Golden Boy, through their paces. Rodeo tickets were distributed to servicepersons. As in the previous year, the Melody Ranch Boys included Jimmy Wakely and Johnny Bond. Gene and Johnny Agee attended a Rodeo Fans of America reception. Informed of a fire at his home while performing at Boston Garden, Gene went on with the show.

Berwyn, Oklahoma, proud to have been selected as Gene's rodeo headquarters, voted to change the town's name to "Gene Autry." November 16, 1941 (Oklahoma statehood day), was designated as "Gene Autry Day." Five state governors headed a crowd estimated at more than 30,000. Gene performed with Champion and the Melody Ranch Boys, and made a remote radio broadcast. Newsreel cameras whirred as the old town sign was replaced.

Pairing Western stars with rodeo looked like a profitable venture; however, Gene entered at a risky time. With World War II looming, some rodeos would be suspended and many contestants would enter military service. The Flying A Ranch Stampede, streamlined and glamorized according to Gene's specifications, had yet to make its first performance when he optimistically tried to book it for the fall 1942 Boston Garden rodeo. Management, however, retained Everett Colborn's World's Championship Rodeo.

In February 1942, Gene debuted as feature attraction of his own rodeo at Houston's Fat Stock Show. Afternoon arrival allowed several hundred school-aged youngsters to join rodeo officials at the airport. Surrounded, Gene rejected offers to be "rescued," saying, "That's all right. These boys and girls are my friends, and I'm proud to have them here to welcome me to Houston." At City Hall, he had the mayor autograph his Stetson. He attended to Champ and Robin Hood, who had arrived in their air-conditioned van. He checked out the arena, held a press reception and posed for pictures. Mrs. Autry also made the trip. A newspaper printed Gene's life story in four installments. On opening day, youngsters, dismissed early from school, were admitted for only the five cents tax. Organizers accommodated disabled and disadvantaged children, and every child who wanted to see Gene. Special consideration was accorded uniformed servicepersons and Future Farmers of America. Gene rode Champ in the rodeo parade, joining the governors of Texas and Oklahoma before a crowd of 60,000. Herbert J. Yates and Republic Studios executives saw the rodeo and hosted a reception for Gene.

At the rodeo, the Melody Ranch Boys (Jimmy Wakely, Johnny Bond, Dick Rinehart, Carl Cotner, Frankie Marvin and Paul Sells) provided music. Buff Brady, Jr., and Polly Mills Burson were trick riders. Most of the population of Gene Autry, Oklahoma, arrived by bus to view the rodeo. At each performance, Gene put Champ through his routines, climaxed by a jump through a flaming hoop, and sang surrounded by a herd of longhorns. His songs included "Deep in the Heart of Texas." Grand entry riders were outfitted with matching flags and shirts treated to glow. Gene's shirt was also illuminated. "Saturday Night in the Gay 90's at a Country Square Dance" featured horse-drawn buggies. In "Cavalcade of the Men Who Made America," mounted figures in costume represented George Washington, Sam Houston, Davy Crockett, Andrew Jackson, Kit Carson, Teddy Roosevelt and Buffalo Bill. Their stories were read, and a huge American flag was lowered. As a wartime finale, participants with clothing aglow formed a V in the arena as lights dimmed for the National Anthem.

Melody Ranch was broadcast from Houston's Music Hall on the two Sundays Gene was in town. He warmed up the studio audience before airtime and sang after the program. Poem and letter contest winners earned rodeo passes. He sponsored and helped judge a youth essay contest on the topic, "Why I Am Proud to Be an American." Boy and girl first-place winners were his luncheon guests and viewed the rodeo from his private box. Gene gave second place winners autographed hats and he presented autographed record albums for third place. Newspapers pictured Gene with winners. Two-thirds of the entries were from girls, some ending, "P.S. I love you." He visited hospitals, civic and charitable organizations and schools. Reporters noted that he shook hands with children who waited in line to meet him at the Coliseum, his hotel or other locations. He opened bids on a stock show lamb and bought a $50 ticket to the Arabia Temple's annual Crippled Children's Ball, singing two songs for ticket sellers. Following the final performance, he co-hosted a breakfast party for rodeo and radio performers, singing for 30 minutes. The rodeo drew 20,000 more spectators than the previous year.

Gene's new rodeo traveled east, with incentives for contestants. Competitive points earned counted toward the R.A.A. world championships. Five indoor spring rodeo stands, of approximately one week each, ran nearly consecutively from April 8 through May 26. The cities (in order, Pittsburgh, Philadelphia, Washington, D.C., New Haven and Providence) allowed short travel between sites. For completing the full circuit, each event winner received an additional $250 and the all-around cowboy winner received a bonus of $750. The Melody Ranch Boys included brothers Eddie and Jimmy Dean. Buff Brady, Jr., Tex Cooper, Larry Finley and Gerald Roberts participated. Gene scheduled community activities and war bond rallies.

Over the July Fourth holiday, Gene rewarded the area of his Flying A Ranch by presenting his rodeo at Ardmore, Oklahoma. He led the parade, invited the public to a *Melody Ranch* rehearsal and drew 30,000 rodeo spectators in two days. Unfortunately, his rodeo ranch would soon become irrelevant. During Gene's Chicago rodeo engagement later that month, his Army Air Corps induction at a new Merchandise Mart recruiting station was re-enacted on his *Melody Ranch* broadcast from WBBM studios in the Wrigley Building. He was permitted to finish the rodeo prior to his initial assignment as a Technical Sergeant at Bolling Field, Washington, D.C. Evelyn Finley trick-rode at the Everett Colborn–directed rodeo. Soon, a full-page ad in *Hoofs and Horns* proclaimed the "Greatest announcement in rodeo history." Gene's Flying A Ranch Rodeo had combined with Everett Colborn's World's Championship Rodeo to create America's biggest rodeo, with Colborn as manager and arena director. Gene inscribed a photo, "To Everett, Today we start as partners. Here's

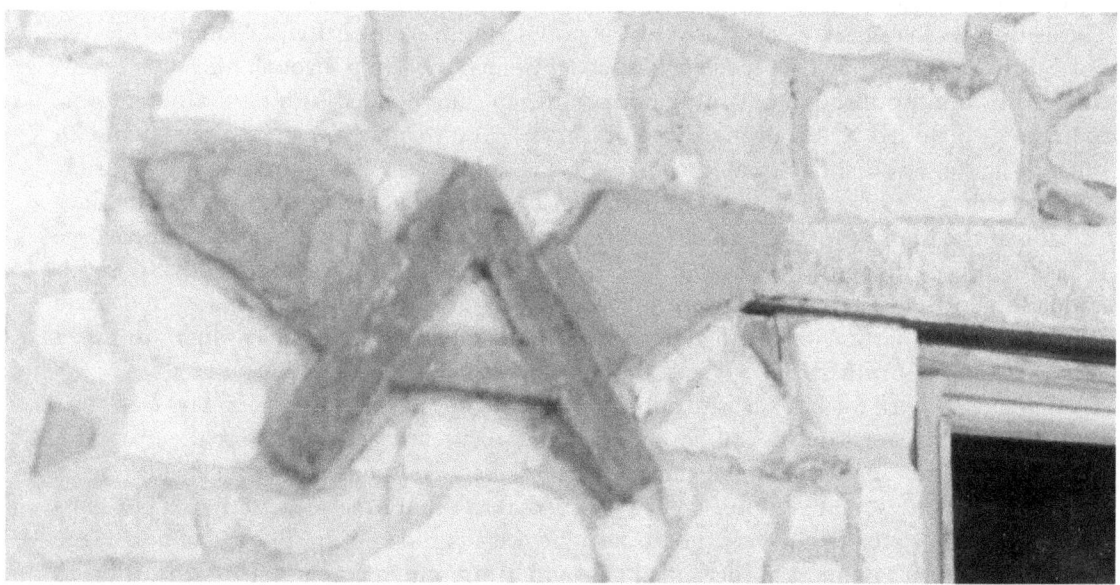

Flying A logo on stone barn of Gene Autry rodeo ranch. Barns are still standing at Gene Autry, Oklahoma, as of this writing (photograph by the author, © 2004 Autry Qualified Interest Trust and The Autry Foundation, provided courtesy Gene Autry Entertainment).

hoping it grows bigger and better." Gene's rodeo livestock was integrated with the Lightning C Ranch at Dublin, Texas, effectively marking the end of the Flying A Ranch in Gene Autry, Oklahoma.

While in the service, Gene remained somewhat involved in rodeo. He appeared at service rodeos, including California's two-day Camp Roberts Roundup. Tech Sergeant Autry, with partner Everett Colborn, watched Cheyenne Frontier Days from the judges' stand. The wartime Madison Square Garden and Boston Garden rodeos, with Gene now part owner, were headlined by Roy Rogers. Polly Mills Burson was a trick rider. In uniform at New York, Gene joined Babe Ruth and Jack Dempsey as spectators. At Boston, he led the rodeo parade and, unscheduled, sang Western and wartime songs at the opening performance. In November, he was transferred to Phoenix. He appeared at Houston's 1944 rodeo. In the fall at Madison Square Garden, Flight Officer Autry responded to opening night youngsters by climbing over the rail to sing. On leave in 1945, Gene visited the Houston rodeo and the one-day Los Angeles Coliseum rodeo starring Roy Rogers. Formally discharged in June, he continued to work for the defense effort. At Madison Square Garden, he signed to headline the 1946 rodeo.

In 1946, Gene returned to films, radio and rodeo. His new act, rehearsed at his home arena and introduced at Fort Worth, included jumping Champion atop a prop baby grand piano, from which Gene sang "Back in the Saddle Again." The Cass County Kids (later the Cass County Boys) musical group joined the Melody Ranch Boys to support most of Gene's post-war rodeos. Champion, Jr., was added. Gene rode in the parade, entertained at a Rotary luncheon and made a "Breakfast in Hollywood" broadcast. From a miniature chuckwagon drawn by two white Spanish mules as part of a simulated trail drive of longhorn steers, he sang "Wagon Wheels." Another production was the "Cavalcade of Texas Pioneers." In the spring, he headlined the Phoenix rodeo and some eastern JE Ranch Rodeos, including Cleveland and Washington, D.C. He starred at the SQ Ranch Rodeo at Toronto. Los Angeles' Pan-Pacific Auditorium hosted a 23-performance Autry-Colborn rodeo in June, featuring many Hollywood-connected rodeo personalities. In the fall, Gene headlined at Dublin, Texas, missing one matinee for his radio broadcast. At City Hall, New York's mayor welcomed Gene's return to Madison Square Garden. Gene, with trick ropers Nancy Sheppard and Gene McLaughlin, greeted a *New York Times* children's reading program. At one Garden performance, Gene fell from Champ. The rodeo drew the largest Garden crowd to date. During the follow-on Boston Garden run, Gene autographed records at Sears, visited City Hospital patients and entertained youths working for the Greater Boston Community Fund. At the end of the year, the original Champion passed away.

In early 1947, Gene flew his Beechcraft aircraft to the Houston rodeo. He rode Champion, Jr., in the rodeo parade while youngsters walked alongside. Two thousand youths were guests at the opening performance. *Melody Ranch* was broadcast from the Music Hall. Gene headlined a one-day Los Angeles Coliseum rodeo in March and rode in the Helldorado Days parade in Las Vegas. At Oklahoma City, he joined an all-star tornado relief rodeo. He drew the largest rodeo crowd in Lubbock, Texas, history, and starred at Ogden, Utah. Headlining August's Los Angeles Sheriff's Rodeo, he attracted nearly 87,000 spectators to the Coliseum. In September, Gene began an association with Montana stock contractor Leo Cremer. Their first rodeo in St. Paul, Minnesota, drew a record 90,000 fans. Ray Whitley joined Gene's musical group for the fall Garden rodeos. While in New York, Gene, Champion and the Cass County Boys, met by Cardinal Spellman, entertained over 1,000 youngsters (including those from four nearby schools) celebrating October birthdays at the Lincoln Hall

Gene Autry autographs for youngsters in his dressing room at the 1948 Boston Garden rodeo (*Herald-Traveler* photograph by Dan Murphy, obtained from Boston Public Library, Print Department, © 2004 Autry Qualified Interest Trust and The Autry Foundation, provided courtesy Gene Autry Entertainment).

School. In his autobiography, *Back in the Saddle Again*, Gene noted that kindness at Boston Garden to children of baseball's Joe Cronin at this time may have years later aided his bid for the California Angels franchise.

Joined on parade by "Wild Bill" Elliott, Gene starred at the 1948 Houston rodeo. Rufe Davis and movie horse *Gallant Bess* entertained. Champion appeared in a department store window. Rodeo fans braved winter weather. Between rodeos at which he starred, Gene's company produced rodeos in other cities, and he toured with his stage show.

In June, he led the parade and headlined a rodeo at San Francisco's Cow Palace to benefit the Optimist Club Boys Welfare Fund. On this, his first appearance in the area, he visited media, met with the mayor and toured Letterman General Hospital. In September, he arrived in his private plane to headline the Fort Madison rodeo and broadcast *Melody Ranch* from the high school auditorium. At Madison Square Garden, Gene performed with Champion, Jr., and Little Champ. He brought Little Champ in a taxi to the Bellevue Hospital show. Overhearing a nine-year-old wheelchair patient's wish to pat the horse, he arranged for children to do so. At one rodeo performance, Gene in his white suit was forced to scramble up a chute gate to avoid a bronc. In Boston, Little Champ made a big hit. Gene visited Massachusetts General Hospital, hosted newspaper delivery boys and met department store contest winners.

Aircraft mechanical problems delayed Gene's arrival for Mandan, North Dakota's,

1949 rodeo, but airport fans waited. He led the parade and checked out a horse purchase, perhaps a future Champion. With the Cass County Boys, he entertained at a private party where he peeled potatoes. Later that month, he starred at Salt Lake City's Days of '47 Rodeo. Champion appeared at a local department store. Gene and the Cass County Boys entertained at children's hospitals. He awoke one night to find a building ablaze near his horse trailer, but the fire was extinguished. His third July rodeo, at the Cow Palace, benefited the Boys Club. Following the one-day Los Angeles Sheriff's Rodeo, he headlined at Ardmore, Oklahoma, where a county fair building was named for him.

Later that month, he returned to Fort Madison, riding in the parade and crowning the rodeo queen. His radio show had been transcribed. For New York and Boston rodeo appearances, Gene introduced Tony Whitecloud's Jemez Pueblo Indian dancers, and the song "Rudolph, the Red-Nosed Reindeer." He presented perhaps rodeo's most dramatic production number, singing, in a luminous shirt, "Ghost Riders in the Sky" while riders drove a herd of steers with hooves and horns aglow. One competing rodeo cowboy wrote, "I would find a different place in the grandstand for every performance to watch this act." A Bellevue Hospital boy got to sit on Little Champ. At New York's special matinee, disabled and underprivileged children loudly joined Gene in song. In Boston, he awarded a pony to a rodeo contest winner.

In 1950, movie and TV filming limited Gene's availability for rodeos. He impressed the town with his friendliness at July's Snake River Stampede in Nampa, where a new stadium was named for him. Champion appeared at a music store, and Gene tapped out a Morse code rodeo invitation to railroad telegraphers. With the Cass County Boys, he attended a Buckaroo Breakfast in the park. Unscheduled, he rode in the rodeo parade. He visited the Boise Elks convalescent home, introduced the Kiwanis Kid's Day king and queen, and met junior riding club members. An infected toe caused swelling and a limp. He borrowed an oversized boot from Cass County Boy Jerry Scoggins and spent an afternoon receiving hospital treatment. At the rodeo, Champion marched to the Army Air Corps song. Gene varied his song selection at each of five sell-out performances, inviting audience participation on "I'm Looking Over a Four-Leaf Clover." In the fall, Gene presented the same well-received Garden shows as the previous year. At New York's matinee for disabled and underprivileged children, he carried a four-year-old boy from his special bus to an arena seat.

In June 1951, Gene headlined the rodeo at Miles City, Montana. Visiting a hospital, he sang over the intercom system and presented a get-well stencil for each patient's breakfast tray. He also made a home visit, talking from their porch to twin boys with measles. In July, he starred at Mandan, North Dakota's, rodeo. Following a Hollywood recording trip, he appeared at Leo Cremer's home area of Big Timber, Montana. His plane's landing gear was damaged en route, so a borrowed plane made the return trip. He brought Tony Whitecloud's Indian dancers to the Los Angeles Sheriff's Rodeo, drawing 87,577 spectators. He returned to Madison Square Garden and Boston Garden. For the latter rodeo, he drove a stagecoach for publicity. Two extra matinees met the demand of children. Gene's personal check supported Children's Free Clinic holiday parties.

In 1952, Gene's filmmaking permitted only three rodeos. On opening night at Nampa's Gene Autry Stadium, he introduced 16-year-old singing rodeo queen Judy Voiten (later rodeo headliner Judy Lynn). Theaters played four of his films. He shared the Buckaroo Breakfast, visited the Boise Elks hospital and presented a pony mare and colt to a contest winner. In the arena, he sang nine to 12 songs per performance, responding to requests.

Attendance set a record. August saw Gene and Mrs. Autry at the Pikes Peak or Bust Rodeo. He awarded a Shetland pony to the "name the pony" contest winner and visited St. Francis Hospital, including the cerebral palsy ward. At a matinee, a helicopter delivered a Spencer Penrose buckle for presentation to Gene, but had difficulty lifting off. Gene and spectators watched pick-up men on horseback tow the chopper out of the arena. In the fall, Gene starred at Denver's Rocky Mountain Empire Rodeo, registering with Champ at the Brown Palace Hotel. There were contests to "name the pony" and to devise "the best question to ask Gene." He recorded radio programs with youth, met with Colorado's governor and visited Children's Hospital, including iron lung polio patients. In 1953, Gene gave priority to his stage show, except for the Madison Square Garden rodeo. There, suffering from bronchitis, he joined the Range Rider and Dick West, who headlined Boston's rodeo.

In Gene's arena act, Little Champ's disobedience sometimes exceeded the script. In 1949, at New York's Bellevue Hospital, Little Champ broke through his roped ring and headed toward the stands of ill and disabled children. The announcer calmed the crowd, saying, "Looky here, Little Champ wants to say hello to the children." Evading pursuers, Little Champ returned to the ring on his own. At Nampa, frisky Little Champ broke away from his rope ring, entangling and stirring Champion. Down went the ropes, the props and Gene. The crowd loved it. Gene calmly collected the horses and completed the act.

In January 1954, Gene purchased a half-interest in the rodeo company of Leo Cremer, killed in a November accident. Represented by partner Harry Knight, Gene, with the Cremer family, fulfilled Leo's rodeo schedule. He and the Cass County Boys starred at rodeos in Miles City, Montana, and Casper, Wyoming, and then entertained a crowd of 95,000 at Los Angeles' Sheriff's Rodeo. With Mrs. Autry, he arrived for Colorado's State Fair Rodeo. Youngsters enjoyed seeing Gene, Champion and Little Champ register at the hotel. Gene led the parade and did a bit of work in each newspaper department. Champ was photographed looking on with disapproval as Gene drove a Corvette. Laryngitis hampered Gene's singing voice. At the Iowa Centennial State Fair Rodeo, he kept a promise made four years earlier. Visiting at home, Gene had told an ill boy that when he got well, he could ride Champ. In front of the rodeo crowd, Gene made good on his promise to the now eight-year-old lad. He also visited the local hospital. At Houston's 1955 rodeo, Gene and Gail "Annie Oakley" Davis made their first joint rodeo appearance. They rode on the Salt Grass Trail Ride and drew 171,000 rodeo spectators. The duo headlined fall rodeos at Des Moines and Chicago. At the latter, Gene and the Cass County Boys cheered patients at the County Children's Hospital.

In early 1956, Gene, with Harry Knight, established the Flying A Ranch, on acreage near Fowler, Colorado, to accommodate former Cremer rodeo livestock, now fully owned. For summer and fall rodeos in 1956, Gene made tandem appearances with Gail Davis. The two headlined the Mollala (Oregon) Buckaroo Rodeo, the Spokane (Washington) Diamond Spur Rodeo, the Colorado State Fair Rodeo and the Kentucky State Fair Rodeo. Johnny Western joined Gene's musical troupe at Pueblo. Scheduled to share the Ak-Sar-Ben Rodeo tanbark in Omaha with Miss Davis, Gene was forced to drop out and seek medical attention for persistent voice problems. Gail, the Cass County Boys and Gene's horses carried on. Returning for Chicago's Dairy Show "Golden Spurs" rodeo, Gene celebrated his twenty-fifth anniversary as a singing star, having started in 1931 in that city.

Gene and Gail headlined six 1957 rodeos in addition to Boston Garden. At Fort Madison, the Riders of the Purple Sage provided musical back-up, and the rodeo drew its largest crowd. In 1958, Gene and Gail made their final joint rodeo appearance at San Antonio. Gail continued to appear solo at rodeos. Gene, over 50 years of age, had made his final theatrical film and TV episode. On a risky rodeo trip with Mrs. Autry to Cuba, active in revolution, he was assigned bodyguards. According to his autobiography, Gene assessed the situation and departed when stock contractor Tommy Steiner was paid. That spring, he headlined a Milwaukee rodeo, where Johnny Bond and Merle Travis were part of the musical aggregation. A coloring contest earned youngsters rodeo tickets and a meeting with Gene. That year, he backed the Brussels World's Fair Wild West Show, which closed early.

Most of Gene's subsequent rodeo dates were not as an entertainer. For the 1960 Ellensburg (Washington) rodeo parade, he rode a borrowed palomino as parade grand marshal. His non-riding arena visit showed he could still draw a crowd. Twice in the 1960s, he was grand marshal of Palm Springs' rodeo parade. As late as 1980, he was parade marshal and Man of the Year there. In 1983, he accepted a Buffalo Bill Award in conjunction with North Platte's rodeo. Gene was a leader in rodeo, as well as in other areas.

GENE BARRY (1921–) Gene Barry, star of NBC-TV's *Bat Masterson*, headlined the 1959 Mid-South Fair at Memphis, Tennessee, and appeared at the Calgary Stampede.

NOAH BEERY, JR. (1916–94) Seen in Western features, serials and TV series, Noah Beery, Jr., starred at the 1952 Arkansas Livestock Show Rodeo in Little Rock.

Western actor Noah Beery, Jr.

Gene Barry, of NBC-TV's *Bat Masterson*.

WALLACE BEERY (1886–1949) Kansas City–born Wallace Beery left school to experience show business with the circus, musical stage shows and stock companies. A screen test in 1913 led to more than 250 films. He progressed from early comedies to villain and rough "good guy" roles. He lent story, screenplay and/or direction to several early silent films. He was under contract to MGM for 20 years, making films, as star or supporting player, with many of that studio's greats. Nominated for an Academy Award in 1930, he won a Best Actor Oscar in 1931. He piloted his plane to vacation at a Wyoming ranch home. Several of his films were Westerns. A lieutenant commander in the U.S. Naval Air Reserve, Wallace died of a heart attack.

Academy Award–winning actor Wallace Beery (courtesy Eddie Brandt's).

Wallace Beery on the Rodeo Trail

At rodeos, Wallace preferred the chutes and competing cowboys to the role of dignitary. He was among celebrities attending rodeos at Salinas in 1929 and 1932, and Pendleton in 1936. He presented a championship saddle at the 1936 Reno Rodeo. In 1937, he crowned Cheyenne's "Miss Frontier" and participated in a historical pageant. In 1941, he was the first star featured at Colorado Springs' Rodeo. A newspaper stated, "He rides, shoots, and is an accomplished master of ceremonies." He appeared in the rodeo parade and, with his ten-year-old daughter Carol Ann, galloped into the arena immediately following the grand entry.

REX BELL (1903–62) Rex Bell debuted as a silent Western star in 1928. Re-cast temporarily as a romantic lead, he married the famous "It" girl, Clara Bow. At his Walking Box Ranch near Searchlight, Nevada, he raised livestock. He made low-budget sound Westerns through 1936 and, later, played supporting roles. Following retirement from films, he attended to his ranch, his family and his western clothing stores in Las Vegas and Reno. Elected in 1954, he served eight years as Nevada's lieutenant governor. While campaigning for governor, he suffered a fatal heart attack.

Rex Bell on the Rodeo Trail

Rex, as a young man, rode bareback broncs and roped at amateur rodeos. Later active in lending his celebrity to rodeos, he participated in each of Las Vegas' 28 Helldorado Days

Rex Bell and Ruth Mix in a lobby card scene for *Saddle Aces* (Resolute, 1935) (courtesy of Eddie Brandt's).

celebrations in his lifetime. He first appeared at the Reno Rodeo in 1932, and he was a regular from 1955 onward. In 1958, he told a reporter that he attended 15–18 rodeos a year. These included rodeos at Denver, Pendleton and Red Bluff. Rex was a familiar rider in rodeo parades.

"BOBBY BENSON" Beginning in 1932, 12-year-old cowboy Bobby Benson was the title character of a radio program. British-born Easterner Herbert C. Rice created and developed *Bobby Benson* to promote H-O Oats, a cereal produced by the Hecker H-O Company of Buffalo, New York. Bobby, an orphan brought up by old Bart Benson, lived in Texas Big Bend country on his H-Bar-O Ranch.

Bobby Benson was broadcast on the CBS network from 1932 to 1936. About 1934, production moved to New York City. In 1949, a new Mutual network sponsor made Bobby's ranch the B-Bar-B.

Bobby Benson on the Rodeo Trail

Various actors appeared at rodeos in Bobby's name. The *Bobby Benson* radio show advertised in 1930s Madison Square Garden rodeo programs. In 1934, on a rodeo date designated "Bobby Benson Day," "Bobby" appeared at the Garden with the H-Bar-O cowboys.

1936 RODEO

Bobby Benson Speaking To...

Boys and girls by the thousands who are all Rodeo, ranch and radio followers

by BOBBY BENSON
· H-Bar-O Ranch ·

HOWDY, everybody!
Say, does it make me feel good to be back in New York and at the Rodeo again! I could hardly wait to roll my blankets, saddle up and ride East!

And this year it's more fun than ever because I feel like I'm giving a party! When I ride around the arena and look up and see all the boys and girls — and hear them, too — say, it's a grand and glorious feeling to know I was able to help a bunch of them get their tickets. There's only one thing that isn't so good.

When the Rodeo is over October 25, I've got to leave New York and head back to the H-Bar-O ranch in the Big Bend Country of Texas. But, that'll be fun too, because you know they say anything can happen in Texas and it usually does.

I guess you know about the cowboys I brought with me. Some of the best riders, ropers and bull doggers in the west are among them. And you can count on the H-Bar-O boys to stay right in there and pitch, when the bronchos come busting out of the chutes.

And we'll be riding and roping for you because we feel that all of you fellows and girls sitting up there in The Garden every Monday, Wednesday and Friday nights at 6:15 are our guests at the H-Bar-O ranch — when we're on the air over WABC and a Columbia network — so we're going to do our level best for you!

I'll be wavin' my hat at you — so you wave right back, will you? And we'll all wish the H-Bar-O boys best o' luck.

Gracias! Which is the way we say thank you down on the Rio Grande.

Bobby Benson advertisement and message from the 1936 Madison Square Garden rodeo program.

In 1936, he made matinee appearances. Ivan Cury, radio's Bobby Benson in the early 1950s, recalled with pleasure appearing as guest star at the 1950 Pony Express Rodeo in St. Joseph, Missouri. Reportedly voted the cowboy children most wanted to see, Bobby and other cast members were in the rodeo parade. Bobby rode a palomino in the grand entry, ranch foreman Tex Mason sang, Hanka the Indian demonstrated archery and Windy Wales provided comedy. Bobby led a B-Bar-B yell contest, awarding Bobby Benson merchandise to winners. Saturday matinee fans received a Bobby Benson singing lasso.

JOHNNY BOND (1915–78) Born in Enville, Oklahoma, Johnny Bond was in the school brass band and played stringed instruments. He performed in church and in a local band before graduating from high school. He played with a band on radio and at dances, joined Jimmy Wakely in a trio and composed the Western song "Cimarron." In September 1940, the trio joined Gene Autry's *Melody Ranch* radio program. From 1939 through 1947, Johnny provided music and/or composed songs for more than 35 films. When Gene Autry returned from service, Johnny resumed providing music and comedy on *Melody Ranch*.

Johnny Bond on the Rodeo Trail

Johnny accompanied Gene's 1940 and 1941 fall rodeo tours to Madison Square Garden and Boston Garden. He continued to perform at rodeos, solo and with Gene Autry.

RICHARD BOONE (1917–81) Richard Boone starred as Paladin on TV's *Have Gun Will Travel* and on *Hec Ramsey*. He also appeared in several Western feature films.

Johnny Bond, singer, musician and comedian, supported Gene Autry on radio's *Melody Ranch* and played rodeos.

"Paladin" on the Rodeo Trail

Richard Boone starred at a 1958 Texas Prison Rodeo and received the TV award at the 1959 California Rodeo. In 1961, he was grand marshal of Los Angeles' Sheriff's Rodeo, and accepted a Silver Spur Award at Reno, Nevada.

Richard Boone, Paladin of CBS-TV's *Have Gun Will Travel*, compares draws with a correctional officer while appearing at a 1958 Texas Prison Rodeo (courtesy of Texas Department of Criminal Justice).

WILLIAM BOYD (1898–1972)   William Lawrence Boyd was born in Hendrysburg, Ohio. Upon his father's death, he left school to travel and work at a variety of jobs. Based on his looks, he was advised to give Hollywood a try. After appearing in silent films, he made the transition to sound. A 1931 Hollywood scandal involved an actor with the same name, but some newspapers ran photos of the innocent William Boyd, and this sent his career into a tailspin. Boston-born Harry "Pop" Sherman produced a Paramount film series based on Clarence E. Mulford's Hopalong Cassidy novels. Prematurely white-haired William Boyd experienced a career revival when chosen for the glamorized lead role. He rode his white horse Topper in 66 Hopalong Cassidy pictures (1935–48) and modified his personal life to conform to his heroic screen image. Foreseeing the potential of television, he risked his financial resources to purchase rights to the Hopalong films and character. Soon the films were playing nationwide on TV, gaining a new generation of fans. In 1950, he began a *Hopalong Cassidy* TV series and radio program. Licensed juvenile products met the demand of a Hoppy craze that swept the nation. In his fifties, William Boyd appeared on magazine covers as a national hero. He made a number of personal appearances. In 1993, Mrs. Boyd accepted an "In Memoriam" Golden Boot Award for her late husband. Hopalong Cassidy Museums opened at Wichita, Kansas, and Cambridge, Ohio.

"Hopalong Cassidy" on the Rodeo Trail

William Boyd reportedly turned down overtures to headline rodeos at Madison Square Garden and Boston Garden, supposedly doubting his ability to carry a live show before

William Boyd as Hopalong Cassidy.

thousands of spectators. Soon, Hopalong Cassidy attained even greater popularity, and Mr. Boyd gained confidence.

Mrs. Boyd frequently accompanied her husband to rodeos. Hoppy appeared in the parade and at the opening of the 1948 Pony Express Rodeo at St. Joseph, Missouri. At Philadelphia's 1949 rodeo, he shared billing with the Sons of the Pioneers. In early 1951, he headlined the Houston rodeo with singer Eddy Arnold. That same year, astride Topper, he was in Tucson's La Fiesta de los Vaqueros rodeo parade, meeting and holding youngsters. At opening day of the Grand National Junior Livestock Exposition at San Francisco's Cow Palace, he rode Topper and talked about the virtues required of a young cowboy or cowgirl. Children got a Hoppy photo and a chance to win a white pony, Little Topper. In 1953, he was grand marshal of the Los Angeles Sheriff's Rodeo, and he was at Las Vegas' 1956 Helldorado Days Rodeo. A Hopalong Cassidy Trophy offered at the Spokane (Washington) Diamond Spur Rodeo, beginning in 1950, was retired in 1960 by three-time all-around champion Pete Crump.

WILFORD BRIMLEY (1934–) Raised on a California farm, Wilford Brimley spent summers riding in Idaho, where he later worked as a farrier. A Western film extra in the mid–1960s, he rode, did saddle falls and drove wagons. He became a notable character actor in major films and on NBC-TV's *Our House* (1986–89). He co-starred with Richard

Farnsworth on TV's *The Boys of Twilight* (1992) and was featured in the TNT movie *Crossfire Trail* (2001). He has also been featured in TV commercials.

Wilford Brimley on the Rodeo Trail

Wilford Brimley team-roped with his son and, for charity, has hosted roping competitions on his ranch. He participated in Ben Johnson celebrity rodeos. Grand marshal of the 1985 Snake River Stampede parade, he received the 1987 Buffalo Bill Award at North Platte. Later that year, in Las Vegas, he helped "roast" Casey Tibbs. In 1988, he was Reno Rodeo parade grand marshal and recipient of the Silver Spurs Award. He is an honorary PRCA member for his contributions to the sport. He helped raise funds for Casey Tibbs' statue and paid tribute to his friend at the statue's unveiling. He volunteered at exceptional rodeos and appeared in the PRCA video "Animals and Rodeo: A Closer Look."

Wilford Brimley leaves the outdoor podium at the ProRodeo Hall of Fame following his tribute at the 1989 unveiling of Casey Tibbs' statue, "The Champ" (photograph by author).

JOHN BROMFIELD (1922–2005) Born in South Bend, Indiana, Farron Bromfield moved with his family to the California coast. His lifelong love of fishing was often incorporated into his show business career. Through college years, he was active in football and boxing. He served in the U.S. Navy between stints in commercial fishing. He made feature films before being named TV's Sheriff of Cochise, as contemporary Western lawman Frank Morgan. The syndicated show was filmed in Cochise County, Arizona. Following two seasons (1957–58) with composer Stan Jones as Deputy Olsen, the show was re-titled *U.S. Marshal*. John, as the same character, was promoted and given state-wide jurisdiction.

Young fans get the drop on John Bromfield (second from right), "Sheriff of Cochise," and Joe Bodrie (right), "Fastest Gun Alive," stars of Boston Garden's 1958 rodeo (*Herald-Traveler* photograph courtesy Boston Public Library, Print Department).

James Griffith became Deputy Tom Ferguson. The change extended the show another two years (1959–60). John returned to TV in outdoor sports-oriented shows. He made personal appearances at fairs, circuses and rodeos.

"Sheriff of Cochise" and "U.S. Marshal" on the Rodeo Trail

John Bromfield joined social activities surrounding the 1957 La Fiesta de los Vaqueros rodeo at Tucson. That year, he was a star at the Los Angeles Sheriff's Rodeo. At Las Vegas' Helldorado Days celebration in 1958, he was featured on a first-place parade float. That fall, supported by Joe Bodrie, "Fastest Gun Alive," he was the last Western star to headline Boston Garden's World Championship Rodeo. John and Joe were co-billed with Dale Robertson at the 1964 Eastern States Exposition Rodeo at West Springfield, Massachusetts. John brought along his familiar white station wagon.

JOHNNY MACK BROWN (1904–74) Johnny Mack Brown was born in Dothan, Alabama. His gridiron prowess as a University of Alabama scholar-athlete led his team to consecutive Rose Bowl victories (1926 and 1927) and won him All-American honors. A crew filming in Alabama afforded him his first contact with the motion picture business. In Hollywood, he began as a romantic leading man in silent films. His title role in MGM's

Billy the Kid (1930) led to Western stardom in over 100 action pictures, including serials. He and his horse Rebel retired from picturemaking in 1953. In the mid–1960s, he returned to the screen for a few character roles. Johnny Mack passed away in Los Angeles of kidney failure.

Johnny Mack Brown on the Rodeo Trail

In 1949, Johnny Mack Brown appeared at Las Vegas' Helldorado Days Rodeo. In Lubbock, Texas, he headlined the 1950 ABC-Boys Club Rodeo, leading the parade and drawing an estimated 34,000 rodeo spectators. He was in the 1952 Palm Springs Rodeo parade. As star of Fort Madison's 1956 rodeo, he arrived two days early to publicize the rodeo through the media and at civic luncheons. He registered under an assumed name at a hotel in a nearby city but, as word leaked out, youngsters surrounded him. At the rodeo, he presented a pony, Rebel, Jr., to a lucky child. Following each performance, he passed out autographed photos to kids. In 1957, he headlined the American Legion Rodeo in Washington, D.C. Johnny Mack also appeared at the Calgary Stampede.

Western film star Johnny Mack Brown.

PETER BROWN (1935–)   Peter Brown was born in New York City. On a California ranch, he gained experience in riding and rodeoing. During U.S. Army service, he participated in stage productions. He studied drama at the University of Southern California and with Jeff Corey. From California theater he moved to TV drama. Under contract to Warner Brothers, he worked in feature films and TV series. On *Lawman* (1958–62), he played Deputy Johnny McKay. John Russell, who played Marshal Dan Troop of Laramie, Wyoming, on that series, appeared at Camp Pendleton's Marine rodeos in 1963 and 1964. He died in January of 1991. Added to the *Lawman* cast for the second season, attractive Peggie Castle played well-dressed Birdcage Saloon owner Lily Merrill. She later passed away at a young age.

Following *Lawman*, Peter Brown made additional films and another Western TV series, *Laredo* (1965–67), on which he played Boston-born, revenge-seeking Texas Ranger

The cast of TV's *Lawman*: (left to right) John Russell, Peggie Castle and Peter Brown.

Chad Cooper. Western actor Philip Carey played Ranger Captain Parmalee. Other rangers were Neville Brand (1920–92) and William Smith. Following his two Western series, Peter made additional films and enjoyed an extended stint on soap operas. Golf and tennis, as well as horsemanship, have made him a regular on the celebrity tournament and rodeo circuit supporting various charitable causes. He received a Golden Boot Award.

Peter Brown on the Rodeo Trail

Peter Brown and Peggie Castle arrived in Albuquerque wearing Western dress as headliners at the 1960 New Mexico State Fair Rodeo. A newspaper publicity picture showed Castle in one of her fancy saloon girl dresses. Their act included songs, jokes, Johnny McKay's gun handling and Lily's beauty. Peter later toured with fellow *Laredo* cast members. Neville Brand sometimes joined the group, but was absent when the other three stars headlined the 1966 Louisiana State Fair Rodeo at Shreveport.

SMILEY BURNETTE (1911–67) Lester Alvin Burnette was born in Summum, Illinois, to minister parents. After moving to Astoria, he showed youthful musical talent. By his high school years, he was involved in school musical activities and had his own band. He performed in vaudeville and on radio. Gene Autry hired him as an accordionist. From WLS radio's *National Barn Dance*, the pair went to Hollywood. Following appearances in *In Old Santa Fe* and *Mystery Mountain* (1934) with Ken Maynard, they starred in a 12-chapter serial, *The Phantom Empire* (1935), combining musical, Western and science fiction elements. Moviegoers welcomed them. Smiley was Gene's comic sidekick Frog Millhouse in about 50 Republic films. His comedy included remarkable voice range from high to froggy low. Additional characteristics included his girth, checkered shirt, battered black hat with turned-up front brim and his horse, Ring-Eyed Nellie. Gene and Smiley established the singing cowboy and his sidekick as standard screen fare. Smiley's song compositions ranged from the classic "Ridin' Down the Canyon" to novelty ditties.

With Gene in World War II service, Smiley supported other cowboy heroes, including Charles Starrett as the Durango Kid in 56 Columbia films. After filling in for injured Pat Buttram in *Whirlwind* (1951), he rejoined Gene for a final six features. He had supported Gene Autry and Roy Rogers in their initial starring films, and backed both Charles Starrett and Gene Autry in their final features.

He often commented that he went unrecognized until he put on his familiar battered black hat. He claimed that he bought his hats new, then broke them in by letting a few horses run over them. Smiley and his wife Dallas raised four adopted children. Smiley had been listed among the top ten Western box office stars. He had his own radio program and comic book. He appeared at theaters, fairs, midways and store openings. Beginning in 1963, he was a regular on TV's *Petticoat Junction*. He once offered this insight into his philosophy: "Tomorrow's a promissory note, yesterday's a canceled check, and just this minute's all the cash I've got." Smiley Burnette, a man who had brought audiences much enjoyment, died of leukemia.

Smiley Burnette on the Rodeo Trail

From the late 1940s through the early 1960s, Smiley entertained at rodeos. He played some of the larger rodeos, such as the St. Louis Fireman's Rodeo and Omaha's Ak-Sar-Ben Rodeo. He was the first Western star at Sikeston's Jaycee Bootheel Rodeo. More often, he appeared at small-to-medium locations. His show was relatively simple, making him affordable to smaller venues or rodeos experimenting with Western star entertainers. Sometimes

Western movie sidekick Smiley Burnette poses between rodeo clowns Jimmy Schumacher (left) and Wiley McCray (right) at Omaha's 1960 Ak-Sar-Ben Rodeo (Pep-Tone Studio, Omaha, Nebraska, photograph, used with permission of Jack Pepitone. Obtained from Ak-Sar-Ben/River City Rodeo, Omaha, Nebraska).

another horse represented Ring-Eyed Nellie. Smiley's act consisted of a comedy routine, skits with children and comedy songs. Mainly directed toward youngsters, his presentation also generated roars of laughter from adults. He imitated sounds such as a motorboat, or a fly landing on a pile of sugar. He delighted crowds with his voice changes. Calling a group of youngsters from the stands, he gave them cowboy star names and staged a mock gun battle. Following his performance, he met youngsters and signed autographs.

JAMES CAAN (1940–) Raised in New York City, James Caan attended Hofstra University and trained as an actor. Seasoned on stage and on TV, he gained nominations for an Emmy in *Brian's Song* (1971) and for an Academy Award in *The Godfather* (1972). He starred in the Western *Comes a Horseman* (1978). After an absence from the screen to resolve personal problems, he returned to filmmaking and television.

James Caan on the Rodeo Trail

James Caan presents an unusual case of an established actor of some reputation who, while making movies, became a serious rodeo contestant. In 1972, he became a PRCA member,

Actor and rodeo roper James Caan, as seen in *Comes a Horseman* (United Artists, 1978) (courtesy Eddie Brandt's).

team-roping at rodeos for about nine years as filming allowed. Roping partners included rodeo cowboy-stuntmen.

HARRY CAREY (1878–1947)   In 1915, Harry Carey and Hoot Gibson worked at Universal. Young John Ford honed his directorial skills on Harry's early Westerns. Harry starred in silent and sound films, mostly Westerns, for various studios. Later a noted character actor,

Western film star Harry Carey.

he earned an Academy Award nomination as Best Supporting Actor. In the 1940s, he acted in Broadway plays, toured with a circus and appeared in four films with John Wayne. He is an inductee of the National Cowboy Hall of Fame.

Harry Carey on the Rodeo Trail

About 1927, the Newhall-Saugus American Legion asked Harry to hold a charity rodeo on his ranch. Son Harry Carey, Jr., recalled riding in a grand entry with his dad as marshal at an all–Indian rodeo on the premises. The Carey ranch was damaged in a 1928 flood and destroyed a second time by fire. The Carey ranch rodeo became part of the Saugus area rodeo tradition. As late as 1942, Harry was president of the Newhall-Saugus Rodeo Association.

SUNSET CARSON (c. 1924–90) Star of 20 action Westerns for Republic and Astor in the 1940s, Sunset Carson was reputed to have been a third generation rodeo competitor and all-around champion at Buenos Aires in 1941 and 1942.

Western film star Sunset Carson.

ALLEN CASE (1935–86) Born at Dallas, Texas, Allen Jones left college to pursue a career in show business. His baritone singing voice brought work on TV, in nightclubs and on Broadway. In Hollywood, he acted in episodes of TV Westerns. To avoid confusion with musical star Allan Jones, he changed his name. In the Western TV series *The Deputy*, he played the title role, sharp-shooting shopkeeper Clay McCord, who preferred to avoid violence. Henry Fonda was Chief Marshal Simon Fry, a strict law-and-order man. Allen later starred as Frank James in *The Legend of Jesse James* (1965–66). He followed with more stage productions. Allen died of a heart attack.

"The Deputy, Clay McCord" on the Rodeo Trail

Allen Case's rodeo act was primarily singing. He sang folk songs (popular at the time) as well as Western songs. Young fans enjoyed shaking the hand of *The Deputy* as he circled the arena on horseback. In the summer of 1960, he appeared at Sidney's Iowa Championship Rodeo. That fall, he performed at the Texas Prison Rodeo. In 1961, he headlined rodeos at Shreveport and Lafayette, Louisiana, and the Buffalo Bill Rodeo in North Platte, Nebraska. At Austin, Texas, that fall, he split headliner dates with Dale Robertson. A newspaper report indicated that Allen left fans "clamoring for more."

Allen Case, co-star of the TV Western *The Deputy*.

ROBERT CONRAD (1935–) Conrad Robert Falk was born in Chicago, Illinois. He got his show business start as a singer at age 17 and studied drama in college. As Robert Conrad, he signed a Warner Brothers contract in the early 1960s. He had guest roles on TV series, including Westerns. A continuing role on TV's *Hawaiian Eye* made him a well-known star and led to some films. At 5'9" and 174 pounds, Robert was not your "long, tall Texan" type, but his interest in physical conditioning, including pumping iron and running, gave him a trim, muscular physique. On CBS-TV's *The Wild, Wild West* (1965–70), he played James West, an undercover special agent for President Grant. Ross Martin played his partner Artemus Gordon, a master of dialect and disguise. Robert did many of his own stunts. The show demanded hard work, and routinely left its share of bumps and bruises. His later TV series included *The D.A.*, *Baa Baa Black Sheep* and *High Mountain Rangers*. He returned for two TV movie revivals, *The Wild, Wild West Revisited* (1979) and *More Wild, Wild West* (1980).

Advertisement for Robert Conrad's appearance at the 1969 Waco, Texas, rodeo.

"Jim West" on the Rodeo Trail

An accomplished singer, Robert Conrad did his best to present an action-oriented rodeo act. As he rode into the arena, a shot rang out and James West dropped to the ground. A black-clad dry-gulcher (played by a stuntman) would then approach the fallen hero. When the villain was upon him, West leaped up and began a fistfight across the arena floor, finally besting the bad guy in a gunfight. He varied the act and might conclude by singing. At one performance, he sang from different locations on the arena railing. He brought a young girl out of the audience to sing with him, and left his hat with her.

Robert headlined rodeos at Sikeston, Fort Madison and Cheyenne Frontier Days, fulfilling the busy schedule expected of a visiting Western rodeo star. For the 1969 Heart O'Texas Rodeo in Waco, he arrived a day early, held a press conference, attended a luncheon with 60 area students, made local media appearances, chatted with hospitalized children and stopped by Baylor University. Rodeo organizers were impressed with the star's friendly informality, and happy that fan interest was boosting ticket sales. He and stuntman Dick Cangey did fights and stunts for TV and for personal appearances. Singing, though, came in handy. Robert told interviewers that he preferred to minimize singing. He avoided describing his arena act, hoping for surprise, but the surprise was on him. Kicking during a stunt fight at the first performance, Dick injured his knee, curtailing further action sequences and forcing Robert to sing more.

CAROLINA COTTON (c. 1927–97) Carolina Cotton was born Helen Hagstrom in Cash, Arkansas. Moving with her family to San Francisco, she took dancing and music lessons, and yodeled from an early age. While still in school, she filmed a Hollywood movie

Western singer-actress Carolina Cotton.

during a break and worked early mornings and some evenings on radio and television. She acquired the name Carolina while working with Dude Martin. Moving to Hollywood, she sang with Spade Cooley's band and made more films. Pretty, vivacious and full of fun, she sang, danced and yodeled. Al Jolson named Carolina the greatest natural show woman he had ever met. From 1944 to 1952, she appeared in films with country music and Western stars. She performed with the Sons of the Pioneers, Jimmy Wakely and Bob Wills and the Texas Playboys. She entertained U.S. military forces at the Hollywood Canteen, at bases and on overseas tours. During the Korean Conflict, *Carolina Cotton Calls* was broadcast over the Armed Forces Radio Network. Military audiences received her with enthusiasm. Later in life, she earned a Masters Degree in special education and served about 25 years as an elementary schoolteacher. She passed away from cancer.

Carolina Cotton on the Rodeo Trail

From the 1940s into the '50s, Carolina Cotton appeared at rodeos, including the Los Angeles Sheriff's Rodeo, and rodeos at San Bernardino, Riverside and Palm Springs, California. Other rodeos included Las Vegas' Helldorado Days, Truth or Consequences, New Mexico and Tucson, Arizona. She was rodeo queen, featured in parades, judged queen competitions, and entertained in the arena or at nightclubs. As she performed in a Silver Slipper show during Las Vegas' 1953 Helldorado Days, a newspaper article heralded her as "that little piece of dynamite in the saddle." The article further stated, "[S]he can sing and dance and yodel and ride a horse and make you feel like YOU are the star of the show." Interests in rodeo and military personnel combined in Carolina's project to send *Hoofs and Horns* to rodeo cowboys serving in the armed forces.

Western film star Buster Crabbe.

BUSTER CRABBE (1908–83) An Olympic swimming champion, Buster Crabbe played Hollywood's Tarzan, Flash Gordon and Buck Rogers. With sidekick Al "Fuzzy" St. John in the 1940s, he starred in 36 B-Western films. In the spring of 1951, he worked his horse Tarzan at a Garrison, New York, dude ranch rodeo, attracting turn-away crowds.

ROBERT CULP (1930–) Actor Robert Culp returned from New York to his home state of California to star as Hoby Gilman in Four Star Production's Western series *Trackdown* (1957–59), which derived from an episode of *Zane Grey Theater*. Mr. Culp wrote and/or directed several of the series' episodes, which were based on files of the Texas Rangers. He later achieved greater fame co-starring with Bill Cosby on TV's *I Spy*. In addition to

Western and non–Western film credits, he has played many TV guest roles.

"Hoby Gilman" on the Rodeo Trail

In 1958, Robert Culp received the first TV award presented by the California Rodeo at Salinas for his series *Trackdown*. He also led the rodeo's parade and grand entry. That same year, he starred at the Texas Prison Rodeo.

GAIL DAVIS (1925–97) Betty Jeanne Grayson was born in Little Rock, Arkansas. As a youngster, she shot at targets with a rifle, rode horses, engaged in sports and studied dance. She attended Harcum Junior College for Girls in Bryn Mawr, Pennsylvania, and the University of Texas, where, as a Blue Bonnet Belle, she performed in shows for military personnel. Put under Hollywood contract in the mid–1940s as "Gail Davis," she entered studio training programs and debuted on screen in 1947. With MGM and RKO studios, she gained experience but little screen exposure. Primarily interested in musicals, Gail's association with Westerns began with Roy Rogers in *The Far Frontier* (1948). She made West-

The star of TV's *Trackdown*, Robert Culp.

erns with Jimmy Wakely, Tim Holt, Monte Hale, Allan "Rocky" Lane, Charles Starrett, Kirby Grant and Johnny Mack Brown. She was in two films with John Wayne and in episodes of Western TV shows. Her association with Gene Autry productions included 14 of Gene's feature films (1949–53) and an equal number of his TV episodes.

When Flying A Productions conceived the *Annie Oakley* series, executives' familiarity with Gail was a drawback, despite her being under contract. A nationwide tryout failed to identify a young woman deemed right to portray the riding, shooting Annie. Only when Gail appeared before the producer fashioned after the character, and insisted upon being tested, did she win the role. Her youthful good looks aided in playing a character ten years younger. Sponsors were skeptical about a female Western lead. Almost 18 months passed between the signing of Gail's contract and filming of series episodes. Meanwhile, she practiced marksmanship and horsemanship. She experienced large arena crowds on a European tour. Notified of sponsor acceptance, she began filming in September 1953. Brad Johnson played deputy Lofty Craig and Jimmy Hawkins was Annie's younger brother Tagg. The series ceased production in 1956 after 81 episodes. Aimed at youngsters, *Annie Oakley* won the hearts of all. At one point, the series aired on over 200 North American stations. Trailblazing Annie, an idol for young girls, was recalled years later when *Dr. Quinn, Medicine Woman* became popular.

Gail Davis ("Annie Oakley") and Gene Autry wave to admirers at the 1957 Fort Madison, Iowa, rodeo (photograph obtained from, and used with permission of, Tri-State Rodeo, Fort Madison, IA, © 2004 Autry Qualified Interest Trust and The Autry Foundation, provided courtesy Gene Autry Entertainment).

Gail did TV guest spots and a cameo in Bob Hope's, *Alias Jesse James* (1959). Typecasting as Annie Oakley limited further show business opportunities. In later years, she worked in computer sales and personal management. She attended Western film fan gatherings and arranged for *Annie Oakley* episodes to be made available to the public. In 1954, *Annie Oakley* was nominated for an Emmy as "Best Western or Adventure Series." Gail was later honored with a star on Hollywood's Walk of Fame. In 1994, she received a Golden Boot. Gail passed away from cancer.

"Annie Oakley" on the Rodeo Trail

Gail began making rodeo appearances as "Annie Oakley" in 1955. For a time, she spent about half the year filming her TV show and the remainder making personal appearances. Most of her earlier rodeos were with Gene Autry, but she headlined a number of rodeos as a solo performer. For TV, Gail called on the services of stuntwomen for potentially dangerous physical action. At arena performances, to live up to such press descriptions as "the hardest-riding, straightest-shooting, most lovable cowgirl on American television," Gail assumed the rigor and risk of doing her own riding and shooting, both of which required considerable practice.

Following her rodeo arena introduction, Gail entered aboard her palomino TV horse, Target, urging the horse at a fast pace around the arena. She then stopped for a bow. Her next speedy pass featured handgun shooting at a half-dozen targets in the form of matches to be lit. Dismounting, she proceeded with trick rifle shooting. Despite her petite size, Gail made her mounts and dismounts look good. Sidekick Pat Buttram stated that Gail at 50 paces could shoot a gnat off a poppy seed roll. From youthful experience, Gail preferred a rifle, but she was also handy with a pistol. She doused the flame of a small candle at 30 paces, perhaps by firing the rifle over her shoulder using a mirror for sighting. She shot at four balls on a revolving target, firing at two with her rifle sighted conventionally and at the other two holding it upside down.

Gail didn't typically sing in movies or on TV, but she vocalized at rodeos, for many one-night Gene Autry stage shows and on recordings. At rodeos, she sang selections from Western or popular songs such as "Y'all Come" and "You Caint Git a Man with a Gun." Some tunes, such as "Annie Oakley" and "Ten Gallon Hat," were written especially for her. For solo performances, she sang additional songs. Gail concluded her act by riding Target around the arena rail, shaking youngsters' hands.

Wherever Gail traveled, her glamorous wardrobe contrasted with her black-and-white TV show costume (multiple copies of the same standard outfit). She had input into the design of her 20 or so colorful, eye-catching arena costumes, created by Nudie of Hollywood. Materials included kid, garbardine, satin and cashmere, in colors such as red and white. A Kelly green outfit was decorated with brilliants, rubies and sequins and trimmed with a gold calf yoke and collar, with golden fringe by the belt. Another outfit was pink with silver trim. Set off with rhinestone fringe and white accessories, some of her outfits included deep fringed or sequined cuffs in matching colors. White boots (size 4½) trimmed with appliqués, blended with individual costumes. Gail had a special trunk for hats, all white with flat crowns and broad brims, some trimmed with pearl and bugle bead medallions. One hat was edged with pearls and had a hatband of four strings of pearls. Her trademark pigtails displayed bows tied in jewel-studded ribbons. Decorative designs on Gail's outfits often featured a target crossed by a rifle (her TV show logo) or Indian symbols. Duplicates of some outfits, sized to fit, were made for her young daughter.

Glamour wasn't the only feature of being "Annie Oakley." Co-workers in the filmmaking business respected Gail for her friendliness, good humor and spunk in enduring sometimes-harsh conditions on location. At rodeos, she was recognized not only for her looks and personality, but also for her ability to withstand the rigors and occasional dangers of life in the arena. Despite the effort required by rodeos, she found live audience response rewarding and the experience fun.

Early in 1955, Gail accompanied Gene Autry on horseback on part of the Salt Grass Trail Ride and appeared with him at Houston's big rodeo. In July, she, Gene and the Cass County Boys appeared at Salt Lake City's Days of '47 Rodeo. She also played rodeos in Des Moines and Chicago. During her Des Moines entrance, her mount shied as she raced onto the track in front of the grandstand. She recovered and continued her act. Said Annie later, "I su'ah thought I was going to get down from the wrong side." The next year, 1956, Gail played a minimum of eight rodeos, most with Gene, but some solo. Backed by the Cass County Boys, she shared Snake River Stampede billing with the Sons of the Pioneers. She visited a school, the Elks rehabilitation center and a Veterans Administration hospital. The Cass County Boys supported at Casper's Central Wyoming Fair Rodeo, where the winner of a junior Annie Oakley contest greeted Gail's airport arrival. Gail met all contestants and their mothers at a party, and she sang for patients at Natrona Memorial Hospital.

Later that month, drawing record crowds to the Colorado State Fair Rodeo, Gail joined Gene Autry in meeting an eight-year-old boy who had lost an eye in a fishing accident. At

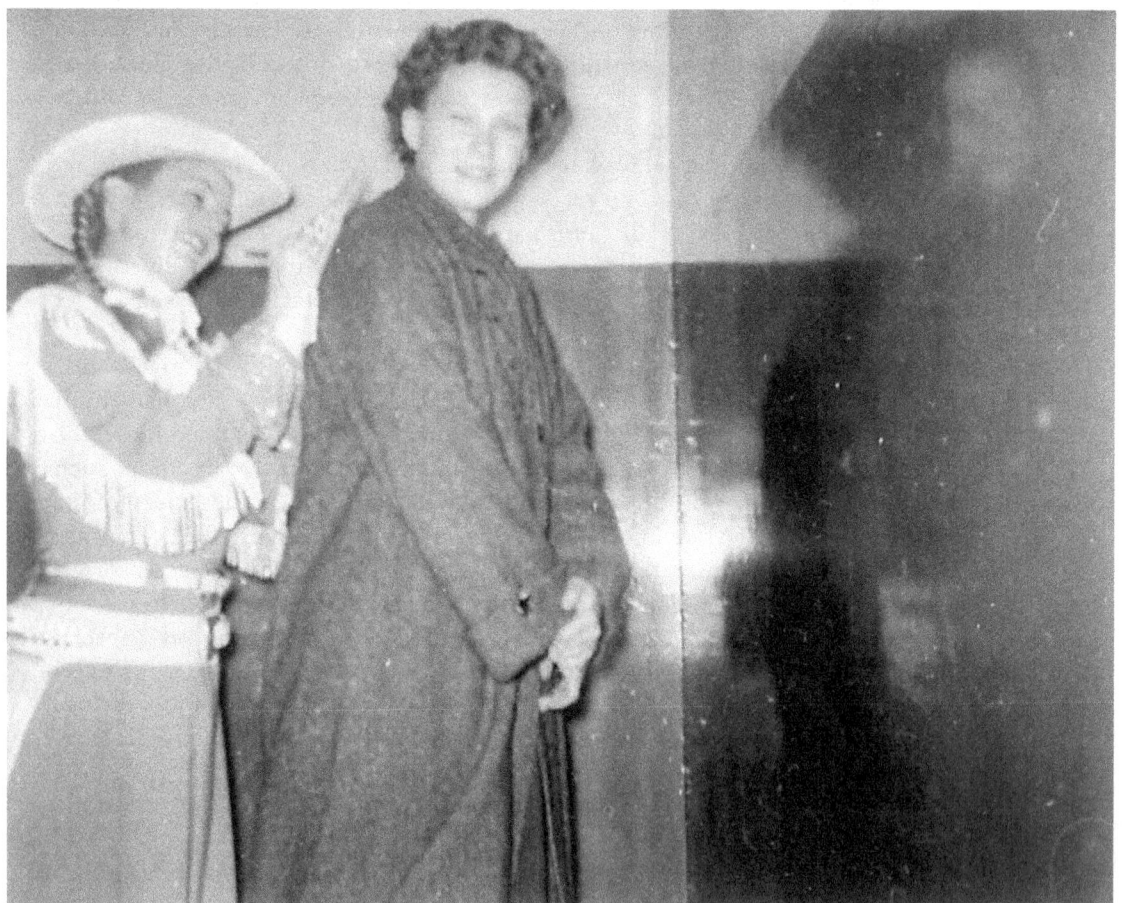

At Boston Garden's 1957 rodeo, Gail Davis autographs a program for fan Eleanor Eaton (courtesy Richard and Eleanor Eaton. Used with permission).

the Kentucky State Fair Rodeo, Gail and Gene visited patients at the Kosair Crippled Children's Hospital where she compared pigtails with a seven-year-old patient. Gail and Gene landed in Omaha, Nebraska, to appear at the Ak-Sar-Ben Rodeo. When health reasons forced Gene's return to Los Angeles, Gail carried on alone. With the Cass County Boys, she visited polio patients at St. Joseph's Hospital, meeting a young woman who shared her Little Rock birthplace. She judged the junior rodeo contests, met with 4-H queens and presented a saddle to the junior queen.

By 1957, the *Annie Oakley* series had ceased broadcasting original episodes. Gail made

While headlining the 1958 Fort Worth Stock Show Rodeo, Gail Davis meets Susan Ann Oakley, relation of the historical Annie Oakley (courtesy *Fort Worth Star-Telegram* Photograph Collection, University of Texas at Arlington Libraries, Arlington. FWST #3925).

joint rodeo appearances with Gene, accompanied by Foy Willing and the Riders of the Purple Sage. They presented a 45-minute show at the spring Louisiana State Fair Rodeo. In the fall, giving a pair of young cowgirls a ride on Champion, they set an attendance record at Fort Madison, Iowa. They performed at Pomona's Los Angeles County Fair. Gail then traveled home for a solo rodeo appearance at Little Rock. Next was the rodeo at Boston Garden. While at the St. Louis Fireman's Rodeo, Gail and Gene rode a fire truck as honorary firefighters.

Most of Gail's remaining rodeo appearances were solo. She began the 1958 season at Lafayette, Louisiana, and arrived at her next rodeo, Fort Worth, fresh from a visit with her parents in Little Rock. She wore a mink wrap and high heels, topped off with her trademark braids and Western hat. She met the governor, but a sore throat kept her from the parade. Backing out of the arena at the end of one performance, Gail was waving goodbye when her horse slipped and fell. She was helped to a stretcher, but a truck blocked the exit. As the stretcher was being passed under the vehicle, she was confused seeing the bottom of the truck. Medical exam showed no broken bones, only bruises. She gave way on the rodeo's final day to Roy Rogers' TV Chevy Show troupe. She wrapped up her early season rodeos at Lake Charles, Louisiana.

Gail in 1959 continued solo rodeo appearances, accompanied by the Ernie Felice Trio. On this Southern tour, she sang "Is It True What They Say About Dixie?" and "Wabash Cannonball." She returned to the Louisiana State Fair Rodeo. When she headlined at Montgomery, commentary suggested to local girls that Annie Oakley was a model of dress and decorum. However, Gail experienced the nightmare of all traveling performers, announcing how happy she was to be in Shreveport (the previous stop), prompting such newspaper headlines as, "Your slip is showing" and "Annie Misses Mark." A year earlier, she had made a similar gaffe in Fort Worth. At Winston-Salem, western-dressed dairy bar waitresses served her a rodeo sundae. She was visited by Smiley Burnette, met the governor and passed out recordings. Dale Robertson briefly shared her final performance. She was billed with Dale at Charlotte, and publicized a cerebral palsy march, but missed performances while hospitalized for a kidney ailment. In a newspaper drawing, a nurse warned her against wearing spurs in her hospital bed. At Raleigh, she led Target so fans could see him, but shook hands from a convertible. Fully recovered for the Kentucky State Fair Rodeo, she put on a musical show on the terrace of the Kosair Crippled Children's Hospital, and talked and sang to bedridden children. Gail concluded her rodeo year at Madison Square Garden, co-headlining with the *Rin Tin Tin* TV cast.

Gail returned to rodeo arenas in the early 1960s, at the Shrine Championship Rodeo at Peoria, Illinois. At Kansas' largest rodeo at Coffeyville, her shooting exhibition was omitted because of an eye condition. Due to flight problems, she barely arrived in time for her first performance, and weather cancelled her last performance. She entertained at Parsons State Hospital and School. As late as 1968, she headlined the rodeo at Pine Bluff, Arkansas. Gail was not only the first cowgirl to have her own national TV show, she was a rare female TV star to headline a rodeo solo.

EDDIE DEAN (1907–99) Edgar Dean Glosup was born at Posey, Texas, the seventh son of a seventh son. Acquiring a guitar in his youth, he performed within his family, at community functions and in school drama and musical productions. Still in his teens, he toured with a singing quartet. Later, with his brother Jimmy, he "played nearly every [radio] station in the Midwest" as a singer and guitar player. In the early 1930s, the duo settled at

Singing cowboy film star Eddie Dean.

WIBW in Wichita; they then moved to Chicago's WLS, where their shows included *National Barn Dance*. Eddie recorded in 1933. He told author David Rothel that he acted character parts on radio, including a soap opera lead. To decide whether New York City or Hollywood offered the greater opportunity, he flipped a coin and then headed for Hollywood.

Eddie sang on radio and in nightclubs. After about a year, he began getting bit parts in Westerns. In 1942, he was reunited with brother Jimmy, providing musical back-up as a member of Gene Autry's "Melody Ranch Boys." He next sang on Judy Canova's radio show. In 1944, he was featured in Ken Maynard's last starring film. Helping pioneer the Cinecolor process, he became the first B-Western cowboy to star in a series of color films, beginning with *Song of Old Wyoming* (PRC, 1945). The film gave Lash LaRue a start. Eddie made another 14 black-and-white films through 1948. His voice is generally rated the best among singing cowboys. In 1946 and 1947, he was listed among the top ten Western stars at the box office.

Eddie recorded for a number of labels and had a hand in writing approximately 100 songs, including "On the Banks of the Sunny San Juan," co-written with Glenn Strange. With his wife Dearest and Hal Blair, he co-wrote "One Has My Name, The Other Has My Heart," a 1948 Jimmy Wakely hit. In 1961, Tex Ritter recorded "I Dreamed of a Hillbilly Heaven," co-written by Eddie and Hal Southern in 1955. Eddie starred briefly in the 1950 ABC-TV series *The Marshal of Gunsight Pass*. He sang at nightclubs and at overseas military clubs. With his rich voice and ability to provide his own accompaniment, he stayed in demand as a performer into his eighties.

Eddie did TV spots, continued to compose songs and recorded for small companies, including Jimmy Wakely's Shasta label. He performed at Western film festivals, convincing fans that his singing had improved with age. For several years he concluded the Golden Boot Awards by singing his trademark "Wagon Wheels," and then leading stars and guests in singing cowboy themes. On episodes of TV's *The Beverly Hillbillies*, he was a yodeling policeman. In later years, he performed in the Los Angeles area at outdoor concerts that included his celebrity impressions. Eddie was a founder of the Academy of Country Music. In 1982, his saddle plaque was placed in Newhall, California's, Western Walk of Fame. He received a Golden Boot Award and was inducted into the Western Music Association Hall of Fame. Posthumously, a star in his honor was unveiled on the Palm Springs Walk of Fame. Eddie passed away as a result of emphysema at Thousand Oaks, California.

Eddie Dean on the Rodeo Trail

In 1942, Eddie Dean and brother Jimmy, as "Melody Ranch Boys," performed at Flying "A" Ranch Stampedes in Houston and in eastern cities. In July, the rodeo performed at Ardmore, Oklahoma, and in Chicago, where Gene Autry enlisted in the Army Air Corps. Eddie made remote broadcasts of the *Melody Ranch* radio program from rodeo cities.

In the mid–1940s, Eddie, as a singing cowboy movie star, became a rodeo headliner. In 1947, he was the Snake River Stampede's first celebrity guest star. His film *West of Glory* showed downtown. The rodeo queen and her court, officials and local businessmen met him at planeside. He headed a parade through the business district to arrive at City Hall at noon. There, before a crowd of several hundred, the mayor welcomed him with a key to the city. Eddie told the crowd he was "just an old cowboy who got a little break." His five-piece band, the Rodeo Revelers, provided music. By one that afternoon, he was guest of honor at an Elks Club buffet luncheon. Then he hosted a party for youngsters at Lakeview Park. He and his band entertained, concluding with "Boogie Woogie Cowboy." He distributed paper cowboy hats to youngsters. He crowned the new rodeo queen, and performed nightly at the Majestic Theater with "Eddie Dean's Golden West Revue," preceding a showing of his film *Tumbleweed Trail*. He autographed records at a music store. He impressed the public, particularly youngsters, as easygoing and friendly.

Eddie continued rodeo appearances at least into the late 1950s, ten years after his last Western film. In 1954, he was guest star at the Jaycee Frontier Days Rodeo, a feature of the Wichita Territorial Centennial. He was a division marshal of the 1955 Palm Springs Rodeo parade. In 1956, he made several rodeo appearances in Louisiana. He often rode a Tommy Steiner–provided palomino, Buddy. At Lake Charles, he rode in the parade. At Shreveport, he cheered young patients at the Shrine Hospital. A review of his arena performance stated:

> The biggest crowd-pleaser of the evening was cowboy movie and TV star Eddie Dean, who received a tremendous ovation from the crowd. Dean, riding his beautiful Palomino horse, "Buddy," gave the big responsive audience a full taste of the singing that has made him one of the most popular of Western film stars. His numerous selections included the ever-popular "San Antonio Rose" and "You Are My Sunshine." Dean further delighted the many youngsters in the crowd by riding around the arena to shake the many extended hands of his small admirers.

He split West Monroe's billing with Tex Ritter and Smiley Burnette, and appeared at Springhill's rodeo.

That year, Eddie starred in at least two Texas rodeos, at Henderson and at Waco. At the latter engagement, he shared billing with Preston Foster. At various performances, he sang "Cry of a Broken Heart," "Fool's Gold," "On the Banks of the Sunny San Juan," "Walk

Beside Me" and "One Has My Name, The Other Has My Heart," among others. Again, he received good press:

> All the wild rodeo stock in the world couldn't have stolen the show from Eddie Dean, America's golden-voiced singing cowboy, as far as the youngsters were concerned. With the spotlight on him in the center of the arena, Dean invited the young cowboy fans into the arena to share the spotlight with him. It took all the cops, cowboys, and [Tommy] Steiner himself, to lift the youngsters over the arena fence and down on the dirt floor to gather around Dean. Together the youngsters and Dean sang "You Are My Sunshine" and the crowd loved it.

In early 1957, local dignitaries met Eddie upon his arrival for the Mid-Winter Fair Rodeo at Lafayette, Louisiana. Generating record advance ticket sales, he visited hospitals. In the arena, he rode Buddy and invited youngsters to join him. He sang folk, cowboy and rock'n'roll songs. Youngsters braved cold rain to see him at the coliseum and to follow him after the rodeo. Later that year, Eddie returned to headline a second consecutive Lawton, Oklahoma, rodeo. Upon his evening arrival, met by the mayor and rodeo officials, he leaped from the airliner steps into the saddle of the waiting Buddy. Eddie rode to the rodeo arena where he and Buddy went through a quick workout under the stars before police escorted him to his hotel. The next morning, he began receptions and personal appearances in and around the city. To his list of songs, he added, "I Dreamed of a Hillbilly Heaven," and again circled the arena shaking hands with fans of all ages. That same year, he was invited back to Waco. Killeen, Texas, was one of his stops in 1958. Still on the rodeo trail in 1959, Eddie worked the Red Willow County Fair Rodeo at McCook, Nebraska, where he judged a youngster quick-draw contest, the prize for which was an outfitted pony.

DON DURANT (1932–2005) Donald Allison Durae was born in Long Beach, California. As a youngster, he had to deal with his father's death in an accident and his own year-long hospitalization for bicycle mishap injuries. He spent some of his youth on a ranch in Nevada. He had a high school radio program, and later pursued little theater groups and music study. From entertaining in Las Vegas, he was drafted into the military. Discharged, he sang with Ray Anthony's band. He appeared in films and on TV drama, comedy and Western shows. Offered roles in more than one Western series, he chose *Johnny Ringo* (1959–60), featuring him as the character he first played on an episode of *Zane Grey Theater*. With a name borrowed from a historical gunman, the TV Johnny was a gunslinger turned sheriff. Mark Goddard played his young deputy and Karen Sharpe was Durant's love interest. Don composed, sang and recorded the theme song. He carried an unusual French-made weapon, the Le Mat Special, which combined a six-gun with a shotgun barrel. He mastered drawing the gun from a special clamp-type holster. Traveling about 150,000 miles on personal appearances in 1960, he endeared himself to fans. A guest star on a few later Westerns, he went on to success in real estate.

"Johnny Ringo" on the Rodeo Trail

Don Durant sang Western songs, including the *Johnny Ringo* theme, in his 1960 rodeo act. In addition to songs and commentary, Don brought two Hollywood stuntmen, Tom Sweet and Whitey Hughes, for the action component of his act. Following Don's opening song, a tough hombre approached, riding and shooting at him. Shot from his horse, the villain was dragged by a foot caught in the stirrup. There was a stuntman skit. Don's act ended with a hand-shaking ride around the arena. On rodeo tours, Don presented a fine,

Don Durant, star of TV's *Johnny Ringo*.

clean-cut Western hero image. At one stop, he awarded prizes for a drawing contest. He visited schools and signed many autographs. His wife Trudy accompanied him on the road. Johnny Ringo appeared at the San Angelo Stock Show Rodeo, the Colorado State Fair Rodeo and the Jaycee Bootheel Rodeo, as well as rodeos at Mercedes, Texas, and Pine Bluff, Arkansas. Arriving at San Angelo, Texas, sleepy and non-costumed, he was greeted by a group of youngsters, many in Western outfits. Later, outside the arena, attendants had to hold back a crush of autograph seekers.

BILL ELLIOTT (1903–65)   Bill Elliott was born Gordon Nance on a ranch near Pattonsburg, Missouri, on October 16, 1903. As a youngster, he rode horses and dreamed of becoming like his screen hero, William S. Hart. At age ten, he moved to Kansas City, where his father was a stockyard official. Rural upbringing and stockyard experiences educated him in the cowboy arts. Completing his education, he headed for Hollywood. He trained in acting at the Pasadena Playhouse until a motion picture scout spotted him. About 1925, he obtained small parts in silent films, adopting the screen name Gordon Elliott. In 1928, he appeared in two Westerns, but not until the mid–1930s was he again cast in a Western film. Bill told a reporter that casting officials felt he didn't look enough like a cowboy. Fans appreciative of Bill's resonant voice may be surprised by reports that his career temporarily stalled during the transition to talkies. Employed by various studios, he was under contract to Warner Brothers for a time, acting in films with some of the era's biggest stars.

Following supporting parts in Westerns, Columbia Pictures cast him in the title role of the 12-chapter serial *The Great Adventures of Wild Bill Hickok* (1938). The serial's success earned him a starring series of Columbia Westerns and, shortly, a name change to Bill Elliott. In five years (1938–42) at Columbia, Bill starred in two more serials and 24 Western

"Wild Bill" Elliott and stock contractor Leo Cremer at a rodeo (Doubleday photograph courtesy Center for the Study of Western Experience, National Cowboy and Western Heritage Museum, Oklahoma City, OK).

features, including eight paired with Tex Ritter. Dub Taylor was his most frequent sidekick. In some of his films, Bill was called "Wild Bill." On-screen, he portrayed a hard-riding, tight-lipped, strong-voiced, no-nonsense "peaceable man," until riled into forcible action. He experimented with wearing the butts of his six-shooters facing forward.

Republic Studios, building a quality reputation in the production of B-Westerns, signed Bill in 1943. They promoted him in a series of eight action Westerns with the billing and character name of "Wild Bill" Elliott. Beginning with *Calling "Wild Bill" Elliott* (1943), the entire series co-starred George "Gabby" Hayes. In 16 films from 1944 through 1946, Bill portrayed comic artist Fred Harman's Red Ryder, supported by Bobby (later Robert) Blake as young Indian sidekick Little Beaver. These two series are counted among the best B-Westerns made. Bill made a guest appearance in Roy Rogers' film *Bells of Rosarita* (1945).

Republic studio boss Herbert J. Yates then cast Bill as "William Elliott" in higher-budget Westerns. Bill had the acting ability and carried a fan following to these films. At first, however, he wasn't enthusiastic about the "promotion." He later told reporters he didn't like the name change (and all that entailed), and he regretted that additional filming days meant less rodeo time, but increased salary outweighed other concerns. From *In Old Sacramento* (1946) through *The Showdown* (1950), Bill made ten of these Westerns, working with many fine supporting actors. Two were filmed in color, and Bill's own production unit made two.

In 1950, Bill had a radio program and a comic book. With so many Westerns on the market, his TV pilots failed to attract a sponsor. Bill departed Republic for a series of more traditional B-Westerns at Monogram Studios, soon called Allied Artists. Again billed as "Wild Bill" Elliott, he starred in 11 films, from *The Longhorn* (1951) to *The Forty-Niners* (1954), his last Western. At this time, television was coming into prominence, and big-screen B-Westerns were on the decline. Bill finished his film career in a series (1955–57) of five modern-day police detective dramas.

In a movie career that lasted over 30 years and more than 70 films, Bill Elliott flourished as an action Western star for two decades despite the concurrent popularity of singing cowboys. Recalling his horsemanship, propensity for slam-bang action, his style of wearing and firing his six-shooters and his personality, fans have kept Bill high in popularity rankings. He had a reputation as a "regular guy." Pierce Lyden, veteran Western supporting player, told of Bill arranging for a retake to be postponed until Pierce recovered from an on-set injury. Pierce observed, "Not many stars would have done this—not for a mere extra." Bill, who worked in pictures for 13 years before getting his first starring role, was quoted as saying, "I can remember when I was an extra myself. I haven't changed inside so why should I try to put on airs?" Retired from movies, he moved to Nevada, continuing his interests in ranching and cutting horses. He said, "The original reason I tried to break into pictures was to make enough money to buy a ranch." Fans saw him in TV commercials and hosting Nevada TV showings of his films. In Las Vegas, Bill passed away from cancer on November 26, 1965.

"Wild Bill" Elliott on the Rodeo Trail

Still in his teens, Bill Elliott competed at rodeos. Visiting Cheyenne Frontier Days in 1947, he stated that, en route to Hollywood in the 1920s, he ran out of money in Wyoming. When working odd jobs provided less than he needed, he won enough money at Cheyenne Frontier Days to continue his journey to the Coast. In Hollywood, Bill developed his horsemanship. Once established in Western films, he frequented rodeos as a star attraction. In

1941, he joined other Hollywood stars at the Reno Rodeo. In June 1943, he starred at the Sunset Ranch Rodeo in Fresno, California, including special shows at military installations and at a hospital. In March 1944, after two rain postponements, a Sunset Ranch Rodeo was held at Los Angeles' Gilmore Stadium, with Bill, on Thunder, as parade marshal. Mrs. Tom Mix, Stuart Hamblen, Don Stewart and Don Reynolds appeared. Jim Thorpe led a mock Indian raid on a stagecoach. Lina Basquette and Tex Cooper were in the parade. Bill was grand marshal for July's Roy Rogers Rodeo, held at the Los Angeles Coliseum.

With Monte Hale, Bill was introduced to the crowd at Bakersfield's 1945 California Patrolman Rodeo. The next month he appeared at Roy Rogers' Coliseum rodeo. In the fall, at the "Wild Bill" Elliott Rodeo and Barbeque in Lancaster, California, he rode Thunder as grand marshal, in the grand entry and during each performance. Early in 1946, rodeo star Tex Ritter introduced him to applause at Houston's rodeo. Bill starred at the Louisiana State University Rodeo and Livestock Show. In May of 1947, he announced a Gilmore Stadium rodeo, at which Dick Farnsworth won the bareback riding event. That year, accompanied by leading lady Vera Ralston, studio head Herbert J. Yates and the Sons of the Pioneers, Bill was at Cheyenne Frontier Days for the premiere of his film *Wyoming*. He was grand marshal of August's Los Angeles Sheriff's Rodeo.

At the end of January 1948, weather cleared for Houston's rodeo parade, in which Bill joined rodeo star Gene Autry. Spring of that year brought Bill back to Baton Rouge for the L.S.U. Rodeo and Livestock Show, publicized as the world premiere of Bill's Bar Bar A Ranch Rodeo. Arriving a few days early, he supervised preparations. The rodeo featured Bill's horses Thunder and Stormy Night. He hosted a "gold rush" for more than 3,000 youngsters. On three roped-off acres of campus were scattered 1,000 gold-colored cardboard discs of stated value. Preliminary ceremonies were broadcast on the radio. Bill explained the rules, emphasizing sportsmanship, then fired all 12 shots from his six-shooters to start the contest. The ropes dropped, and youngsters swarmed over the field. When discs were found and tabulated, prizes included a bicycle (Bill's personal prize) and a "Wild Bill" Elliott shirt. Bill presented his horse and other rodeo acts in a show for local orphans.

In May 1948, Bill and Thunder toured with Col. Jim Eskew's Ranch Rodeo to Cleveland, Columbus and Toledo, Ohio. He put Thunder through a repertoire of tricks and introduced a musical troupe that included Doye O'Dell and his Radio Rangers. Bill was a member and office holder in national organizations of both quarter horse and cutting horse enthusiasts. In addition to competing, he frequently served as director or judge at individual contests. He announced the 1949 Palm Springs Rodeo of the Stars. He reportedly entered into a rodeo partnership with Lysle Greenman, producer of this rodeo and others, mainly in the Los Angeles area. Bill and Lysle initially combined for a May rodeo at Rolling Hills, near Long Beach. About this time, *The Buckboard* displayed advertisements for "Wild Bill" Elliott's Championship Rodeo. In December, he directed and participated in cutting at the Pacific International Horse Show and Rodeo at North Portland, Oregon.

In July of 1950, Bill, with movie horse Thunder and cutting horse Stormy Night, was the featured rodeo attraction at Mandan, North Dakota. Texas Rose Bascom also performed. He and the governor led the rodeo parade, and Bill competed in cutting. He called two boys and two girls from the stands to join in his act. At August's Southwest Championship Junior Rodeo at Post, Texas, Bill was guest star and served as judge for both the quarter horse and cutting horse competitions. Arriving early, he made appearances on several radio programs. He was star of the rodeo at Big Spring, Texas, and at the Quay County Sheriff's Posse Rodeo at Tucumcari, New Mexico, both produced by Tommy Steiner. Bill, on Thunder, led the rodeo parade.

"Wild Bill" Elliott stops to chat with young fans at Colorado Springs' Antlers Hotel in 1951, en route from Denver's National Western Stock Show to the Fort Worth stock show (photograph by Stan Payne, courtesy Pikes Peak Library District Local History Collection, Colorado Springs, CO. Stan Payne #7213).

Next on Bill's schedule was the Young County Rodeo at Graham, Texas, which proved important. By his own account, Bill first saw the cutting horse Red Boy in action about 1947 when he was entering cutting horse contests with his horse, Stormy Night. For three years, he wanted to buy Red Boy, but could not meet the owner's asking price. Bill turned down a salary for the Graham rodeo, saying he was on vacation and wanted to be there. Halfway through the final performance, Red Boy was led into the arena and presented as a gift to Bill from rodeo officials in appreciation for his presence. Bill expressed his gratitude and wasted no time entering Red Boy in competitions, often at rodeos at which he was the star. At California's King County Fair at Hanford in October, Bill and Red Boy tied for first place. At the cutting horse finals at San Francisco's 1950 Grand National, Red Boy was named the season's Reserve Champion. Bill began the 1951 rodeo season competing on Red Boy in cutting at Denver, Fort Worth and San Antonio. He contributed an article on Red Boy to *Hoofs and Horns*.

From the summer of 1950, Bill entered into partnership with Tommy Steiner, an Austin, Texas, rodeo stock contractor 25 years his junior. Bill combined his livestock with Steiner's at Mineral Wells, Texas. Bill's bankroll and star power allowed the partners to add stock. Beginning in the spring of 1951, they produced about 20 rodeos: two each in New Mexico and Oklahoma, and the remainder in Texas.

Bill had definite ideas about putting on a rodeo, as reflected in quotes at various times and places:

II. Individual Movie and Television Actors at Rodeos 157

As an actor and showman, I think the art of showmanship is being neglected in many rodeos. I plan to produce a show that will be spectacular and colorful in addition to having all the elements of other rodeos... In order to make a name for ourselves, we plan on putting on just as good if not better shows at the small rodeos as are produced at the bigger shows in the country [Colorado Springs, January 1951].

I've always had an ambition to produce big-time rodeos... [W]hen Tommy Steiner and I decided to form a partnership, that ambition materialized. We were determined to have the best rough stock in the West, and frankly, we've spent far more time and money than common sense should have allowed. Since specialty acts and clowns, spectacular grand entries and showmanship are so essential to the success of any rodeo, as far as the paying public is concerned, we both decided we'd spare no expense in equipping our company with the most colorful costumes, horses and equipment possible to get, and to contract for the very best trick riders and other specialty acts in the business [Kerrville, Texas, July 4–7, 1951].

There is a lot of work behind a good rodeo... A rodeo should be colorful... We are trying to put color back in rodeos along with the contests themselves... That is why Mr. Steiner and myself let the kids actually participate in our shows [Lawton, Oklahoma, August 1–4, 1951].

Every phase of a show like this needs constant attention. With other kinds of shows you hold rehearsals; we can't do that. It all has to be done by preparation [Lake Charles, Louisiana, February 8–25, 1952].

"Wild Bill" Elliott presents a ribbon to a young competitor at the 1952 Fort Worth Stock Show and Rodeo (courtesy *Fort Worth Star-Telegram* Collection, University of Texas at Arlington Libraries, Arlington. FWST #2662).

In each of the two years (1951–52) that Bill was aligned with Tommy, he spent about three months in Hollywood and nine months with the rodeo. A typical rodeo appearance involved travel between engagements by Cadillac and living in a trailer, usually accompanied by his wife Helen. He rode Thunder in rodeo parades and presented him in the arena. Not a singing cowboy, Bill devised a different type of arena act. In the past, he arranged for a few youngsters from the audience to join him in the arena. Why not invite all the boys and girls who wanted to be part of the show? One advertisement read, "Kiddies, help 'Wild Bill' handle Thunder." Assuring parents that Thunder was quite accustomed to youngsters, Bill was remarkably at ease with gatherings of kids that ranged from a small group to a large assemblage. His warm, comfortable personality when dealing with children carried the day. He apologized at each performance that not all kids could ride Thunder. Nevertheless, young fans were assured of close contact with their movie hero and his horse.

Youngsters formed a circle as Bill led Thunder through his tricks: picking up a hat, running sideways, playing lame, kneeling in prayer, dancing the jitterbug, walking on his knees, picking up the mail and bowing. Thunder might hold one end of a rope in his mouth while Bill held the other end so youngsters could jump the rope. Bill swung four or five youngsters onto Thunder, maybe placing one additional child at the base of Thunder's tail as he held up the tail for support. Several boys and girls led Thunder around the arena. Bill might then have kids lead Thunder backward by the tail. More youthful participation came in the event "'Wild Bill' Elliott and his Junior Posse." Rodeo advertisements encouraged youngsters to wear Western dress and to bring their cap pistols. "Wild Bill" demonstrated his style of drawing and firing his six-shooters. Then, it was announced that a local bank had been robbed, and the robbers had been spotted approaching the rodeo arena. Rodeo clowns played the robbers. Bill led his young posse through a mock bandit chase and shootout, giving each the satisfaction of having helped his or her cowboy hero. The kids loved it, and the adults enjoyed watching them.

ProRodeo Hall of Fame inductee Tommy Steiner, who passed away in 1999, commented about his years with Bill Elliott:

> Probably, we were ten years ahead of our time for the kind of rodeos we were putting on and for the kind of money we were spending. Bill Elliott was ... kinda my idol... No, he didn't sing like Roy Rogers or Gene Autry. As a matter of fact, that was one problem we had. All he could do was be a cowboy. He rode cuttin' horses and he was real flashy. He had an act where he would get all the kids out in the arena and they had a big shootout. It was a lot of fun and it was a unique act in the rodeo field... Bill got all the kids involved and it went really good for us [PRSN, September 20, 1978].

Bill frequently made a cutting contest part of a rodeo so that he could compete on Red Boy. Entering cutting contests at rodeos he headlined was unique. That he was able to accept whatever standing was adjudged, says something about the man's self-assurance and character. Indeed, he rarely placed first in these contests. As noted in Jerry Armstrong's column in *The Western Horseman*, "There is ... no favoritism shown the boss and his mount in these events; in fact, just the opposite appears to be the rule. It is our opinion that Bill himself probably made the rule. He appears to be that kind of guy."

In 1951, Elliott-Steiner productions included May rodeos at Henderson and Burnet, Texas. In June, the rodeo stopped at Plainview, Texas, for the Bar-None Rodeo. Then Bill went on to Sulpher, Oklahoma's, Hereford Heaven Stampede. At one performance, he called a group of young fans from the stands, but the cowboy shoot-out had to be called off because youngsters were getting stuck in the mud. The fourth of July saw the troupe return to Texas for the Kerrville Jaycee Rodeo, where Bill judged a contest for the best-dressed juvenile cowboy. A boy with an incurable blood disease shook Thunder's hoof. Bill and Red Boy placed fourth in cutting. From Kerrville, the rodeo moved to Coleman. At Levelland, rain cleared just in time for the late afternoon rodeo parade, and a record crowd viewed the opening performance. Weatherford's Parker County Frontier Days Rodeo closed out the month of July. Bill attended a Lion's Club meeting. He and Red Boy won the cutting horse contest.

Kicking off the August schedule was the Lawton Rangers Rodeo, part of that community's fiftieth Jubilee Celebration. The announcer introduced Bill's kiddie shoot-out, saying, "A Lawton bank has been robbed and two desperate characters were seen heading for the rodeo grounds." The all-too-realistic announcement sent city and military policeman rushing to the highway to intercept the bandits. Following his visit to a seriously ill 13-year-old at the Fort Sill hospital, Bill said, "It's strange how a sick child will turn to a cowboy. They identify themselves, I guess, with the free healthy life of the range." In a newspaper ad, he wore a locally manufactured Bulldogger Panama hat. The Elliott-Steiner rodeo was highly acclaimed by fans and organizers, set an attendance record and was scheduled for a return engagement. Bill's schedule took him to rodeos in Lamesa, Colorado City and Graham, Texas, Elliott-Steiner's home rodeo. The winner of a Western dress contest for youngsters was awarded a "Wild Bill" Elliott gun and holster set. The rodeo next stopped at Georgetown and Cleburne, Texas.

Early in 1952, at Fort Worth's Southwest Exposition and Livestock Show, Bill and Red Boy tied for second place. In February, Bill began his second season with Tommy Steiner. To the organization's credit, the schedule repeated many of the previous season's locations. By this time, the company's rodeo livestock was valued at $250,000. A newspaper photo showed a Lake Charles youngster on a bowing Thunder. Veteran rodeo man Fog Horn Clancy described the rodeo as "fast, snappy ... with plenty of thrills." Despite rainy weather, the rodeo drew big crowds. At Jasper, Texas, Bill's latest film, Waco, was shown by special request. Hundreds were turned away from the rodeo's sold-out opening night. In May, Bill went back to Hollywood for film business.

The Elliott-Steiner rodeo made return visits to Sulpher's Hereford Heaven Stampede, Lamesa, Kerrville and Weatherford. The Lawton Rangers Rodeo led off the month of August. Bill and Thunder rode on parade. He and Red Boy entered a three-way cutting horse contest with each entrant putting up $500. Following was the Quay County Sheriff's Posse Rodeo at Tucumcari, New Mexico, where Bill and Red Boy won the cutting competition. There was also a return engagement in Graham, Texas. Additional rodeos produced during the 1951 and 1952 seasons omitted Bill's personal appearances. In September, Elliott-Steiner closed their season and their partnership at Memphis' Mid-South Fair Rodeo. Ads asked kids to dress up, bring their pistols and help "Wild Bill." At one matinee performance, 2,500 persons were turned away. This engagement was a breakthrough to "the big time" for Tommy Steiner, who went on to many successful years as a top rodeo producer in larger cities featuring a variety of Western stars. Bill Elliott had concluded his closest association with rodeo.

In 1953, Bill concentrated more on moviemaking and cutting horses. At the fall horse show at Devonshire Downs in Northridge, California, on Red Boy, he joined Audie Murphy for a cutting horse demonstration to benefit youth clubs. At the 1954 California

Rodeo at Salinas, Bill judged cutting. By the end of that year, Red Boy was sold. Bill made his last films, and retired from movies. In 1960, he severed ties to California, settling on a Nevada ranch with Stormy Night and other equine friends. He planned to raise cutting and rodeo horses. He was marshal of Elko's 1960 Silver State Stampede.

DOUGLAS FAIRBANKS (1883–1939) Douglas Fairbanks was born in Denver, Colorado, and lived close to mining camps until his father abandoned the family when Doug was five. Doug's mother maintained the father's interest in theater. Following success on Broadway, Doug became a star in silent films that displayed his physical abilities. His Westerns showed his riding and roping. Yakima Canutt coached Doug in trick mounts for the film *The Gaucho* (1927). From 1920 to 1934, Doug was married to Mary Pickford. He created swashbuckling films from *The Mark of Zorro* (1920) to *The Iron Mask* (1929). He received a posthumous special Academy Award.

Douglas Fairbanks on the Rodeo Trail

In 1917, filming scenes in Wyoming for *The Man from Painted Post*, Douglas Fairbanks stood on horseback to lead the rodeo band at Cheyenne Frontier Days and presented a trophy saddle. Visiting the chutes at a 1919 Los Angeles rodeo, Doug doubled the purse offered

Douglas Fairbanks, lobby card for ***The Gaucho*** (United Artists, 1927) (courtesy Eddie Brandt's).

Yakima Canutt in his successful ride of the bronc Pancho Villa. In 1925, a Douglas Fairbanks trophy saddle was awarded Cheyenne's calf-roping winner. He donated a prize at Calgary, and appeared at Tex Austin rodeos.

TEX FLETCHER (1909–87) Researchers believe that Tex Fletcher was born as Jerry Bisceglia in New York City. His family moved when he was ten years old to Harrison, New York. To help his ill father and eight siblings, he became, at age 16, a horse handler with a circus Wild West show and sent money home. In the Depression, he hitchhiked to South Dakota, finding conditions so bleak that he survived only through Western hospitality, a kindness he never forgot. Eventually he worked as a ranch cowboy, rode broncs and bulls, and played banjo in a cowboy band. After his father's death, Tex helped his mother in New York. As "The Lonesome Cowboy from South Dakota," he sang in amateur contests and at a nightclub, playing guitar left-handed. Stage shows, dude ranches, small rodeos, radio and a Broadway show led Tex to Hollywood, where he appeared in several short musical films. He starred in a single Western feature, *Six Gun Rhythm* (1939), and went into the Army in World War II.

Wounded in Italy, a hospitalized Tex wrote a song about the area of South Dakota where he had been a cowboy. At a U.S. hospital, he met a nurse he later married. Upon recovery, Tex made recordings in New York, was a guest star on various programs and joined the cast of the Bobby Benson radio show. He later had a TV show, *Frontier Diary*. For such songs as "The Black Hills Roundup" and "Tipperary," the governor named him "the official singing cowboy of South Dakota." Tex performed for crippled children, boys clubs and the March of Dimes.

Tex Fletcher on the Rodeo Trail

Tex provided pre-rodeo music and publicity for the Madison Square Garden and Boston Garden rodeos. He also played some Col. Eskew rodeos as well as children's hospitals and benefits. In 1954, a Spearfish, South Dakota, racetrack was converted to the Tex Fletcher Rodeo Bowl. Tex attended the first three Tex Fletcher Rodeos (1954–56). In 1955, he began a new six-day-a-week radio show, *Tex Fletcher Wagon Train*, over the Mutual Network, providing rodeo news. He made TV films of ranch life and rodeo.

DICK FORAN (c. 1910–79) Warner Brothers 1930s singing cowboy Dick Foran participated as a Western celebrity from

Left: Warner Bros. singing cowboy star Dick Foran.

1938 through 1948 at Las Vegas' Helldorado Days Rodeo, and was a parade marshal for the 1941 Palm Springs Rodeo.

GLENN FORD (1916–) Star of many Western films and of CBS-TV's *Cade's County*, Glenn Ford received Reno's Silver Spurs Awards in 1957 and 1958, and he appeared at the 1961 Camp Pendleton rodeo.

PRESTON FOSTER (c. 1903–70) Sometime Western actor Preston Foster was on hand for the 1941 Reno Rodeo and the 1948 Los Angeles Sheriff's Rodeo. He starred at the 1956 Heart O' Texas Fair Rodeo at Waco.

Star of Western films, Glenn Ford.

PEDRO GONZALEZ-GONZALEZ (1926–2006) Pedro Gonzalez-Gonzalez had roles in *The Sheepman* (1958) and *Rio Bravo* (1959). He headlined the 1962 Colorado State Fair Rodeo, starred with Rex Allen at Ardmore's 1971 rodeo and appeared at Rex Allen Days in Willcox, Arizona.

TITO GUIZAR (1908–99) Mexico's singing cowboy, Tito Guizar was in three 1940s films with Roy Rogers. He was at the 1945 Roy Rogers Rodeo at the Los Angeles Coliseum. In 1952, he headlined San Antonio's rodeo and the Arkansas Valley Fair Rodeo night show in Rocky Ford, Colorado.

Left: Preston Foster (courtesy Jerry Ohlinger's).

Left: Latin musical star Tito Guizar. *Right*: Western supporting actor Pedro Gonzalez-Gonzalez.

MONTE HALE (1921–) Born in Ada, Oklahoma, Monte Hale was raised in San Angelo, Texas. His entertaining led to nightclub and radio engagements. On a U.S.O. tour, a contact led him to Hollywood, where he starred in a series of 19 Westerns (1946–50) for Republic Studios. Monte was the first Republic cowboy star to have a film series in color. Adrian Booth was his most frequent leading lady, Paul Hurst was his most common sidekick. He began as a musical Western star and finished as an action star. He was handsome, had a fine singing voice and exuded friendliness. He had a long run of successful comic books. Songs he wrote included "That Statue in the Bay." On tours, he made hospital visits. He appeared in *Giant* (1956). Monte is modest about his Western stardom, but fans remember him with great affection. He received a Buffalo Bill Award at North Platte, Nebraska, and a Golden Boot Award. His saddle plaque was placed in the Newhall (California) Western Walk of Fame. He received stars on the Palm Springs and Hollywood Walks of Fame.

Monte Hale on the Rodeo Trail

In spring of 1945, Monte Hale, with Bill Elliott, was introduced to the crowd at the California (Kern County) Highway Patrolman Rodeo at Bakersfield. With Jimmy Wakely, he headlined the 1949 March of Dimes benefit rodeo at the Oklahoma Stockyards Coliseum. Early the next year, he rode a buckboard in the Palm Springs Rodeo parade. When bad weather delayed completion of Penny Edwards' filming, Monte solo-headlined the 1950 Arkansas Livestock Show and Rodeo in Little Rock, sharing arena billing with Bob Wills and the Texas Playboys.

Republic singing cowboy star Monte Hale.

STUART HAMBLEN (1908–89) Singer, composer and radio personality Stuart Hamblen appeared at Jute Smith's 1943 Sunset Ranch Rodeos in Los Angeles and San Diego. In 1944, he rode his pinto Natchee at a Gilmore Stadium rodeo. In 1980, he and his family appeared at Palm Springs' Rodeo.

TY HARDIN (1930–) TV's *Bronco* (1958–62), Ty Hardin headlined the 1962 Arkansas-Oklahoma Rodeo, visiting the U.S. Army's Fort Chaffee, where he had earlier been stationed. In the arena, Ty demonstrated his fast draw, joked and sang.

Ty Hardin in *Bronco* (Warner Bros., ABC-TV).

WILLIAM S. HART (c. 1864–1946)

William S. Hart, born in Newburgh, New York, and introduced to acting on the eastern stage, traveled as a boy with his family to the Midwest, where he experienced ranchers, cowboys and Indians.

His 1929 autobiography tells of riding broncs and bulls. In silent Western films, with his loyal steed Fritz, he portrayed his concept of a realistic West. Drawing many fans, his stern style gave way to the more flamboyant heroics of Tom Mix and others. He retired from films in 1925. Upon his death, Hart left his home to the people of California as a museum and park.

William S. Hart on the Rodeo Trail

During the 1920s, William S. Hart kept in contact with rodeos. Unable to appear at Cheyenne in person, he once sent a check to purchase 1,000 feet of whale line rope, silver-mounted bits and other trophies. In 1926, the actor donated a bronze "Bill Hart Trophy" to be awarded to Cheyenne's top bronc rider. Rodeo stock contractor Leo Cremer's personnel escorted Mr. Hart when he visited Billings, Montana, for the 1927 unveiling of "A Range Rider of the Yellowstone," a statue for which Bill posed. His greetings were included in the 1931 World Series Rodeo program. Bill joined Tim McCoy and Tom Mix at a 1932 Hoot Gibson rodeo in California. In 1936, Bill, announcer Abe Lefton and Western star Rex Bell helped organize an amateur rodeo at Victorville, California, dedicated to Bill.

"The Bill Hart Trophy" ("Two-Gun Man" by C.C. Christodoro) awarded to 1926 Cheyenne Frontier Days champion bronc rider, Mike Stewart (from the collection of the Cheyenne Frontier Days Old West Museum, Cheyenne, WY. Used with permission).

GEORGE "GABBY" HAYES (1885–1969)

George Francis Hayes, born in Wellsville, New York, was involved in theater as early as age eight and joined a stock theater company at age 17. Before appearing in his first film role in 1929, he had accumulated a quarter century of show business experience, including comedy, singing and dancing. He eventually supported a galaxy of Western stars. In the 1930s and 1940s, he became well-known as sidekick to John Wayne, William Boyd, Roy Rogers and Bill Elliott. His scene-stealing performances as a grizzled, crotchety oldtimer thoroughly entertained Western fans. His final film was *Caribou Trail* (1950) starring Randolph Scott. In the early 1950s, he gained new fans as a TV personality.

George "Gabby" Hayes on the Rodeo Trail

In 1946, Gabby Hayes joined fellow cast members on location in Las Vegas, Nevada, to film scenes for the Roy Rogers film *Heldorado*, set amidst the Helldorado Days celebration and rodeo. Gabby was introduced at each performance to a hearty ovation when the Roy Rogers troupe headlined the 1947 Chicago Stadium rodeo. Early in 1950 at Houston,

Ranger Roy Rogers cautions George "Gabby" Hayes concerning placement of rodeo posters in *Heldorado* (Republic, 1946), the duo's final film together (courtesy Eddie Brandt's).

Gabby appeared with Roy Rogers, Dale Evans and Foy Willing and the Riders of the Purple Sage. The rodeo drew a record attendance of 493,000 fans. In 1958, Gabby, Roy and Dale broadcast *The Chevy Show* from the Fort Worth rodeo. Gabby presented "Hound Dog," complete with gyrations.

Invited to the 1959 Heart of the North Rodeo in Spooner, Wisconsin, 74-year-old Gabby replied, "Oh, you don't want me. I can't do anything except tell stories." Told, "That's just what we want you to do," he made the drive from California to Spooner in his Cadillac convertible. He promoted the rodeo in the nearby cities of Eau Claire and Duluth, and treated his rodeo group to a harbor boat tour on Lake Superior. The local newspaper reported, "[Y]ou could hear a pin drop in the sandy arena so completely did Gabby hold his audience with his tall tales... His ride around the arena and his session of signing autographs at the conclusion of each performance gave rodeo fans ample opportunity to get a close-up [view] of Gabby." At one performance, the sheriff pinned a deputy badge on Gabby, who accepted with a pitch for safe driving. He proved to be a powerful draw. Record attendance overflowed accommodations, seating capacity and highways. Gabby agreed to return.

In the fall of 1959, Gabby appeared at the rodeo in Pine Bluff, Arkansas. He wanted no greeting upon his airport arrival; however, a group was on hand. He sat and signed autographs for youngsters at the airport. He rode in a buckboard in the rodeo parade. He signed more autographs at the Sunshine School, where photographers clicked away as children sat in his lap.

Seating capacity was increased for Gabby's 1960 return to Spooner. He arrived a week prior to the rodeo and stayed for about a month, bringing his brother Clark. Plans included fishing and relaxing. Both he and his brother were fly-fishing enthusiasts, and Spooner was renowned as an outdoor vacationland. Gabby became part of the family at the same lodging place, often sitting in the kitchen chatting with the lady of the house as she went about her chores. He took some meals at the home of his host rodeo committeeman. The mayor presented him a key to the city. Following the rodeo's run, he hosted a party at a lakeside cottage for rodeo committee members and his local friends. Following his departure, Gabby kept in touch with Spooner.

At planeside, Roy Rogers admires Gabby Hayes' beard. The two were in Fort Worth to televise *The Chevy Show* at the 1958 Stock Show Rodeo (Al Panzera photograph courtesy *Fort Worth Star-Telegram* Collection, University of Texas at Arlington Libraries, Arlington. FWST #3925).

TIM HOLT (1919–73)   Charles John (Tim) Holt, Jr., was born February 5, 1919, in Beverly Hills, California, the son of actor Jack Holt. Younger sister Jennifer was a leading lady in Westerns. After his parents' separation, Tim grew up on his father's ranch, learning to ride and rope. He played his dad's character as a boy in a 1928 film. Tim was active in sports and drama at Indiana's Culver Military Academy. Graduating *cum laude* in 1936, he won the Gold Spurs horsemanship award. On loan to RKO Studios, Tim supported Harry Carey in *The Law West of Tombstone* and George O'Brien in *The Renegade Ranger*, both in 1938. Liking his work, RKO took over his contract.

Tim demonstrated early that he could hold his own in "A" features. He was a memorable cavalry lieutenant in the classic Western *Stagecoach* (1939), an unpleasant character in Orson Welles' *The Magnificent Ambersons* (1942) and a Nazi officer in *Hitler's Children* (1943). Following 18 starring B-Westerns (1940–43) for RKO, he saw wartime service in the Army Air Corps. Commissioned as a lieutenant, he served as trainer, and was decorated for combat bombardier missions in the Pacific Theater.

Discharged in 1945, Tim returned to filmmaking in the role of Virgil Earp in John Ford's *My Darling Clementine* (1946). Settling into his post-war (1947–52) RKO series, he completed 29 additional starring Westerns with Richard Martin as his Irish-Mexican sidekick Chito. In one film, *The Arizona Ranger* (1948), Jack Holt played Tim's father. In Warners' *The Treasure of the Sierra Madre* (1948), Tim earned an Academy Award nomination as Best Supporting Actor for his portrayal of a bewhiskered gold prospector.

A no-nonsense cowboy star, Tim favored workmanlike garb and displayed superior horsemanship skills. Obvious rapport with sidekick and real-life friend Richard Martin contributed to fans' enjoyment. His films, showing exemplary production values, won favor with the public and made a profit for the studio until TV began to replace theater B-Westerns. He ranked in the list of top ten Western stars before and after his military service.

In later years, Tim began living away from Hollywood, commuting for picturemaking. Plans for a Tim Holt–Richard Martin TV series fell through when the airwaves became overbooked with Westerns. From Oklahoma City, Tim hosted *The Tim Holt Western Theater*, showing his own films. In retirement from films, he operated a livestock supply store, constructed homes and dealt in automobile parts. He also toured with a Western stage show. His few forays into film projects seem to have been done as favors for friends. One better-remembered exposure for Western fans was a guest role on TV's *The Virginian*. Tim was a radio executive when he passed away from cancer on February 15, 1973. He was inducted into the Hall of Great Western Performers at the National Cowboy Hall of Fame. An "In Memoriam" Golden Boot Award was presented in his honor.

Tim Holt on the Rodeo Trail

At age five, Tim viewed his first rodeo with his dad. Watching Abe Lefton as a rodeo clown, he aspired to that profession. In 1924 he was crown prince of the Fresno, California, rodeo, where his dad was king. Tim and sister Jennifer joined Hollywood stars at the July 4th Reno Rodeo in 1941. He attended the rodeo dance and rode in the parade. For the first 12 of Tim's pre-war Westerns, Ray Whitley, an old hand at combining film and rodeo work, supported him as a musical sidekick. Ray may have talked up the potential for an entertainer on the rodeo circuit. Whatever the impetus, Tim maintained a long-standing interest in rodeo.

In December 1947, Tim bought into a rodeo-producing partnership with stock contractors Joe Jennings and Carl Lamar of Norman, Oklahoma, allowing the company to augment their livestock. Planning to actively manage and publicize rodeos for the 1948 season, he scouted the market with Jennings and met rodeo committees. He also assumed the hardworking position of arena director for each rodeo performance. Concerning his director duties, Tim said, "I'll be working from the first minute until the finish. It's my responsibility to see that the cowboys get the stock they draw, that competition is absolutely fair, and the rules observed. I have to line up the calves in the chutes, get the steers out, and make certain that everything runs smoothly. There's a lot more to rodeo than a spectator may realize." The Holt-Jennings-Lamar company donated to the 1948 RCA saddle bronc-riding champion a Bohlin $1,000 "Tim Holt saddle." The prize saddle was a duplicate of one designed and made for Tim in 1940.

About his rodeo appearances, Tim was once quoted as saying, "I can't play a 'gittar.' And if I had to sing for a living, I'd go hungry. But we do have a first-class rodeo…" A typical rodeo date for Tim meant participating in radio broadcasts, including those in nearby towns, and speaking at civic luncheons. He rode in rodeo parades and crowned queens. He visited orphanages, veterans' and children's hospitals, and individual sick and disabled chil-

II. Individual Movie and Television Actors at Rodeos 169

Tim Holt presents his trophy saddle to 1948 world champion saddle bronc rider Gene Pruett (O.J. Hebrank photograph, used with permission of Mrs. May Hebrank. Obtained from Imogene Veach Beals).

Tim Holt appears at the Temple Theater while headlining Mangum's 1948 Old Greer County Pioneer Reunion Rodeo. Tim frequently visited theaters playing his films in rodeo towns (courtesy Old Greer County Museum, Mangum, OK. Used with museum permission).

dren. He paid for buses and tickets to bring orphans to the rodeo. He usually made at least one appearance at a local theater showing a film of his. He met with individuals, young and old, and was gracious in signing autographs. In the arena, he rode in the grand entry, worked continuously as arena director during the contests and put on his star act.

Early in 1948, Tim and company produced the week-long Oklahoma 4-H and FFA Livestock Show and Rodeo at Oklahoma City's Stockyards Coliseum. Despite snow and freezing temperatures, near-capacity crowds flocked to see Tim, his movie palomino Lightning and his trained Lipizzan dancing horse Sheik. The Austrian Lipizzan was a gift to Tim following World War II. Following a spring rodeo stop in Okemah, Oklahoma, the Red River Valley Livestock Exposition Rodeo celebrated Sherman, Texas,' one-hundredth anniversary. On the courthouse steps, the sheriff presented Tim an honorary Grayson County sheriff's badge. The six-day rodeo drew capacity attendance. Tim's next two rodeos, Pine Valley and El Centro, were near his California home. Tim's comic book "Scrapbook" page showed pictures of El Centro's rodeo.

Following a mid-year rodeo at Pecos, Texas, Tim used a substitute horse for the Greer County Pioneers Rodeo at Mangum, Oklahoma (Lightning had hurt his leg filming a movie). From the chutes, Tim returned youngsters' greetings. He attended, and was interviewed at, the queen selection finals at a theater, an event broadcast on radio. Despite a rained-out performance, the three-night rodeo drew more people than it had in previous years. In a local newspaper ad, Tim endorsed Lee Riders jeans.

During Tim's next rodeo at Shawnee, Oklahoma, he had to leave Lightning in a veterinarian's care. Of his blue cowpony, Pecos Bill, Tim said, "Bill isn't much to look at, but he knows his business. I was trying to get a calf in a cattle car down at Pecos and the little rascal ran by the door four times. I didn't want to rope it and knock the breath out of it, but old Bill solved the problem. He ran alongside that calf, reached down and bit it on the shoulder and pushed it in the car." When a California forest fire destroyed residences not far from Tim's newly built home, downed telephone lines delayed word that his home was safe. The rodeo's opening performance attracted a standing-room-only crowd, the largest ever to attend that rodeo. Due to an impending film worker's strike, Tim left Shawnee hastily to film *Stagecoach Kid*. In late August, he starred with Lightning and Sheik at the Lions Club Rodeo in Alexandria, Louisiana. At a combined Lions-Rotary luncheon, he spoke on the value to a community of rodeo and 4-H competition.

In early September, Tim wrapped up his season at the Labor Day Exchange Club Rodeo in Brookhaven, Mississippi. There, he sat outside his hotel chatting with passersby and had a four-hour autograph session at a local shop. Tim performed at the rodeo with Sheik. He gave talks and answered questions at three different local forums. Officials acclaimed the smoothness of the rodeo, a financial success despite hurricane-induced rains, which forced the final night's contestants and performers to work in foot-deep mud. When weather kept the governor from crowning the queen, Tim obliged. Following the rodeo, he returned to Hollywood for movie work.

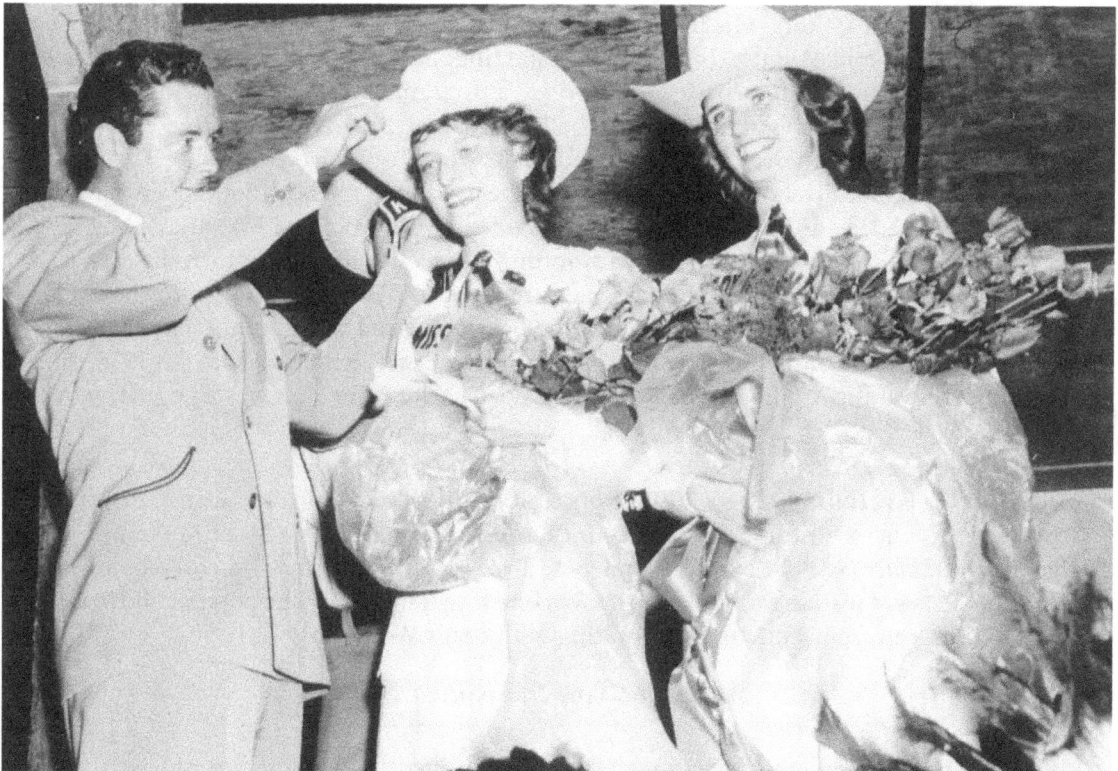

Tim Holt places a hat on Miss Frontier Joy Vandehei as part of the 1950 Cheyenne Frontier Days crowning ceremony. The Lady-in-Waiting is Laura Bailey (courtesy Wyoming Division of Cultural Resources, Cheyenne. Neg. #26389/H56-28).

Tim resumed his association with Jennings-Lamar for the 1949 rodeo season, during which he was scheduled to appear at another ten rodeos. His season began at Oklahoma City's Livestock Show and Rodeo. At one rodeo there, he met his future wife, Berdee. At the spring 89'er Rodeo at Guthrie, Oklahoma, Tim's movie sidekick, Richard "Chito" Martin, joined him on parade and in the arena. The occasion commemorated the sixtieth anniversary of the Oklahoma Territory opening. Oklahoma's governor was on hand, as was Lynn Unkefer, RKO's assistant publicity director. Tim appeared at May's Bar-None Rodeo in Plainview, Texas, and the June rodeo in Clovis, New Mexico.

In early July, Tim left Hollywood on a Friday morning for a three-day, four-performance rodeo at Levelland, Texas. The mayor and rodeo officials met him at Lubbock's airport. In the arena, Tim performed with his Lipizzan stallion. Rodeo attendance exceeded 10,000 spectators. Tim flew back to Hollywood on Tuesday. During the 1948 and 1949 rodeo seasons, the Holt-Jennings-Lamar Company produced additional rodeos at which Tim did not star.

In 1950, Tim was no longer associated with Jennings-Lamar. However, the cover story of the spring *Western Stars* magazine was a first-person account titled "Tim Holt's Rodeo Story." That year, Tim was a guest, officially opening the 54th Cheyenne Frontier Days by crowning "Miss Frontier" and her "Lady in Waiting." He rode the traditional train and participated with Lightning in the first week of rodeo parades and grand entries.

In 1951, Tim reportedly bought an interest in the Harley Roth-Jim Madden rodeo of Rapid City, South Dakota. His first appearance was at the Black Hills Range Days Rodeo in Rapid City in mid–August. In addition to starring, he served as arena director. A news photo showed Tim on horseback swamped by autographed seekers at one of the three parades in which he rode. Tim and folk balladeer–actor Burl Ives presented ribbons to junior horse show winners. Tim also starred at the Key City Rodeo over Labor Day weekend in Sturgis, South Dakota. Later that month, he headlined the Mid-South Fair in Memphis, Tennessee. Then, in early October, he starred at the Arkansas Livestock Show and Rodeo in Little Rock, sharing billing with Johnnie Lee Wills' band. He introduced a new mount, Sun Dance. In early 1952, there was a report that Tim would return to the Dakotas for a July 4 rodeo at Belle Fourche and the Labor Day rodeo at Sturgis. These appearances could not be confirmed. He did appear that year at Wichita, Kansas. In 1953, Tim headlined the Southwest Louisiana Rodeo at Lake Charles. Tim Holt was a popular working cowboy at rodeos.

WILL HUTCHINS (1932–) TV drama roles led Will Hutchins to a Warner Brothers contract. His character of Sugarfoot (Tom Brewster) had been introduced in the film *The Boy from Oklahoma* (1954). Mild-mannered, Tom was studying law by correspondence. Once his sense of justice was violated, he was one tough hombre. The popular show, laced with humor, ran from 1957 to 1961, rotating with other Westerns.

"Sugarfoot" on the Rodeo Trail

Will Hutchins' rodeo appearances were usually confined to rodeo grand entries. In the summer of 1958, he appeared with other Western stars at the U.S. Marine Rodeo at Camp Pendleton. Then, he was grand marshal of the Los Angeles Sheriff's Rodeo. At the 1962 Seattle World's Fair rodeo, he shared billing with Guy Mitchell, performing on street corners to encourage attendance. In 1999, at the Nebraskaland Days/Buffalo Bill Rodeo at North Platte, Will was parade grand marshal and received a Buffalo Bill Award.

STAN JONES (1914–63) A former park ranger, Stan Jones composed "Ghost Riders in the Sky" and many other Western songs. He also had movie and TV roles. As leader of the Wagonmaster quartet, he appeared in 1961 at the Old Santa Fe Trail and Colorado State Fair rodeos with Frank McGrath and Terry Wilson.

Will Hutchins as TV's *Sugarfoot*.

DOUGLAS KENNEDY (c. 1918–73) Veteran of several Western films and the lead in TV's *Steve Donovan— Western Marshal* (1955–56), Douglas Kennedy starred at the 1956 Shasta County Sheriff's Posse Rodeo at Redding, California.

JACK LORD (1921–98) New York–born Jack Lord learned to ride on his grandfather's Hudson Valley farm. His father's steamship business gave him a lifelong interest in the sea. He studied both art and drama. Jack said he had never been near a rodeo until cast as *Stoney Burke* in that one-season series. In April of 1963, at the National Cowboy Hall of Fame, North Dakota's governor presented Jack with an award. The museum displays his Stoney Burke costume, saddle and tack. In 1968, Jack became Steve McGarrett in the long-running series *Hawaii Five-O*. He retired to pursue his art in Hawaii.

"Stoney Burke" on the Rodeo Trail

Having filmed the last *Stoney Burke* episode, Jack Lord was asked to entertain at rodeos. He stated, "I didn't have any kind of act ... but I wanted to get out and play before a live audience." More accomplished at riding, he prepared to sing at rodeos. At Sidney, Iowa,

Jack Lord, TV's *Stoney Burke*, appears on the cover of the 1964 Snake River Stampede program (used with permission of Snake River Stampede).

he sang with a folk-type band. Attendance of 97,000 broke a 40-year record. At Lake Charles and Shreveport, Louisiana, he vocalized such favorites as "When the Saints Go Marching In" and "Jambalaya." He met the former president while performing at the Truman Rodeo in Independence, Missouri. At Nampa's Snake River Stampede, he traveled to his motel by stagecoach. He appeared at the New Mexico State Fair Rodeo (as a substitute) and at Pine Bluff, Arkansas.

TIM MCCOY (1891–1977) At age 28, Tim McCoy was named Adjutant General of the Wyoming Army Guard, holding office for two years. He was technical advisor and coordinator of Native American players for the film *The Covered Wagon* (1923). He and his troupe promoted this and other films. Between 1926 and 1929, he made 16 silent Westerns for MGM. From 1931 into 1941, he made films and toured with circuses. He teamed with Buck Jones for a series of "Rough Riders" Westerns before World War II service in Europe. He returned to films, circuses and, in later years, a medicine show. He is an inductee of the National Cowboy Hall of Fame.

Western film star Tim McCoy.

Tim McCoy on the Rodeo Trail

Secretary of the publicity committee for the 1920 Cheyenne Frontier Days, Tim McCoy supervised bulldogging and snubbed for bronc riding. He returned as a frequent Frontier Days visitor. In 1930, he appeared at the Los Angeles Stockyards Rodeo. He received a Buffalo Bill Award in connection with North Platte, Nebraska's, rodeo.

FRED MACMURRAY (c. 1908–91) In his 50-year acting career, Fred MacMurray played in classic dramas, comedies and Westerns and on TV's *My Three Sons*.

Fred MacMurray on the Rodeo Trail

In 1951 at Cheyenne Frontier Days, Fred MacMurray rode the special train, crowned Miss Frontier and rode in a parade and grand entry. At the 1959 Reno Rodeo, he received

Fred MacMurray (left) and Chill Wills in a lobby card scene from *Gun for a Coward* (Universal-International, 1957).

a Silver Spurs Award and rode a stagecoach on parade. In 1962, he was grand marshal of Los Angeles' Sheriff's Rodeo.

STEVE McQUEEN (1930–80) Indiana-born Steve McQueen survived a rough childhood. Honorably discharged from the U.S. Marines in 1950, he studied acting on the G.I. Bill in New York City. He appeared in stage productions, TV drama shows and a few films. *Wanted: Dead or Alive* was introduced as an episode of the Western series *Trackdown*. Steve starred as the offbeat loner Josh Randall, with the unsympathetic occupation of bounty hunter. His distinctive, powerful weapon was a sawed-off Winchester .44–40 shotgun called the "mare's leg," or "maire's laig." The weapon's hammer was built up, so that a shot could be fired by "fanning," or striking the hammer with the palm of the hand in lieu of pulling the trigger. He became adept with the weapon.

On one TV filming break, Steve made the war film *Never So Few* and got positive notices. Steve again worked for director John Sturges in *The Magnificent Seven* and *The Great Escape*, progressing from TV personality to international stardom. In March of 1961, *Wanted: Dead or Alive* was canceled, allowing him to focus exclusively on feature films, which included four Westerns. Ben Johnson was in three of Steve's films; Slim Pickens was in two.

Richard Farnsworth, whom Steve had earlier fired as a stuntman from *Wanted: Dead or Alive* for a kidding remark, had a featured role in *Tom Horn*. Steve passed away of a heart attack following cancer surgery.

"JOSH RANDALL" ON THE RODEO TRAIL

Steve McQueen's rodeo act consisted primarily of gun-handling and explaining his weapons. He demonstrated fast and fancy draws with his cut-down "mare's leg" and a revolver. When the weapon misfired during his show, Steve coolly remarked, "I guess the ammunition they used in the Old West was more reliable than this Hollywood ammunition." At New Mexico's 1959 State Fair Rodeo, he visited with two men he had known from the Marine Corps and expressed admiration for Albuquerque stage actress Kim Stanley, with whom he had toured in *A Hatful of Rain*. He posed for a newspaper photo "covered" by his own "mare's leg" weapon in the hands of a five-year-old boy. Reports said that he kept fair officials entertained with his wisecracks. In response to Jimmy Wakely's offer of music for his arena entrance, Steve said he didn't mind as long as the horse didn't dance. Later that fall, he was at the Texas Prison Rodeo.

Steve McQueen, Josh Randall on CBS-TV's ***Wanted: Dead or Alive***, with "mare's laig" weapon at a 1959 Texas Prison Rodeo (courtesy Texas Department of Criminal Justice).

Steve headlined the 1959 St. Louis Fireman's Rodeo. Proceeds from this event, in a state where he had spent positive time in his formative years, went to the Uniformed Fireman's Relief Association, aiding widows and orphans of deceased firemen. He arrived at the airport in a suit and tie, waving to fans. He was greeted by the public safety director and the fire chief. In an interview, he commented on his "mare's leg" weapon and his TV horse Ringo. The rodeo hosted 3,000 underprivileged children from St. Louis and outlying areas at a matinee.

Steve's last known starring rodeo appearance was in Orange, Texas, at the 1960 Southeast Texas Championship Rodeo. Despite a growing reputation as "difficult to work with," he represented the cowboy hero image well. Junior Chamber of Commerce sponsors met him at the airport. For a breakfast interview, he dressed in white pants and shirt, and was barefoot. He showed his "mare's leg" weapon to a young boy seated on his knee. He provided autographed pictures, congratulated the rodeo queen and visited children at a local hospital. His hosts took him on a boat tour of the Sabine River. His agent, Hilly Elkins, relates in Marshall Terrill's book *Steve McQueen, Portrait of an American Rebel* that, for his finale, Steve fired the "mare's leg" from horseback at a coin tossed in the air. At that moment, arena lights were shut off, and he made a hasty exit without anyone knowing whether he hit the coin or not. As Steve achieved big-screen stardom, rodeo appearances were discontinued. However, after filming the rodeo-related film *Junior Bonner* (1972) at the 1971 Prescott Frontier Days rodeo, Steve returned in 1973 as Prescott's grand marshal.

JAN MERLIN (1925–) Jan Merlin played Confederate Lt. Cullen Kirby on the ZIV-TV series *Rough Riders* (1958–59). In 1959, with Kathy Nolan and Tom Tryon, he led the rodeo parade and grand entry at Elko's Silver State Stampede.

Jan Merlin as Lt. Cullen Kirby on ZIV-TV's *Rough Riders*.

BETTY MILES (1910–92) Horsewoman Betty Miles was a trick rider at rodeos and circuses. Between 1941 and 1944, she was a leading lady in Monogram Westerns. At the 1941 Prescott Rodeo, she and Gene Alsace competed in team tying and exhibited stunt riding.

GUY MITCHELL (1925–99) Born in Detroit, Michigan, Guy Mitchell desired to be a cowboy, and herded cattle on his uncle's ranch. When he was a boy, his family moved to San Francisco. As a teen, he roped calves, worked on ranches, broke horses and competed in rodeos. Following U.S. Navy service, he resumed rodeoing, but not successfully. His parents urged him to pursue show business. Carrying his $10 Gene Autry guitar in a pillowcase, he went to a San Francisco Western music radio station, where he won a job with Dude Martin's band. For a time,

Betty Miles, horsewoman and Western film leading lady (courtesy Eddie Brandt's).

Guy Mitchell (left) as Detective George Romack in support of Audie Murphy in NBC-TV's *Whispering Smith* (courtesy Eddie Brandt's).

he sang with the Carmen Cavallaro orchestra. In New York, he spent two and a half lean years mostly making demonstration records for songwriters. In 1949, Guy won the "Arthur Godfrey Talent Scouts" contest and was signed by Columbia Records. In the 1950s, his string of hit recordings included 16 million-sellers. His popularity led to two Paramount films and a TV show. He had a California ranch, and was fond of saying, "I'm singing so I can go back to cowboying." In 1961, he supported Audie Murphy on the Western TV series *Whispering Smith*.

Guy Mitchell on the Rodeo Trail

At rodeos, Guy Mitchell returned to his cowboy image. In 1952, he provided a musical complement to the Cisco Kid's rodeo appearance at Cleveland. In 1958, he headlined the Colorado State Fair Rodeo. At the Fair, he toured cattle and horse barns, ate Rocky Ford watermelon and performed lariat tricks. He signed autographs wherever he went. He was also featured at the 1962 Seattle World's Fair rodeo.

AUDIE MURPHY (1924–71) Audie Leon Murphy was born at Kingston, Texas, one of nine children. Life was difficult and became tougher when Audie's father left the family. Audie developed his marksmanship by hunting game for food. After the fifth grade, he quit school to work, providing

Advertisement for Guy Mitchell's appearance at the Colorado State Fair Rodeo.

Audie Murphy appearing on "Audie Murphy Day" at the fall 1945 Corsicana (Texas) Agricultural and Livestock Show Rodeo (courtesy *Fort Worth Star-Telegram* Photograph Collection, University of Texas at Arlington Libraries, Arlington. FWST #1831).

some support to his family. Upon the death of his mother, he enlisted in the Army, seeing two years of World War II action in the European Theater. At the war's conclusion, having received the Congressional Medal of Honor among many other awards, and a lieutenant's commission, he was identified as the war's most highly decorated soldier. Upon Audie's return from service, actor James Cagney provided some Hollywood drama schooling. Audie made his film debut in *Beyond Glory* (1948). Under contract to Universal-International, he removed his younger siblings from an orphanage and placed them in the care of his sister. With his first Western, *The Kid from Texas* (1950), it was obvious that he was well suited to the genre. In 1951, he earned recognition for his role in *The Red Badge of Courage*. Audie's autobiography *To Hell and Back* was published in 1949, became a best-seller and, in 1955, was made into a Universal film starring Audie as himself.

In the 1950s, Audie raised quarter horses for racing and cutting, making a number of appearances with his horse Joe Queen. He acted in some television dramas and starred in the Western TV series *Whispering Smith* (1959–61). He wrote poetry and collaborated in writing country songs. On a business trip, Audie was killed in a private plane crash in Roanoke, Virginia. Survived by his wife and two sons, he was buried at Arlington National Cemetery with full military honors.

Audie Murphy on the Rodeo Trail

Audie Murphy's biographer, Col. Harold B. Simpson, expressed the opinion that, next to military and patriotic functions, Audie's favorite activities were rodeos and horse-related events. In 1945, when Audie was being welcomed home from wartime duty, he participated

Audie Murphy (right), special guest at Fort Worth's 1949 rodeo, with Ray Woods (courtesy *Fort Worth Star-Telegram* Photograph Collection, University of Texas at Arlington Libraries, Arlington. FWST #2140).

in two rodeos. Attracted by a bond rally, he was guest of honor at a rodeo held at McKinney, Texas, over the Fourth of July holiday. That fall, he appeared at the Corsicana, Texas, Agricultural and Livestock Show. For the combined Audie Murphy Day and rodeo, as previously, he led the parade on horseback and the rodeo's grand entry. In 1948, a Kaiser-Frazier auto executive, Ray Woods, built the Audie Murphy Arena on his ranch at Euless, Texas. There, an Audie Murphy Rodeo was held annually through 1951, with Audie as guest of honor three of the four years. Beginning in 1952, Audie Murphy Rodeos were relocated to Stephenville, with Audie's occasional attendance, until discontinued in the mid–1950s due to Woods' poor health.

In January 1949, Audie and his bride, actress Wanda Hendrix, were two-day guests of the Fort Worth rodeo. He remained in Texas to promote his film *Bad Boy*. This marriage lasted less than two years. Audie, in 1951, married Pamela Archer. He was guest star at the 1957 Caldwell (Idaho) Night Rodeo. The governor and mayor jointly declared August 6 Audie Murphy Day. Audie arrived early to participate in the selection and crowning of Miss Rodeo Idaho. He rode in the parade and appeared at each rodeo performance with his quarter horse Joe Queen. A week later, he was grand marshal of the Los Angeles Sheriff's Rodeo at the Coliseum. Early in 1958, he was grand marshal for the Rodeo of the Stars parade in Palm Springs, California. In the summer of 1961, he returned to Texas as the community of Falfurrias celebrated its fiftieth anniversary with the Brooks County Golden Fiesta, and honored Texas Rangers. Audie, as marshal, led the parade on horseback, received an honorary Texas Ranger commission, participated in meals at local ranches and officially opened the evening rodeo.

HUGH O'BRIAN (1925–) Stuart Lake, author of *Wyatt Earp, Frontier Marshal* and script advisor for a new TV series about Earp, favored Hugh O'Brian for the part because of his physical resemblance to the historical Wyatt Earp. Hugh developed a fast draw with the extra-long barrels of Wyatt's trademark Buntline Special .45 revolvers. *The Life and Legend of Wyatt Earp* (1955–61) edged *Gunsmoke* as the first adult Western and led to an Emmy nomination for Hugh. He received a Golden Boot award.

"Wyatt Earp" on the Rodeo Trail

In June 1957, Hugh O'Brian appeared at Livermore, California's, rodeo. Then, early in 1958, he headlined Houston's Fat Stock Show Rodeo. In a poll, he led other nominated guest stars by two to one. His "official arrival" by helicopter increased excitement among the 3,000 fans assembled to greet him outside his hotel. As he stepped from the aircraft, smiling and waving his distinctive black hat, the seat of his pants ripped. Ordinarily, his long coat would have provided cover, but the combination of high winds and the helicopter's wake presented a problem. U.S. Marines escorted him to the speaking platform. He paused to greet a four-year-old, Wyatt Earp–outfitted youngster who drew a cap pistol on him. The mayor awarded Hugh a silver badge naming him honorary mayor. Two men walked close behind as kids mobbed him en route to his hotel.

Hugh made three appearances along the Salt Grass Trail Ride. He had an opening night midnight breakfast with the governor and mayor. He held interviews, was guest at a press dinner, visited a TV station, rode horseback in the downtown rodeo parade, visited hospitals, attended special events and appeared before children's groups. A Houston Press Club–sponsored contest challenged elementary school children to complete a verse of the *Wyatt Earp* theme song. Hugh presented the arena director with an engraved copy of a Buntline

Hugh O'Brian, star of ABC-TV's *The Life and Legend of Wyatt Earp*.

Special six-shooter. He introduced special guest Hoot Gibson to the crowd, saying, "He was my inspiration for becoming what I was to become."

In his rodeo act, Hugh demonstrated prowess with a regular Colt six-shooter and with the Buntline Specials. An accomplished fast-draw artist and a true marksman, he showed that the Buntline could fire accurately from a distance. In a hay wagon with a group of youngsters, he re-entered to sing, accompanied by young helpers firing cap pistols. He closed using his Buntline Special to "shoot" a stuntman off his horse, and then rode around the arena to shake hands. In the fall of 1960, Hugh appeared at the Jaycee Bootheel Rodeo at Sikeston, Missouri, splitting dates with Don Durant. The rodeo was considered the most successful edition in eight years of the rodeo's operation.

DOYE O'DELL (1912–2001) Singer Doye O'Dell appeared in Western films. In 1948, he and his Radio Rangers made a rodeo tour with "Wild Bill" Elliott. He was a parade marshal at Palm Springs' 1955 Rodeo.

MICHAEL O'SHEA (1906–73) Michael O'Shea made Western films and was active on TV. In 1945, he and his wife Virginia Mayo were at the Phoenix rodeo. In 1947, he was in the Salinas rodeo parade and headlined the rodeo at Dublin, Texas. He participated in the Los Angeles Sheriff's Rodeo and was on hand for the 1957 Camp Pendleton Marine Rodeo.

Michael O'Shea and his wife Virginia Mayo (courtesy Eddie Brandt's).

Fred Harman as "Red Ryder," and "Thunder" (courtesy Fred Harman Art Museum, Pagosa Springs, Colorado. Used with permission of Fred Harman III).

"RED RYDER"— FRED HARMAN The fictional character of Red Ryder initially appeared in Fred Harman's syndicated comic strip, and expanded to products, a radio program and films. Hollywood's adaptations began in 1940 with the 12-chapter serial *Adventures of Red Ryder*, starring Don Barry as Red and Tommy Cook as his young sidekick Little Beaver. Bill Elliott was Red Ryder for a series of 16 Republic films (1944–46). Beginning in 1946, Allan Lane became Red for an additional seven Republic films until

1947. Bobby Blake (later known as Robert Blake) played Little Beaver in all of Republic's Red Ryder features. In 1949, Eagle-Lion released four Red Ryder films starring Jim Bannon as Red and Don "Brown Jug" Reynolds as Little Beaver. Three of the named actors are known to have appeared at rodeos in character. At Gilmore Stadium's 1944 Sunset Ranch Rodeo, Bill Elliott was billed as the "Star of Republic's *Red Ryder* series." Bill retained ties to the role throughout his rodeo career. A rodeo performer before playing Little Beaver, Don Reynolds kept the designation at rodeos. Jim Bannon appeared with Don at the 1949 Union Stockyard Rodeo in Los Angeles.

The individual who appeared at more rodeos than any other as Red Ryder was Fred Harman (1902–82). Born in St. Joseph, Missouri, Fred soon moved with his family to Colorado. From 1938 when newspapers first carried the Red Ryder strip, to 1962, when he devoted his talents full-time to fine art, Fred was associated with Red Ryder. During the 1940s and '50s, dressed as Red Ryder, mounted on Thunder and frequently accompanied by a Little Beaver, Fred made personal appearances as Red Ryder.

Fred Harman as "Red Ryder" on the Rodeo Trail

Drawing his strip and other commitments usually kept Fred close to home, limiting rodeo appearances to Colorado. Mrs. Harman usually accompanied him. Fred drew special Red Ryder cartoons to promote rodeos. Photos of Fred astride Thunder announced a rodeo's arrival. The Red Ryder Round Up, held in Pagosa Springs, celebrated its fiftieth anniversary in 1999 and is still active as of this writing.

Fred Harman III assumed his dad's interest in this event. For years, an annual Little Beaver Rodeo, featuring Indian competition, was held in nearby Dulce, New Mexico. Beyond those, Fred was most closely aligned with Monte Vista's Ski Hi Stampede (where he was an honorary committeeman), the Colorado State Fair Rodeo at Pueblo and Durango's rodeo. During Denver's National Western Rodeo in early 1949, steer wrestlers contracted in Fred's hotel room for a match at that year's Ski Hi Stampede, adding interest to an already exciting rodeo. At that rodeo, Fred greeted visiting rodeo queens; he was guest celebrity at a luncheon for Colorado rodeo queens.

At the 1949 Colorado State Fair Rodeo, Fred on Thunder led two parades. For Colorado Springs' Pikes Peak or Bust Rodeo in 1950, Fred as Red Ryder rode the Denver Post's special Denver and Rio Grande train, carrying Colorado's governor and more than 400 supporters from Denver to Colorado Springs for the initial rodeo performance. Fred and Little Beaver rode in the rodeo parade. At the 1951 Colorado State Fair Rodeo, Fred led two parades and was made an honorary member of the Navajo Indian tribe. He and Mrs. Harman arrived at the 1957 State Fair after a military tour of Japan and the Far East. He joined Colorado's governor and Rex Allen in two parades. Renowned as a cartoonist and artist, Fred also contributed to rodeo.

JEANNINE RILEY (1941–) Billie Jo on CBS-TV's *Petticoat Junction*, Jeannine Riley joined *Gunsmoke*'s Ken Curtis at the 1964 Kentucky State Fair Rodeo, and split dates at the Arkansas State Fair Rodeo with that show's Doc and Festus. In 1965, she and *Rawhide*'s Paul Brinegar teamed for the Arkansas-Oklahoma Rodeo.

TEX RITTER (1905–74) Interest in music, both as a performer and as a student of historic Western ballads, prevailed over law studies for Murvaul, Texas, native Woodward Maurice Ritter. In 1928, he became the first singing cowboy to perform on radio. The early 1930s found him in the New York City stage production *Green Grow the Lilacs*, a play with songs that evolved into *Oklahoma!* Here, Tex acquired his nickname. Hank Worden and Everett Cheetham, from Madison Square Garden's rodeo, answered an audition for cowboys; the three shared an apartment and their careers intertwined. Hank provided comic relief in several of Tex's early Westerns and introduced Tex to his (Tex's) future wife.

Everett composed Tex's popular recording "Blood on the Saddle," based on an actual 1926 rodeo ride in which bronc rider Orville Fisher drew Bolshevic at Florence, Arizona, and stayed on nearly to the buzzer. The horse then pitched forward, landing on the rider, resulting in "blood all around" and a fall that "mashed his head." Cheetham never learned that Fisher survived multiple head fractures, living into his eighties. Fisher hummed the song, unaware for many years that it was about him.

In New York, Tex performed on radio, at a rodeo and, on weekends, at a dude ranch. One of the first to popularize Western music in the East, he was invited to Hollywood. From 1936 through 1945, he starred for several studios in more than 50 B-Westerns, marked by action as well as singing. A gentleman, he displayed a plausible toughness on-screen, particularly in fights with villain Charles King. Tex's screen personality built a loyal fan following. During his filmmaking years, Tex met and married Dorothy Fay (Southworth). The union produced two sons: Tom, a lawyer, and John, an actor (the star of the sitcom *Three's Company*). In 1939, Dorothy made four films with Tex.

Tex was a much-traveled Western star, performing for many years at a variety of venues. His background singing of the Oscar-winning theme for *High Noon* (1952) boosted his career. A hit recording, the song was most requested by live audiences. Shortly, Tex headlined the show *Texas* in London for a nine-week engagement. White Flash and rodeo contract performers Buff and Ruby Brady, Pat Paul and Jerry Ann Portwood were in the cast. Tex was a TV guest and had his own musical programs: *Town Hall Party*, *Five-Star Jubilee* and *Ranch Party*.

In his later years, Tex was a Nashville song publisher and president of the Country Music Association. He stood for traditional principles of God, country and family. He worked tirelessly at benefits for cerebral palsy, twice entertained U.S. troops in Vietnam and in 1970 ran unsuccessfully for the U.S. Senate. He died of a heart attack while visiting a friend at the Nashville jail. He was inducted into the Country Music, Songwriter's and National Cowboy Halls of Fame. He received a posthumous Golden Boot Award. A Tex Ritter Museum is located in Carthage, Texas.

Tex Ritter on the Rodeo Trail

Tex Ritter brought a crew to the 1937 Las Vegas Helldorado Days to film scenes for his rodeo-themed film *Frontier Town* (1938). He returned to that celebration and rodeo several times. Tex rode in the 1941 Palm Springs Rodeo parade. He headlined Houston's 1946 rodeo with his horse White Flash, sharing billing with radio's Lone Ranger. In August, Capitol recording artist Wesley Tuttle and sidekick Arkansas Slim Andrews joined Tex and White Flash at the first annual North Texas Fair at Arlington Downs. Following the opening rodeo performance, Tex broadcast from the arena nationwide on CBS radio. He and his Hillbilly Jamboree starred at the 1947 Caldwell (Idaho) Night Rodeo, supported by movie sidekicks Dub "Cannonball" Taylor and Arkansas Slim Andrews. At a music store, Tex signed his recordings. In 1949, he starred in a Wild West Show at Michigan's State Fair in Detroit. In April 1950, he was featured at San Antonio's rodeo. He starred at Redwood City, California's, 1952 rodeo, providing dance entertainment as well.

In 1953, Tex starred at the Lawton (Oklahoma) Rangers Rodeo, the Los Angeles Sheriff's

Singing cowboy star Tex Ritter (courtesy Eddie Brandt's).

Rodeo and the Wichita, Kansas, rodeo. At Vernal, Utah's, 1955 rodeo, he entertained in the arena and at the local dance hall all three nights. He split fall rodeo dates with Eddie Dean and Smiley Burnette at West Monroe (Louisiana). In 1960, he entertained at Omaha's pre–rodeo show honoring charity volunteers. Returning as star of the 1962 Ak-Sar-Ben Rodeo, he was inducted into that rodeo's Western Hall of Fame.

Tex entertained at Fort Madison's 1963 pre-rodeo show. At a Birmingham, Alabama, rodeo, he learned there was no dressing room. With his guitar, he sat in rainy stands with a blanket for cover, but was never called to perform. Tex's recollection: "One fellow, his wife and kids came by, saying, 'Tex, we drove a hundred and fifty miles just to hear you sing.' 'Well, podner,' I said to him, 'I came 2000 miles to sing. And I don't know why they didn't call on me.'" Tex popularized the rodeo-related song "Bad Brahma Bull."

DALE ROBERTSON (1923–)   Dale Robertson was born at Harrah, Oklahoma, and moved with his family to Oklahoma City. Family friend Will Rogers, recognizing young Dale's star potential, advised him to avoid drama lessons and stay natural. Training horses on his father's ranch, Dale became an expert horseman. At Oklahoma Military College, he studied law. He earned multiple athletic letters and was named the school's outstanding athlete. In later years, he became an outdoor sportsman. During college summers and subsequently, he trained polo ponies and worked as a ranch hand, among other jobs. He compiled a winning record as a professional boxer. During World War II, he served with U.S. Army combat engineers attached to Gen. Patton's Third Army. In the European Theater, he received a knee wound from shrapnel. Discharged in 1945, he had earned the rank of first lieutenant and decorations for valor, but had to abandon serious pursuit of athletics.

Dale had appeared in college dramatic productions. While he served in the Army in California, a photo studio displayed a portrait made for his mother, prompting his first movie contact. After discharge, he sought to break into the movies as an actor, but faced increased post-war competition. He was successful on his tenth attempt: In 1949, producer Nat Holt cast Dale in his first movie, *Fighting Men of the Plains*. He earned favorable notice and a contract with 20th Century-Fox. Additional Westerns were *The Caribou Trail* and *Two Faces West*, both in 1950. In 1951, Dale was named one of Hollywood's "Stars of Tomorrow." From 1951 into 1953, the studio showcased his talents primarily as a non–Western leading man opposite top female stars. Freelancing beginning in 1954, he made films for various studios. He studied filmmaking, wrote scripts and, for a time, was involved in film production.

Initially reluctant, Dale accepted Nat Holt's offer to appear in a 1956 pilot broadcast that led to the Western TV series *Tales of Wells Fargo*. As Jim Hardie, he became familiar in households across the country. Viewers quickly accepted a Western star of his distinctive carriage, bearing and voice, authentically "born to the saddle" and mounted on his horse Jubilee. Doing most of his riding, fighting and action scenes, Dale called on doubles, including Dean Smith, for high-risk stunts. Steve McQueen was one of many guest stars. Following its original run, the show continued in widespread syndication.

Dale also made nightclub appearances. In the early 1960s, he helped establish a Texas summer camp for boys. He produced a fully animated Western feature film, *The Man from Button Willow* (1965). Following additional Western movies, he starred in a new TV series, *Iron Horse* (1966–68). When friend and fellow rancher Robert Taylor passed away in 1965, Dale became host of TV's *Death Valley Days* until the early 1970s. In the '70s, Dale made additional movies and recorded an album of vocal music. He helped develop, and made appearances on, TV's *The American Sportsman*. In the 1980s, he was a guest on several TV

Western star Dale Robertson tips his hat to fans along the 1959 Pikes Peak or Bust Rodeo parade route (courtesy Pikes Peak Library District Local History Collection, Colorado Springs, CO. Stewarts #2378).

shows. In 1987, he starred in the series *JJ Starbuck*. Dale and his brother bred and trained quarter horses on their Haymaker Farm in Oklahoma. He was a pilot, participated in celebrity golf tournaments and enjoyed photography, as well as hunting and fishing.

Dale has been honored in his home state with the Will Rogers Award, and he was the first inductee into Oklahoma's Motion Picture Hall of Fame. He was inducted into the Hollywood Stuntmen's Hall of Fame. In 1965, he received the Buffalo Bill Award at North Platte, Nebraska. He was inducted into the Hall of Great Western Performers at the National Cowboy Hall of Fame and received a Golden Boot Award. In subsequent years, he served as presenter or master of ceremonies for the Golden Boot. He was honored with a saddle plaque in Newhall, California's, Walk of Western Stars. He is a popular guest at Western film festivals.

Dale Robertson on the Rodeo Trail

During the time Dale was starring on *Tales of Wells Fargo* and beyond, he was a major star on the rodeo circuit. He saw rodeo appearances as a natural extension of his role as a Western series star, although he termed rodeo performances "the toughest kind of show business." He respected competing rodeo cowboys. He often rode in rodeo parades. At rodeos, he occasionally purchased a local horse or showed his horses in stock competition.

Like most action stars, Dale, more than adequate as a vocalist, sang as a major part of his rodeo act. He was also quick-witted with stories. Knowledgeable rodeo fans recognized him as an accomplished rider. In a typical appearance, he galloped into the arena on his horse Jubilee to the strains of *Oklahoma!* He usually wore a black outfit similar to his TV garb, only a bit fancier. He told of his rodeo and TV steed, whose ancestry included the Thoroughbred racer Man O' War. He talked about his six-shooter and shooting ability, with perhaps a demonstration of his fast left-handed draw. He explained that his right-handed draw got too fast for the cameras to capture. He joked about his show's outlaw-catching rivalry with other Western series. Occasionally, he fired his weapon. Dale delivered renditions of "You Don't Know What Lonesome Is," "El Paso," "The Hanging Tree," "Open Up Your Heart," "Cowboy Blues," "Cool Water" and "He's Got the Whole World in His Hands." He recited his poem "The Man with the Face." To close out his spot, Dale rode around the arena's perimeter shaking hands with all the eager youngsters he could reach. Frank Laswell often served as his wrangler.

Winston-Salem, North Carolina, in April of 1958, marked Dale's introduction to the busy schedule of a rodeo headliner. He arrived later than expected, missing a party in his honor hosted by a rodeo sponsor, the Hanes Knitting Company. Upon arrival, he excited employees by touring the Hanes plant and took in the sights at Old Salem. On a local TV program, he was presented with a Peacemaker hand weapon. In an interview, he promoted Western TV shows, citing *Cheyenne* and *Maverick* as among his personal favorites. He appeared at the local Buick dealership. He signed a photo of their old outfit for his former Army cook. Stuntman-double Tom McDonough served as his wrangler. The Men from Wells Fargo provided musical accompaniment.

Dale occasionally appeared in the rodeo arena with such stars as Gail Davis, Molly Bee or the LeGarde Twins. He played rodeos at many cities across the country and was often invited to return. He made at least two appearances each at the Texas Prison Rodeo; Charlotte, North Carolina; Louisville, Kentucky; Lafayette, Lake Charles and Shreveport, Louisiana; San Antonio, Texas; and Albuquerque, New Mexico.

Dale Robertson, star of TV's *Tales of Wells Fargo*, rides the arena perimeter to shake hands with admirers at the 1959 Pikes Peak or Bust Rodeo (photograph courtesy Pikes Peak Library District Local History Collection, Colorado Springs, CO. Stewarts #2390).

Dale Robertson at the 1959 rodeo at Fort Madison, Iowa (courtesy, and used with permission of, Tri-State Rodeo, Fort Madison, IA. Photographer unknown).

Dale often posed with, or was transported via, stagecoach. He greeted and exchanged gestures of affection with youngsters, visited disabled fans and led rodeo troupes to hospitals. At Charlotte, North Carolina, he met a six-year-old boy who shared his name, and greeted fans at a shopping center. At Winston-Salem in 1959, he supported headliner Gail Davis at the rodeo's final performance. At Sidney, Iowa, he sat in box seats with winners of a letter-writing contest. In Waco, following a welcome by the mayor and a group of Baylor coeds, he was guest of honor at a media luncheon with postcard writers and students representing area schools. He posed with inmate rodeo participants at the Texas Prison Rodeo, where a favorite among his songs was "Show Me the Way to Go Home." At Shreveport, he visited the Wells Fargo Bank Museum. In 1960, Dale and Rex Allen alternated daily stints as arena director at the National Roping Finals in Scottsdale, Arizona. That year, he appeared at Los Angeles' one-day Sheriff's Rodeo and at the ten-day Grand National at San Francisco's Cow Palace. At Nampa, he presided over the award of a pony. He was photographed with rodeo queens, suffered the indignity of faulty sound amplification systems, and performed in rain and mud, as necessary. Wherever he went, Dale drew sizable, enthusiastic crowds.

Dale experienced his share of strange happenings at rodeos. At Charlotte in 1959, it was reported that Dale "was lifting his voice in a pleading rendition of the ballad, 'Cool, Clear Water,' unaware that one of the rodeo clowns was perched high in the rigging of the Coliseum. As Robertson bore down on the chorus, the clown upended a tub of water that brought the song to a gurgling halt. With the customary nonchalance that has made Robertson a threat to the bad men of the West, he shook himself and continued his act."

The location of the following story has a way of changing; however, the principles remain the same. Hall of Fame rodeo announcer Mel Lambert was giving Dale a big build-up prior to the star's galloping entry into the arena. The crowd was stunned when he concluded with, "Ladies and gentlemen, Dale Evans." Mel counted this as his most embarrassing moment; the misidentified star told the crowd that anyone could make a mistake. Wells Fargo investigator Dale arrived for an Austin rodeo in 1961 to find a case waiting. His dressing room-horse trailer, on site earlier, had been burglarized and a transistor radio removed. At that rodeo, a roar from the crowd interrupted Dale's song performance when a little girl ran into the arena to ask for his autograph. At Houston, Dale was the rodeo headliner, but not directly involved, when snakes belonging to Indian dancers escaped from their handlers.

Often, the timing of Dale's airport arrivals and his appearances at local events were purposely kept secret or rescheduled to avoid his being mobbed by fans, but crowds greeted him anyway. He provided quotable comments to interviewers whether on the subject of a Western star's responsibility to uphold a wholesome image for young fans, the riding ability (or lack, thereof) of TV cowboy stars or the benefits to children of pets. In his peak rodeo years (1958–60), he performed at 10–12 rodeos per season. By 1961, when his TV series expanded to one hour, he had time for fewer rodeos. He continued rodeo appearances beyond the run of *Iron Horse*, appearing at the Brawley, California, Cattle Call and Imperial Valley Rodeo in November 1969. Rodeo fans fortunate enough to see Dale Robertson at a rodeo saw one of the finest riders of all Western stars.

ROY ROGERS (1911–98) Leonard Franklin Sly(e), born November 5, 1911, in Cincinnati, grew up on a houseboat near Portsmouth, on a farm at Duck Run, and then back in Cincinnati, all in Ohio. Early family life ingrained a strong work ethic, along with musical skills. By age ten, he was a square dance caller and shortly mastered yodeling. He rode the family horse Babe, raised a prize-winning 4-H pig and became an excellent marksman. He left high school to join his dad in shoe factory work. First on a family visit and then for good, Len went to California. As he landed Depression jobs driving a gravel truck and picking fruit, his family's musical talents found expression around migrant campfires. Len's musical ambitions were strong. He first performed at social events with his cousin. A talent show led to his joining the first of several musical groups. Following lean times, he formed the Pioneer Trio with noted Western composers Bob Nolan and Tim Spencer. The group, soon augmented by Hugh and Karl Farr, evolved prior to 1935 into the Sons of the Pioneers. Opportunities opened for radio, recordings and movies.

In the fall of 1937, Republic Studios signed Len, for $75 per week, as a singing cowboy. He arranged for Pat Brady to take his place with the Pioneers. Under the screen name Dick Weston, he appeared in a few films. When studio conflict with top Western star Gene Autry left a film without a leading man, Dick Weston became Roy Rogers and was elevated to stardom in *Under Western Stars* (1938). Shortly, Roy purchased Trigger, billed from 1943 as "The Smartest Horse in the Movies." He made personal appearances to publicize his films. Early films often took place in the historical Old West, and, in several, Roy was assigned a character name. Beginning in 1939, George "Gabby" Hayes boosted Roy's pictures for 27 consecutive films until *Ridin' Down the Canyon* (1942). Gabby not only lent lovable comic presence, but his reference to their past heroics gave youthful Roy added stature. Bob Nolan and the Sons of the Pioneers contributed to Roy's films starting with *Red River Valley* (1941), a film that signaled other changes: higher budgets, contemporary settings, calling Roy by his own name and a heavier emphasis on music.

Republic promoted Roy's career during Gene Autry's wartime military service. Art Rush's management also aided his success. Billed as "King of the Cowboys," he starred in a film with that title. With studio-generated publicity, Roy was the number one box office moneymaker among Western stars (by theater poll) from 1943 throughout his picturemaking career. *Life* magazine's cover showed him upon a rearing Trigger. He supported the war effort by selling bonds and entertaining servicepersons. He was heard on radio and recordings, made public appearances and marketed merchandise.

Band and radio singer Dale Evans began appearing in Roy's movies with *Cowboy and the Senorita* (1944). Shortly, she joined him on radio and at rodeos. When Gabby returned for *Lights of Old Santa Fe* (1944), the ensemble of Roy Rogers, Dale Evans, Gabby Hayes and the Sons of the Pioneers remained intact for 14 films through *Heldorado* (1946). When Roy's wife Arline died in November 1946 within days of giving birth to Roy Rogers, Jr., grieving Roy became a single father of three young children. His professional relationship with Dale became a personal friendship that grew into love. The two were married on New Year's Eve, 1947. As mother to Roy's children, in addition to a grown son from a previous marriage, Dale stayed home for a while, developing a strong Christian faith. She made six more films with Roy in 1949–50, and then left again to have a baby. She co-starred in Roy's final two Republic Westerns, making a total of 28 films with Roy. Dale composed the couple's theme song, "Happy Trails." Baby daughter Robin died in 1952 from complications resulting from Down's Syndrome. The couple subsequently adopted three children and took on a ward.

Apache Rose (1947) began a series of 19 films in Trucolor, a process that favored Trigger's golden palomino coat. Andy Devine was Roy's sidekick for nine films (1947–48). The Sons of the Pioneers bowed out with *Night Time in Nevada* (1948), having supported Roy in 41 pictures. For the next 13 films, Foy Willing and the Riders of the Purple Sage provided musical back-up. In the late 1940s and early '50s, Jane Frazee and Penny Edwards, among others, were leading ladies in Dale's absence. Roy's Republic series ended with *Pals of the Golden West* (1951). Between 1951 and 1957, more than 100 episodes of *The Roy Rogers Show* were filmed for TV, starring Roy, Dale, Pat Brady, Trigger, Bullet the dog and Nellybelle the Jeep. Comic books and extensive lines of merchandise continued to be big sellers. The TV show was syndicated through 1964. Roy starred in *Son of Paleface* (1952) with Bob Hope and Jane Russell. Roy and Dale's Christian values and patriotism became part of their public performances. They visited hospitals, orphanages, and special homes and schools for disabled children. The Sons of the Pioneers often joined them on personal appearances.

Two of Roy and Dale's adopted children died in separate tragedies in the 1960s. Dale authored several books on facing life's difficulties with faith. She witnessed at religious crusades and had a long-running Christian TV show, *A Date with Dale*. On TV, the couple starred in musical and rodeo specials, and made guest appearances. In the 1960s, Roy loaned his name to roast beef restaurants, some still serving as of this writing. The couple visited U.S. troops in Vietnam and made recordings. In 1976, Roy starred in *Mackintosh and TJ*. In the mid–1980s, Roy and Dale introduced their films on the Nashville Network's *Happy Trails Theater*. One of Roy's final recordings was the album "Roy Rogers Tribute," featuring duets with contemporary country artists. In later years, Roy greeted fans at his Victorville museum. On July 6, 1998, Roy died of congestive heart failure. Despite suffering a stroke and other health problems, Dale continued to make public appearances until she passed away on February 7, 2001. The Roy Rogers-Dale Evans Museum relocated to Branson, Missouri.

Roy Rogers on the Rodeo Trail

In the fall of 1939, immediately after completing *Saga of Death Valley*, Roy Rogers flew to Little Rock. In a visit sponsored jointly by Arkansas independent theater owners and the rodeo director, he attended a meeting of local roundup clubs, met the rodeo queen, and was present for a matinee rodeo performance and the night revue. Roy was Palm Springs rodeo parade marshal in 1940 and 1941. He also appeared at 1941 California rodeos, which attracted numerous film stars. In the summer of 1942, Roy toured with Col. Jim Eskew's eastern rodeos. At Baltimore's outdoor arena, he earned respect by performing in a heavy downpour.

Upon Gene Autry's entry into the armed forces in 1942, Roy headlined the Garden rodeos with the Sons of the Pioneers. His wife Arline accompanied, visiting New York's sights. Wearing cushioned shoes into the hotel lobby, Trigger, holding a pencil in his mouth, "registered" by making an X. He then rode the elevator and sat down in a restaurant to eat oats. In the arena, Trigger performed tricks, Roy and Trigger joined a dramatic sketch with six Texas sponsor girls and Roy called a Gay Nineties square dance. In addition to his songs, Roy participated in the patriotic finale, "Cavalcade of the Men Who Made America." Roy and Trigger entertained at Bellevue Hospital and at the rodeo performance for disabled and underprivileged children. The rodeo drew record attendance. Roy and the Pioneers were guests at the Rodeo Fans of America convention and at the Stage Door Canteen.

While at Boston Garden, Roy visited Children's Hospital and the Chelsea Naval Hospital. He helped judge a coloring contest offering a pony, and autographed hats and rodeo tickets. He was a guest at the Coconut Grove nightclub, where less than a month later a horrific fire killed nearly 500 people, including Western star Buck Jones. The rodeo next was engaged at Buffalo, New York. Each child who bought a half-price ticket received a color photo of Roy and Trigger. Republic Pictures held a party in Roy's honor. Roy and Trigger performed for defense workers at the Curtiss-Wright aircraft plant, where Trigger was taken aboard a large troop transport plane. Trigger also rode an elevator to perform for children's hospital patients. Roy was exhausted by his first long-running, big-time rodeos and their extra demands. One day, so as not to be disturbed, he took a nap in his publicist's room. Contrary to his instructions, he was not awakened in advance of his performance. At the arena, his spot arrived and was postponed before frantic organizers roused him to appear.

In May 1943, Roy and Trigger led Las Vegas' Helldorado Days parade. In June, the National Council of Rodeo Fans of America, based on a poll of youngsters, was named for Roy. In July, Roy's one-day rodeo at the Los Angeles Coliseum featured Dale Evans and Allan Lane. At Madison Square Garden in the fall, a matinee was added to accommodate turn-away crowds. The rodeo included Polly Mills Burson, Buff Brady, Jr., and Jack Knapp. Roy sang "Home on the Range" with the ranch girls and a herd of longhorns. He entertained at the New York Infirmary for Women and Children and at Bellevue Hospital. At the performance for disabled and underprivileged children, contest animals were named for comic strip characters. The rodeo was telecast to area military hospitals. Roy's schedule included war bond drives, China Relief, servicemen's canteens, orphanages and hospitals. Trigger celebrated his birthday in the Dixie Hotel's Plantation Room. Roy attended the Rodeo Fans of America convention. Boston Garden followed.

Roy and the Cactus Cowboys starred at 1944 spring JE Rodeos, to include Akron, Pittsburgh, Washington, D.C., and Providence. In Washington, Roy visited Walter Reed Army

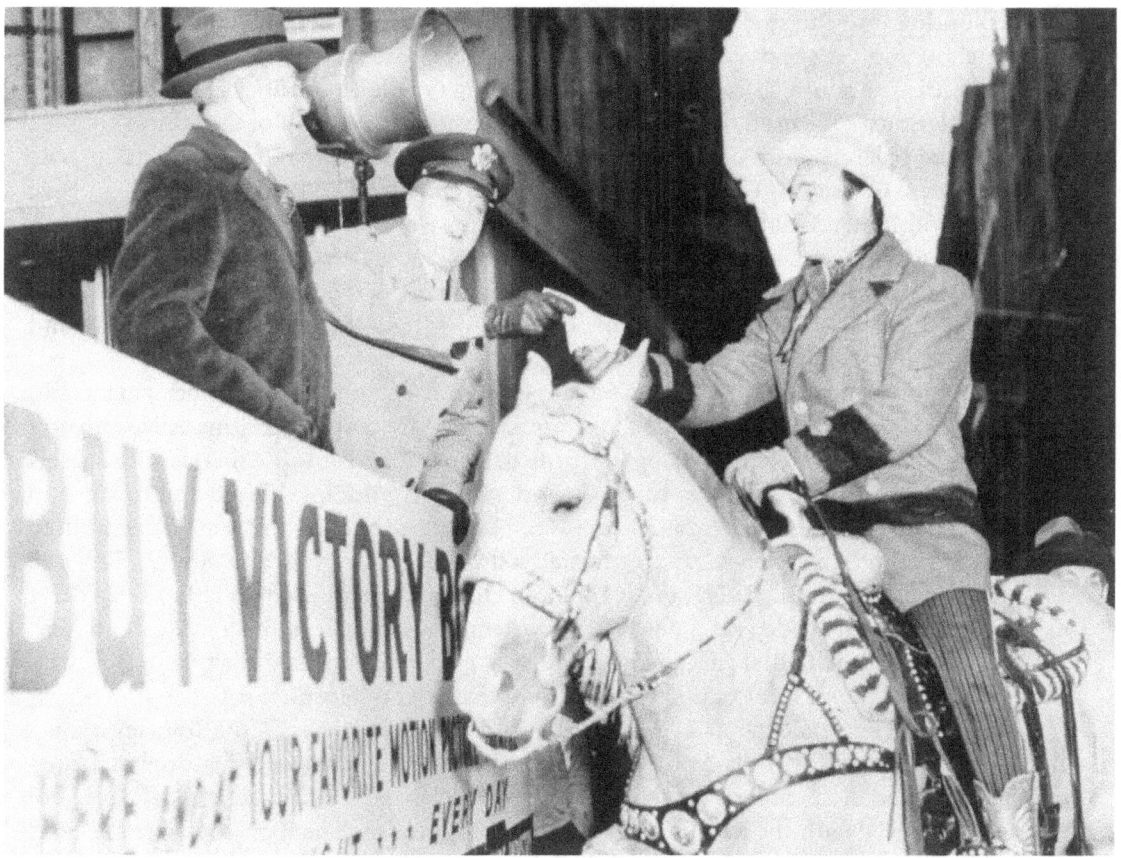

Headlining the 1945 Boston Garden rodeo, Roy Rogers and Trigger publicize the sale of Victory bonds by re-tracing Paul Revere's ride. Here, Roy accepts a bond from the drive chairman (*Herald-Traveler* photograph courtesy Boston Public Library, Print Department).

Hospital. Later, at Montreal's Forum, he split rodeo dates with radio's Lone Ranger. In July, his one-day rodeo at the Los Angeles Coliseum featured Dale Evans, the Sons of the Pioneers, "Wild Bill" Elliott and Hoot Gibson, with many other stars on hand. Roy presented a check for $23,000 to the Joe E. Brown fund for servicepersons' recreation. At Madison Square Garden in October, Foy Willing and the Riders of the Purple Sage backed Roy. Guest of honor at a party in the hotel's Grand Ballroom, Trigger performed dances and tricks. Roy entertained for *The New York Times* children's book program. He and the Sagers were a hit at the performance for underprivileged children and at Bellevue Hospital, where one lucky girl got to sit on Trigger. Roy was guest of honor at the fourth annual Rodeo Fans of America gathering. He attended a World Series game and the Broadway show *Oklahoma!* At Boston, he and rodeo personnel visited hospitals. Trigger ate from a "Victory" feed bag denoting a diet supporting the war effort.

Roy turned down a 1945 spring rodeo tour as his wife was expecting her first baby. In May, Roy, Dale, Gabby and the Sons of the Pioneers filmed *Heldorado* in Las Vegas during Helldorado Days. One detail to be worked out was a title acceptable to the movies' Hays censorship office. Las Vegas' officials rejected Republic's proposal to call the film *Eldorado*, as that meant loss of publicity for their celebration and rodeo. The solution: *Heldorado*, with one L removed. The Helldorado rodeo parade route was reversed so that movie cameras could avoid shooting into the sun. When Roy, Dale and other stars were scheduled to entertain in the Helldorado Village dance hall, thousands of spectators crowded the ground floor and the balconies. The south balcony collapsed, throwing people to the floor and injuring several, none seriously. Ground floor spectators were saved by a row of slot machines that kept the collapsed balcony from crushing them. Roy's second one-day rodeo was held in June at Los Angeles' Coliseum. Hoot Gibson was again arena director. Polly Mills Burson, Faye Johnson and Montie Montana performed. Celebrities were participants and spectators. A Victor McLaglen team participated in a chuckwagon race. Roy battled Leo Carrillo and "Wild Bill" Elliott in the chariot race finale. Proceeds supported Joe E. Brown's All-Pacific Recreation Fund. Roy performed at Col. Jim Eskew's Texas Rodeos at Philadelphia and Montreal.

Roy's fourth consecutive Madison Square Garden rodeo presented 49 performances in 33 days, a record. Ray Whitley and the Oklahoma Wranglers supported him. Alice Van and Buff Brady, Jr., trick-rode. Jack Knapp performed. The Rodeo Fans of America met in New York for the final time. At their special performance, two underprivileged children got to meet Roy and sit astride Trigger backstage. U.S. Navy personnel in uniform were admitted free to a special matinee. Dude ranches hosted a dinner for Roy and Mrs. Rogers. Roy and Trigger entertained disabled veterans at Halloran Hospital and opened a Victory Loan drive at Times Square. The rodeo set a new Garden attendance record. In Boston, Roy and Mrs. Rogers were guests at a hotel party. Roy appeared at a sporting goods department, was master of ceremonies for a local radio broadcast and visited City Hospital patients.

Introduced by Tex Ritter at a 1946 Houston rodeo performance, visitor Roy sang a song. In early September, Roy, Dale Evans and the Sons of the Pioneers were featured at a two-day Sheriff's Rodeo at the Los Angeles Coliseum. Later that month, allied with Col. Jim Eskew, Roy toured with the Roy Rogers Championship Rodeo. The first stop, with the Sons of the Pioneers and Rex Rossi, was at Philadelphia. At the next city, St. Louis, Dale Evans joined. Roy began broadcasts of a radio show from the road. At the final stop, Chicago, Gabby Hayes took a bow. Roy was guest at a fan club dinner. The day after this rodeo closed, Mrs. Arline Rogers gave birth to Roy Rogers, Jr. Six days later, she died.

In September 1947, the Roy Rogers Rodeo toured Philadelphia, Detroit (where Roy and Dale introduced their red, white and blue plastic saddles), St. Louis and Chicago. At this last stand, over a thousand were turned away. Youngsters became unruly, but calmed down when given ice cream and Roy Rogers buttons. The Sons of the Pioneers were on hand. Roy proposed to Dale during their arena introduction.

In August 1948, Roy and Dale headlined the one-day Los Angeles Sheriff's Rodeo, drawing that event's largest-ever attendance, over 100,000. Glenn Randall's Roy Rogers Liberty Horses were introduced to rodeo. In September, the Roy Rogers Rodeo toured with Col. Jim Eskew as arena director. The rodeo featured Dale Evans, as well as Foy Willing and the Riders of the Purple Sage. A vehicle driven by Glenn Randall caught fire on the turnpike, but there were no injuries to personnel or horses. At Detroit, a strike by ushers forced the cancellation of one performance. A sold-out Indianapolis rodeo performance accommodated a busload of 20 additional children when contestants' wives graciously shared their seats. At Chicago, Roy and Dale entertained at hospitals, including those for veterans. Roy made his annual $1,000 donation to RCA contest winners.

Roy curtailed his rodeo activity for the next few years. In the fall of 1949, Roy and Dale attended the Cal Farley Boy's Ranch Rodeo at Amarillo, Texas. In late January 1950, they were Fort Worth rodeo guests en route to headlining Houston's rodeo. Roy made time

Roy Rogers circles Boston Garden shaking hands with youngsters crowding the rail at 1955's rodeo (*Herald-Traveler* photograph courtesy Boston Public Library, Print Department).

for a coon hunt. Roy, Dale, Gabby, and Foy Willing and the Riders of the Purple Sage entertained, as did Trigger, Trigger, Jr., the Roy Rogers Liberty Horses and the Red Pony. In August, he headlined the Los Angeles Sheriff's Rodeo, telling a crowd of over 89,000 that his daughter Robin had been born the previous day. In 1951, Roy, Dale and Trigger entertained at Camp Pendleton's Marine Rodeo.

In 1952, Roy and Dale headlined two big rodeos. With Pat Brady, the Whipporwills, Trigger and the Roy Rogers Liberty Horses, they played the Houston rodeo despite concern over daughter Robin's health. Roy turned down a purchase offer of $200,000 for Trigger and introduced religious music to his arena act, singing "Peace in the Valley" while spotlights formed a cross. At one performance, he publicly answered a boy's letter asking whether or not Sunday school was for sissies. In August, Robin passed away. Shortly, Roy and Dale were rehearsing for their fall Madison Square Garden booking. Roy and Trigger, Dale and Buttermilk, Bullet, Pat Brady and Nellybelle performed, with music by the Whipporwills. A young English lad, writer of the winning essay "Why I would like to visit Roy Rogers," was Roy's guest for a week. Despite cautions, Roy sang, "How Great Thou Art." Such religious selections became a standard part of his personal appearances. After a six-year absence, he set a new Garden attendance record. Roy returned to Madison Square Garden in the fall of 1954. Trigger, Jr., and the Sons of the Pioneers were added. As he had in 1952, Roy donated a saddle to the champion bronc rider.

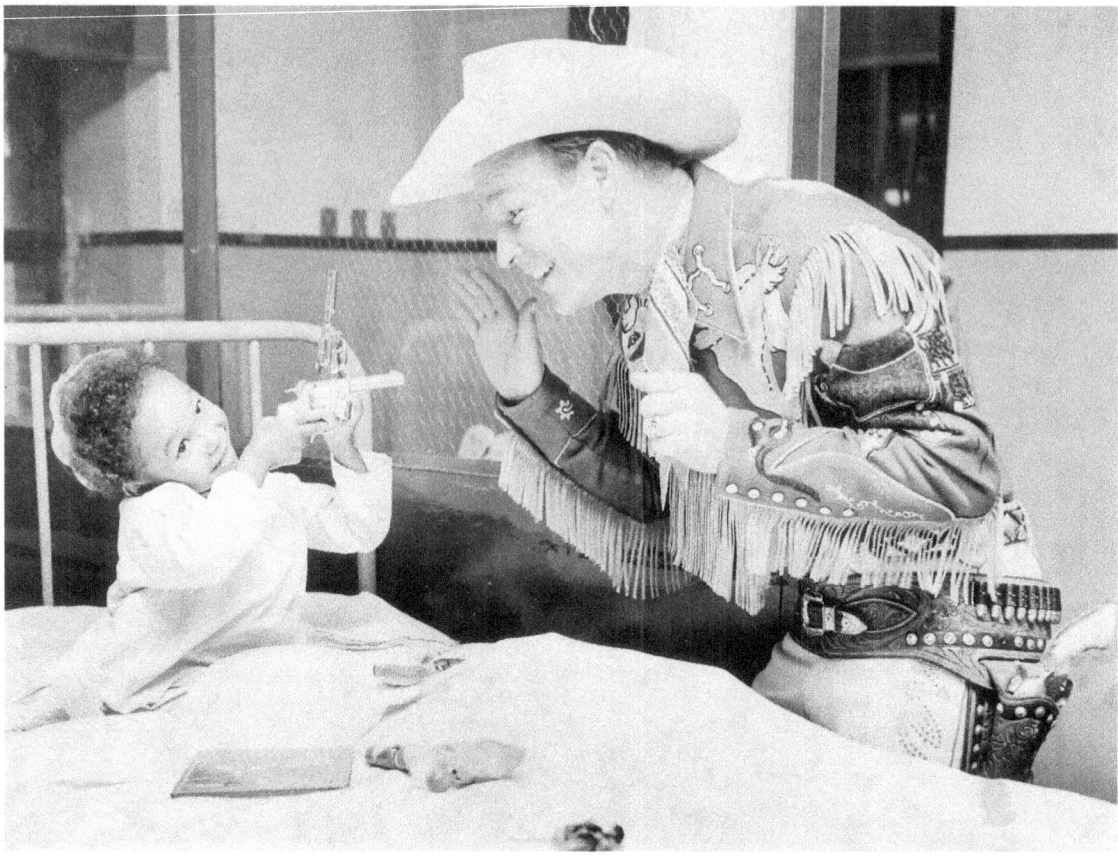

A three-year-old Boston City Hospital patient appears to have the drop on Roy Rogers, star of the 1955 Boston Garden rodeo (*Herald-Traveler* photograph by George Hoyt, courtesy Boston Public Library, Print Department).

A potentially dangerous incident occurred when a Garden rodeo gate was apparently intentionally narrowed as Dale Evans was making her brisk entrance into the arena. Her leg striking the gate drew blood, and Roy's ire let those in the vicinity know he meant business. Trigger, Jr., had an annoying habit of biting Roy's back when Roy was standing at the arena microphone, resulting in welts on the star's back and tears in his shirts. So cute was the horse in other ways that Roy could not bring himself to punish him.

In June 1955, the Roy Rogers Rodeo with the Sons of the Pioneers packed in spectators at San Antonio. NBC–TV made from the rodeo a one-hour program that was the network's first coast-to-coast telecast, reaching an estimated 50 million viewers. Roy and Dale headlined that summer's Los Angeles Sheriff's Rodeo. Fall brought Roy's troupe, less Dale, back to Madison Square Garden. Roy was selected for the Garden's Hall of Fame. After a ten-year absence, Roy returned for Boston Garden's silver anniversary rodeo.

Roy and Dale, leading fan voting, headlined Houston's 1956 rodeo, drawing standing-room-only crowds. The Sons of the Pioneers supported. In disguise, Roy visited livestock exhibits. Later that year, at the Iowa State Fair, Trigger took a spill on muddy ground as Roy was about to mount, but there were no injuries. The Roy Rogers troupe returned for Houston's 1957 silver anniversary rodeo. They completed a one-hour telecast of *The Chevy Show* and set a new attendance record. In the fall, Roy and cast headlined the twentieth

Dale Evans and Roy Rogers in a Houston rodeo parade, circa 1950s (photograph copyright Houston Metropolitan Research Center, Houston Public Library, Houston. Press #6158B).

anniversary of Albuquerque's New Mexico State Fair Rodeo, drawing huge crowds to the rodeo parade. Daughters Dodie and Debbie sang "Jesus Loves the Little Children," and Carl "Alfalfa" Switzer was in the cast. Roy's songs saluted various New Mexico towns. Meeting the owner of Trigger's grandfather, Roy learned that a Trigger ancestor was a Kentucky Derby winner. Roy entertained at an orphanage, a V.A. hospital and a hospital–training school. He visited Bernalillo County Indian Hospital and Presbyterian Association for Retarded Children. The rodeo broke attendance records.

Early in 1958, Roy, Dale and the Sons of the Pioneers were reunited at Fort Worth's rodeo with Gabby Hayes for an hour-long NBC *Chevy Show*. Rated highly, the show reached an estimated 8,000,000 viewers. Additional *Chevy Show*s were telecast at intervals from San Francisco's Cow Palace. Roy announced that Trigger, Jr., would succeed Trigger on personal appearances. Daughter Cheryl's high school graduation delayed Dale's arrival. In June, Roy, Pat Brady and the Sons of the Pioneers starred at Waco's Heart O'Texas Rodeo. Following the opening performance, Dale left for additional California graduations. In the fall, Roy and Dale made their seventh and final appearance at Madison Square Garden, with Pat Brady and the Sons of the Pioneers. Roy's shooting act was at times subject to sabotage. Sidekick Pat Brady modified shells to cause temporary embarrassment, and rodeo clowns were known to throw dead pigeons from the arena rafters.

Roy Rogers on bowing Trigger, Jr., at the Houston rodeo, circa 1950s (photograph copyright Houston Metropolitan Research Center, Houston Public Library, Houston. Press #6158B).

In the summer of 1959, Roy, Dale and four of their children arrived for Salt Lake City's Days of '47 Rodeo. Roy received a key to the city and attended a fishing rodeo for disabled children. The stars were provided first-class mobile living quarters adjacent to the arena. A pebbled path, lined with stones and potted plants, led to the arena entrance. To provide a little competition, rodeo clowns moved Jimmy Schumacher's well-worn trailer adjacent and installed a walkway decorated with old tires and tin cans planted with weeds. Roy and Dale responded with more amusement than rodeo officials. Fall brought them to the Iowa State Fair Rodeo. In 1960, Roy and Dale returned to Houston for one performance only. San Antonio's 1961 rodeo was nationally televised. In Houston for a physical check-up, Roy observed Rex Allen at that city's rodeo. In 1962, Roy and Dale celebrated the Calgary Stampede's fiftieth anniversary. In 1967, they headlined the Arkansas State Fair Rodeo. They appeared in 1968 and 1969 at rodeos in Houston's Astrodome, and at the 1969 Colorado State Fair Rodeo.

In the fall of 1970, Roy and Dale returned to Little Rock, Arkansas,' rodeo. In midsummer 1971, the couple's night shows celebrated Cheyenne Frontier Days' seventy-fifth anniversary. In 1972, they repeated at Houston's rodeo, followed by the Southeast Livestock Exposition Rodeo at Montgomery. With son Dusty, they headlined the 1973 Jaycee Bootheel Rodeo at Sikeston, Missouri, and Nampa's Snake River Stampede. Dusty joined Roy and

Dale in 1977 for the fiftieth anniversary of Omaha's Ak-Sar-Ben Rodeo, where the couple was inducted into the Western Hall of Fame. They returned to Omaha's rodeo in 1979. For most rodeo engagements in the 1960s and '70s, the Sons of the Pioneers accompanied Roy and Dale. By 1979, Roy was winding down his rodeo career. Dusty, who performed with his parents for several years, headlined Nampa's rodeo in 1986.

Roy's rodeo practices reflect the nature of the man. Often, he had trainer Glenn Randall exhibit Trigger outside the arena so that youngsters who couldn't afford a ticket could see his famous horse. Although rodeo organizers sought speedy performances, Roy typically took time circling the arena to touch as many outstretched hands as possible. When fatalities occurred among rodeo participants, he saw to proper arrangements, personally assisting with services and expenses. In addition to hospital visits, he telephoned and sometimes made home visits to ailing children. Roy signed many autographs, but was wary of signing for a never-ending crowd lest someone be disappointed. Finally, he stood for belief in God and country, singing inspirational songs and encouraging youngsters to attend Sunday school and say their prayers.

WILL ROGERS (1879–1935) The life of America's humorist Will Rogers has been chronicled in several books, a film and a Broadway musical. William Penn Adair Rogers was born in Indian Territory, now Oklahoma. His Cherokee heritage derived from both parents' ancestors. Will's father, a prosperous cattle rancher and a member of Oklahoma's constitution-drafting convention, gave Will his own pony at age five. Youthful advantages did not spare Will tragedy. By age ten, he had lost his older brother and his beloved mother. Growing up among Native American and black children, he learned riding and roping from a black cowboy in his father's employ.

With his father at Chicago's 1893 World's Fair, Will was inspired by a display of Mexican fancy roping at Buffalo Bill's Wild West Show. His restlessness and preference for roping led him shortly to abandon school. He honed his cowhand skills on ranches and trail drives, at riding and roping contests, and on the Argentine pampas. With Wild West Shows in South Africa, New Zealand and Australia, he was billed as "The Cherokee Kid." At the 1904 St. Louis World's Fair and at Madison Square Garden in 1905, Col. Zach Mulhall's Wild

America's humorist Will Rogers (courtesy Jerry Ohlinger's).

West Show put him in the company of Tom Mix and Bill Pickett. Will's roping expertise led to vaudeville, European tours, musical shows and the Ziegfeld Frolics and Follies for nearly 20 years. Over time, his acclaim and salary increased. Eventually his act relied on humorous observations on current events as he held his everpresent rope.

In 1908, Will married Betty Blake. In 1919, he made the first of 46 silent films in a three-year period. In *The Ropin' Fool* (1922), he demonstrated more than 50 rope tricks. Upon his return to the eastern stage, he supplemented performances with writing, radio broadcasts and speaking engagements. In 19 sound motion pictures for Fox studios, he avoided the role of action hero. By 1934, he was the top film star in terms of salary and box office receipts. He moved permanently to the West Coast. For recreation, he played polo and roped. He contributed to charitable fund-raising activities. His kindness to friends was renowned. When a 1928 airplane accident sidelined Fred Stone just prior to a show opening, Will stepped in, ad-libbing and singing for a number of performances.

Will, a frequent air traveler, died when a plane piloted by aviator Wiley Post crashed on a flight from Fairbanks to Point Barrow, Alaska. His death prompted an outpouring of public grief and honors. Statues by Jo Davidson stand in the U.S. Capitol and at Claremore, Oklahoma's, Will Rogers Memorial, dedicated in 1938 to honor Will's life. Oklahoma City's airport carries his name. The Rogerses' California ranch is a state park.

Will Rogers on the Rodeo Trail

As a young man, Will practiced and competed at roping and riding contests. Later, he attended rodeos across the country. Squatting on his haunches to jaw with contestants, observing from a fence rail or chatting with children, he shunned the celebrity role. At times, he added to the roping purse. Among Will's effects upon his death was a rodeo program from the last day he spent with his family.

THE SONS OF THE PIONEERS In 1931, the singing Rocky Mountaineers included Leonard Slye and Bob Nolan. When Bob left the struggling group in late 1932, Tim Spencer took his place. The aggregation underwent name changes. In late 1933, Len and Tim convinced Bob to rejoin them as the Pioneer Trio. The three rehearsed long and hard to perfect their harmony, timing and phrasing. Bob and Tim were accomplished composers, as well as vocalists. Bob's classic "Tumbling Tumbleweeds" became the trio's radio theme song. Fiddler Hugh Farr joined in 1934 to strengthen the instrumental background. Rechristened "The Sons of the Pioneers" by a radio announcer, the group (no longer a trio) began making radio transcriptions and recordings. By 1935, they had appeared in a motion picture. Guitarist Karl Farr was added in 1936. Bob Nolan wrote "Cool Water," and the Sons of the Pioneers appeared in more films. Tim Spencer left the group in the fall of 1936, but returned in 1939. His replacement was Lloyd Perryman.

In 1937, when co-founder Leonard Slye left to become Republic Pictures' star "Roy Rogers," Pat Brady filled the vacancy. Through 1941, the group supported Charles Starrett in his Columbia films. Bob and Tim composed songs to fit movie storylines. Following a tour, the group spent a year on radio in Chicago and made more recordings. From 1941 through 1948, they joined Roy Rogers in Republic musical Westerns.

In 1948, the Pioneers began to meet a rising demand for live performances. Neither Tim nor Bob enjoyed touring. Tim retired as a performer in 1949, although he remained the Pioneers' manager. Ken Curtis took over his spot. Shortly, a replacement for Bob was found in the person of Tommy Doss, whose voice was remarkably similar to Bob's. When

Early Sons of the Pioneers group (clockwise from lower left): Tim Spencer, Hugh Farr, Pat Brady, Bob Nolan, Karl Farr and Lloyd Perryman.

Roy Rogers tapped Pat Brady to be his movie and TV sidekick, Shug Fisher served in Pat's stead. The musical trio now consisted of Lloyd Perryman, Ken Curtis and Tommy Doss. Shug, on bass, provided comedy. Of the early pioneer aggregation, only the Farr brothers remained.

In 1950, the Pioneers joined Rex Allen's radio show, which in time became their program, *The Lucky U Ranch*. The group provided background music for the film *Wagonmaster* (1950), singing a number of Stan Jones' compositions, and for *Fighting Coast Guard* (1951). They appeared in *Everybody's Dancin'* (1950) with Spade Cooley and in the John Ford–John Wayne film *Rio Grande*. In 1951, the Pioneers performed in concert at New York City's Carnegie Hall and on national TV shows. In early 1953, they left the radio show to Ken Curtis and Shug Fisher. To replace Ken, the group selected Dale Warren, who leads the Pioneers at this writing. The recording Pioneers did not always match the touring group.

Hugh Farr took leave of the Pioneers in the latter part of 1958. Karl Farr suffered a fatal heart attack in 1961 while performing. The departure of Tommy Doss opened a spot for young Rusty Richards to serve the first of two tenures with the group. Rusty had ridden bulls in rodeos, served in the Marines and worked as a movie stuntman. He yodeled, in addition to his tenor vocals. As one solid performer left the group, another joined to carry on the Pioneer tradition.

Celebrating their seventieth anniversary in 2004, the Sons of the Pioneers still perform as of this writing. In later years, they alternated between a chuckwagon dinner spot in Tucson, Arizona (winters) and a theater in Branson, Missouri (summers). Continuing to win acclaim from fans old and new, the Pioneers have accumulated many honors and tributes. The National Cowboy Hall of Fame presented the group with a Wrangler Award and later inducted them into the Hall of Great Western Performers. They were honored with a star on Hollywood's Walk of Fame. In 1979, they were declared a "national treasure" when they performed at the Smithsonian Institution in Washington, D.C. In 1980, the original Sons of the Pioneers were inducted into Nashville's Country Music Hall of Fame. The current group received a Golden Boot Award.

The Sons of the Pioneers on the Rodeo Trail

Bob Nolan and the Sons of the Pioneers supported Roy Rogers in 1942 and 1943 at the World Championship Rodeos in New York and Boston. They performed for patients at Bellevue Hospital, for underprivileged and disabled children, and for Rodeo Fans of America conventions. In 1942, additional dates in Buffalo extended the rodeo tour to nearly two months. Lloyd Perryman and Pat Brady saw wartime service. In 1946 at Las Vegas, the Pioneers, with Roy and cast, filmed scenes for *Heldorado* around the Helldorado Days rodeo. They joined Roy Rogers at the one-day Los Angeles Sheriff's Rodeo and for his fall tour with Jim Eskew's rodeo. In 1947, they and "Wild Bill" Elliott were at Cheyenne Frontier Days. In the fall, they again supported Roy's big-city rodeo appearances. In 1949, they provided music for William "Hopalong Cassidy" Boyd's Philadelphia rodeo. They played at Elko's Stockman's Hotel during the 1951 Silver State Stampede. Headlining the Snake River Stampede at Nampa, Idaho, they varied song selections each night. Solos were appreciated, and the group drew calls for encores. Fans admired them for viewing the rodeo from the announcer's stand when not performing.

In 1952, the Pioneers' performances included rodeos at Mandan, Pueblo and Miles City. Following the latter rodeo, they rode out on the stock contractor's ranch to help round up horses. Stock handlers had a laugh at their expense as the singers' real cowboy skills left

A later Sons of the Pioneers aggregation, circa 1970s. (Top, left to right) Dale Warren, Rusty Richards, Billy Liebert; (bottom, left to right) Roy Lanham, Rome Johnson (courtesy Snake River Stampede, Nampa, ID).

something to be desired. One got lost for a time, the legs of others were skinned and, for a spell, all had a reluctance to sit down. At Pueblo, the press noted Ken Curtis' Colorado birth. Shug Fisher and Lloyd Perryman were pictured greeting parade guests Fred Harman (as Red Ryder) and Little Beaver. That year, the Pioneers supported Rex Allen at Los Angeles' Sheriff's Rodeo.

A 1953 engagement was the rodeo in Ranger, Texas, acclaimed as the home of the Farr brothers. The group entertained at the Pikes Peak or Bust Rodeo, the Central Wyoming Fair Rodeo and the Colorado State Fair Rodeo. At Colorado Springs, the group performed at an Alamo hotel luncheon, at Camp Carson hospital wards and at an in-home concert for an invalid woman. By popular demand they were signed for the second consecutive year at the State Fair Rodeo. For a publicity photo, Colorado's governor watched a 4-H girl milk a cow to Hugh Farr's fiddle accompaniment. In 1954, the group backed Gene Autry at the Los Angeles Sheriff's Rodeo. Later that fall, they performed at Madison Square Garden with Roy Rogers, Dale Evans and former Pioneer Pat Brady, now known for driving the Jeep Nellybelle.

In 1955, the Pioneers supported Roy Rogers at San Antonio's rodeo. The final day's performance was telecast. They headlined the Charles M. Russell Rodeo at Great Falls, Montana, appeared with Roy Rogers and Dale Evans at the Los Angeles Sheriff's Rodeo, and supported Roy and Pat Brady at Madison Square Garden and Boston Garden. Early in 1956, the Pioneers joined Roy and Dale to entertain packed houses at Houston's rodeo. That summer, they shared billing at the Snake River Stampede with Gail Davis. Tommy Doss completed his song at a veteran's hospital before leaving for his mother's funeral.

The 1957 Houston Silver Jubilee Rodeo brought back Roy, Dale, Pat and the Sons of the Pioneers. The troupe starred in the first of a series of hour-long *Chevy Show*s broadcast from rodeos at Fort Worth, Houston and San Francisco. In the fall, the same stars reunited for the New Mexico State Fair Rodeo, where Karl Farr was acclaimed as a onetime state resident. Capacity and standing-room-only crowds set attendance records. The stars put on shows at an orphanage, a veteran's hospital and a training school. In 1958, the billing "Roy Rogers and the Sons of the Pioneers" still held magic for fans. At Fort Worth's rodeo early that year, the hour-long NBC-TV *Chevy Show* telecast from the rodeo's final performance reunited the Pioneers with Roy, Dale and Gabby Hayes. The Pioneers supported Roy at Waco, Madison Square Garden and the Cow Palace's *Chevy Show*.

In 1959, the Pioneers did two TV *Chevy Show*s with Roy and Dale, one from the Fort Worth rodeo, the other from the Cow Palace. Between these events, they performed at Salt Lake City's Days of '47 Rodeo. Another *Chevy Show* was telecast from the Cow Palace in 1960. Through the 1960s, the Sons of the Pioneers entertained at rodeos as the headline attraction, or supporting Roy Rogers. Occasionally they shared the arena spotlight with other Western stars such as Rex Allen (at Casper), Fess Parker (at Little Rock and Camdenton) and James Drury (at Fort Worth). Twice they joined Roy and Dale at the Houston Astrodome. They entertained at rodeos at Jasper and San Angelo, Texas, and at Clear Lake, South Dakota. They played return engagements at the New Mexico State Fair Rodeo and the Pikes Peak or Bust Rodeo. Twice each, they returned to rodeos at the Colorado State Fair and Burwell, Nebraska.

The 1970s found the Pioneers still working rodeos. They performed twice at Montgomery, Alabama's, rodeo, with Doug McClure and with Roy Rogers, respectively. In 1971, they joined Roy and Dale at the seventy-fifth edition of Cheyenne Frontier Days. They supported Roy at the Jaycee Bootheel Rodeo and at the Snake River Stampede. They also backed

Rex Allen in Nampa and Rex Allen, Jr., at the Pikes Peak or Bust Rodeo. Twice they appeared with Roy at the Ak-Sar-Ben Rodeo in Omaha. In 1974, the Pioneers were inducted into the Ak-Sar-Ben Western Hall of Fame. They starred at the Days of '47 Rodeo. In 1979, they performed with Rex Allen and other celebrities at the ProRodeo Hall of Fame's opening gala.

Dale Warren recalled the mechanism breaking down on a revolving rodeo stage, tilting the stage so far that the group had to stand uphill to perform. During a lightning storm at Colorado Springs, the Pioneers huddled in a booth, trying to make "Cool Water" heard above the crash of thunder. That song being a standard part of their repertoire, the Pioneers were victims of water dumped by rodeo clowns. Still filling rodeo bookings in the 1980s, the Pioneers celebrated 50 years in show business.

Personnel change; however, the name is legendary and the sound touches a responsive chord in fans' hearts. They made return appearances at several rodeos, such as Colorado Springs, Montgomery, Salt Lake City, San Francisco and Fort Worth (twice). In 1986, they went to Nampa for a sixth time to support Roy "Dusty" Rogers, Jr. Fans who experienced the Sons of the Pioneers entertaining in the rodeo arena know that they have heard the best Western singing group of all time.

FRED STONE (1873–1959) Fred Stone was born in a sod house on a ranch near Valmont, Colorado. By age five, he could ride a horse and shoot a rifle. An athletic lad, he began show business at age 11 as a circus acrobat and tightrope walker. From vaudeville, he became a musical comedy stage star, delighting audiences with new physical stunts in each show. He appeared in silent and sound films and on radio. He and Will Rogers were friends, sharing interests in riding, roping, polo, flying and rodeos. In a 70-year career, Fred was best known for his athletic influence on the musical stage, but he also had strong cowboy credentials. In Hollywood, he made silent films, doing his own stunts, whether circus aerial work or riding a bucking horse. A heart attack claimed his life.

Fred Stone on the Rodeo Trail

Frequenting rodeos, Fred Stone considered himself just another cowboy. He had worked on a Texas ranch and competed at the Dewey (Oklahoma) rodeo. His company filmed the Western *The Duke of Chimney Butte* in Wyoming in 1919. Fred could pick up a handkerchief at a gallop and vault from one side of a horse to the other. For this picture, he learned in a day to bulldog a steer. He competed in a ranch rodeo, and then entered bulldogging, bronc riding and steer roping events and the wild horse race at Cheyenne Frontier Days. He presented the champion steer rider with "the Fred Stone Trophy," a Colt single action revolver. Among other rodeos, he viewed the 1941 Madison Square Garden rodeo.

Actor Fred Stone.

MERLE TRAVIS (1917–83)

The son of a coal miner, Merle Travis was an influential guitarist and a composer of popular songs, including "Sixteen Tons." He headlined Ardmore, Oklahoma's, 1956 rodeo and performed at a 1957 Milwaukee rodeo with Gene Autry.

JIMMY WAKELY (1914–82)

James Clarence Wakeley was born at Mineola, Arkansas, and known in early years by his middle name, Clarence. His family moved, residing in different Oklahoma towns. He grew up in hard country during hard times, picking cotton with his parents and farming. He walked behind a mule and plow, slept on a dirt floor pallet and watched families' livelihoods destroyed by dust storms. To help his family eke out a living, he left school to work on the road or in the fields. Slight of build, he was not well-fed and had bouts of disease,

Merle Travis, singer, guitarist, composer.

including malaria. Through determined effort, he followed his love of music to a better life. He learned to play guitar as a youngster. When the family was given a piano, he taught himself to play. Although music was not a typical home activity, his parents liked to hear him play and sing.

In 1932, Clarence made his first 15-minute radio performance. The family sharecropped, and at church he sang, taught music classes, directed the choir and played the organ, accepting meals as payment for lessons. He performed with quartets and published some gospel compositions without payment. He sang duets with Inez, who played piano at church and was one of his vocal students. Meanwhile, he worked at a gas station. In 1935, he married Inez, a source of support and a musical partner throughout his life. Together they raised four children. He reverted to his first name of James, and then went by Jimmy, while shortening his last name to Wakely. A Stillwater talent contest led to radio work. By 1936 he played piano in Oklahoma City on weekends with Merle Salathiel and his Barnyard Boys. On a 15-minute radio spot during the week, he sang popular and cowboy songs for meager pay. He hitchhiked through snow to see Gene Autry in performance.

Jimmy joined The Bell Boys, a trio sponsored by Bell Clothing Stores, on a 15-minute Oklahoma City morning radio show. Johnny Bond soon joined the trio. The show expanded to five days a week and lasted about three years. The trio was an opening act for visiting stars. In Hollywood, they made recordings and appeared in a Roy Rogers film. By late 1939 they had made transcriptions and had appeared on television. Jimmy was ambitious, a convincing spokesman, and learned the music business. Back in Oklahoma, Jimmy had his trio perform on stage with Gene Autry and got Gene to appear on their radio show. Gene invited them to try out for his *Melody Ranch* radio program. In Hollywood, the group found spots in Western films with the Range Busters and others. When their audition failed to win sponsor acceptance, Gene arranged for a two-week trial that won Mr. Wrigley's approval. For two years, as Melody Ranch Boys, they worked with Gene on radio and on personal appearances.

Jimmy wrote songs, recorded transcriptions and played some weekends with a Western band at the Aragon Ballroom. He had a hit recording of his composition "Too Late." The trio appeared in films with Western stars. Shortly before Gene Autry entered military service, Jimmy left for additional Western films. Jimmy and Gene remained lifelong friends. During World War II, Jimmy was active in celebrity war bond drives. He appeared in support of Western film stars. His rising screen presence and a recommendation from Phil Isley (Jennifer Jones' father) helped secure a contract with Monogram studios. Beginning with *Song of the Range* (1944), he starred in a series of 28 singing cowboy films, building a loyal fan base and giving a start to cowboy star Whip Wilson. In 1949, following a period of unfair treatment, his relationship with the studio ended.

As Jimmy wrapped up his film series, his recording career was on the rise. Following a string of hit records, his 1948 Capitol recording of Eddie Dean's composition "One Has My Name, The Other Has My Heart," rose to number one on the country charts. In 1949, "Slipping Around" was a smash hit for the duet of Jimmy and Margaret Whiting. The two made several hit records. Jimmy's recording success led to a career as a popular singer, although he never totally lost his cowboy image. He had a CBS radio show for several years, toured military bases with Bob Hope and provided music for a few Western films. He was featured, often with his family, on Armed Forces Radio beamed to service members overseas, and appeared on Tex Ritter's musical TV show. He founded Shasta Records, served as a music publisher, recorded songs and performed at nightclubs. After suffering from a lung condition for several years, Jimmy passed away of heart failure at Mission Hills, California.

Jimmy Wakely on the Rodeo Trail

Jimmy entertained with Gene Autry at Madison Square Garden, Boston Garden and other rodeos in 1940 and 1941. According to the 1992 biography *See Ya Up There, Baby* by daughter Linda Lee, Jimmy missed his family while on the road. With Johnny Bond at Madison Square Garden in 1940, he co-wrote the song "I've Got Those Gone and Left Me Blues." In an interview with author David Rothel for *The Singing Cowboys*, Jimmy rated his time with Gene Autry as the most personally satisfying of his career.

Jimmy provided music for the Sunset Ranch Rodeo and Dance in June 1943. In 1946, he was on hand for Las Vegas' Helldorado Days. In 1947, Jimmy Wakely and his Saddle Pals starred at the Lakeland, Florida, rodeo. In the parade, he rode in an open convertible. Billed as "Monogram's Sensational Singing Star," he starred at the Chicago Championship Rodeo at Soldier Field that same year. A theater played his film *Song of the Wasteland*. Wesley Tuttle and his Texas Stars supported. The American Legion–sponsored rodeo benefited a convalescent center for disabled veterans. Provided a horse and a $2,500 saddle for the engagement, Jimmy, with his Saddle Pals, headlined the 1948 Will Rogers Rodeo at Claremore, Oklahoma, entertaining at a Chamber of Commerce luncheon. That year,

Jimmy Wakely on the program cover for the 1954 Snake River Stampede (used with permission of the Snake River Stampede).

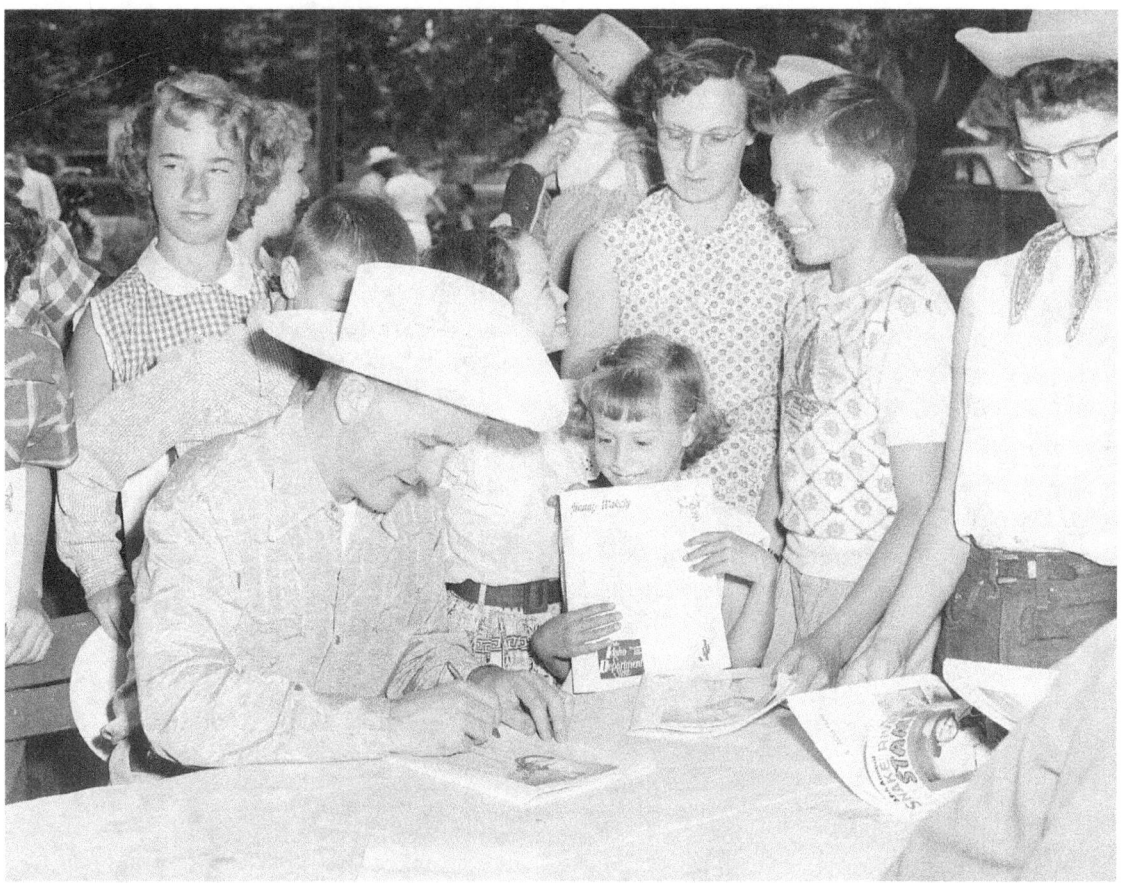

Jimmy Wakely autographs for fans at the 1954 Snake River Stampede (Photo Shop photograph courtesy, and used with permission of, the Snake River Stampede, Nampa, ID. Photographer unknown).

at Dallas' State Fair of Texas rodeo, Jimmy and Western leading lady Wanda McKay starred and visited the Children's Hospital polio ward. They drew record crowds despite poor weather. With Monte Hale, Jimmy headlined Oklahoma City's 1949 March of Dimes Benefit Rodeo.

Jimmy and his Saddle Pals starred at the 1954 Snake River Stampede at Nampa, Idaho. He chatted with youngsters at the Buckaroo Breakfast. He sang a medley of songs from the 1940s onward. One evening, he called upon a 14-year-old local girl to join him in duets, keeping his voice low to better showcase her talent. Prior to exiting the arena on horseback, Jimmy confessed to the crowd that he hadn't been on a horse in a year and had not practiced in preparation for the rodeo. He commented, "You've seen movie cowboys ride — I've seen 'em thrown." To close out his act at another performance, he said, "You've seen movie cowboys shoot from the hip and kill a bandit at 150 yards." Then, with the help of the light operator, he "shot" out the lights. He visited patients at Samaritan Hospital. At the final performance, he introduced rodeo producer Gene Autry. Children joined Gene in singing "Rudolph the Red-Nosed Reindeer." Attendance for the rodeo was the largest to date for that locality.

In the fall of 1956, supported by The Three Rays, Jimmy headlined the Arkansas Livestock Exposition Rodeo. Early the following year, he starred at the Southwest District Livestock Show Rodeo at Lake Charles, Louisiana. At one performance, he spent 20 minutes

Singing cowboy Jimmy Wakely (right) performs with The Three Rays at the 1956 Arkansas State Fair and Livestock Show Rodeo (Johnnie M. Gray photograph, obtained from the Arkansas State Fair and Livestock Show, Little Rock, AR, used with permission of Kermit Gray).

convincing a doorman that he should be allowed to enter the arena without a ticket. In his act, he shunned horseback riding. He sang such songs as "Young Love," "Ghost Riders in the Sky," "Singing the Blues," "Heartbreak Hotel" and "Slipping Around." He updated his repertoire, finding that recently popular hits drew the warmest response. Jimmy visited area schools and hospitals. A record crowd attended the second performance, with 600 would-be patrons turned away. A month later, he appeared at the Phoenix rodeo. That summer, he was star of the Central Wyoming Fair Rodeo at Casper, where he visited a hospital children's ward. In 1958, Jimmy starred at the Shasta County Sheriff's Rodeo at Redding, California, finding a name for his record company, originally called Shastone.

In 1958, 1959, 1961 and 1963, Jimmy was associated with the New Mexico State Fair

Rodeo, serving in various capacities. As a scout and organizer of talent, he helped bring in TV Western stars and such popular singers as Margaret Whiting and The Andrews Sisters. He toured the state providing publicity, served as master of ceremonies or starred. For the parade, he rode in a red sports car. In 1963, he, Rex Allen and others did a special show on the V.A. hospital lawn. Jimmy starred at the 1960 San Joaquin County Fair Rodeo. In the fall of 1964, 15 years after he last starred in a singing cowboy movie, he headlined three days of Omaha's Ak-Sar-Ben Rodeo. Daughter Linda Lee and son Johnny joined him. Jimmy omitted boots, but wore a Western tie. He sang Western-flavored songs such as "Cool Water," "Tumbling Tumbleweeds" and "Tennessee Waltz." He was inducted into the Ak-Sar-Ben Western Hall of Fame. In 1975, he performed one day at the California Rodeo at Salinas.

CLINT WALKER (1927–) Born Norman Eugene Walker in Hartford, Illinois, Clint grew up in Alton. After-school jobs left no time for sports. He left high school for full-time employment. Following Merchant Marine service from 1944 to 1947, Clint found meager earnings in Texas construction and ranching. As a Las Vegas law officer and bouncer, he made Hollywood connections. Following his 1954 film debut, he played a pharaoh bodyguard in *The Ten Commandments*. Warner Brothers bought his contract and changed his name. He won the part of Cheyenne Bodie, a character (like Clint) of partial Native American heritage, on TV's *Cheyenne*, the lone success in a group of rotating shows. When his situation became intolerable, Clint gave notice and walked out on the series in 1958, returning in 1959. He concluded the show's run of 108 episodes in 1962.

Clint starred in the films *Fort Dobbs* (1958), *Yellowstone Kelly* (1959) and *Gold of the Seven Saints* (1961). Following the *Cheyenne* series, his additional films included *The Night of the Grizzly* (1966), a family adventure story he suggested. On the set, he accidentally cut his foot with an axe. Clint was said to be an expert pistol shot and handy at throwing a knife and lariat. He returned to TV in the 1970s for the series *Kodiak* and the mini-series *Centennial*. He made an occasional film into the 1980s. He appeared in commercials and the TV film *The Gambler Returns: The Luck of the Draw* (1991). In a skiing accident, a pole pierced Clint's heart. Scar tissue led to later complications and open-heart surgery. As film roles became less frequent, Clint retired to a modest Northern California ranch. He attends Western film fan gatherings. He received a Golden Boot Award and co-authored a Western novel.

"Cheyenne" on the Rodeo Trail

Clint Walker was grand marshal of the 1956 Los Angeles Sheriff's Rodeo. During the 1958 Fort Worth rodeo, he was in town promoting *Fort Dobbs*. After his walkout, Clint reportedly received an improved share of rodeo receipts. He was a solid performer who could be counted upon to raise interest and rodeo ticket sales. In his rodeo act, he sang, and played the guitar and harmonica. About his rodeo singing, he quipped, "I'll scare the stock a little." He typically rode a horse in and out of the arena, and circled the arena on horseback to shake hands.

Shortly after injuring his back on a *Cheyenne* episode, Clint arrived at the 1961 Arkansas-Oklahoma Rodeo in Fort Smith. On doctor's orders, he did not ride. So as not to disappoint fans, he walked the fence line to shake hands. He hosted an informal party for rodeo queens and contestants. In the arena, his singing and friendly personality were well-received, and he signed autographs following each performance. Johnnie Lee Wills

Clint Walker of the "Cheyenne" series and a young pony contest participant at the 1962 Snake River Stampede, Nampa, Idaho. (*Idaho Free Press* [Nampa, ID] photograph by Chapin Studio, obtained from Snake River Stampede and used with permission of Idaho Free Press).

band provided additional music. At the J Bar H Rodeo in Camdenton, Missouri, Clint split headlining duties with the team of Lorne Greene and Dan Blocker. That summer, he played the Northwest Championship Rodeo in St. Paul, Minnesota. In 1962, he entertained at Sidney, Iowa, and at Nampa's Snake River Stampede, which his father attended.

In 1963, Clint appeared at the Southwest District Stock Show Rodeo at Lake Charles, where he substituted for Dan Blocker, who was ill. For four performances, fans were treated to the pairing of Clint and Lorne Greene. He headlined the Phoenix (Arizona) Jaycee Rodeo and the Mid-South Fair Rodeo in Memphis, where he told crowds he watched *Gunsmoke*. At the 1963 Heart O'Texas Fair Rodeo, Clint replaced *Laramie* star John Smith, who left for Europe to film *Circus World*. Clint proclaimed upon arrival in Waco, "I know he would have done the same for me, so here I am." He held an arrival press conference, rehearsed at the arena, hosted a dinner party for area students, worked out at a health studio, posed for pictures and toured fair exhibits. At the arena microphone, he dedicated songs to polio patients and other invalids. When questioned about his size, Clint expressed his view that it is more important "how big a man is on the inside." On the rodeo trail, Clint Walker was a man to be respected for more than his imposing frame.

JOHN WAYNE (1907–79)   John Wayne starred in low-budget Westerns and serials in the 1930s. He experienced a major career break playing the Ringo Kid in John Ford's *Stagecoach* (1939), and then established himself as a star, mostly in war movies and Westerns. He remained in Hollywood's top ten for 16 years, winning a Best Actor Oscar for *True Grit*

John Wayne in the stands at a 1960 Texas Prison Rodeo at Huntsville. On the right is his *The Alamo* co-star, Frankie Avalon (courtesy Texas Department of Criminal Justice).

(1969). In his final film, *The Shootist* (1976), he portrayed a gunfighter facing terminal cancer, but determined to go out with dignity. Wayne had survived earlier surgeries for cancer and heart problems, but succumbed to a recurrence of cancer. Five decades of screen fame gave John Wayne the status of legend.

John Wayne on the Rodeo Trail

In 1939, John Wayne visited the Saugus (California) Rodeo and rode around the arena. Harry Carey was grand marshal. Director John Ford, Ward Bond and Montie Montana were on hand. In 1946, Wayne and Joanne Dru led a rodeo grand entry at Sonoita, Arizona. Grand marshal Wayne and rodeo queen Jane Russell led the grand entry at the 1948 Los Angeles Sheriff's Rodeo, where Wayne's children met rodeo headliner Gene Autry. Spring of 1950 saw Nevada's governor present Wayne and John Ford with Reno's first Silver Spurs Awards for *She Wore a Yellow Ribbon* (1949).

In the fall of 1960, following Texas location filming for *The Alamo*, John Wayne and co-star Frankie Avalon were present for the Texas Prison Rodeo. John joined Mrs. Bond at Reno, Nevada, in June 1961 when the Silver Spurs Award was presented posthumously to old friend Ward Bond. In 1966 in Reno, he received his second Silver Spurs Award, the last presented for several years. Prescott, Arizona's, rodeo honored him in 1974 with a program cover showing Bill Nebecker's bronze of Wayne cast by Ernie Phippen. The rodeo's champion all-around cowboy received a copy of the bronze. On the Fourth of July weekend of the bicentennial year 1976, in Cody, Wyoming, Wayne helped dedicate the Winchester Arms Museum at the Buffalo Bill Historical Center, served as parade grand marshal for the Cody Stampede and awarded prizes of Winchesters to the rodeo's champions. He was presented a Winchester model 94, .22 caliber rifle at the final rodeo performance. The 1980 Prescott rodeo was dedicated to his memory.

RAY WHITLEY (1901–79) Born in Atlanta, Georgia, Ray Whitley shortly moved to a ranch near Ashland, Alabama. He attended country school, sang in the church choir and rode 50 miles for supplies. Following U.S. Navy service, he married and traveled, pursuing such occupations as electrician, structural steel worker and ranch hand. Music was an avocation. In 1929, he moved to New York City, where his labor contributed to such landmarks as the Empire State Building and the George Washington Bridge. When the Depression slowed construction, he pursued his vocal and guitar talents on radio and with bands. He continued steel construction, when available. From the early 1930s, he made recordings and films and performed on radio. An accomplished horseman and bullwhip expert, he was sidekick to Western action stars George O'Brien in the late 1930s, Tim Holt in the early 1940s and Rod Cameron in the mid–40s. He starred in 18 short musical films, making more than 50 films in all. In several of the early films, Ray's Six Bar Cowboys included the Phelps Brothers (Willie, Earl and Norman) from Virginia.

Ray composed a number of successful songs—some by himself, some in collaboration with Gene Autry and others in collaboration with Fred Rose. During World War II, Ray sold war bonds and entertained servicepersons at bases and hospitals, including in the South Pacific. Troops tuned in his *Melody Round Up* on the Armed Forces Radio Service. During the war years, he formed a Western swing dance band, The Rhythm Wranglers, attracting crowds to Los Angeles–area ballrooms. Following the war, he resumed touring and radio broadcasts. At various times, Ray had managed his own groups, The Sons of the Pioneers and Jimmy Wakely. His final film role was as Watts, manager of James Dean's character in *Giant* (1956). He gradually withdrew from performing to tend to business interests, including music publishing and recording. Ray was inducted posthumously into Nashville's Songwriters Hall of Fame.

Ray Whitley on the Rodeo Trail

In 1932, dressed in construction work clothes, Ray convinced promoter Col. W.T. Johnson to allow his Western musical group to entertain at Madison Square Garden's rodeo. In gratitude, Ray later changed his group's name to The Six Bar Cowboys after the colonel's Texas ranch. Ray played New York and Boston Garden rodeos off and on into the 1950s, and starred

Western singer Ray Whitley.

at other rodeos. At the 1937 Madison Square Garden rodeo, Ray discussed with a Gibson executive his ideas for an improved acoustic guitar. His original prototype for Gibson's SJ–200 guitar series, used by singing cowboys and country music artists, is displayed at the Country Music Hall of Fame. Ray's song "Back in the Saddle Again," sold and slightly reworked, became Gene Autry's theme song. Gene contributed to "Ages and Ages Ago," drafted by Ray and Fred Rose at Madison Square Garden's 1945 rodeo. One of the earliest singing cowboys to entertain at rodeos, Ray urged rodeo promoters and Western stars to recognize rodeo's potential as a Western entertainment venue.

By the early 1950s, approaching 20 years as a rodeo entertainer, Ray performed at rodeos with Western star Monte Hale and formed a family act with his wife and daughter. Ray Whitley and Family were featured at Fort Madison's 1951 rodeo and at Dublin, Texas, rodeos in 1951 and 1952. Ray publicized rodeos in person, and with radio and TV spots. He also entertained disadvantaged and hospitalized children. As late as 1976, he performed at a Montana all-girl rodeo.

GUY WILLIAMS (1924–89)

Guy Williams in Walt Disney's *Zorro*.

Physically qualified, skilled in a Spanish accent and adept at fencing, Guy Williams won the TV role of Walt Disney's Zorro. Spoiled Don Diego de la Vega took on the secret identity of the caped and masked hero Zorro, who battled injustice in early Los Angeles. *Zorro* (1957–59) produced a merchandising campaign, and reruns extended into recent times. The show earned good ratings but the studio decided to cancel. Guy reprised his Zorro role occasionally through 1961 on *Walt Disney Presents*. When reruns of *Zorro* became popular in Argentina, he made personal appearances there.

"Zorro" on the Rodeo Trail

In spring of 1959, Guy Williams as Zorro headlined his first rodeo, the Arkansas-Oklahoma Rodeo at Fort Smith. He told an interviewer that he took two fencing lessons per week. His arena act included swordplay with a member of the *Zorro* TV troupe and the traditional ride around the arena to shake hands with youngsters. He was mobbed for autographs. In the fall, Zorro starred at a rodeo held at the Eastern States Exposition in Springfield, Massachusetts.

TEX WILLIAMS (1917–85)

Tex Williams sang and played with Spade Cooley's band and with his own Western Caravan, enjoying several hit recordings. With Smokey Rogers and Deuce Spriggins, he starred in a series of short musical Western films, some of which were combined into features.

Tex Williams on the Rodeo Trail

In the fall of 1955, Tex Williams headlined the Arkansas State Fair and Livestock Show Rodeo at Little Rock. He and his band played for dances held in conjunction with the 1956 Emerald Empire Rodeo in Eugene, Oregon. In 1957, he performed, with Eddie Dean and Louise Duncan, at Salt Lake City's Days of '47 Rodeo. As part of his arena act at the 1959 J Bar H Rodeo at Camdenton, Missouri, Tex sang "That Little Boy of Mine" while a three-year-old boy in a Nudie outfit entered under the arena spotlight. The musical group The Texans backed Tex. Slim Pickens and Casey Tibbs also lent their celebrity.

Singing Western star Tex Williams in a performance at the 1955 Arkansas State Fair and Livestock Show Rodeo (Johnnie M. Gray photograph, obtained from Arkansas State Fair and Livestock Show, Little Rock, AR, used with permission of Kermit Gray).

BOB WILLS (1905–75) AND JOHNNIE LEE WILLS (1912–84)

Born near Kosse, Texas, Bob Wills, as a youth, followed in the footsteps of his fiddle-playing father, often playing for dances. He also competed at local rodeos. He worked as a barber before displaying his musical talents in a medicine show. He later joined the Light Crust Doughboys. In 1933, he formed The Texas Playboys. Younger brother Johnnie Lee was a member. Bob Wills and the Texas Playboys, making recordings and radio broadcasts, became synonymous with Western swing and appeared in some Western films. They played Cain's Ballroom in Tulsa and one-night stands. Bob performed into the 1960s when his health began to decline. Bob was inducted into Nashville's Country Music Hall of Fame and received a special award from the National Cowboy Hall of Fame. He was honored by the Texas and Oklahoma legislatures. In 1970, Tulsa honored him with a Bob Wills Week tribute at the Tulsa Fairgrounds Pavilion, with Tex Ritter, Jimmy Wakely and Chill Wills in attendance. His final recording, "Bob Wills and His Texas Playboys: For the Last Time," earned a Wrangler Award from the National Cowboy Hall of Fame. A Bob Wills monument and museum are located in Turkey, Texas, where "Bob Wills Day" is still held.

Bob Wills and Johnnie Lee Wills on the Rodeo Trail

To entertain delegates at a 1939 convention, the Tulsa Jaycees planned entertainment representative of the area. They approached Bob Wills and O.W. Mayo, Bob's band manager and master of ceremonies, about producing a rodeo. The rodeo featured Marge Greenough, John Jordan and Don Stewart. The FBI's J. Edgar Hoover attended. Bob Wills and the Texas Playboys provided music. Even with free tickets for convention delegates, the Bob Wills Rodeo showed a small profit and began an annual tradition. In 1942, Hoot Gibson attended all performances. Following the rodeo, Bob returned to Hollywood to make a series of eight Western films with Russell Hayden for Columbia Studios. He then entered military service.

A Doubleday picture of Bob (in uniform), Johnnie Lee, O.W. Mayo and their horses

Left to right: Tex Ritter, Bob Wills and Leon McAulliffe, with other Texas Playboys, including Johnnie Lee Wills (with guitar, foreground) in a scene from *Take Me Back to Oklahoma* (Monogram, 1940).

appeared on *Hoofs and Horns*, August 1943 cover. The setting was the Fifth Annual Bob Wills Stampede, held in May. The rodeo parade featured Bob (on furlough) and Johnnie Lee on their respective Palomino mounts, Punkin and Victory. At the rodeo, 11 empty chairs represented band members in the service. Mayo hosted children from the Boy's Home and Welfare facility as well as newsboys of Tulsa. Performers included Alice and Marge Greenough, Cecil Cornish and Nancy Bragg, age 15. Johnnie Lee was co-producer.

In 1944, Will's son Jimmy Rogers was part of the opening night crowd. That year, Bob was on the road. Johnnie Lee, leader of a Tulsa band, took over the rodeo, called the Johnnie Lee Wills Tulsa Stampede, for the next 41 years. Across the country, Bob and Johnnie Lee's bands headlined rodeos, played for rodeo dances and played clubs during rodeo dates. Johnnie Lee, based in Tulsa, operated a Western clothing store. He was proud to have made nearly all rodeo performances. In later years, son John Wills, Jr., assumed more responsibility. When Johnnie Lee died in October 1984, a decision was made to terminate the Tulsa rodeo. Spin-off musical organizations continued to perform at rodeos after the Wills brothers' demise.

CHILL WILLS (1902–78) Born in Texas, Chill sang as a young man in church choirs and at local events. Beginning as a teen, he seasoned his musical comedy talent in burlesque, minstrel, medicine and tent shows, and then progressed to New York vaudeville and nightclubs. From the 1930s, he obtained film roles. He appeared in many Westerns and received an Academy Award nomination for *The Alamo* (1960).

Chill Wills (left) and a young helper feed stock at the 1974 Fort Worth Stock Show (courtesy ***Fort Worth Star-Telegram*** Photograph Collection, University of Texas at Arlington Libraries, Arlington. AR 406 2-121-42).

Chill Wills on the Rodeo Trail

Chill Wills initially entertained at rodeos, including the 1935 Reno Rodeo, as a member of the musical-comedy group The Avalon Boys. At Cheyenne Frontier Days in 1951, Chill and other cast filmed *Bronco Buster*. Chill also promoted the film *Francis Goes to the Races*, in which he provided the voice of Francis the Talking Mule. He, Francis and xylophone-playing Dub "Cannonball" Taylor appeared at a downtown theater. To assist entrants in a "Shoot at Chill Wills" photo contest, Chill's itinerary was broadcast on the radio. Early in 1959, he rode a buggy in the Tucson rodeo parade, conversing via loudspeaker with spectators, and posed with winners of the whiskers-growing contest. Chill and his wife attended social events at Houston's 1961 Fat Stock Show. A year later, he was a special guest at that event. He joined other celebrities at the 1970 Reno Rodeo dance. He and Guy Madison were special guests at Fort Worth's 1971 Diamond Jubilee rodeo. In 1972, he rode in a stagecoach in Reno's rodeo parade. At Oklahoma City's 1972 National Finals Rodeo, he displayed his Western-customized automobile. July 1974 saw Chill as grand marshal of Prescott's rodeo parade.

WHIP WILSON (1911–64) Whip Wilson starred in 22 films for Monogram Studios, beginning with *Crashing Thru* (1949) and ending in 1952. Andy Clyde was his most frequent sidekick. He generally wore a white hat, light shirt and jeans, and rode a white horse. He occasionally sang, but his films stressed action.

Whip Wilson on the Rodeo Trail

Whip's studio biography stated falsely that he had been a rodeo champion. In October 1949, he purchased a white Tennessee Walking Horse to serve as his movie steed. Known as Rajah in its hometown of Amarillo, Texas, the horse had for five years

Monogram Western star Whip Wilson.

led parades, often with state governors aboard. As part of his sales agreement, Whip agreed to appear at Amarillo's annual Will Rogers Range Riders Rodeo the following July. By rodeo time, the horse had Hollywood training and had appeared in its first film, *Arizona Territory*, making a "world premiere" at Amarillo's Rialto Theater. A local celebrity, the horse, (movie name: Rocket) was as much publicized as the star. Whip led the rodeo parade and, with his wife Monica Lane, entertained rodeo crowds with his snake whip proficiency. With his whip he threw a calf, caught a horse, snatched a six-shooter from a villain's hand, unbuttoned his wife's sweater and snapped a cigarette from an assistant's lips. In 1952, Whip appeared in Palm Springs' rodeo parade and at Camp Pendleton's Marine Rodeo.

III

Television Casts Performing at Rodeos

"The Big Valley" Cast

BARBARA STANWYCK (1907–90) Barbara Stanwyck played Victoria Barkley, widowed matriarch of the Barkley family of three sons and a daughter. She had a long, distinguished motion picture career. Barbara's *Big Valley* costume is displayed at the National Cowboy Hall of Fame, where she has been inducted into the Hall of Great Western Performers.

Barbara Stanwyck on the Rodeo Trail

Stanwyck served as Queen of the 1958 Los Angeles Sheriff's Rodeo and as Hostess of the 1959 Palm Springs Rodeo of the Stars parade.

Veteran screen actress Barbara Stanwyck played Victoria Barkley on *The Big Valley* (ABC-TV) (courtesy Eddie Brandt's).

PETER BRECK (1929–)   Peter Breck was born in Rochester, New York. He performed as a nightclub singer, dancer, comedian and master of ceremonies until he served on U.S. Navy ships. He studied drama at the University of Houston, and was associated with theater groups in Houston and Dallas. He toured in over 100 stage productions. Cast in the film *Thunder Road* (1958), he followed with several films. He played TV supporting roles and starred in the TV series *Black Saddle* (1959–60). He joined *The Big Valley* (1965–69) as youngest son Nick Barkley. In more recent years, he has conducted drama schools in Vancouver, British Columbia.

RICHARD LONG (c. 1927–74)   Born in Chicago, Richard Long moved to California as a teen. Universal-International spotted him in a high school play and signed him to a contract. His first starring role was in *Air Cadet*. He also acted on TV drama shows. Following U.S. Army service, he made additional films and TV shows. On *The Big Valley*, he was older brother Jarrod Barkley, a lawyer.

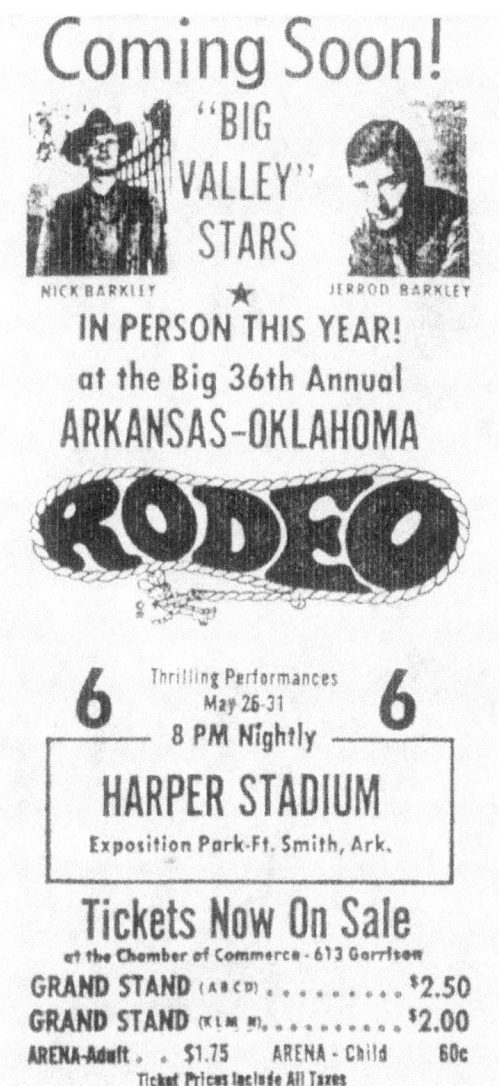

"Nick and Jarrod Barkley" on the Rodeo Trail

In 1967, Richard Long, accompanied by his wife Mara Corday, was grand marshal at the Palm Springs Rodeo of the Stars. He then co-starred with Clu Gulager at the Dixie National Rodeo at Jackson, Mississippi. Peter Breck was "Mr. Rodeo" at the Palm Springs rodeo parade in 1969. That same year, Peter and Richard were stars of the Arkansas-Oklahoma Rodeo in Fort Smith and the Pikes Peak or Bust Rodeo. The popularity of *The Big Valley* and the duo's showmanship insured a rousing audience reception for their arena act of dialogue and singing. They soloed, and then joined their back-up group, "The Frontiersmen and Joanie," for a hand-clapping, audience-participation rendition of "When the Saints Go Marching In." Their humor consisted primarily of Peter making his "brother" the butt of his jokes. They led an audience hog-calling contest. Richard commented to reporters, "We're not real cowboys, but rodeos are a lot of fun, and Pete and I enjoy playing them." In 1998, Peter Breck received the Buffalo Bill Award, in connection with North Platte's rodeo.

Advertisement for the Peter Breck and Richard Long appearance at the 1969 Arkansas-Oklahoma Rodeo.

Left: Richard Long as Jarrod Barkley (courtesy Eddie Brandt's). *Right:* Peter Breck as Nick Barkley (courtesy Eddie Brandt's).

Bonanza Cast

PERNELL ROBERTS (1928–) Born in Waycross, Georgia, Pernell Roberts served in the U.S. Marines. Drama studies in college led to acting in stage plays, to Broadway and, eventually, to Hollywood, where he appeared in *Desire Under the Elms* (1958). In 1959, he joined *Bonanza* as eldest son Adam Cartwright. Well-received by fans, he left midway through *Bonanza*'s run to pursue other acting opportunities. He starred in another successful TV series, *Trapper John, M.D.* (1979–86). Western fans continue to remember him for Adam Cartwright and other Western roles.

"Adam Cartwright" on the Rodeo Trail

In 1960 and 1961, Pernell Roberts, with *Bonanza* co-stars, appeared at Camp Pendleton's Marine Corps rodeos. In the summer of 1961, he paired with Michael Landon at Eugene, Oregon's, Emerald Empire Roundup. Direct from *Bonanza* filming, the two, unshaven and weary, arrived about dawn. After Pernell put his ten-year-old son to bed,

Bonanza cast members Pernell Roberts (Adam), Michael Landon (Little Joe), Lorne Greene (Ben Cartwright) and Dan Blocker (Hoss). All, plus David Canary, made rodeo appearances.

the pair submitted to a press interview before resting for their evening performance. They participated in a breakfast, the Roundup Dance and the rodeo parade, which drew the largest crowd in nine years. They also made time to visit young patients at Sacred Heart Hospital and to sign autographs. In the fall of 1962, Pernell made a solo appearance at the 101 Ranch Rodeo in Ponca City, Oklahoma. A newspaper account stated that he rode into the arena to thunderous applause. Moving to the microphone, he asked the crowd to stand and relax. Completing his remarks, he sang a few songs, mostly in the folk vein popular at the time. After the Saturday night performance, he stayed to sign autographs, but departed immediately after Sunday's matinee to resume family and *Bonanza* responsibilities.

LORNE GREENE (1915–87) An only child, Lorne Greene was born in Ottawa, Canada. He acted while attending Lisgar Collegiate Institute, and acted and directed for the Drama Guild while earning a degree in languages from Queen's University in Kingston, Ontario. After two years of training at New York City's Neighborhood Playhouse School of the Theater, he entered radio, becoming the Canadian Broadcasting Company's lead news broadcaster. Following service in the Royal Canadian Air Force, he founded an academy for training radio broadcasters and led a repertory theater company, acting in, or directing, over 50 productions. He frequently acted on radio. In New York City in 1953, a television producer friend cast him on *Studio One*. His interest in acting rekindled, he relinquished business interests to appear on Broadway and in Shakespeare's plays in Canada. He did TV roles and was cast in films.

A 1959 *Wagon Train* episode led to Lorne's casting as Ben Cartwright on NBC's color

Western series *Bonanza*. He molded his character, based somewhat on his father, into the fair, caring patriarch millions enjoyed watching. Telecast from 1959 to 1973 (260 episodes), the show is still watched in reruns as of this writing. Top-rated in the United States, *Bonanza* expanded its audience through showings in many countries and languages. For a time, Lorne had a nightclub act. His Arizona home was a replica of the Ponderosa ranch house. Successfully investing earnings, he became a wealthy man, and joined fellow cast members in several business deals. He enjoyed reading, tennis, swimming, bridge and maintaining a stable of racing horses.

Having lost Dan Blocker, its sponsor and its time slot, *Bonanza* was canceled in January 1973. Upon recovery from a mild heart attack, Lorne starred in additional TV series. Devoted to wildlife causes, he produced two syndicated wildlife series. He was also involved in historical-patriotic specials. He was a TV guest star, served as host or narrator for several projects and made commercials. He had roles in *Earthquake* (1974), made-for-TV movies and the TV mini-series *Roots* (1977).

Lorne received several awards for his charitable activities, including the Heart Award from Variety Clubs of America and the John Swett Award from the Los Angeles Teachers Association. *Radio-TV Mirror* named him "Most Popular TV Star" and the Foreign Press Association cited him for Best Performance by an Actor. He served as chairman of the National Wildlife Federation. Rodeo organizers found him one of the most pleasant celebrities. Lorne passed away from a heart attack following surgical complications.

DAN BLOCKER (1928–72) Dan Davis Blocker (at 14 pounds, said to be Bowie County's largest baby) was born near DeKalb, Texas, and raised in O'Donnell. Entering first grade, he weighed 105 pounds and was five feet tall. By age ten, he was doing adult manual labor, working at grain elevators, loading grain trucks, picking cotton and doing construction work. At Texas Military Institute, he weighed 200 pounds and attained six feet in height. Known as "The Big'n," he was a football lineman and a fighter. From about age 13, Dan took on challengers, including older youths, on a roped-off part of Main Street. He later entered Golden Gloves competition.

At 6'4" and 275 pounds, Dan worked as saloon bouncer and truck driver. Majoring in physical education and playing football at Sul Ross State, he was selected, based on his physical strength, for a non-speaking role in the college's production of *Arsenic and Old Lace*. He then directed *Mister Roberts* with a cast of football teammates. Becoming a drama major, he played the title role in Shakespeare's *Othello* and "De Lawd" in *Green Pastures*, for which he won 1949 national recognition for Best College Acting. He graduated from Sul Ross in 1950 with a BA in drama and a minor in physical education.

Turning down a professional football offer, Dan acted in summer stock. From there, he performed on Broadway. Following military service in Japan, he taught school and coached football. Completing a Master's Degree in drama and English at Sul Ross, he taught at a New Mexico elementary school. In 1956, he began doctoral study in Shakespeare at UCLA. Finding acting roles available and lucrative, he left graduate school and began acting in TV dramas and on Western series, often as a villain. He had a continuing role on the Western TV series *Cimarron City* (1958–59). A part on *Restless Gun* led to his role as middle son Hoss Cartwright on *Bonanza*. An oversized, uncreased Western hat topped the somewhat rumpled appearance of his powerful, big-hearted character. While in *Bonanza*, Dan appeared in a few theatrical and TV movies.

Dan was a people-oriented person. He excused himself from a rodeo press conference to spend a half-hour chatting and joking with fans. As he entertained at rodeos around the country, friends and neighbors responded. Louisiana welcomed him as near-home territory. In Oklahoma, he told stories of native friends. In Texas where he was raised or New Mexico where he had taught school, he hosted hospitality suites at his lodging place, entertaining hundreds of acquaintances who traveled to greet him. His friendly manner and remarkable memory for faces and names engendered some talk of his entering politics, but he refused to capitalize on his TV fame. He felt that scientists and others who made a difference to society were more deserving of attention. He told reporters that he longed to return to the classroom. He died from a blood clot on the lung following gall bladder surgery and was buried in his hometown of DeKalb. O'Donnell erected a bust in his memory.

"Ben and Hoss Cartwright" on the Rodeo Trail

Lorne Greene and Dan Blocker typically appeared together at rodeos. In 1961 and 1962, they joined other cast members at Camp Pendleton's Marine Rodeo. Typically, crowds welcomed their airport arrival. Newspaper reports often pictured them signing autographs or holding children. Despite a tight filming schedule, they made time to accommodate autograph seekers, visit youngsters in hospitals and pose for photographs with kiddie dress-up winners, rodeo queens, visiting dignitaries, etc. Unfortunately, they seldom had time to enjoy a rodeo or fair. In a rodeo parade, Lorne said, "Don't take off the hat, Dan, people won't recognize us." Distinctive, cube-shaped luggage held Dan's trademark big hat (but, on one occasion, did not keep the hat from being stolen).

Lorne Greene (left) and Dan Blocker (right) pose with visiting mayors at the 1963 Pikes Peak or Bust Rodeo (courtesy Pikes Peak Library District Local History Collection, Colorado Springs, CO. Stewarts #5115).

III. Television Casts Performing at Rodeos 233

Bonanza stars Lorne Greene and Dan Blocker entertain in the arena at the 1963 Pikes Peak or Bust Rodeo (courtesy Pikes Peak Library District Local History Collection, Colorado Springs, CO. Stewarts # 5167).

Lorne and Dan rode into the arena, dismounting at the microphone. Hoss excused his entrance ride being slower than that of his TV dad as resulting from his weight handicap. Their makeshift stage might be a flatbed trailer or a platform pulled into place by a tractor. The act typically began with praise for the locality. They said they valued the opportunity to visit their loyal viewers. Hoss observed that, with TV, he had the advantage as viewers could see him, but "I don't have to look at you." Dan's size was the subject of quips. It was commonly said that *Bonanza* was telecast in color to promote sales of color TV sets, but casting Hoss encouraged viewers to buy large-screen sets. Dan cited his real-life dad's comment when he was younger, "I was too big to ride and too little to hitch to a wagon — no good for anything." He also stated, "I'm the only guy that's six feet, four inches any way you want to measure me." He referred to Lorne as "Big Daddy." Dan told arena crowds he had once been a teacher: "I'll learn 'em English if they'll listen to me." The duo acted out a *Bonanza*-related skit, perhaps a parody of how the show appeared on foreign TV.

At one rodeo, a reporter quoted Lorne as saying, "We sometimes wonder what we are doing here with all these cowboys. We can't ride, can't shoot, can't rope and we certainly can't sing." Wary of horses, Lorne sometimes lamented "strange horses and strange saddles." Dan had his own problems with horses. At an early horse show appearance, his horse spooked and jerked its head back sharply, striking and cutting Dan's forehead and knocking the big man to the turf. In 1962 while filming a *Bonanza* episode, he broke his collarbone in a fall from a horse. A car racing enthusiast, he said, "I learned my lesson. Cars can have roll bars, but horses don't."

Lorne apparently started singing when fashioning a rodeo act. His familiar, deep voice, singing and reciting such selections as "Ringo" and "An Old Tin Cup," enjoyed success on recordings, as well as at rodeos. One of Dan's hobbies was listening to serious music, but the most complimentary comment about his singing was that he was loud. By staying in character, Hoss won audience approval for his "bellerin.'" He led into his song by saying, "I may not sing so pretty, but no one will go to sleep." A typical opening song was the parody, "I'm an Old Cowhand from TV Land." Following solos and humor, a duet of "Together" closed the act. Back-up musicians were skilled at covering sour notes. Ben and Hoss wound up an appearance by riding around the arena.

Extended at Ardmore, Oklahoma, for a kiddie matinee, their act fulfilled its purpose of drawing crowds. At Colorado Springs in 1963, they set a new attendance record for opening night when boards were set over bales of hay to accommodate the overflow crowd. At Houston, they set a new attendance record for indoor rodeos, drawing 55,000 patrons in two performances on a single Saturday. They seemed to be having fun as they sang and joked through their act, and the audience was entertained.

During the 15 years Lorne Greene appeared at rodeos as Ben Cartwright, he also performed solo. He headlined alone such rodeos as Palm Springs, the Independence (Missouri) Civic Rodeo (where President Truman led him on a tour of his library) and the St. Louis Fireman's Rodeo in 1963; Edmonton's Canadian Western Exposition and San Francisco's Grand National in 1965; Cheyenne Frontier Days in 1970; the Snake River Stampede in 1971; and the Southeastern Livestock Exposition Rodeo at Montgomery, Alabama, in 1976. On one solo stage, a wagon pulled by six horses, he had to spread his feet for balance when the horses' shifting caused the stage to wobble. In 1963, Dan became ill prior to a joint booking at Lake Charles, Louisiana. Lorne and Clint "Cheyenne" Walker combined for the first four performances, and then Michael Landon flew in for the final two. Of his annual six-week *Bonanza* filming hiatus, Lorne often spent five weeks on tour.

Dan Blocker worked Sidney, Iowa's, 1961 rodeo with Michael Landon. He performed solo at the 1962 Texas State Prison Rodeo and received Silver Spurs Awards at Reno in 1962 and 1965. Just prior to a night performance with Lorne at Colorado Springs' 1963 Pikes Peak or Bust Rodeo, Dan received news that his six-year-old son was in a coma in an Oklahoma City hospital with a ruptured appendix. Dan completed the act, tried until the next morning to learn details of his son's condition and stayed near the telephone during the day. He performed as expected at that evening's rodeo, learning only the following morning that his son was out of danger.

MICHAEL LANDON (1936–91) Eugene Orowitz was born at Forest Hills, New York, and moved shortly to Collingswood, New Jersey. His parents' religious differences, and dissatisfaction with their vocations, led to unhappiness at home. Personal slights, some from anti–Semitism, poisoned peer relationships. In his only drama experience, in a Japanese role, he overcame shyness pretending to be someone else. He found his niche as a javelin thrower in track and field competition. Although studies suffered, athletic prowess gained him scholarship offers. At the University of Southern California at Los Angeles, an arm injury ended his sports and college careers. To help family finances, he unloaded freight at a North Hollywood warehouse. A co-worker invited him to a reading, which led him to Warner Brothers' acting school. He worked at odd jobs while doing some acting, selecting the name "Michael Landon" from the telephone book. He had roles on TV drama shows and Western series, and in the films *I Was a Teenage Werewolf* (1957) and *God's Little Acre* (1958).

In 1957, Michael appeared on the *Schlitz Playhouse of Stars* pilot for the Western series

Restless Gun. Producer David Dortort remembered and invited him when casting in 1959 for Little Joe Cartwright, the youngest son on *Bonanza*. Initially not interested in being tied to a series, he was persuaded by the attractive salary and by his rapport with Lorne Greene and Dan Blocker. He also grew to admire the show's reliance upon old-fashioned values. He preferred TV to feature films or stage plays because he could go home to his family each evening. After a slow start, *Bonanza* enjoyed a long, popular run, making stars of the actors and putting them in demand for personal appearances. Once dubbed "the happiest Cartwright," he said that he would like to see the show last until he was old enough to play the father role.

Bonanza was only the beginning of Michael's TV contributions. While sometimes difficult to work with, he used his experience on *Bonanza* to become a better actor and to expand his filmmaking skills. He eventually wrote 30 original *Bonanza* teleplays, re-wrote scripts for additional episodes and directed a dozen episodes. When *Bonanza* was cancelled in 1973, he was deluged with offers to star in a variety of TV series. He rejected them as unworthy of his ideals. He did not want to tarnish the image of family-oriented entertainment established on *Bonanza*. In 1974, he found in *Little House on the Prairie* an appropriate outlet for all of his talents. In *Father Murphy*, *Highway to Heaven* and the TV movies *It's Good to Be Alive— The Roy Campanella Story*, *The Loneliest Runner*, *Sam's Son* and *Where Pigeons Go to Die*, he addressed sensitive issues with a strong family orientation. In 1991, he completed a new series pilot, *Us*; the series never came to pass. On July 1, 1991, Michael succumbed to cancer of the liver and pancreas. Over a quarter century, he had progressed from TV cowboy and rodeo star to create and shape a body of television film that probably represents the finest exploitation of the medium for positive values by any individual.

"Little Joe Cartwright" on the Rodeo Trail

Major *Bonanza* cast members appeared together at Camp Pendleton's Marine Rodeo in 1960 and 1961. Michael returned in 1962. He occasionally starred with other Cartwrights, and sometimes with such personalities as Johnny Crawford or the Sons of the Pioneers, but he usually did a solo act. "Little Joe" was a sufficient draw to fill the stands with devoted fans. One result of appearing alone was the comment that he looked taller in person than on television. Of normal size, "Little Joe," alongside Lorne Greene or Dan Blocker, looked short by comparison. He told reporters that he liked to watch rodeos but seldom attended because of being mobbed.

Michael admitted that he did little horseback riding except on the show, and that riding when the show began was a painful experience. His ready reply was, "I'd rather ride in a Chevrolet" (the show's sponsor). Although he was proud of having performed many of his own stunts on *Bonanza*, he confessed to doing less riding as the years progressed. He had occasional problems with horses on personal appearances and, like other Western entertainers, he sometimes endured the barbs of rodeo cowboys. Gun handling, on the other hand, was part of his training as an actor. At one point, Michael did a dozen rodeos a year. Appearances helped support his family and his lifestyle. His absences, though, reportedly took a toll on his first marriage. His second wife, Lynn, frequently accompanied him on the road. In later years, he was doing three or four rodeos a year, mostly over weekends. *Bonanza* filming schedules meant that the week-long St. Louis Fireman's Rodeo was an exception. At some long-running rodeos, he split the duration with other entertainers. Personal appearances were credited with boosting *Bonanza*'s TV audience.

Michael Landon, Little Joe of *Bonanza* in the 1964 Houston, Texas, rodeo parade (photograph copyright Houston Metropolitan Research Center, Houston Public Library, Houston. Press #1039).

Michael described his rodeo act as "storytelling and singing." For his arena entrance, accompanied by the *Bonanza* theme, he rode a borrowed horse, fired shots from his six-shooter and approached the microphone. In a variation of this phase, he fired blank rounds into the ground, and then grabbed his foot in mock alarm, asking, "Who put in that extra bullet?" His quick wit and proficient ad-libbing made his rodeo press conferences as entertaining as his stage work. The *Bonanza* boys had an early reputation of simply "winging it" through a performance. This is possible; however, it is also the mark of a good performer to make the act appear effortless. Michael evoked laughter and cheers by remarking on the size of his older TV brother: "Hoss is so big, he couldn't get through the airplane door to come with me." "When Hoss does the twist, he looks like a runaway truck ... and trailer." "Hoss eats only once a day—from 9 a.m. to 6 p.m." "The other night Hoss dreamed he ate a 25-pound marshmallow and, when he woke up, his pillow was gone."

Daughter Cheryl, in her book *I Promised My Dad*, relates that Michael had once traveled with Jerry Lee Lewis as a singer. At rodeos, he sometimes sang, "Gimmie a Little Kiss Will Ya, Huh?," an earlier recording. She added that, on occasion, he called her on stage to dance. Other selections included "Jambalaya" (accompanied by audience handclapping), "Danny Boy" and "I Believe in Music." A segment of his spotlight time was an "acting contest": Prior to the rodeo, five or six boys and girls were selected from the crowd. Michael called them forward at the appropriate time. He asked them to act the role of a villain and "die" his or her own way, and acted out a shootout scene with each one. Audience applause selected the best

III. Television Casts Performing at Rodeos 237

Michael Landon (right) poses with the pony contest winner at the 1967 Snake River Stampede (Idaho Free Press [Nampa, Idaho] photograph, used with permission. Obtained from Snake River Stampede).

"dying" actor as winner of a savings bond. Michael then circled the arena on horseback and retired to an autograph booth. The Vernon (Texas) *Daily Record* reported, "For a young man whose forte is writing, directing and acting, [Landon] came off extremely well, proving to be a tremendous crowd pleaser." He was invited back for repeat engagements.

Some observers saw Michael as overly sentimental when during his arena act he remarked, "Say a prayer that a lot of little boys and girls not here tonight will be here next year." His genuine concern for young people took him out of his way to visit with the ill or disabled at hospitals, centers, special schools and at the rodeo. Knowing they were interested in "Little Joe" of the Ponderosa, he approached them in character in a manner that was entertaining and comforting. They looked upon him as their friend. In *I Promised My Dad*, daughter Cheryl tells of Michael visiting a Mississippi hospital, then traveling 90 miles to spend an afternoon with a terminally ill high school boy and his family at their home.

Michael's time was consumed immediately upon arrival. Crowds met him at the airport. For press interviews, he was typically friendly, candid and full of fun. At Cheyenne Frontier Days in 1967, 250 newspaper carriers interviewed him. He related that the Cartwrights were expected to show zesty appetites for meals, even though the food may have been prepared hours in advance. Insisting on a horse other than the one offered, he fell at one performance from his horse of choice. Only his dignity was hurt. Interviewers asked, "Did you fall off your horse on purpose?" Good-naturedly, he replied, "I wish I did." He rode horseback in rodeo parades. At Houston, he made an unusual hospital visit to a woman whose fingertip was bitten off as she visited his horse's stall. He was guest of honor at organizers' welcoming receptions, judged a beard-growing contest and was photographed with various individuals and groups. He received plaques, keys to cities and honorary law enforcement badges. He liked to fish, and sometimes he was invited to play golf, but there was seldom time.

The hectic pace of filming *Bonanza* all week, and flying away many weekends, took a toll. Michael appeared outdoors in all kinds of weather, from Phoenix mud to Alaska's ice to chilly Texas winds. Some locals were eager to pick a fight. He made a hit with rodeo fans and with people he met; however, there was pressure in having to carry the show and to be "up" much of the time. Energy-boosting substances weren't the answer. On one return flight to Los Angeles, he collapsed from exhaustion.

Michael made extra money and frequently drew the crowds rodeo committees sought. At Fort Madison, organizers credited his appeal for the near-capacity turnout. In Vernon, over a thousand people had to be turned away from a Saturday performance. At Sikeston, he drew over 30,000 spectators in four performances, with 1,500 turned away for lack of seating capacity. When *Bonanza* was cancelled, he continued to appear at rodeos. According to daughter Cheryl in *I Promised My Dad*, he felt that honest rodeo work, manure and all, was preferable to appearing on screen in some inferior vehicle. At one point in 1973, he established arena records for attendance and box office receipts at four consecutive rodeos.

DAVID CANARY (1938–) David Canary was born in Elwood, Indiana, and moved at age five with his family to Massillon, Ohio. At the University of Cincinnati on an athletic scholarship, he made the Pop Warner All-American football team and earned a music degree. He studied at the Cincinnati Conservatory of Music, developing a strong lyric baritone voice. He declined a professional football contract to try his hand as a musical entertainer and actor. Beginning with a musical stock company, he proceeded to New York City. Off-Broadway, he worked his way up from chorus and bit parts to a role in *The Fantasticks*. During U.S. Army service, he acted in and directed little theater groups. He won the 1963 All-Army entertainment contest as a singer. Following discharge, he joined San Francisco and Los Angeles productions of *The Fantasticks*. He was cast in the film *The St. Valentine's Day Massacre* (1967). On TV, he was in *Peyton Place* and on episodes of Western series. A role in the film *Hombre* (1967) led to his casting as the young loner, "Candy," who joined the Ponderosa. On *Bonanza* from 1967 to 1971, he left to try writing and directing films, but returned for a final season when Dan Blocker passed away. Later, he did commercials, returned to the stage and acted on the TV soap opera *All My Children*.

"Candy" on the Rodeo Trail

Bonanza co-stars, with less polished voices than his own, were supplementing their incomes by singing at rodeos. Beginning in 1969, David Canary made solo rodeo appearances at Fort Worth, Phoenix, Fort Smith, Alexandria, Lake Charles and Spooner. He arrived at the end of the era of cowboy star rodeo headliners; however, audiences warmed to his act. He said that his greatest trick was staying on the horse. His vocal talents were unmistak-

David "Candy" Canary of *Bonanza*.

able, even while rendering "Jambalaya" to the accompaniment of a rock band. At rodeos, he visited students in a special school class, as well as hospital and nursing home patients. He signed thousands of autographs and concluded his act by riding around the arena to shake hands with youngsters.

THE CISCO KID CAST

DUNCAN RENALDO (c. 1904–80) Duncan Renaldo's real name, as well as his date and place of birth, are unknown. Possibly a European foundling, he had talent in art and music. He entered the country on a 90-day seaman's permit when his merchant freighter burned about 1921 at Baltimore. He stayed well beyond that limit. Interested in writing, producing and directing, he designed sets. He acted on stage and for eastern film companies. In Hollywood in the mid–1920s, he produced and starred in a series of silent short films, paying with difficulty, but integrity, his debt to Herbert J. Yates' processing laboratory. He established himself as a film actor in *The Bridge of San Luis Rey* (1929). He went to Africa to make *Trader Horn* (1931), but fell victim to a vindictive wife and studio head. Charged with being in the country illegally, he was found guilty of perjury and served 18 months in a penitentiary until pardoned by President Roosevelt in 1936. He was reduced to working at Republic studios as janitor and prop man, when Mr. Yates, now head of that studio, offered him a five-year acting contract. For about seven years, Duncan supported Western stars in feature films and chapter serials.

The Cisco Kid circles the arena to shake hands with youthful fans at the 1952 Jim Eskew Ranch Rodeo, Cleveland, Ohio (courtesy Duncan Renaldo Collection, Neg. #29547, American Heritage Center, University of Wyoming, Laramie, WY).

The character of Cisco Kid originated in O. Henry's 1904 short story, portraying him as an Anglo bandit and killer. As Hollywood adaptations evolved, the Cisco Kid became a Mexican. In the mid–1940s, Monogram chose Duncan to star as the Cisco Kid. His revised image of the Kid, inspired by the Spanish tale of Don Quixote and Sancho Panza, was more acceptable to Latin Americans. After three films, Duncan left the role. In 1948, a new Cisco Kid series was produced. Duncan, restoring his Cisco Kid concept, starred, with Leo Carrillo as sidekick Pancho, in five films (1949–50) and a syndicated TV series of 156 color episodes (1950–56). Duncan incorporated elements from a variety of Latin American countries into his costume. Cisco, astride his steed Diablo, and Pancho, on Loco, outsmarted villains in mostly non-violent ways and became idols of youngsters across the country. In addition to rodeos, the Cisco Kid made personal appearances at circuses, trade shows, stores, stage shows and fairs. Battling cancer, Duncan passed away of heart failure in California.

LEO CARRILLO (1881–1961)   Leo Antonio Carrillo was born in Los Angeles, California, of mixed Mexican and Italian heritage. His great-grandfather was the first governor of California. Following attendance at the University of St. Vincent at Loyola, Leo

Rodeo star Leo Carrillo autographs for fans at the 1953 Arkansas State Fair and Livestock Show, Little Rock, Arkansas (Johnnie M. Gray photograph, used with permission of Kermit Gray. Obtained from the Arkansas State Fair and Livestock Show, Little Rock, AR).

worked as a newspaper cartoonist. Overheard telling stories in dialect, he was urged to try show business. His early career included vaudeville, Broadway and touring in stage plays. When one production was made into a film in 1929, he retained his part, beginning a movie career that lasted three decades. That same year, he reportedly suggested unemployed Warner Baxter to director Raoul Walsh for his Academy Award–winning role as "The Cisco Kid" in *In Old Arizona*. Leo appeared in various film genres, including some Westerns, for a number of studios. Duncan Renaldo was a friend.

Cautious that playing the part of Pancho for laughs would demean Hispanics, Leo accepted the film role reluctantly. He grew to enjoy the role, and the films were popular north and south of the border. He gained even greater popularity on TV's *The Cisco Kid*. In addition to helping Cisco round up the bad guys, he contributed accented, fractured dialogue, reportedly adopted from his home caretaker. He endeared himself to youngsters across the nation, advising them to go to church and to be good Americans. He regularly rode in Pasadena's Tournament of Roses Parade. Following his years as Pancho, he was a member of the Los Angeles Parks Commission, hosted a troupe of Hispanic musicians and dancers, and did some writing. Leo died of the cancer he had battled for several years.

"The Cisco Kid and Pancho" on the Rodeo Trail

Leo Carrillo had extensive rodeo experience prior to *The Cisco Kid*. In 1939 and 1940, he appeared at the California Rodeo at Salinas. In the early 1940s, he headlined annual rodeos in several California cities. From 1943 through 1945, Leo Carrillo Rodeos held at the Los Angeles Coliseum featured a number of performers with Hollywood connections. At his 1944 Coliseum rodeo, Montie Montana was parade marshal, Andy Jauregui was arena director and young Universal star Gloria Jean was the rodeo queen singing "God Bless America." This star-studded event foreshadowed the Sheriff's Rodeo, which began a year later. For *Hoofs and Horns*, Chuck Martin wrote, "No doubt about it, Leo Carrillo sure brings 'em through the admission gates. Mounted on his beautiful pinto stallion, he had the crowd in his expressive hands, and they took him to their hearts. [He] had a roving mike on his saddle, ad-libbing between announcements to the delight of the fans." Leo joined other Hollywood stars at Roy Rogers' 1945 Coliseum rodeo, where he, Roy Rogers and Bill Elliott contested in a harness race, and at Sheriff's Rodeos. In 1947, he was on parade at Las Vegas' Helldorado Days.

During the popular run of *The Cisco Kid*, Duncan Renaldo and Leo Carrillo made rodeo appearances, mainly in the years 1951 through mid–1955. At one time, Leo's contract called for equal billing. Age didn't deter Duncan and Leo from devising a rodeo act based on vigorous action. They enacted a stagecoach holdup that demanded energy and risked injury.

The Cisco Kid (left, center) and Pancho (right, center) on the Salt Grass Trail Ride in conjunction with their appearance at Houston's 1954 Fat Stock Show Rodeo (courtesy Duncan Renaldo Collection, Neg. #29553, American Heritage Center, University of Wyoming, Laramie, WY).

III. Television Casts Performing at Rodeos

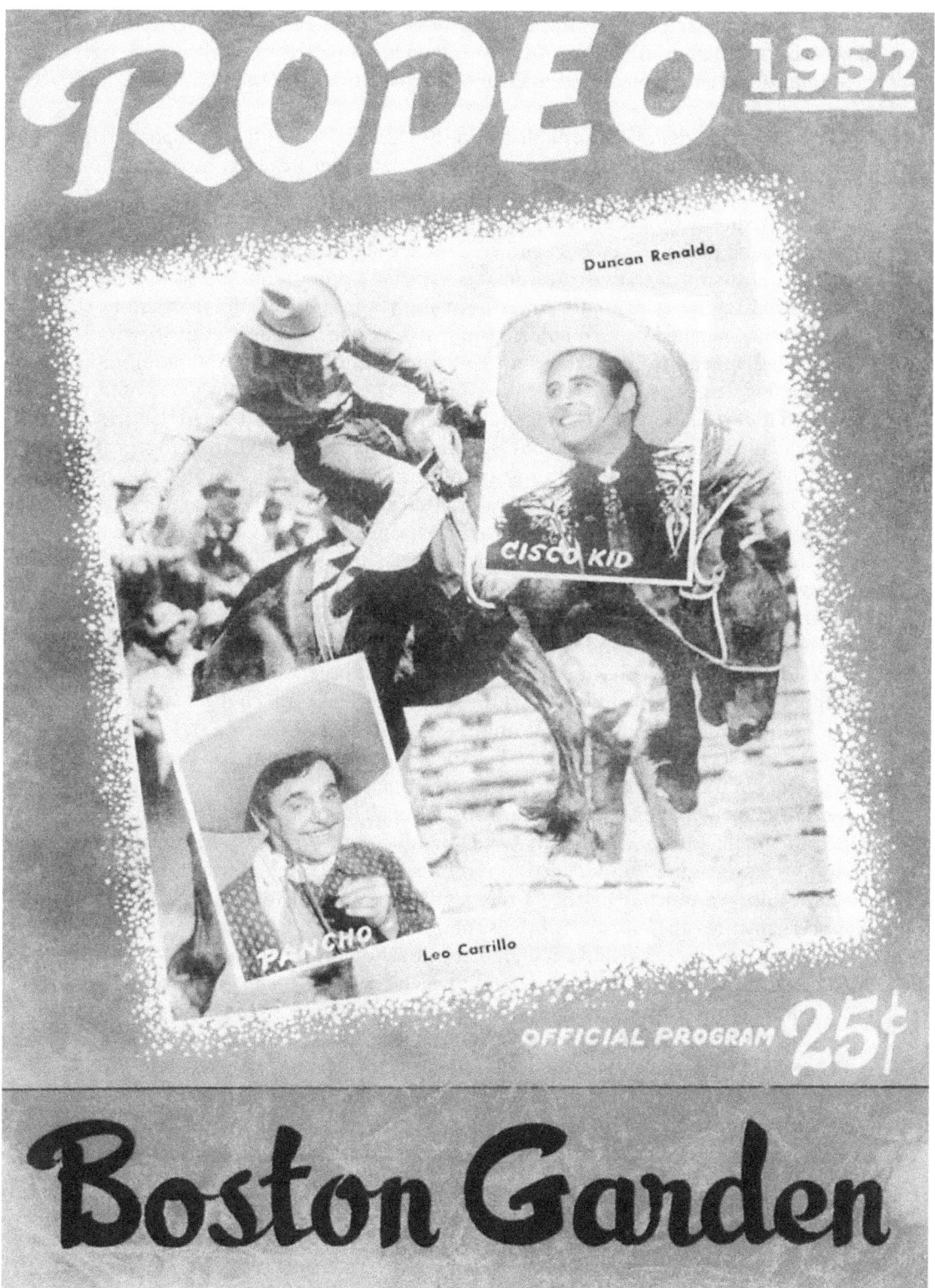

Boston Garden 1952 rodeo program cover.

Their performance varied over time and depended upon the host organization providing a stagecoach, a surrey or other horse-drawn wagon appropriate for wealthy passengers. To provide additional action players, the act employed stuntmen, often Bill Catching and Troy Melton.

Certain characteristics were established early. Duncan frequently corresponded directly with local rodeo organizers concerning his arrival date, logistics (e.g. borrowed horses or handling of his personal trunk) and the sequence of his act. He traveled and appeared in costume. He requested scheduling of as many hospitals and institutions as possible, so he could visit young patients, veterans and seniors. He signed autographs, shook hands and passed out photos until the last person was satisfied. Upon request, Cisco and Pancho recorded publicity spots prior to arrival. For early appearances, horses were borrowed locally. Duncan specified desired coloring to resemble the TV horses, but they took what was available. Duncan shipped ahead a trunk containing his saddle, blank ammunition, saddle blankets, Pancho's serape and other props. The saddle was not to be used or displayed until his arrival to avoid damage to its delicate décor. He also asked that the ammunition, loaded to his specifications, be secured. Duncan and Leo sought repeatedly to improve the details of their act. On one occasion, Leo observed Duncan's solo performance and provided his partner with several written suggestions.

Following is a description of the act as it was once scripted: Cisco and Pancho made a fast entrance on horseback, shooting and waving. Then, both dismounted, they handed their horses to a wrangler and approached a microphone to greet the crowd. Pancho entertained with dialogue, Cisco gave a short safety talk and the two prepared the audience for a "surprise." They mounted and exited the arena. The announcer described perils faced by early West passengers as a coach entered at a fairly fast pace. Suddenly, the narration was interrupted by gunshots. Bandits chased the speeding stage a full circle of the arena, firing their six-guns and taking return fire from the stage guard (Bill Catching). Finally, the bandits stopped the stage. While henchmen held personnel at gunpoint, the head bandit (Troy Melton) ordered passengers out of the coach, searched and robbed them. One attempted to interfere, but the bandit knocked him sprawling. The head bandit then mounted and grabbed the mailbag from the guard. As the bandit reached to take the female passenger with him, the stage guard bulldogged him off his horse. A spirited fistfight followed, but the bandit knocked out the guard. As the bandits were about to make their getaway, the announcer lamented the injustice of the situation.

Just then, the Cisco Kid and Pancho, firing gunshots, approached the scene, and Cisco chased away the henchmen. The head bandit began chasing Pancho on horseback and was about to shoot him. Instead, Cisco shot at the bandit, causing him to fall off his horse. Pancho rushed the bandit on the ground, covered him with his serape and sat on him. The bandit, only playing possum, jumped up and swung at Pancho, who fended him off with his serape in the manner of a bullfighter while yelling for his partner who was helping the stage people. As Pancho was about to be subdued, Cisco rushed to his aid, making a quick dismount. He joined Pancho in engaging the head bandit in a short, acrobatic fight sequence, throwing the bandit over his shoulder and forcing him into submission. Pancho grabbed a (breakaway) pitchfork and broke it while prodding the bandit's behind as he chased him out of the arena. Cisco and Pancho mounted their horses and, waving to the audience, circled the arena. It became a trademark of personal appearances for Duncan (and Leo, if co-starring) to personally hand out photos and shake each youngster's hand.

Beginning in 1951, Duncan and Leo held the Cisco Kid Rodeo and Big Top Circus at baseball stadiums in Chicago, Cincinnati and Baltimore. At the latter rodeo, they shared billing with Western star Johnny Mack Brown. In Cleveland for a 1952 JE Rodeo shared with Guy Mitchell, the duo greeted sponsor employees at the Ward Baking Company plant. At Des Moines, Duncan and Leo rehearsed at the arena as two boys in Cisco-like outfits watched from atop a fence. Cisco and Pancho joined downtown businessmen for a hotel luncheon. Doug O'Donnell and Hank Mills, rodeo pick-up men, were part of the stage holdup gang. The Sons of the Pioneers shared billing. Later that season, youngsters mobbed Cisco and Pancho upon their arrival for the St. Louis Fireman's Rodeo.

The 1952 Boston Garden rodeo (11 days, 18 performances) marked the first time that a star other than Gene Autry or Roy Rogers headlined the rodeo. Locally, the *Cisco Kid* show ranked number one among youngsters. Newspaper photos showed the mayor, wearing a Western hat, getting the drop on Cisco and Pancho. Pancho was photographed with a bevy of cowgirls. Cisco and Pancho enjoyed dinner with heavyweight boxer Rocky Marciano and his family, and Duncan saw his first hockey game. The two helped the Park Commissioner open a new city swimming pool. Youngsters surrounded them at Boston Garden. At Norwood Hospital, Cisco, with cowgirls, chatted with a young girl who had recently lost a leg. Duncan traveled 24 miles to a hospital to meet a five-year-old terminal cancer patient. He gave the boy an autographed model horse, a cartridge from his belt and a cowboy hat. Telling him, "Remember, I always am with you," he presented photos to the boy and his three brothers. He visited and shook hands with all patients, and then spent more than an hour at another hospital.

In 1953, Duncan suffered a broken neck when struck by a fake boulder during filming of his TV show. His many well-wishers received an autographed photo and a picture of Duncan in his Cedars of Lebanon Hospital bed. His first public appearance following the accident was at the Tri-State Fair Rodeo at Bristol, Virginia, in late August. He was still in a neck cast from his injury. Leo's wife had died a few weeks earlier. Duncan announced that this would be his only rodeo appearance until fully recovered. He credited prayers of boys and girls all over the country with speeding his recovery, noting that a thousand get-well wishes had come from the Virginia area. He advised youngsters, "Remember little amigos, be good, do kind to others, and mind your elders and have faith in God and you'll be all right." He promised to shake hands with, and provide a photo to, every child, "even if it takes until three in the morning." Troy Melton and Boyd Stockman provided stuntman assistance. At an October non-rodeo appearance, Duncan was still not riding.

Cisco and Pancho in their rodeo act emphasized safety and accident prevention, yet seemed to experience more than their share of mishaps. In 1951, en route to Windsor, Ontario's, rodeo, Duncan had his gun confiscated by Canadian customs officials. On the last night of a 1952 Des Moines rodeo, the villain tossed a satchel from the stagecoach directly in front of Pancho's horse, which spooked and threw Leo. Unhurt, he laughed off the incident. At Chicago, a wagon substituting for a stagecoach tipped over on a turn, injuring a young woman passenger.

Cisco and Pancho began 1954 at Houston's rodeo. They rode on parade and on the Salt Grass Trail Ride. Stuntmen included Bill Catching, Troy Melton and Boyd Stockman. A young lady reporter was a stagecoach passenger rescued by the Cisco Kid and Pancho. In the fall, the stars entertained at the Indiana and Michigan State Fair rodeos, and at Chicago's Dairy Show Rodeo.

Leo was featured as a solo guest star at Detroit's 1948 Michigan State Fair rodeo; at Fort Madison, Iowa, in 1950; and at the Arkansas Livestock Show and Rodeo in Little Rock in 1953. He appeared at the Roswell, New Mexico, rodeo in 1955 and, from 1956 through 1958, at Camp Pendleton's Marine Rodeo. He continued other appearances but, beginning in the fall of 1955, Leo no longer worked the rodeos with the Cisco Kid.

In addition to those with Pancho, Duncan Renaldo made solo appearances at Grand Rapids, Michigan, in 1950, and at Windsor, Ontario, in 1951. At Windsor, he awarded a Cisco Kid outfit to a six-year-old contest winner who guessed the number of words in a letter from Pancho to Cisco. He was adopted into the Iroquois tribe and recognized a young man who diverted a runaway horse from the grandstand. He rode in a convertible in the parade and was photographed with the rodeo queen. In 1952, questionable practices of a Washington, D.C. rodeo promoter delayed granting of a license. When the way was cleared, Duncan said, "I had to come. I couldn't disappoint all the kids." At the St. Louis Shriner's Hospital, Cisco raised the spirits of a seven-year-old fan suffering from a rheumatic heart condition, and visited other confined children. He set a record at two non-rodeo shows on Children's Day at Memphis' Mid-South Fair in 1954, drawing 50,000 fans. Squeezing in an interview by youthful reporters and visits to four hospitals, he received invitations to return as rodeo headliner in subsequent years.

Beginning in the fall of 1955, Duncan worked rodeos as a solo act. At Col. Selby's Border Legion Rodeo in Detroit, a massive crowd surrounded him as he stood atop a vehicle. Arriving for Col. Jim Eskew's Hero Scholarship Rodeo in Philadelphia, where he drew 75,000 fans, the Cisco Kid was photographed on a motorcycle as youngsters greeted him at the airport. At Waco's Heart O' Texas Rodeo, he put on the stagecoach robbery skit he had previously performed with Pancho, and visited patients at the Crippled Children's Hospital. He promoted gun safety, and in 1956 he had the barrel of his six-gun inscribed, "Do not touch me. I don't want to hurt you." Dedication to his public was again illustrated at the Big Brother's Rodeo at Saginaw, Michigan. On the eve of the rodeo's final day, he became ill. He got little sleep and awoke at 7:30 that rainy morning with a nosebleed and a headache. He kept a commitment to visit the Crippled Children's Hospital. For the matinee performance, which had drawn a sizable crowd, he went on early as harder rain threatened. When a downpour cancelled the evening performance, he remained an extra day at no cost to the organizers.

Duncan's arrival for Eugene's 1956 Emerald Empire Rodeo was two hours late. En route, his various flights, including a charter, suffered engine trouble, a damaged propeller and grounding. The delay increased to 1,500 the cheering crowd, many in Western outfits, meeting him at the airport. He kissed the cheeks of official rodeo beauties, chatted with the crowd and shook fans' hands before launching on a busy schedule that included lunch with the governor, a show at the Sacred Heart Hospital auditorium and a tour of the children's and polio wards. He visited the Crippled Children's Hospital and crowned the rodeo queen. At the rodeo, he presided over the awarding of a pony each to a boy and a girl. Rex Rossi and his brother Jim supported Duncan by hauling his horse Diablo and serving as stunt men.

At Memphis, Duncan visited the Variety Club's Home for Convalescent Children, stopping at every bed. He saw patients at Le Bonheur Children's Hospital and at the Crippled Children's Hospital. He appeared on local TV during the intermission of the *Cisco Kid* show, and talked to 800 junior safety patrolmen. His arena act now involved a fight with three bandits who robbed an old prospector. In rehearsal, he tore a back muscle throwing the villain over his shoulder, leaving him in pain and requiring taping. Rodeo organizers suggested he announce the injury and just make an appearance. Insisting that nothing be said, Duncan did his show as planned.

Duncan renewed rodeo appearances in 1958, arriving at the Calgary Stampede four days early for promotion. Black Jack Watts cared for Diablo. James Gray, Stampede historian, cites the Cisco Kid as one of Calgary's most successful celebrity experiences, noting that Duncan spent "days on end" visiting shut-ins. The same year, at the Snake River Stampede, Duncan awarded a trained child's pony to a ten-year-old boy. He appeared at civic meetings, on local TV and radio programs, and in the rodeo parade. He attended a Rotary/Lion's Club joint luncheon and visited the Elks Convalescent Home and the Boise Veteran's Hospital. He had the rodeo queen play the prospector's niece in his arena act. Upon return to Memphis' Mid-South Fair, he again toured care facilities. In 1963, Duncan appeared at Silver Springs, Maryland, for a special rodeo sponsored by the Ambassador of Nicaragua on the grounds of the Holy Family Seminary.

The popularity of the *Cisco Kid* TV show, the esteem in which youngsters held the characters of Cisco and Pancho, the pair's distinctive costumes, the opportunity to meet them up close and the actors' personalities, made their appearances exciting and satisfying events.

Daniel Boone Cast

FESS PARKER (1924–)   Fess Parker was born in Fort Worth, Texas, and raised in San Angelo. His name Fess, meaning "proud" in Old English, was shared with his father and later his son. He played sports in high school. After graduating in 1942, he served on a U.S. Navy minesweeper. At the University of Texas, Austin, he performed with amateur drama groups and played trumpet with local dance bands to meet expenses. Visiting actor Adolphe Menjou encouraged him to try Hollywood. Upon graduation, Fess enrolled in a Masters program at the University of Southern California. He soon joined a touring company of *Mister Roberts*. His first film was *Untamed Frontier* (1952). Over the next three years, he appeared in additional films and on TV.

Walt Disney selected 6'5", 215-pound Fess to play TV's Davy Crockett. Buddy Ebsen was his sidekick, Georgie Russell. Three *Davy Crockett* TV episodes led to a national phenomenon. Radios played "The Ballad of Davy Crockett" and youngsters bought from a landslide of merchandise items, including coonskin caps. Broadcast in black-and-white, the shows were filmed in color to heighten their appeal when they were edited together into a feature film, *Davy Crockett, King of the Wild Frontier* (1955). Fess achieved international fame and a share of commercial tie-ins, including his own theme song recording. He made personal appearances across the country and in Europe. Additional TV episodes were combined for a second film, *Davy Crockett and the River Pirates* (1956). Fess made additional films, including *The Great Locomotive Chase* and *Westward Ho! The Wagons* (1956), *Old Yeller* (1957) and *The Light in the Forest* (1958). His recording of Stan Jones' song "Wringle Wrangle" sold a half-million copies. Leaving Disney, Fess made other films. A guest role on Bob Newhart's TV show displayed his flair for comedy and led to his starring for one season on TV's *Mr. Smith Goes to Washington*.

The Disney organization, which retained the Davy Crockett character rights, vetoed Fess' idea for a Crockett series, so he turned to another legendary historical frontiersman. *Daniel Boone*, with Fess as producer-star, began on NBC-TV in September 1964. Although a history major, Fess never taught in a classroom. He felt that his fictionalized exploits of Davy Crockett and Daniel Boone brought history to life and sparked interest in the heroes'

Star Fess Parker ("Daniel Boone") is met upon arrival for the 1966 Fort Madison, Iowa, rodeo by general chairman Mike Howard (Fort Madison [Iowa] *Evening Democrat* photograph, used with permission. Obtained from Tri-State Rodeo, Fort Madison, IA).

real lives. The supporting cast included Patricia Blair as his wife, Ed Ames as the educated Indian Mingo and Jimmy Dean as trapper Josh Clement. *Daniel Boone* ran six years for 165 episodes, some in color, until 1970.

Fess was an outdoorsman who raised and rode horses, played polo, hunted, sailed and golfed. He held a civilian pilot's license and often commuted to the studio in his own plane. As an entertainer, he had credits as an actor, writer, producer, director, singer and composer. A strong family man, specializing in family-type entertainment, he imprinted his portrayals of Davy Crockett and Daniel Boone forever in the public minds. He was honored with a Golden Boot Award. He enjoyed further success in real estate, and now operates a resort and winery in Santa Barbara, California.

"Daniel Boone" on the Rodeo Trail

The popularity Fess gained as Davy Crockett and sustained as Daniel Boone made him a welcome performer on the rodeo circuit. At rodeos, he presented a polished show of songs and conversation. Personal appearances for Walt Disney prepared him for crowds.

Parker performs at the 1966 Fort Madison rodeo with the Boonevilles (Fort Madison [Iowa] *Evening Democrat* photograph, used with permission. Obtained from the Tri-State Rodeo, Fort Madison, IA).

The Sons of the Pioneers, the Boonevilles or the New Establishment provided musical support. When asked to describe his act, he simply replied, "I'll sing some, talk some and shake hands." His wife and children often accompanied him on the road.

Over a period of about seven years, roughly parallel to telecasts of the *Daniel Boone* show, Fess played many rodeos that employed Western stars, including Little Rock and Fort Smith, Arkansas; Salt Lake City, Utah; Fort Madison and Sidney, Iowa; Louisville, Kentucky; Cheyenne Frontier Days; Waco and Odessa, Texas; Shreveport, Louisiana; and the Texas Prison Rodeo. His attire upon arrival in a city was usually casual business dress. This was also true for his occasional participation in rodeo parades, in which he rode in an automobile. This made his arena entrance in Daniel Boone buckskins all the more impressive. He brought to the stage his long rifle ("Old Betsy" or "Ole Tick Licker") and included "The Ballad of Davy Crockett" in his musical selections. He told reporters that he looked forward to filming breaks that allowed for rodeo appearances. Rodeos were a challenge, and he sought to constantly improve his act. Still, he welcomed the change of pace and the opportunity to show his talent. He enjoyed meeting fans and getting their input regarding his show.

At Jackson's Dixie National Rodeo in early 1966, Fess, appearing with the Sons of the Pioneers, visited Mississippi's governor, Senate and House of Representatives, as well as a cerebral palsy school. The governor commissioned him an honorary staff colonel. That summer, when he appeared with the Sons of the Pioneers at the J Bar H Rodeo in Camdenton, Missouri, Rex Allen was the announcer. In the fall of that year at the Mid-South Rodeo at Memphis, Tennessee, the governor interrupted the rodeo to make Fess an honorary colonel on his staff. At the New Mexico State Fair Rodeo in the fall of 1968, 30 of Fess' relatives from New Mexico and West Texas met him for a family reunion. Relatives of Daniel Boone's brother met him at the 1969 Fort Worth Stock Show rodeo, where Fess introduced his mother in the arena. He arrived with his wife and children at July's Snake River Stampede, where he presented a pony to a contest winner. At Omaha's Ak-Sar-Ben Rodeo in September, Fess was inducted into the rodeo's Western Hall of Fame. Promoters were impressed with Fess' popularity and support in making rodeos a success.

ED AMES (1927-) Boston-born Ed Ames began in show business as a member of the singing Ames Brothers, formed in 1947. The group had hit records and, at one point, their own TV show. With the group and solo, Ed sang some title songs for movies. In the 1960s as a solo performer, Ed had top-20 hit recordings. His voice also gained him Broadway credits. As Daniel Boone's Indian sidekick Mingo until 1968, Ed was pictured with Fess Parker on the covers of Daniel Boone comic books. He made a memorable tomahawk-throwing appearance on *The Tonight Show* with Johnny Carson. Following *Daniel Boone*, Ed had guest roles on other TV series.

"Mingo" on the Rodeo Trail

Ed Ames as Mingo headlined the Phoenix Jaycee Rodeo in March 1967. In November of that year, flu-stricken Fess Parker could not continue beyond the opening performance of the St. Louis Fireman's Rodeo. Ed as Mingo stepped in for the duration of the rodeo.

OTHER CAST *Daniel Boone* supporting player Jimmy Dean frequented the rodeo circuit, but as a country music singer rather than as his series character. Fess Parker's earlier *Davy Crockett* sidekick Buddy Ebsen made some rodeo appearances as Jed Clampett of *The Beverly Hillbillies*.

Forrest Tucker as Sgt. O'Rourke of ABC-TV's *F Troop*.

"F Troop" Cast

F Troop cast members Forrest Tucker (as Sgt. O'Rourke), Larry Storch and Ken Berry headlined the 1966 Jaycees Rodeo in Phoenix, Arizona.

Gunsmoke Cast

JAMES ARNESS (1921–) James Arness (originally Aurness) was born near Minneapolis, Minnesota. Younger brother Peter Graves also had TV stardom in his future. Jim spent summers hunting, fishing and sailing, but did some acting and singing during his school years. A World War II Army draftee, he suffered a severe leg wound in Italy, endured a long recovery and acquired a residual limp. Following discharge, he was a radio announcer and acted in stage plays prior to relocating to Hollywood. A stage appearance led to Jim's screen debut in *The Farmer's Daughter* (1947). He was in *Wagonmaster* (1950), *The People Against O'Hara* (1951) and (unrecognizable under makeup) *The Thing from Another World* (1951). In 1954, he appeared in another cult favorite, *Them!*

His appearance in the film *Hellgate* (1953) led to his TV career. Charles Marquis Warren, who wrote, produced and directed the film, later produced *Gunsmoke*. More immediately, the part earned a contract and roles with John Wayne's production company. Nearly half of his films were Westerns. His size (6'6", 230 pounds) relative to other leading men sometimes caused him to be passed over for roles. In *Battleground* (1949) and *Stars in My Crown* (1950), future *Gunsmoke* co-star Amanda Blake was a fellow cast member. *Horizons West* (1952) featured Dennis Weaver. Jim starred in *Gun the Man Down* (1956).

Gunsmoke traced its adult Western lineage back to 1952 on CBS radio, where William Conrad's strong voice represented Matt Dillon. A "John Wayne type" was the image CBS-TV executives sought to star in their adaptation. Wayne recommended Jim, helped him overcome doubts, released him from his contract and volunteered to introduce the new series. *Gunsmoke*, first telecast on September 10, 1955, immediately set new standards of complexity and quality for Western series. When shooting to kill was the only recourse, TV's thoughtful but determined Matt Dillon was not a man to be taken lightly. The supporting cast of Dennis Weaver, Amanda Blake and Milburn Stone was outstanding. Beginning at 30 minutes in length, the show later (1961) expanded to 60 minutes. *Gunsmoke* earned high ratings and, during its record-setting 20-year run, garnered awards.

Following *Gunsmoke*, James Arness was Zeb Macahan on *The Macahans*, renamed *How the West Was Won* (1976–79). He was in a pair of TV movies, *The Alamo: 13 Days to Glory* (1987) and *Red River* (1988). He also starred in five *Gunsmoke* TV movies from 1987 to 1994. He was inducted, along with other *Gunsmoke* cast members, into the Hall of Fame of Great Western Performers at the National Cowboy Hall of Fame. He received a Golden Boot Award and the Autry Museum's Western Heritage Award. In 2001, his autobiography was published.

"Matt Dillon" on the Rodeo Trail

In his early years as Matt Dillon, James Arness embarked on personal appearances, some at rodeos. It was said that a Western star at a rodeo resulted in children dragging their parents to the contests expressly so the youngsters could see their cowboy hero in person. Would this apply to the star of an adult Western? Despite *Gunsmoke*'s conscious appeal to a more mature audience and its being telecast at a later hour, it attracted the younger set, as well as adults. Perhaps it helped that *Gunsmoke*, for most of its run, was scheduled on Saturday evening, or that there was a *Gunsmoke* comic book. Whatever the reason, Jim attracted crowds of youngsters and adults on his limited rodeo trail excursions. With other *Gunsmoke* cast members, he was at Camp Pendleton's 1957 U.S. Marine Rodeo. His appearance in 1958 helped put Sikeston's Jaycee Bootheel Rodeo on the map. Advance ticket sales were five times greater than those of the previous year, and Jim drew record crowds. In the arena spotlight, he spoke about

James Arness, Matt Dillon of *Gunsmoke*, in Houston's 1959 rodeo parade (courtesy Metropolitan Research Center, Houston Public Library, Houston. Press #1164).

Gunsmoke. With film stuntman Al Wyatt, he demonstrated the staging of movie fights and he closed by reciting "The Cowboy's Prayer." He and Al Wyatt visited the home of an invalid.

Early in 1959, Jim began a two-week engagement at Houston's rodeo, one of the nation's biggest. About 500 fans welcomed his official railroad arrival. Reporters commented that he looked about 15 years younger than Matt Dillon did on TV. Fans commonly hobbled up to Jim with one stiff leg (mimicking Chester) to ask for an autograph. Houston's weather, sometimes bad at rodeo time, was cooperative this year, as Jim participated in the Salt Grass Trail Ride and rode horseback in the downtown rodeo parade. He met with the press, made the radio and TV rounds, visited the Spring Branch Dad's Club and greeted riders on the Sam Houston Trail at Memorial Park. He didn't have a special weapon or trick horse, but he did kick his way out of a man-sized TV box to a "deafening" cheer. He gave details about the *Gunsmoke* show, staged a fight scene, sang a couple of Western songs and rode around the arena to greet youngsters. On Kid's Day, he stopped to shake hands with a group of young polio patients. In August 1959, he was grand marshal of the Los Angeles Sheriff's Rodeo. Later that year, he shared billing with Johnny Cash at the Texas Prison Rodeo. For reasons unknown, Arness, though popular at rodeos, didn't continue his rodeo appearances.

DENNIS WEAVER (1924–2006)

Dennis Weaver dealt with horses on the family farm in Joplin, Missouri. A top high school athlete in football and in track and field, he attended Joplin Junior College. In 1943, he enlisted in the U.S. Naval Reserve, serving in naval aviation, continuing in track and field, and earning a commission. Following discharge, he worked his way through the University of Oklahoma. A drama major, he appeared in college productions. Showing championship form in track and field competition, he narrowly missed a spot on the 1948 U.S. Olympic decathlon team. Completing his degree, he understudied the role of Turk in Broadway's *Come Back Little Sheba* before playing the part with a road company. Actress Shelley Winters noticed him at the Actor's Studio and recommended him to Universal-International.

Universal's further training in filmmaking arts and horseback riding led to a number of supporting roles, some in Westerns. Failing to achieve a breakthrough at the studio, Dennis freelanced. He played the male lead in *A Streetcar Named Desire* on stage in Los Angeles, where he operated the Dennis Weaver Actor's Workshop. He appeared in four films released in 1954–55, taking odd jobs during periodic acting lulls. In 1955, he was delivering flowers when he auditioned for the role of Chester on *Gunsmoke*. He was the first *Gunsmoke* actor cast. The show's director suggested that Chester have a disability to emphasize that he was less vigorous than Marshal Dillon. Making Chester a classic character, Dennis adopted a limp, maintaining stiffness of limb through natural muscle control. Filling out the character from his own resources, he gave Chester an exaggerated drawl common to his home area. *Gunsmoke* made stars of its players.

Despite opportunities to direct episodes and acknowledgment of his contribution, Dennis in the early 1960s felt constrained by his single *Gunsmoke* characterization and wanted to expand his acting range. Following nine seasons as Chester, he left *Gunsmoke* in January of 1964. Thereafter, he made the transition from sidekick to leading man in several TV series, achieving his objective of playing a variety of characters. In *Kentucky Jones* (1965) he was a veterinarian, on *Gentle Ben* (1967–69) he was a game warden and on *McCloud*

Publicity photo of "The *Gunsmoke* Trio," c. 1959 (courtesy Southeastern Livestock Exposition Rodeo, Montgomery, AL).

(1971–77) he was a New Mexico lawman transplanted to New York City. He guest-starred on series and appeared in TV films, including the mini-series *Pearl* (1978) and *Centennial* (1978–79). In *The Great Man's Whiskers* (1969), he played Abraham Lincoln, and in *The Ordeal of Dr. Mudd* (1980) he portrayed the physician alleged to have aided Lincoln's assassin. In the 1980s, he starred in three series: *Stone* (1981), *Emerald Point N.A.S.* (1983–84) and *Buck James* (1987–88). He continued to appear in TV productions, including Westerns, and he introduced films on the Encore Westerns Channel. In late 2001, his autobiography was published.

In 1972, Dennis spoke at a fundraiser that yielded $1,000,000 for a hospital in his hometown, where a street is named for him. He served two years as president of the Screen Actors Guild. He vigorously promoted health and environmental issues. For his role on *Gunsmoke*, he received an Emmy nomination in 1957. In 1959, he won an Emmy as Best Supporting Actor in a Dramatic Series. He received two additional Emmy nominations (1974 and 1975) for his starring role in *McCloud*. With other *Gunsmoke* cast members, he was inducted into the Hall of Great Western Performers at the National Cowboy Hall of Fame. He received a Golden Boot Award.

AMANDA BLAKE (1929–89)   Amanda Blake was born Beverly Louise Neill in Buffalo,

New York, where she acted in a grade school production. In 1943, she moved with her family to California, completing high school and attending Pomona College. Entering the acting profession, she returned east to appear in New England summer stock and on radio in Buffalo. She broke into films with *Stars in My Crown* (1950), a Joel McCrea Western. She appeared in several additional films and in episodes of TV dramas.

Familiar with the radio *Gunsmoke* character, Amanda's persistence landed her the TV role of Miss Kitty of Dodge City's Long Branch Saloon. The red-haired, blue-eyed Blake played Kitty Russell for 19 of *Gunsmoke*'s 20 years. At first her period costume was authentic down to the lace-up shoes, but more comfortable apparel soon replaced invisible items. Amanda's dressing room sported Dodge City décor, including a refrigerator made to look like a period safe. Later, executives presented her a pair of prop lamps from the set. She was nominated for a 1959 Emmy Award as Best Supporting Actress in a Dramatic Series.

Following her departure from *Gunsmoke*, Amanda did some TV guest spots and appeared in the TV movie *Gunsmoke: Return to Dodge* (1987). She was inducted into the Hall of Great Western Performers at the National Cowboy Hall of Fame and received a Golden Boot Award. She traveled, and supported wildlife conservation and animal welfare causes. She suffered from throat cancer, but it was revealed that her passing resulted from AIDS–related complications.

Milburn Stone as Dodge City's "Doc" on television's *Gunsmoke*.

MILBURN STONE (1904–80) Milburn Stone was born in Burrton, Kansas. Moving with his family to Fort Larned, even closer to Dodge City, he gained a thorough background in the area and its people. His father, a country storeman, wanted him to become a doctor. Milburn turned down an Annapolis appointment to join a traveling repertory company, the Allen Mames Players, touring the Midwest as an actor, director, musician and handyman. For a time, he was a partner in a vaudeville act, "Stone and Strain—Two Loose Pages from the Book of Harmony," offering "songs, dances, and snappy chatter." Milburn said the act kept him fed. It also honed talents that later entertained rodeo fans. He performed in little theater and repertory groups prior to his 1932 Broadway debut in Sinclair Lewis' *The Jayhawkers*. Other Broadway roles followed. His first film was *Ladies Crave Excitement* (1935). Gas station earnings supplemented his initially meager film income. From 1943 to 1947, he was under contract to Universal Studios. He eventually acted in over 200 films, including *Young Mr. Lincoln*, *Reap the Wild Wind*, *Cass Timberlane* and *The Long Gray Line*. Some of his films were Westerns. He made numerous TV appearances.

In 1955, Milburn was selected as *Gunsmoke*'s Galen "Doc" Adams, Dodge City's only medical professional. He patterned the character partially after his paternal grandfather, Joe Stone, a Civil War veteran who seldom smiled, but had a good sense of humor and a propensity to tease. Another influence was a hometown frontier doctor and family friend, Doc Hampstead. Despite two heart attacks, Milburn stayed the full run of the series (until 1975). Recognizable in his black hat, threadbare jacket and vest, string tie, wire-rimmed glasses

Ken Curtis (left) and Milburn Stone, Festus and Doc on *Gunsmoke*, exit the 1970 Pikes Peak or Bust Rodeo arena in a convertible. This was the duo's third Colorado Springs appearance and one of Mr. Stone's last rodeos (courtesy Pikes Peak Library District Local History Collection, Colorado Springs, CO. Stewarts color neg).

and graying hair, Milburn later revealed that his pocket watch on a chain didn't really run. He often wore a grouchy scowl, and could be cantankerous in conversation. Doc's convincing medical practice provoked fan mail requesting medical advice. In 1960, he was made an honorary member of the Kansas Medical Society. The next year, he became one of only five laymen in that organization's 100-year existence to receive their Outstanding Service Award. He was also made an honorary member of the National Coroners Association.

Senior in acting experience on the set, Milburn was reportedly outspoken in his opinions. Serious about his obligation to his public, he tersely stated that any actor who didn't feel that way should get out of the business. On personal appearance tours, he was genial and laudatory concerning the show and fellow cast members, although fans enjoyed seeing his cantankerous side. In 1968, he was awarded an Emmy as Best Supporting Actor in a drama. When *Gunsmoke* ended, he retired to ranching at Rancho Santa Fe, California. Milburn passed away in La Jolla, California.

The Gunsmoke *Trio: "Chester, Kitty and Doc" on the Rodeo Trail*

Dennis Weaver, Amanda Blake and Milburn Stone joined James Arness at the Camp Pendleton Marine Rodeo in 1957. Amanda and Milburn returned in 1958. The three devised for fairs and rodeos an act comprised of dialogue, songs and dance on the order of an old-time vaudeville act. All three supporting actors were show business veterans who had performed similar bits in the past. Amanda, having done little singing in public, tended to be nervous until she hit the first few notes. Milburn, the acknowledged leader, described the "*Gunsmoke* Trio" act as designed to produce a shock effect on the audience. The actors engaged in humorous dialogue within their familiar *Gunsmoke* characterizations, and then displayed less familiar singing and dancing talents. Kitty's costume, considerably more abbreviated than what she wore on television, included sequined mesh stockings. She sang "The Long Branch Blues" and joined Doc in a duet of "When You and I Were Young Maggie." Chester, typically last to make an entrance, vaulted stiff-legged over hurdles. His song was "What Do You Do When You Don't Know What To Do?" Chester and Doc could be counted on to get into an argument. The three combined for dancing and such songs as "He's Got the Whole World in His Hands" and "May God Be with You." They typically exited in a surrey.

Milburn proudly stated, "We play a date like this to entertain the people, make friends, and go away leaving the people happy... We like to have the public like us when we leave and know they've been entertained." Up to this time, most Western entertainment at rodeos consisted of hero cowboy stars, musical groups and one or two top sidekicks. *Gunsmoke*'s popularity, as exemplified by this troupe, led the way for TV's Western supporting players to headline rodeos. Chester, Kitty and Doc enjoyed success with their show from 1959 through 1961.

Usually backed-up musically by the Frontiersmen and Joanie, the Trio played the rodeo at McCook, Nebraska's, Red Willow County Fair, where Chester met his local counterpart, and they visited patients at St. Catherine's Hospital. At Sikeston, Missouri's, Jaycee Bootheel Rodeo, a kindergarten group met them at the airport and Dennis Weaver's parents visited their son. Forty third-graders awaited their arrival at Charlotte, North Carolina. There, Milburn visited a trumpet player from his 1920s repertory company. Other rodeos included the New Mexico State Fair; Montgomery, Alabama; Camdenton, Missouri; and Little Rock, Arkansas.

Gunsmoke stars also made rodeo appearances as individuals. Dennis Weaver was grand marshal of the 1960 Palm Springs rodeo parade and of the 1996 Calgary Stampede parade. Amanda Blake lent her celebrity to the 1958 Riverside (California) Sheriff's Rodeo. She was the first female Western star honored at the California Rodeo at Salinas (1968) and to be presented the Buffalo Bill Award at North Platte's rodeo (1972). By early 1964, Milburn Stone was making solo rodeo appearances, inviting children to the center of the arena to join him in a dance named for the locality. Once he had completed his act of singing, dancing and humor, he circled the arena in a buggy. Visiting schools, he sat on the floor and joked with the children, leaving time to sign autographs. He also visited young hospital patients.

KEN CURTIS (1916–91) Curtis Wain Gates was born at Mud Creek, near Lamar, Colorado. As a youngster, he moved with his family to Las Animas. When Curtis was 12 years old, his father was elected sheriff. In their jail building home, Curtis' mother cooked for the prisoners as well as for her family. Young Curtis, as an apprentice jailkeeper, had real-life preparation for supporting Marshal Dillon on *Gunsmoke*. He was also immersed in music at local dances and in his home, where his family played various instruments and sang. During his high school years, he played saxophone in a combo, entertaining to aid his dad's re-election. Enrolled in a pre-med program at Colorado College, he performed locally with vocals and guitar, and participated in student musical activities. Writing songs for a college production encouraged him to leave school to try that trade.

In the late 1930s in Los Angeles, Curtis decided to become a singer, performing as staff vocalist for NBC radio. His desire to be a big band singer took him to New York and back to Los Angeles, but he worked mainly in construction. Thanks to his demo record finding its way to bandleader Tommy Dorsey, he was hired as a temporary replacement for Frank Sinatra and changed his name to "Ken Curtis." He then worked on radio and toured with Shep Fields' orchestra. He made recordings with both bands. He served in the Army from 1942 to 1945.

Ken appeared in films as a singing cowboy. He substituted temporarily for Lloyd Perryman with the Sons of the Pioneers and was subsequently asked to replace Tim Spencer. With the Pioneers, he provided music for films. Playing a non-singing, Zorro-type role, he starred in the 12-chapter serial *Don Daredevil Rides Again* (Republic, 1951). He sang in *The Quiet Man* (1952). His work with the Sons of the Pioneers included recordings, the Rex Allen radio show in 1950, tours, rodeo dates, a Carnegie Hall concert and the Lucky U Ranch program. He left the group in early 1953, lending his voice to Pioneer recordings until 1957. He and pal Shug Fisher took over the Lucky U Ranch radio program. With two partners, Ken formed a trio, re-named the program *The Lucky U* and emphasized popular music. Once married to John Ford's daughter, Ken's association with the director led to roles in several of Ford's films. In 1959, he produced three films. He was featured in John Wayne's *The Alamo* (1960) and appeared as guest star on TV series. From 1961–63, he played a skydiver on TV's *Ripcord*.

Ken's Festus dialect evolved over time. When *The Lucky-U Ranch* added comedy in the early 1950s, Ken contrived a character, Dink Swink, endowed with a Festus-like country dialect. For *The Searchers* (1956), John Ford had Ken's character, Charlie McCorry, speak

Composite photo showing Ken Curtis as a singing cowboy film star, c. 1945, and as *Gunsmoke*'s Festus, 1960s.

that way. As a guest star on TV's *Have Gun Will Travel,* Ken, in dialect, was Monk, a muleskinner. The *Have Gun Will Travel* writer, later working on a *Gunsmoke* episode featuring a similar character, thought of Ken. Entitled "Us Haggens," the episode introduced Festus, the only honest member of an outlaw family. The dialect derived from speech common to Ken's native region, not far from the Texas panhandle. He added such expressions as "Gollee Bill" and "Ol' Scudder" from relatives and acquaintances. Milburn Stone put in a good word for his old friend, and Ken began as a *Gunsmoke* regular in the episode "Prairie Wolfer" in January 1964. Viewer reception was favorable, and in April, Chester made his final appearance. Ken was apprehensive about his acceptance, given Chester's long-standing popularity, but Festus won the hearts of viewers. He was a mainstay for *Gunsmoke*'s 11 remaining years. Ironically, a performer blessed with a fine singing voice realized his greatest fame by putting on a comic dialect.

Ken enjoyed playing Festus, feeling that writers accorded him more depth and independence than they had Chester. He was gratified by the laughter he brought his public. He believed that, having found a role that seemed tailor-made for him, he should stay in it. Yet, Festus was too scruffy a character for him to "become" Festus. Ken was known as a cultured gentleman, a "class" individual of high character. He was real, without pretense or conceit, and spoke his mind. When Milburn Stone was ill, Ken often visited his bedside. Ken was patriotic and honored his country. He made announcements for national disease control organizations and highway safety. After *Gunsmoke* left the air, Ken appeared in the TV films *The Shadow Riders* (1982), *Once Upon a Texas Train* (1988) and *Conagher* (1991). He also joined the cast of *The Yellow Rose* (1983–84).

In 1972, Ralph Edwards honored Ken on TV's "This Is Your Life," which recognized the rodeo phase of his career. Ken received the Buffalo Bill Award at North Platte, Nebraska. In the spring of 1981, with the remaining principal cast of *Gunsmoke,* he was inducted into the Hall of Great Western Performers at the National Cowboy Hall of Fame. A year earlier, Ken and the Sons of the Pioneers received a Wrangler award. Ken served several years as a Hall trustee.

After a day at the Clovis Rodeo, Ken Curtis passed away in his sleep at his home in Fresno, California. He left a message for his fans and friends: "If there are to be prayers said for me, let them be said in the hearts of my friends and those whose lives I may have touched during my life time — by all means let there be not sadness or grief. I want my family and friends to remember only the happy times we were together, my attributes (if any) and try to overlook all of my faults— that should keep you all busy until the time we all meet up again."

"Doc and Festus" on the Rodeo Trail

In the summer of 1964, Milburn Stone was a veteran of *Gunsmoke,* while Ken Curtis had only recently replaced Dennis Weaver's Chester with his portrayal of Festus. Both actors had origins in the Arkansas Valley not far from Dodge City and had been friends for about 20 years prior to becoming *Gunsmoke* castmates. Both were show business veterans. Milburn had toured rodeos with "The *Gunsmoke* Trio" and as a solo act. Ken had played rodeo dates with the Sons of the Pioneers. Dedicated, hard-working professionals, they joined for several successful seasons on the rodeo circuit.

Even more than other *Gunsmoke* cast members, Ken was suited to produce the act's desired "shock effect." Rodeo fans loved the patter between cantankerous Doc and scruffy but lovable Festus. Doc could be counted upon to make humorous barbed comments about Festus, whom he introduced as "the world's only kindergarten drop-out." Doc told Festus, "Try to keep your voice low, so it'll match your I.Q." The astonishing contrast between Festus' twangy dialect and Ken's sweet singing voice never failed to "knock out" audiences.

In March 1966, Ken married Torrie Connelly, who had been a sponsor girl and barrel racer at the Madison Square Garden and Boston Garden rodeos, had worked at RCA headquarters and was a rodeo secretary, timer and color bearer for several stock contractors. Mrs. Curtis fixed Ken's favorite foods and frequently traveled to his rodeo engagements. Mrs. Festus also insured that Festus' appearance was thoroughly disreputable before he went out to greet his public.

In 1966, after opening night at Houston's Astrodome, Milburn was disappointed at seeing the unusual sight of numerous empty seats until he was reminded that a half-empty Astrodome represents 25,000 fans, the duo's greatest crowd to date. They played many smaller arenas as well, never failing to please. A sense of their impact is captured in this newspaper quote from Sidney, Iowa:

> The spectacular success of this year's rodeo can be attributed in large part to the popularity of the headline stars, Doc and Festus, from the television series, Gunsmoke.
> Although the long-time crowd pleasers have played at Sidney's rodeo recently, there were thousands and thousands of fans who wanted to see them in person once again.

At Cheyenne Frontier Days in 1969, the Laramie County Medical Society honored both Doc and Festus. Doc's citation read, in part, "Doc Adams is a splendid example of a frontier doctor—self-reliant and capable of making quick decisions. He typifies the doctor whose education consisted of reading medicine for a year and studying with another doctor for one year." Festus' medical accolade required imagination: "[F]or his folklore medicine, superstition, and his will to practice," and "[H]e was the forerunner of medical critics." Both characters were cited for "long and eminent service to the people of Dodge City."

Embarking upon the rodeo trail, Ken became a member of the PRCA. He often said that rodeo tours offered relaxation and a change of pace. One observed, however, that he was a mighty busy man. He was gracious in posing for pictures with individuals and groups, and generous in lending his time for rodeo publicity. He didn't just autograph, he stayed until the last scrap of paper was inscribed. He asked children's names, talked with them and wrote a message for them. Milburn Stone once said, "I think Ken would rather shake hands and sign autographs than eat."

Following a heart attack in 1968, Stone began to curtail rodeo appearances. A second attack in late August 1970 brought his rodeo work to an early end. Fans who watched the Doc-Festus arena show were treated to two "old pros" whose timing was impeccable, and who overflowed with talent. In August 2000, Doc and Festus were inducted into the Pikes Peak or Bust Rodeo Hall of Fame in Colorado Springs. The duo's names are inscribed on a rock in the city's downtown center.

Ken carried on as a solo act, reporting to fans on his pal's medical progress. He began modestly with six or seven rodeos a year. By 1969, he was making over 20 appearances, and in 1970 he made more than 30 personal appearances, most at rodeos. On solo performances, he might shake hands around the arena perimeter from a mule. He performed at children's and veterans' hospitals. He substituted or extended his engagement when other performers cancelled. Once, after he had signed a rodeo contract, Ken learned that a change in *Gunsmoke*'s filming schedule required his presence on set. He immediately chartered a jet to fly to Texas after each day's filming in order to meet his rodeo commitment. Fortunately, a subsequent change rendered that plan unnecessary.

Reverting to normal speech, Ken prompted fans to ask, "What happened to your voice?" He explained that he couldn't talk like Festus all the time, and that he sometimes liked to just be himself. He described rodeo cowboys as the finest athletes in the world and said that rodeo represented everything great about America. He played many different rodeos, and often made repeat engagements. In his home state, he played the Pikes Peak or Bust and the Colorado State Fair rodeos five times each. Promoters, committees, fans and co-workers respected him, and he was deserving of all the success he achieved. Ken played rodeos until the late 1970s.

GLENN STRANGE (1899–1973) George Glenn Strange was born of Irish and Cherokee ancestry in Weed, New Mexico. He worked as a cowboy in his native state and as a lawman in Oklahoma. For a time, he boxed on the Chautauqua circuit. The 6'3" rodeo rider was nicknamed "Pee Wee." He joined the 101 Ranch, and wrestled steers from a motorcycle. In the early 1930s, he was part of Hoot Gibson's rodeo arena crew. He also drifted around the country as a fiddle player, working for radio stations in El Paso and Los Angeles. Later, he joined such singing groups as "The Arizona Wranglers" and "The Singing Riders." He even co-wrote Western songs.

Glenn's musical talents led to Hollywood, where he was a stuntman and extra. When not doing musical bits, he played mostly villains in Western features and serials. A knee injury suffered in a movie stagecoach accident curtailed his riding. In the 1940s, he played Frankenstein's

Glenn Strange as Sam, the Long Branch bartender on *Gunsmoke* (photograph made available in color at rodeos).

Monster in three Universal films. In the 1950s, he performed on many TV shows. For 11 years beginning in 1962, he was Sam, the Long Branch Saloon bartender on *Gunsmoke*. He often had dialogue, but his familiar craggy visage spoke volumes of his place as a Westerner. Glenn died of cancer.

BUCK TAYLOR (1938–) The son of Western sidekick and character actor Dub "Cannonball" Taylor, Buck Taylor was born Walter Clarence Taylor III in Hollywood. While attending high school, he studied art at the Chouinard Institute. He had enjoyed sketching from his earliest years and was inspired by Charles Russell's works. At the University of California he studied theater arts and fine art. Buck's education was cut short when his Naval Reserve unit was called to active duty. He served two years as a Navy fireman in Japan. Upon his return to civilian life, he competed in world-class gymnastics. Buck's athletic background, ranch upbringing and experience as a trail guide made him a natural as a movie stuntman. Doing stunts for TV's *The Rebel*, he injured a shoulder, ending his Olympic aspirations. Stunt work led to TV acting assignments. Cast as Newly O'Brien, Dodge City's gunsmith and deputy, he remained a member of *Gunsmoke*'s cast from 1967 until the series ended in 1975. Later, Buck lent his acting talents to many film and TV Western productions. Returning to his first love, he has toured the country exhibiting his paintings, which mostly reflect Western themes, often inspired by his film experiences.

Buck, his son Adam (who had begun a career in films) and daughter-in-law actress Anne Lockhart frequently participated in celebrity rodeos for charity. In 1994, Buck suffered a double loss when his dad passed away at age 87 and he lost his son Adam to a motorcycle accident.

Buck Taylor, Newly the gunsmith and sometime deputy on *Gunsmoke*.

Buck's son Matthew is a busy Hollywood stuntman and his younger son Cooper participates in rodeos and has worked in films. Buck's grandchildren are now active in entertainment and equestrian events. In 1979, Buck and his father Dub were on hand for opening ceremonies of the ProRodeo Hall of Fame. Buck was presented the Buffalo Bill Award at North Platte, Nebraska. Honored by the National Cowboy Hall of Fame in 1981, Buck participates in ceremonies there. In 1993, he was presented with a Golden Boot Award.

"Sam and Newly" on the Rodeo Trail

In the early 1970s, Buck Taylor ("Newly") and Glenn Strange ("Sam") paired to play a few rodeo dates. Buck credits some of *Gunsmoke*'s success to rodeo appearances of its stars over the years. The duo appeared as a pair or with Ken Curtis ("Festus") as a new *Gunsmoke* Trio. Following their debut in Lovington, New Mexico, the duo was well-received at Spooner, Wisconsin's, Heart of the North Rodeo in July 1971. That same month, Glenn and Buck joined Ken Curtis at Cheyenne Frontier Days 75th Anniversary. All three assisted in crowning Miss Frontier and provided rodeo publicity.

Early in 1972, the three, backed by the Frontiersmen, headlined the seven-performance Dixie National Rodeo at Jackson, Mississippi. At the rodeo, Buck's pleasant singing voice rendered "Everybody's Talkin' At Me" as a solo. He also joined Patti Thompson of the Frontiersmen in a duet of "I Never Promised You a Rose Garden." Glenn Strange played a hot fiddle solo, "Shoofly," and accompanied Buck, first on fiddle, then vocally, on "Take Me Back to Tulsa." Following Festus' comedy and songs, all combined for the patriotic finale, "America" and "God Bless America." Festus and Newly rode around the arena.

"THE HIGH CHAPARRAL" CAST

LEIF ERICKSON (1911–86) Leif Erickson, who played the patriarch of the High Chaparral Ranch, Big John Cannon, was once a band vocalist. In the Pacific during World War II, his Navy reconnaissance planes were twice shot down. He acted in stage productions and in non–Western films. In 1968, Nebraska's governor presented him with the Buffalo Bill Award at the North Platte rodeo.

LINDA CRISTAL (1934–) Linda Cristal played Big John Cannon's wife Victoria, on *The High Chaparral*. She appeared in more than 30 films. Born in Buenos Aires, Argentina, of Italian and French heritage, she was a 1968 "Hollywood Star of Tomorrow."

Left: Leif Erickson of NBC-TV's ***The High Chaparral***.

Linda Cristal of *The High Chaparral*.

MARK SLADE (1939–) Mark Slade played Big John Cannon's son from an earlier marriage, Billy Blue. Mark attended a drama school affiliated with New York University, first acted professionally in a Broadway play, and then landed a film role.

"Victoria and Billy Blue Cannon" on the Rodeo Trail

Linda Cristal and Mark Slade headlined Mercedes, Texas', 1969 rodeo. Shortly thereafter, they played the Louisiana State Fair Rodeo at Shreveport. They were treated to a luncheon of gumbo, and the mayor presented keys to the city. Neither had done much singing in the past, but singing was a part of their rodeo act. When, early in 1970, Cristal and Slade arrived in Jackson, Mississippi, for the Dixie National Livestock Show and Rodeo, Cristal was reported as more beautiful in person than on TV. One factor was that she wore her hair long. In the arena, she wore a striking Western-cut outfit of red and black, while Slade wore his High Chaparral costume and sang such songs as "Gentle on My Mind." Cristal also sang and did a bit of dancing. Slade circled the arena greeting fans from horseback, while Cristal rode in a surrey. The stars exited the arena to an autograph session. Fans were pleased to greet two of their TV favorites.

OTHER CAST On *The High Chaparral*, Cameron Mitchell played the role of Big John Cannon's less serious brother Buck. Henry Darrow appeared as Manolito, Victoria Cannon's brother. Cameron, Henry, producer David Dortort

Right: Mark Slade of *The High Chaparral*.

and other cast and crew appeared in the parade at Tucson's 1968 La Fiesta de los Vaqueros rodeo and at a hotel banquet. Cast members Rudy Acosta and Linda Cristal were in the parade, but not at the banquet. In February 1998, cast members Henry Darrow, Bob Hoy, Ted Markland and Don Collier appeared at Yuma, Arizona's, Silver Spur Rodeo.

"LARAMIE" CAST

ROBERT FULLER (1937–) Robert Fuller, born in Troy, New York, and raised in Key West, Florida, began in Hollywood as a stuntman. He served in the U.S. Army during the Korean Conflict. He co-starred as Jess Harper on TV's *Laramie* with John Smith from 1959 to 1962. He enjoyed acting in Westerns and was good at it. On *Wagon Train*, from 1962 to 1965, he played scout Cooper Smith. His Western films included *Return of the Seven* (1966), *The Gatling Gun* (1973) and *Mustang Country* (1976). He played in TV's *Emergency* for five seasons and did TV commercials. A guest at Western film festivals, he received a Golden Boot Award, has a star on the Hollywood Walk of Fame and has received numerous foreign awards.

"Jess Harper" on the Rodeo Trail

Robert Fuller took to the rodeo circuit with his friend, stuntman-actor Chuck Courtney. Courtney appeared in films (including several Westerns) from the 1950s to the 1990s and had supporting roles in episodes of Western TV series. Courtney was nephew Dan Reid in several episodes of *The Lone Ranger*. In 1970, Nebraska's governor presented Robert with a Buffalo Bill Award at North Platte. Robert presented Courtney with a Golden Boot Award in 1993. Courtney passed away January 20, 2000, after suffering a stroke.

JOHN SMITH (1921–95) John Smith was born Robert Van Orden in Los Angeles. His father died when John was young. He learned to ride at his uncle's ranch. At age 13, he joined the Screen Actors Guild as a member of the Bob Mitchell Boy's Choir, appearing in *Going My Way* (1944) and *The Bells of St. Mary's* (1945). He played football in high school and in junior college. MGM cast him in the film *Carbine Williams* (1952). His agent suggested a name change to "John Smith," liking its "All-American boy" connotation. The star noted that his name evoked the query, "Where's Pocahontas?" At the height of his career success, he named his cabin cruiser, "Pocahontas III." Under contract to John Wayne's company, John had a role in *The High and the Mighty* (1954). He was loaned out for several films, including *Friendly Persuasion* with future *Laramie* co-star Robert Fuller. John was a regular on TV's *That's My Boy* (1954–55) and *Cimarron City* (1958–59). For four seasons, he starred on *Laramie* as Slim Sherman, rancher and operator of a stagecoach relay station. John rode a horse called Alamo, obtained from John Wayne. Following *Laramie*, he appeared on stage, made a few more films and had guest spots on TV shows.

"Slim Sherman" on the Rodeo Trail

At rodeos in his *Laramie* outfit, John Smith, as Slim Sherman, was personable and gracious whether being mobbed by fans at his airport arrival, responding to questions at a press conference or showing his six-shooter to a young admirer. His rodeo act consisted of singing and telling a few jokes before riding around the arena to touch as many young fans' hands as possible. In rodeo interviews, he complimented the cooking of co-star Spring Byington ("Daisy") and praised Western films. He told of touring Japan and hearing *Laramie* dialogue dubbed in Japanese. John's first rodeo appearance was at 1959's Silver Anniversary of the Caldwell (Idaho) Night Rodeo. During his three-day stand at the rodeo, he discussed with Wyoming's governor the soon-to-premiere *Laramie*, set in the governor's state and hometown. He held an autograph party at the arena and was guest at a hotel luncheon. During the rodeo, a Jack Kelly–donated Shetland pony named Maverick was given away.

John appeared at the 1962 Southwest District Fat Stock Show and Rodeo at Lake Charles, Louisiana, where Governor Jimmie Davis rode his own horse Sunshine in the parade. John headlined the fall St. Louis Fireman's Rodeo and the 1963 Sheriff's Posse-Lions Club Rodeo in Lufkin, Texas. Later, he was parade grand marshal at the Reno Rodeo. Met upon his airport arrival by Miss Rodeo America, he rode in the rodeo's grand entry and crowned the new rodeo queen. Contracted for the Heart O'Texas Rodeo at Waco, he cancelled a week prior to accept a role in *Circus World*, about to be filmed in Spain. In the film, he played an ex–rodeo rider starring in a Wild West Show. Asked to fulfill John's rodeo commitment, Clint Walker obliged.

"THE LONE RANGER" CAST

The Lone Ranger, a character based on the imaginations of George W. Trendle and Fran Striker, was brought to life on radio in January 1933 over station WXYZ in Detroit, Michigan. As time went on, *The Lone Ranger* was featured in comic books, comic strips, movies, merchandise and on television. At least once, the *Lone Ranger* creators went to court to enjoin the practice of unscrupulous rodeo promoters using Lone Ranger imposters. Brace Beemer, the radio voice of the Lone Ranger, made personal appearances, including several rodeos. Indian companion Tonto sometimes accompanied him.

BRACE BEEMER (1902–65)   Marcus "Brace" Beemer was born in Illinois. A former station executive and show narrator, he assumed the role of the Lone Ranger upon the accidental death of his predecessor, Earle Graser, in 1941. Beemer, a young World War I veteran (he enlisted at age 14), remained in the role until the radio program ceased original broadcasts in the mid–1950s. At 6'2", weighing 200 pounds and possessing a deep voice, Beemer represented the masked man well on personal appearances. He died of a heart attack.

CLAYTON MOORE (1914–99)   Chicago-born Clayton Moore had been a circus trapeze artist and a model. His Hollywood career was interrupted by two years in the Air Force. He was a veteran of action films and serials when he was chosen to portray TV's *The Lone Ranger* beginning in September 1949. Moore cut an athletic figure as the Ranger. Absent two years because of a contract dispute, he then assumed the role again through 1961, and starred in two Lone Ranger films. The dignity and sincerity of his characterization carried over to his personal appearances.

The cast of the NBC-TV series *Laramie*: (left to right) John Smith, Bobby Crawford, Hoagy Carmichael, Robert Fuller.

Advertisement for Brace Beemer's appearance at the 1951 Madison Square Garden rodeo.

JAY SILVERHEELS (c. 1919–80) Born Harold J. Smith on the Six Nations Indian Reservation in Ontario, Canada, Jay was raised in the traditions of the Mohawk tribe of the Iroquois Nation. Arriving in Hollywood in 1933 with a professional lacrosse team, he boxed and performed bit parts in films. He played Tonto in all *Lone Ranger* TV episodes and two films. He acted or served as technical advisor for a number of additional films. In later years, he was involved in his Indian Actors Workshop and in harness racing. In 1979, he was given a star in Hollywood's Walk of Fame.

"The Lone Ranger" on the Rodeo Trail

Madison Square Garden rodeo programs in 1938 and 1939 carried Lone Ranger bread advertisements. Brace Beemer, in character as the Lone Ranger, appeared at North American rodeos from the early 1940s into the early 1950s. In the fall of 1944, he split dates with Roy Rogers at the Texas Rodeo at the Montreal Forum. Early in 1946, he and Silver shared billing with Tex Ritter and White Flash at Houston's Fat Stock Show Rodeo. He visited crippled children at Arabia Temple Shrine Clinic, where some children got to handle his guns and were given a silver bullet from his cartridge belt. Preceded by an Indian welcoming dance and accompanied by the strains of "The Eyes of Texas," he was awarded a commission in the

III. Television Casts Performing at Rodeos

Clayton Moore, TV's Lone Ranger, rears Silver.

Texas Rangers at a rodeo performance. Beemer's Lone Ranger headlined the Tulsa, Oklahoma, Livestock Exposition in late winter of 1948. A snowstorm closed the carnival portion of the expo, while the rodeo saw near-record attendance.

In 1948, the fifteenth anniversary of the *Lone Ranger* radio program, twice brought Beemer as the Lone Ranger to Cheyenne, Wyoming. For weeks prior to the event, loyal radio listeners nationwide heard references to "Frontier Town" on the *Lone Ranger* program. Youngsters accumulated a layout of a cardboard Western village. A radio contest finally asked for the name of the real-life "Frontier Town" from a clue that referred to "a *shy* girl named *Ann*." During the Lone Ranger's June visit, the mayor read a proclamation changing Cheyenne's name for one day to "Lone Ranger Frontier Town." The Lone Ranger was

Jay Silverheels as Tonto astride Scout.

named honorary mayor. The governor was also on hand. Ceremonies were held at the railroad station and at the state capitol. The Lone Ranger rode on parade and made a special nationwide radio broadcast. Cheyenne children gave the Ranger a giant postcard with over 5,000 signatures. A special postal cachet reading "Lone Ranger Frontier Town, Cheyenne, Wyoming" was issued. The Lone Ranger attended a 4-H dinner and cut a huge birthday cake with a saber. In July, opening day of Frontier Days honored the Lone Ranger, who presented a Western outfit to the "Frontier Town" contest winner, a 15-year-old Cleveland, Ohio, boy.

The Lone Ranger thrilled youngsters at the fall 1950 Championship Rodeo at Chicago's International Amphitheater by galloping across the arena on Silver and addressing them as part of his act. He met the mayor, made TV-radio appearances and visited Chicago-area hospitals. He headlined the first 12 days of the 1951 Madison Square Garden rodeo. The Lone Ranger and Tonto rode in the traditional parade to City Hall to meet the acting mayor. At Bellevue Hospital, he and Tonto toured hospital wards.

Subsequent Lone Ranger rodeo appearances featured TV's Lone Ranger (Clayton Moore) and Tonto (Jay Silverheels). Clayton was grand marshal of the 1955 Sheriff's Rodeo in the Los Angeles Coliseum. Tonto also appeared. Clayton appeared at the 1957 Pendleton (Oregon) Roundup as part of a General Mills–sponsored telecast. That same fall, the Lone Ranger and Tonto headlined dates at Memphis' Mid-South Fair Rodeo. Their act featured quick-draw and gun handling skills and rope tricks, as well as a recitation of Lone Ranger lore. The two also gave away silver bullets. Clayton and Jay starred that year at Madison Square Garden, where they shared billing with Lassie.

"THE RANGE RIDER" CAST

JOCK MAHONEY (1919–89) Jacques O'Mahoney was born to French and Irish parents in Chicago, Illinois, and moved to Davenport, Iowa. He was a multi-sport athlete through high school and two years of pre-medical studies at the University of Iowa. In California, he worked as a swimming coach, dancing instructor and aviation mechanic. He was a civilian instructor at the U.S. Army's flight school at Phoenix. In World War II, he was a U.S. Marine instructor and pilot and served on Atlantic submarine patrol, earning a commission. At 6'4", he became a Hollywood stuntman, doubling major stars. Charles Starrett helped him secure an acting role. Overcoming camera shyness and reluctance to recite dialogue, he performed as a stuntman and actor, often in the same film.

Jock felt that gymnastics training, pursued into adulthood, kept him from getting hurt more often. Nevertheless, he accumulated his share of scars and broken bones. His chest was crushed when a horse ran him into a tree branch while he was carrying a child dummy. He split a kneecap when he dove off a runaway buckboard and landed on a bottle. He had a few close calls, such as flying backward from a punch and off a moving train into rocks. Hit by a fake arrow in the chest, he fell backward onto a net, but was unable to clear before another stuntman's fall.

He also enjoyed successes. For Errol Flynn, he rode into a herd of stampeding cattle. In wet boots he doubled Randolph Scott, climbing a cliff above a mountain waterway cascading over rocks. For one stunt, he ran from behind a building and dove through the window of a moving stagecoach.

Gene Autry chose Jock to star as *The Range Rider*, a buckskin- and moccasin-clad character not previously established on radio or the big screen. On the first day of filming, Jock and sidekick Dick Jones (as "Dick West, All-American Boy") decided to perform their own stunts. The two actors thrilled fans with action-packed riding, fighting, climbing and leaping for 78 black-and-white episodes. The show found success across the country and abroad, enjoying a lengthy syndication run. The Range Rider and Dick West became cowboy heroes solely through TV.

Following *The Range Rider*, Jock's appearances on *The Loretta Young Show* won him acting roles in a number of feature films. In 1958, he starred for one season in the CBS-TV series *Yancy Derringer* as a New Orleans gambler. Jock played Tarzan in two films; however, location shooting in India and Thailand took a toll on his health. He held managerial positions away from Hollywood. In 1973, appearing on the *Kung Fu* series, he suffered a stroke. Subsequently he made few films, but coordinated stunts and had TV guest roles. In his later years, he directed three stage productions. Jock was inducted into the Hollywood Stuntmen's Hall of Fame and received a Golden Boot Award. In 1988, he underwent surgery for an aneurysm. He presented a Golden Boot to Dick Jones in 1989, then suffered a stroke and died before the end of the year.

DICK JONES (1927–)

Richard P. Jones, Jr., was born on a Texas cattle ranch. His mother, a horsewoman, saw to it that he was riding, and then trick riding, at the earliest possible age. By about age five, he did the hippodrome stand, the fender drag and the Cossack drag, as well as vaulting maneuvers. He learned to rope as well. As "Little Cowboy Rambler" on his own WRR Dallas radio program, he sang, recited Western poems and played the ukulele. At rodeos, he was billed as the "World's Youngest Trick Rider and Roper." Noticing him at the Texas State Fair Rodeo, Hoot Gibson advised that the boy give Hollywood a try. Hoot hosted Dick at his home and helped him get a start in movies. Dick made 11 films in the next four years playing a variety of youngster roles. He never made a film with Hoot Gibson, nor as a child actor did he use his trick riding and roping skills. He did many of his own stunts and those of other youthful actors.

Dick's early films included Westerns and comedy shorts. Made with major stars, some of his better-known films as a youngster were released in the years 1939–40. He kept up his studies at public schools or on the set. He appeared in Gene Autry's film *Mountain Rhythm* (1939), provided the voice of Walt Disney's *Pinocchio* (1940) and played child roles until he was 15 years old. With his voice changing, Dick played "Henry Aldrich" on New York radio while Ezra Stone was in wartime military service. He played ice hockey at prep school. He was cast as young Samuel Clemens in *The Adventures of Mark Twain* (1944).

Following discharge from U.S. Army service in Alaska, he established himself as a carpenter. Then Gene Autry wanted him for his first color film, *The Strawberry Roan* (1948). Dick married his high school sweetheart, Betty Bacon. His intent was to make the one film, and then return to carpentry. Signing a five-year contract with Autry, he was featured in a half-dozen of Gene's films and in several TV episodes.

As the Range Rider's youthful sidekick Dick West, Dick provided comic relief, but his role was a far cry from "oldtimer" or "fool" sidekicks. The show's success landed Dick the lead role in the 1954 series *Buffalo Bill, Jr.* In 52 episodes, Harry Cheshire played his guardian, Judge Ben "Fair and Square" Wiley, and Nancy Gilbert was his younger sister,

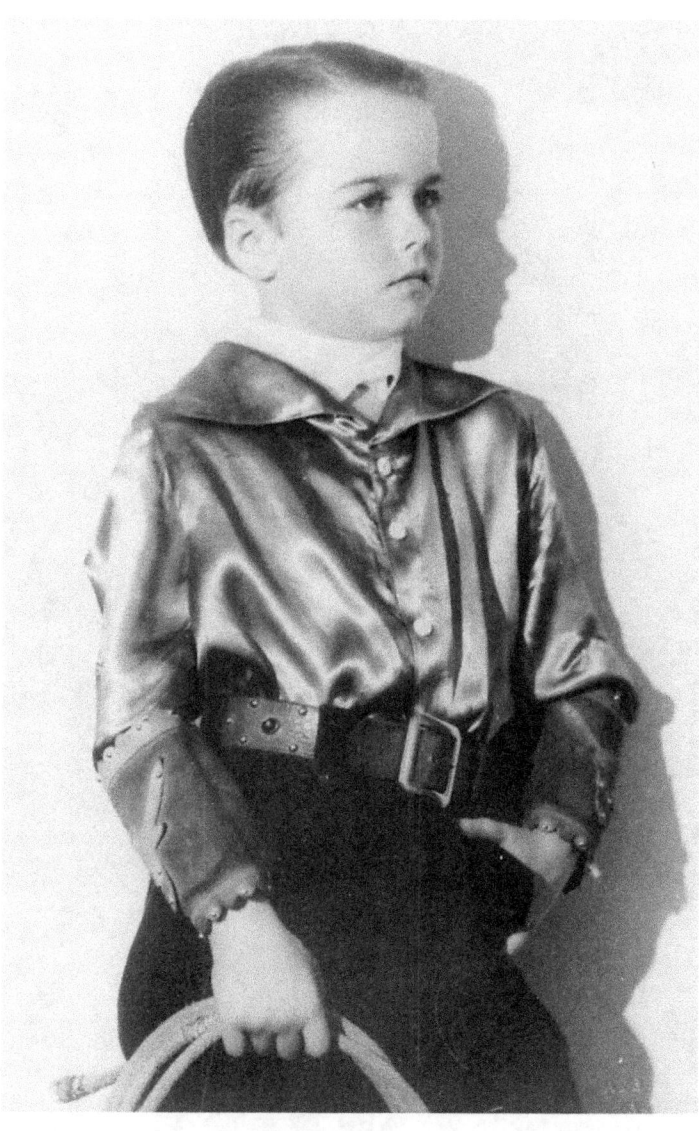

Young Dick Jones, from "World's Youngest Trick Rider and Roper" to Hollywood star (courtesy Eddie Brandt's).

Calamity. At age 29, the handsome, dark-haired Dick Jones appeared no older than his 18-year-old character. He was quoted as saying, "I'm probably the only 18-year-old in history who has been in show business for 22 years." The brash characters he portrayed on TV did not reflect the serious, soft-spoken nature of the performer. Dick made a few films through the 1950s and into the '60s. Successful in real estate and banking, Dick owned for some years a California ranch. He has a star on the Hollywood Walk of Fame, and he received a Golden Boot Award. He is a frequent guest at Western film festivals. Dick lives the part of the Western hero as a role model true to his word.

"The Range Rider and Dick West" on the Rodeo Trail

Jock Mahoney and Dick Jones based their rodeo act around action. When the house lights dimmed and the spotlight focused on the Range Rider and Dick West, the stars' agility was exploited to the utmost in a demonstration of how action elements of TV Westerns were accomplished. They might be shot off their horses by an ambushing villain and forced to regain the upper hand. Fans saw an outlaw bulldogged from his horse. For each performance's fight demonstration, the stars needed one solid, unbreakable table and enough breakaway props to furnish a room. A truckload of props supported the act. Just as the stars' TV stunts carried an element of risk and potential injury, so did the rodeo act. The action sequence was well-rehearsed and oft-repeated; however, the unexpected sometimes happened. Jock and Dick were tough, dedicated performers determined that the show go on. The fact that they were a "team" act and employed an additional stuntman allowed them to carry on under adverse conditions. They brought their own horses to rodeos in order to have support for their stunts and gentle animals used to crowds of youngsters. They created a high degree of excitement,

Jock Mahoney, of TV's ***The Range Rider***, greets a young Houston fan during his 1953 rodeo appearance (photograph copyright Houston Metropolitan Research Center, Houston Public Library, Houston. Press #776).

particularly among younger fans, and then circled the arena on horseback, touching every youngster's hand they could reach.

The 1953 Houston rodeo ran for multiple performances over 16 days. Early in the engagement when the Range Rider was shot and fell from his running horse, he hit heavily, injuring his left shoulder. He got up slowly, but completed the act, including the fight sequence. The next day at Rice Institute, he underwent deep heat diathermy treatments. "The horse was trained to run straight and not to veer," he explained, "but just as I was leaning down, my head a foot off the ground, the horse turned away and I fell and broke my left shoulder." Heavy taping and anesthetic injections got him through the remaining performances. Dick only dislocated four fingers. The duo scored a big hit in Houston.

In the spring, the stars toured eastern cities with Col. Jim Eskew's rodeo. Having appeared in Providence, Philadelphia and Pittsburgh, they made the final stop in Cleveland. For the first time, Dick's wife was in the audience. At the act's conclusion, the stars backed their horses rapidly toward the exit, tipping their hats on the way. Dick's horse suddenly slipped on the arena floor and turned over backwards on him. Already injured from the fall, in which the saddle horn struck his pelvis bone, Dick struggled to extricate himself. The horse reacted by kicking both rear legs, leaving imprints as Dick was struck in the chest and face. Jock helped his pal walk the short distance out of the arena. Put in traction at the hospital, Dick cut himself loose and left to attend a rodeo party.

Less than two months later, Dick was back creating rodeo action with Jock at the Peninsula Celebration Rodeo in Redwood City, California. Jock arrived just in time for the rodeo. Dick was there early to pass out pictures and handle the usual pre-rodeo activities,

While headlining the 1954 Arkansas State Fair Rodeo, the Range Rider (Jock Mahoney) visits a patient at Little Rock Children's Hospital (Johnnie M. Gray photograph, obtained from Arkansas State Fair and Livestock Show, used with permission of Kermit Gray).

such as being the guest at a Lion's Club meeting. Both stars participated in the rodeo parade and judged a local amateur show. In the fall of 1953, they performed at the Oakland Rodeo in a ballpark. During their engagement, I. Magnin and Company advertised Western outfits for boys and girls, "Just as worn by the Range Rider and Dick West…" They immediately moved on to Madison Square Garden, appearing with Gene Autry for a 21-day engagement. Both Jock and Dick had solid praise for their boss, as a man and as a friend. Despite publicity raving, "The Range Rider and Dick West embody the stirring adventurous spirit and action of frontier days," they learned that New York law required even visiting TV cowboys to carry a permit for sidearms, or be detained. During the rodeo's run, the partners staged a fight for Bellevue Hospital patients.

A photo showed Gene Autry saying goodbye to Jock and Dick in New York City as they moved on to headline an 11-day rodeo stand at Boston Garden. Dick limped into Boston from the effects of a horse stepping on his ankle, incurring a "green stick" fracture. He was able to ride better than he could walk. The worst was yet to come. On opening night, while executing a fall from his horse, Jock was kicked, injuring his left side. He announced to the crowd that he was hurt and departed from the arena, stating later that this was the first time he had walked out of a show. It was reported that he had suffered

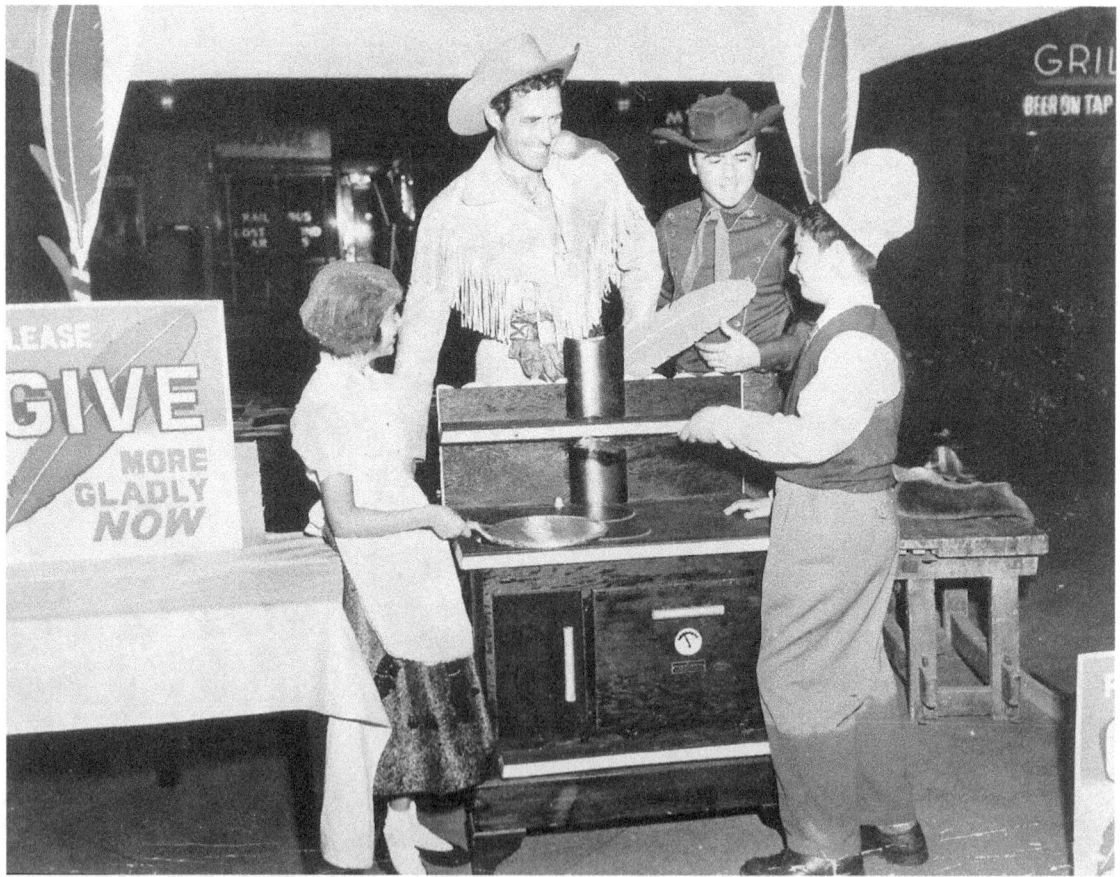

Boston Garden's 1954 rodeo stars, the Range Rider (left) and Dick West, stop at the Red Feather charity booth where youngsters demonstrate cooking skills (*Herald-Traveler* photograph by Robert J. Keller courtesy Boston Public Library, Print Department).

torn ligaments. Jock said, "Pain is nothing new to us... I am going to appear at every rodeo show." Attempting to mount a horse with his chest tightly taped, he passed out. He then had to admit that he had fainted for the first time. After a pain-filled, sleepless night, he quipped, "This is the time I wish I sang instead of doing rodeo stunts." He made every performance, but Dick assumed the action chores. A report stated that Jock had broken ribs. Between performances, TV sponsor Table Talk Pastries assured that the stars would not go hungry (by keeping them supplied with pies).

In 1954, the two starred at spring JE Ranch Rodeos. Toward the end of the first stand at Providence, Jock broke his left elbow in the staged fight with Dick. With Jock's arm in a cast, Dick fought stuntman Richard Smith for the final performance and through the Washington, D.C., stop. Jock, limited to light duty, rode his horse San Souci at each performance and used his good arm for hand-shaking. After Oregon's July 4th Molalla Buckaroo rodeo, they appeared at the one-day Los Angeles Sheriff's Rodeo. Jock related to author David Rothel (*The Gene Autry Book*) that he and Dick were introduced midway through Gene's side pass around the arena. They had to charge into the arena and take their bows, interrupting their boss' moment in the spotlight.

In the fall, Jock and Dick appeared at Fort Madison's rodeo. They were guests at a pancake breakfast, visited the newspaper and unmasked the "Masked Rider." They rode in the parade and visited hospital children's wards. In early October, Jock made a solo appearance at Little Rock's Arkansas Livestock Show. Dick's family had just doubled with the arrival of twins. Jock visited hospitalized children. Later in October, both stars headlined

Nancy Gilbert ("Calamity") and Dick Jones ("Buffalo Bill, Jr.") are greeted upon their arrival for the 1956 Cheyenne Frontier Days (courtesy Brammar Collection, Wyoming Division of Cultural Resources, Cheyenne. Neg. #3923).

Boston Garden's rodeo. Joined by Ray Whitley, they sang to children at City Hospital. At year's end, they donated a trophy saddle to be presented to the RCA's world champion steer wrestler.

At one point on the rodeo circuit, Dick Jones developed complications, including blood poisoning, when a cut on his hand was infected by proximity to ever-present stock droppings. Despite pain and severe swelling, Dick "went on with the show." As near as can be determined, the rodeo days of the Range Rider and Dick West came to an end in May 1955 with an appearance at the Lion's Club Rodeo in Sacramento, California, where they also visited orphanages and hospital children's wards. Hospital boys flexed their biceps for their heroes. Dick recalled how touched the rugged Western stars were by such visits.

In July 1956, Dick (as Buffalo Bill, Jr.) and co-star Nancy Gilbert appeared three days at Cheyenne Frontier Days. At a buffet supper at the Governor's Mansion, the governor presented Dick with a "Bronc Buster" certificate for service to the state. Nancy received a Western charm bracelet. The governor received a Buffalo Bill, Jr., belt buckle and a Calamity Jane doll. The stars visited the children's wards at Warren Air Force Base and veteran's hospitals. At home, they gave a boy, who had been seriously injured in an accident, a Buffalo Bill, Jr., ring, fringe from Calamity's shirt and a box of Mars candy bars. They appeared on Arthur Godfrey's show and presented a $50 savings bond to the youth calf-roping winner. Bill and Calamity attended a Frontier Pavilion children's party. In a newspaper ad, Buffalo Bill, Jr., invited kids to visit the local Robin Hood shoe store to pick up a free ring, "just like the one Bill wears on his TV show."

In August of that year, Dick headlined the St. Louis Fireman's Rodeo. His act now included playing the guitar and singing, backed by Ray Whitley and his musical group. He staged a fistfight with stuntman Fred Krone. Harry Cheshire, Judge Wiley on the TV series, also appeared at St Louis. Dick demonstrated his pistol draw to patients at the Shriners Hospital for Crippled Children. In fall of 1957, he drove from California towing his two horses, Chief and Little Chief, to rodeos at the Kentucky State Fair in Louisville and the Mid-South Fair at Memphis. Not entirely satisfied with his solo rodeo act, he closed the chapter on rodeo appearances.

Jock Mahoney was grand marshal of Palm Springs' Rodeo parade early in 1955, and was on hand for 1956 festivities. In July of 1959, he returned to Redwood City, California, as Yancy Derringer. Rodeo queens met his late flight, and he began a flurry of TV appearances. He participated in the rodeo parade. In the arena, he refrained from stunt work, limiting his appearance to riding and talking. This was Jock's last known appearance as a rodeo headliner.

Dick Jones has a strong personal attachment to rodeo, having contested on bucking horses and bulls. Among his memories are riding bareback broncs with a Dixon rigging. He recalls such dangerous moments as a bull's hook bringing rodeo clown Slim Pickens to his rescue, having a bucking horse run him through a chain-link fence, and another bronc turning upside-down on him. Proud of his RCA membership, he values his possession of a Casey Tibbs RCA button. A gift from rodeo producer Col. Jim Eskew is displayed on his fireplace: a horse-damaged Winchester that looks like it could shoot around corners.

As on their TV show, Jock Mahoney and Dick Jones put everything they had into entertaining crowds during their rodeo appearances. Fans saw unequalled athleticism in their act, as they held nothing back.

"RAWHIDE" CAST

ERIC FLEMING (1925–66)   Eric Fleming was born Edward Heddy, Jr., in Santa Paula, California. From an unhappy home, he spent his youth traveling about the country tackling a variety of jobs to survive during the Depression. He garnered some education by attending half-day school sessions and later completed college courses. During World War II, he served four years as a Navy Seabee. Upon discharge, he worked as a construction supervisor, during which time an accident required extensive facial surgery. Working as a film studio stagehand, he accepted the challenge of acting, beginning serious dramatic study. He acted in stage productions, appeared on TV and made films, largely in the science-fiction and horror realms. On *Rawhide*, conceived by Charles Marquis Warren, he played hard-nosed trail boss Gil Favor, responsible for making decisions, and overcoming natural and man-made obstacles to drive cattle herds to Missouri railheads. An hour-long black-and-white series of 144 episodes (1959–66), *Rawhide* had a realistic, gritty quality that had viewers tasting the dust of a cattle drive. Frankie Laine sang the series' theme song. Eric later made TV guest spots and had a role with Doris Day in *The Glass Bottom Boat* (1966). He lived modestly, and moved to Hawaii. Lured out of retirement for a TV project filming in Peru, he met an untimely death in a canoe accident.

"Gil Favor" on the Rodeo Trail

In Miami for the 1960 Orange Bowl Rodeo sponsored by the Fraternal Order of Police, Eric Fleming visited an 11-year-old girl at home. For a "name a bucking horse" contest, the girl suggested her name in a letter to Gil Favor, inviting the star to "drop by" her house. Police arranged for the girl to be sent home from school early on the pretext that they were to present her prize rodeo ticket. Instead, she received a visit from her hero. Eric presented her with a cowgirl outfit, complete with hat and boots.

As a rodeo headliner, Eric usually worked alone. He did travel with Clint Eastwood to Salinas in the summer of 1960 to accept the California Rodeo's TV Award for *Rawhide*. Following an appearance at Birmingham, Alabama, Eric headlined the fall Heart O'Texas Fair rodeo at Waco. His travel difficulties illustrated the obstacles Western stars sometimes encountered making transportation connections. Scheduled to arrive by air at 10:30 p.m. on a Monday to meet a full schedule of events beginning with breakfast on Tuesday, Eric, lacking sleep for more than 24 hours, did not arrive until shortly after noon on Tuesday. He had to hire a single-engine plane for a hop so that he could make new connections. He took the situation calmly, and quipped, "I should have stuck with my horse." The breakfast and a luncheon were re-scheduled.

In a Waco press reception, he candidly related his life experiences. He told of filming *Rawhide* amid a herd of cattle, spending 14-hour days in the saddle. Asked about Wishbone's cooking, he replied that the horrible faces the cast made on TV didn't require any acting. The session concluded with a siege of autograph and photo seekers. Eric rehearsed his rodeo act, studied a *Rawhide* script and caught a three-hour catnap before his night rodeo performance. The next day, he appeared on radio and TV shows, and toured the city's newspaper plant. He was guest at a luncheon with about 30 students selected by nearby schools. He visited an iron lung polio patient at her home. On Thursday, he spent

Rawhide cast (left to right): Eric Fleming, Clint Eastwood, Paul Brinegar and Sheb Wooley.

two hours on the phone to out-of-state fan clubs. At Baylor University, he attended a reception, toured the Texas History collection, spoke with drama students and visited dormitories. Interviewed, he credited *Rawhide*'s cast and crew for the show's success. He spoke of delays in filming caused by such modern intrusions as airplanes, and of cattle stampeding on a whim, instead of on cue.

For his arena act, Gil Favor drove about 20 head of Mexican steers into the arena with the lights out and the cattle horns glowing from fluorescent paint. In a spot-light, he narrated the history of trail drives. He introduced the owner of the cattle herd used on *Rawhide* as well as additional entertainers. Throughout his visit, Eric was described as totally relaxed and accommodating with regard to autographs and photos. He was gracious in meeting the hospitalized and confined. In June 1961, Eric joined fellow *Rawhide* cast members at Camp Pendleton's U.S. Marine rodeo. *Rawhide* stars were featured at the final (1962) Sheriff's Rodeo at the Los Angeles Coliseum.

CLINT EASTWOOD (1930–) Clint Eastwood was born in San Francisco, California. Like Eric Fleming, Clint was a child of the Depression. He was active in swimming and basketball during his high school years, while his main interest was jazz music. Drafted into the Army in 1951, he served as a swimming instructor at Fort Ord, where he was encouraged to try acting. Discharged in 1953, he enrolled in college on the G.I. Bill. He landed a Universal contract but, after 18 months of bit parts, he was released. Following a period as a lifeguard and as a swimming pool builder, he was chosen, by virtue of a chance encounter, to play Rowdy Yates, a role he played on *Rawhide* for seven years. Rowdy was ramrod of the cattle drives. His job was to carry out the orders of trail boss Gil Favor whether he agreed or not. Conflict often ensued. In 1964, while *Rawhide* was still in progress, Clint made the Italian Western *A Fistful of Dollars*, beginning his rise to international superstar. Forming his own production company, he made a succession of profitable films, including several Westerns. He won an Academy Award as Best Director for *Unforgiven* (1992).

"Rowdy Yates" on the Rodeo Trail

Rowdy Yates typically accompanied other *Rawhide* cast members on rodeo appearances. He joined several *Rawhide* co-stars at Camp Pendleton for the Marine Corps rodeos in 1960 and 1961. In July 1960, he and Eric Fleming accepted the TV Award presented to *Rawhide* at Salinas. He joined Paul Brinegar (his most frequent rodeo co-star) and Sheb Wooley at the 1961 Jaycee Bootheel Rodeo in Sikeston, Missouri. The host community found the trio cooperative and friendly. In their arena act, one of Wishbone's roles was to constantly interrupt the others' talk and music. The three walked the arena perimeter to shake hands. Accommodating their return to Hollywood, the stars were given an early spot on Sunday's program. Upon departure, their plane swooped low and dipped its wings in salute to the audience. The same group played the 1962 Central Wyoming Fair Rodeo at Casper. Later, the *Rawhide* cast closed out a series of annual Los Angeles Sheriff's Rodeos.

Clint and Paul headlined the 1964 Southeastern Championship Rodeo in Montgomery, Alabama. Reports indicated that rodeo fans enjoyed the duo's act. Kids especially warmed to Wishbone's comedy, and lined the rail to shake hands with the pair of stars. That fall, Clint and Paul, backed by Hugh Farr and the Country Gentlemen, entertained at New Mexico's State Fair Rodeo. On this occasion, soon-to-be superstar Clint was overshadowed by Paul, a native New Mexican making a return engagement at his home state's fair. A newspaper caption for a picture of Wishbone stated, "another *Rawhide* star, Clint (Rowdy) Eastwood also will appear..."

PAUL BRINEGAR (1917–95) Paul Brinegar was born at Tucumcari, New Mexico, and moved to several additional towns. Beginning acting in high school plays and operettas, he served as general helper at Santa Fe's Rialto Theater. He later studied at the Pasadena Playhouse. After World War II Navy service as a bomber gunner and radio man, he repaired radios while seeking acting parts. Beginning in 1948, he appeared in numerous feature films and TV shows. From 1956 to 1958, he played "Dog" Kelly, Dodge City saloonkeeper and mayor, on *The Life and Times of Wyatt Earp*. In 1958, his role in *Cattle Empire* led to his being cast for six years as Wishbone, the chuckwagon cook on *Rawhide*. He played ranch handyman Jelly Hoskins on *Lancer* (1969–70). He appeared in support of Elvis Presley and Clint Eastwood. Temporarily breaking out of the Western mold, he played Lamar Pettybone on *Matt Houston* (1982–83). Later, he had roles in *The Gambler IV: The Luck of the Draw* and *Wyatt Earp: Return to Tombstone*. He had a recurring part on *The Adventures of Brisco County, Jr.*, reprised his Wishbone character for a McDonalds's commercial and drove a stagecoach in *Maverick* (1994). He received a Golden Boot Award. Paul passed away of emphysema. He will always be remembered as Wishbone.

"Wishbone" on the Rodeo Trail

Paul Brinegar probably had a more frequent association with rodeo than his fellow *Rawhide* cast members, although most often one co-star or another accompanied him. He was part of the cast assemblage that traveled to Camp Pendleton for Marine Corps rodeos in 1960 and 1961. He appeared with Clint Eastwood and Sheb Wooley at the 1961 Jaycee Bootheel Rodeo in Sikeston. A newspaper headline read, "Wishbone of TV's *Rawhide* Becomes First Casualty." Firing a blank-loaded pistol, he inflicted a painful powder burn on a finger. Following treatment, he returned for the next performance. With Sheb Wooley, he headlined at Cookeville, Tennessee, in 1962. Eastwood joined the two for Casper's Central Wyoming Fair Rodeo. That year, the *Rawhide* cast was at the Los Angeles Sheriff's Rodeo.

Paul's comedy act included entering the arena on a bucking stick horse. As camp cook, he often cooked up a "chef's special" in a cauldron or skillet. Sometimes, there was difficulty getting the fire started; at other times, there was too much fire. There was a bit involving a local "girlfriend" chased from the arena. He twice entertained at the New Mexico State Fair Rodeo, in 1962 with Wooley, and in 1964 with Eastwood. During his 1962 engagement, he visited his parents and his brother. He could rightly claim that New Mexico's governor had been his babysitter. At one performance, Paul's foot got tangled in a rope as he dismounted. His startled horse dragged him about 40 yards along the arena dirt. Cowboys stopped the horse, allowing Paul to continue his act. He and Eastwood headlined the 1964 Southeast World Championship Rodeo at Montgomery, Alabama. He joined Jeannine Riley of *Petticoat Junction* at Fort Smith's 1965 Arkansas-Oklahoma Rodeo.

SHEB WOOLEY (1921–2003) Sheb Wooley was born near Erick, Oklahoma. Learning to ride a horse at age four, he rode at rodeos as a teenager. He formed a touring band and had his own radio show. Beginning with *Rocky Mountain* (1950), he appeared in more than 30 motion pictures, including *High Noon* (1952). After four years on *Rawhide* as drover Pete Nolan, he left the show to concentrate on music, but later returned. A guitarist, singer and composer, his most successful recordings were novelty numbers such as "Purple People Eater." As drunken Ben Colder, he recorded comedy selections. The Country Music Association named him 1968 Comedian of the Year. The following year, he became a regular on TV's *Hee Haw*.

"Pete Nolan" on the Rodeo Trail

Sheb Wooley, in character as Pete Nolan, joined his co-stars at several rodeo appearances. In 1961, he was at the Camp Pendleton and Sikeston, Missouri, rodeos. In 1962, he appeared at Cookeville, Tennessee; Casper, Wyoming; and Albuquerque, New Mexico. At the time he played New Mexico's State Fair Rodeo, he owned a farm in that state.

OTHER CAST Steve Raines as Jim Quince, Rocky Shahan as Joe Scarlett and James Murdock as Mushy, the cook's helper, rounded out the *Rawhide* TV cast at various times. Some of them had a rodeo background, and their horsemanship helped create an air of authenticity. All appeared, either in 1960 or 1961, or both, at the Camp Pendleton rodeo.

"THE RIFLEMAN" CAST

CHUCK CONNORS (1921–92) Kevin "Chuck" Connors earned athletic scholarships to Adelphi Academy and Seton Hall, where he majored in English and Speech. In the U.S. Army from 1942 into 1946, he instructed in armor tactics at West Point. At 6'5", he played seven years with baseball's Brooklyn Dodgers and Chicago Cubs organizations. He also played basketball with the Rochester Royals and Boston Celtics.

While playing and broadcasting for the Los Angeles Angels, Chuck made Hollywood contacts that led to acting in more than a dozen films. He also had some TV guest spots. He learned to ride a horse and grew his hair for Westerns. One fine role was as Burl Ives' bullying son in *The Big Country*. In 1958, Chuck forcefully presented himself for the TV role of Lucas McCain, *The Rifleman*. He helped select Johnny Crawford for his TV son, and the two became lifelong friends. With his modified rifle, rancher Lucas kept the town of North Fork safe from desperados while imparting to son Mark the path of moral behavior. The rifle had a special loop installed on the cocking lever, and a thumbscrew that tripped the trigger each time the weapon was cocked, making it function like an automatic weapon. Lucas' wholesome influence as a single father brought mail requesting his advice on child rearing. On *Cowboy in Africa* (1967–68), Chuck played rodeo world champion Jim Sinclair. He played rodeo cowboy Alabama Dean in the TV film *Balboa* (1983).

In 1967, Chuck received the Buffalo Bill Award at North Platte's Nebraskaland Days rodeo celebration. That same year, he visited U.S. Forces in Vietnam. In 1968, he was "Rodeo King/Mr. Rodeo" at Palm Springs. He received a star on Hollywood's Walk of Fame, a Golden Boot Award and a saddle plaque in Newhall, California's, Western Walk of Fame. In 1991, he was inducted into the Hall of Great Western Performers at the National Cowboy Hall of Fame. Chuck passed away from cancer.

JOHNNY CRAWFORD (1946–) Johnny Crawford was born in Los Angeles to a show business family. At age four, he entertained family and friends with his dancing, singing and imitations, and made his first film appearance. Johnny was an original Disney Mouseketeer. Chuck and the producers thought Johnny, a sixth grader, was right to play son Mark McCain on *The Rifleman*. The father-and-son bond extended to real life as the two became close friends. Fan Johnny was thrilled to be working, and sometimes playing ball, with a

Chuck Connors of TV's *The Rifleman* and his TV son, Johnny Crawford, arrive for the 1963 Houston rodeo (photograph copyright Houston Metropolitan Research Center, Houston Public Library, Houston. Press #1108).

former major leaguer. Chuck invited him to accompany his four sons on camping trips. Johnny was provided with tutors on the set and on personal appearance tours. A parent also accompanied him on tour. He told of bosses and co-workers on the set being appropriately considerate of his welfare. At age 13, he was keeping his room tidy to earn a weekly allowance of $2.50. He stated that he didn't feel the loss of a normal childhood.

Over the course of *The Rifleman*'s run, viewers watched Johnny grow from 12 to 17 years old. At a young age, he had a broad range of interests. He enjoyed baseball, football, basketball and fencing. He learned to play harmonica and guitar, and he collected silent movies as well as coins. He was handy with a rope. His favorite TV show was *Stoney Burke*. He enjoyed riding and participating in rodeo. Like most youngsters, he liked hamburgers and bubble gum. When the series ended, he returned to public school. As the years passed, Johnny worked in live theater, but kept his hand in the filmmaking business. He returned to his love for music, appearing for two years with Vince Giordano's Nighthawks. He then formed his own band, the Johnny Crawford 1928 Society Dance Band, which continues as of this writing.

"Lucas and Mark McCain" on the Rodeo Trail

At age 17, Johnny Crawford was 5'6" and about 122 pounds. He rode in junior rodeos and kept his own horse Two Bits on a friend's ranch north of Los Angeles. At an American Junior Rodeo Association rodeo, he won the all-around cowboy title, competing in his age group in bareback bronc riding and bull riding. Winning money at rodeos barred

Chuck Connors (left) and Johnny Crawford of *The Rifleman* in Houston's 1963 rodeo parade (photograph copyright Houston Metropolitan Research Center, Houston Public Library, Houston. Press #1108).

Chuck Connors (center) and Johnny Crawford (right) and an unidentified cowboy visit a hospital patient while headlining the 1963 Houston Fat Stock Show Rodeo (photograph copyright Houston Metropolitan Research Center, Houston Public Library, Houston. Press #1108).

Johnny Crawford competing in steer wrestling at Cheyenne Frontier Days (Gene Hyder photograph, used with permission. Obtained from PRCA–Media, Colorado Springs, CO).

Johnny's participation in high school varsity sports. He considered making rodeo a major part of his life. A member of the PRCA since the early 1960s, he competed in bareback bronc riding, steer wrestling and calf roping.

As stars of *The Rifleman*, Chuck Connors and Crawford gained experience before large crowds at the 1959 Shrine Circus in St. Louis. That fall, Chuck brought his real-life son to his first rodeo with Johnny, Omaha's 1959 Ak-Sar-Ben Rodeo. At Omaha, a powder flash from his trademark rifle burned Chuck's shirt and seared his skin, requiring first aid. Some other joint rodeos were the 1960 Days of '47 Rodeo in Salt Lake City and, their last, the 1963 Houston Livestock Show and Rodeo. At Houston, youngsters breaking lines to say hello or to ask for an autograph interrupted their parade progress. Houston's organizers remembered Chuck as being easy to work with. He developed a head cold–flu, but made every performance. A thoughtful official, en route to her grandmother's ninetieth birthday party, provided him with some homemade soup. In the midst of the party, Chuck telephoned the grandmother. The family then presented Chuck's autographed photo, impressing all in attendance. Gestures like this solidified fan loyalty. The Houston appearance coincided with the TV show's conclusion. Chuck donated his TV horse, Razor, to rodeo organizers for a scholarship fund auction.

In his rodeo act, Chuck entered on horseback waving his rifle. Dismounting, he described the history of his impressive weapon. He called the rifle modification "a *coup d'etat* of television." He demonstrated his dexterity with the weapon by flipping, twirling and firing blanks, candidly stating that no one on historical record ever twirled a rifle as he did. Family relationship was emphasized by Chuck's recitation of the monologue, "What is a boy?" Johnny sang "Hey Paw!," a reflection of the trouble he got into on *The Rifleman*. Both men were accommodating when it came to signing autographs and visiting children in hospitals.

Rodeos that Chuck played alone included the Texas Prison Rodeo in 1961; the Emerald Empire Roundup at Eugene and the Mid-South Fair Rodeo at Memphis in 1962; and the Tri-State Championship Rodeo at Fort Madison in 1963. On Chuck's solo dates, a local boy led a horse slowly around the arena during his recitation. Johnny also appeared at rodeos without Chuck. Sharing billing with Michael Landon at the 1963 Shrine Club Rodeo in Ardmore, Oklahoma, he told of plans for his upcoming film *Indian Paint*. For photographers, he performed rope tricks, including roping his motel marquee which read WELCOME JOHNNY CRAWFORD. He visited and autographed photos at the Children's Diagnostic Clinic. Johnny headlined a rodeo at Fort Collins, Colorado. In 1967, at Providence, Rhode Island's, rodeo, he strummed his guitar and sang some of his hit recordings from horseback. He also demonstrated his trick roping and calf roping skills. At this time, he was serving with the military. In later years, Johnny competed in celebrity rodeos.

"(THE ADVENTURES OF) RIN TIN TIN" CAST

A boy and his dog form the basis for many good stories. *The Adventures of Rin Tin Tin* was originally broadcast in 164 black-and-white episodes on ABC-TV from 1954 to 1959. The setting was Fort Apache, located in the 1880s Arizona Territory. An Indian raid on a wagon train had left a boy, Rusty, and his German shepherd, Rin Tin Tin, as survivors. Cavalry soldiers brought the two to Fort Apache. When the boy and dog demonstrated their heroism, they were kept at the fort as honorary corporal and troop mascot, respectively.

Rin Tin Tin's 40-year history began in France toward the end of World War I. An American non-commissioned Air Corps pilot and dog fancier, Lee Duncan, discovered in a trench, near an abandoned kennel compound, a German shepherd dog and her pups. Lee adopted a male and a female pup and named them Rin Tin Tin and Nanette, for lovers of French legend. Only Rin Tin Tin lived to reach Lee's home in California. There, following extensive training, Lee's Rin Tin Tin shepherds gained movie fame from the silent era into the 1940s, before starring on TV. Owner-trainer of the movie Rin Tin Tin and copyright owner, Lee was involved in the concept and filming of the TV show. His dog Rin Tin Tin IV was initially used. However, Lee eventually could not do all the training necessary to meet the TV show's heavy demands. Another owner-trainer, Frank Barnes, had a German shepherd, Golden Boy, Jr., or J.R., that succeeded to the role. Frank's training superseded that of Duncan, who continued to be involved in production.

LEE AAKER (1943–) California-born Lee Aaker played Rusty. His show business career began at age four when he performed a song-and-dance act with his older brother at amateur shows. Dancing led to TV appearances. By 1948, he had made his film debut. He compiled a number of film and TV credits. As Rusty, he rode horses, was taken under the wings of the adult stars and enjoyed a warm relationship with Rin Tin Tin. He was educated by private tutors and in public school. Following his acting years, he left show business to live a more reclusive lifestyle. In adult life, he has worked as a building contractor and has taught skiing to disabled youngsters.

JAMES BROWN (1920–92) James L. Brown played the show's adult lead, Lt. Rip Masters. Jim was born in Desdemona, Texas, and attended Baylor University. A California tennis tournament led to a Hollywood contact; however, he returned to Baylor. He was a band vocalist prior to signing for motion pictures. From 1942 through 1946, his films included *Going My Way* (1944). On his first Western, Republic's *The Fabulous Texan* (1947), Jim got on-the-job riding instruction from wranglers. He appeared in Westerns and war films. Enjoying rapport and chemistry with Lee Aaker, he was a father figure. He enjoyed singing on a few episodes. Playing a cavalry officer, he learned to use an English saddle. When the *Rin Tin Tin* series concluded in 1959, he made additional film and TV appearances, and was a partner in a physical fitness equipment company. Jim was a popular guest at Western film festivals. He died following a bout with lung cancer.

JOE SAWYER (1901–82) Joe Sawyer, veteran character actor, played the crusty but good-hearted Sgt. Biff O'Hara. A native of Canada, he grew up in the United States. He accumulated numerous film credits from the early 1930s. Following his casting in *The Adventures of Rin Tin Tin*, he made a few more films and retired. He died of liver cancer at Ashland, Oregon.

RAND BROOKS (1918–2003) Rand Brooks played Corp. Boone. Born in St. Louis, Missouri, he settled with his family in the Los Angeles area. According to biographies, riding skills led to his contesting at amateur rodeos and serving as an all-around performer with the Clyde Beatty Circus' Western show. Prior to World War II Air Corps service, he was in films with Mickey Rooney, had a small but memorable role in *Gone with the Wind* (1939) and acted in support of Western stars. Following discharge, he was cast as young sidekick Lucky Jenkins in the final Hopalong Cassidy films (1946–48). Mostly he was associated with Western films and TV shows. Privately, Rand was a dog enthusiast. He became friends with trainer Frank Barnes and owned a descendant of Frank's Rin Tin Tin shepherd. Following retirement from show business, he ran a successful paramedic-ambulance business and raised horses. Rand passed away of cancer.

"Rin Tin Tin" Cast on the Rodeo Trail

The *Rin Tin Tin* rodeo cast varied from one engagement to another. In the spring of 1955, James Brown was rodeo marshal for the Riverside (California) Sheriff's Rodeo. Prior to embarking on the rodeo trail, the cast practiced their arena routines at the Corriganville movie location. At Eugene, Oregon's, 1955 Emerald Empire Roundup, the stars were Rin Tin Tin, James Brown and Lee Aaker. The entourage included Lee Aaker's mother, Lee Duncan, Frank Barnes and stuntman Doyle Brooks. About 800 fans, mostly young, greeted the stars' airport arrival. Aaker shook dozens of hands and signed autographs along the fence line. In response to children's shouts, Rin Tin Tin de-planed and sat up on his hind legs for photos. Aaker shook hands with the mayor before the party was escorted to town.

Following a TV appearance, Aaker ate spaghetti alongside rodeo clown Slim Pickens. Rin Tin Tin and Aaker were guests of honor in the junior parade. Brown sang at a rodeo

Left to right: Lee Aaker, Rin Tin Tin and James Brown, stars of TV's *The Adventures of Rin Tin Tin*.

dance featuring Bob Wills and the Texas Playboys. Aaker and Brown rode horseback in the grand parade, while Rinty and Frank Barnes rode in an open car. Mobbed when the parade disbanded, the stars greeted youngsters and signed autographs. A local market offered a free picture of Rin Tin Tin and Rusty with purchase of a half-gallon of ice cream. At Sacred Heart Hospital, patients assembled in the auditorium where each child was allowed to pet Rin Tin

Tin. Aaker was excluded from wards because of his age, but Brown and Rinty greeted children at bedside. At the rodeo arena, Rinty shook hands and took bows when introduced. Lee Duncan told the crowd of his experience finding Rin Tin Tin during World War I, and of his career raising and training performing dogs. The *Rin Tin Tin* cast drew 40,000 persons to the rodeo.

In fall 1955, Brown, Aaker and Rinty appeared at Fort Madison's rodeo. Aaker posed for photos with children before he and Brown rode horseback on parade. At one performance, the show went on in a downpour. For the 1956 Madison Square Garden and Boston Garden rodeos, the troupe included Joe Sawyer, Rand Brooks and a cavalry troop. Musical entertainment was by Brown and "The Collins Kids." At New York's City Hall, Rinty delivered rodeo tickets to the mayor. The cast put on a show at Bellevue Hospital and made ward visits. Students from nearby schools, excused for the occasion, were in the audience. An extra Saturday morning rodeo performance was scheduled. Rin Tin Tin entered the arena riding on a buckboard escorted by Fort Apache's Company B, 101st Cavalry. To show what a great actor he was, he sought out the brightest part of the spotlight as it was moved about. At a special performance, Rin Tin Tin was ready to meet a crowd of underprivileged and disabled children, as impatient youngsters chanted, "We want Rinny. We want Rinny." Tardy was Corp. Rusty (14-year-old Aaker was at Yankee Stadium for a World Series game). In Boston, youngsters called a front page telephone number to hear a recorded message from Rusty. Special activities included a Rin Tin Tin paw shake with the president of the Animal Rescue League and a visit to stables at Suffolk Downs racetrack.

Brown, Aaker and Rinty returned in 1958 to Eugene, Oregon. Brown enjoyed the area's fishing, and Aaker planned to water ski. A crowd of nearly 1,000 people greeted them at the airport. Fans found Aaker, now a high school sophomore, considerably more mature than the boy of three years earlier. In the rodeo parade, Brown rode horseback, while Aaker and Rinty rode in a car. In the arena act, Brown sang and Frank Barnes directed a demonstration of Rin Tin Tin's tricks. In a dramatic sketch, Rin Tin Tin rescued Aaker from the villainous Indian Joe (Doyle Brooks). Frank presented a narration on dog training. The troupe visited Sacred Heart Hospital for nearly two hours.

In 1959, the *Rin Tin Tin* cast, including Rand Brooks, but not Joe Sawyer, headlined the San Angelo (Texas) Stock Show Rodeo. Despite a secret arrival time, 50 youngsters were waiting at the airport. Rinty had received a pin for logging 100,000 air travel miles. Six eight-year-old boys chosen by area elementary schools to serve as extras (one each performance) in the Rin Tin Tin act received Corp. Rusty uniforms. Schools dismissed students for the rodeo's "Kid's Day." Three young winners of the pet parade also got Corp. Rusty uniforms. Cast members were guests at a private home reception, entertained patients from the Handicapped Children's Suez Temple Treatment Center and visited Baptist Memorial Hospital. In the fall of 1959, the Rin Tin Tin troupe, with Gail Davis, headlined Madison Square Garden's final World's Championship Rodeo. In 1962, Rand Brooks was grand marshal and presented a trophy belt buckle at the San Bernardino County Sheriff's Rodeo.

"Sky King" Cast

From 1946 to 1954, radio audiences enjoyed *Sky King*. Schuyler "Sky" King of the Flying Crown Ranch went about his adventures at the controls of his twin-engine Cessna, *Songbird*.

KIRBY GRANT (1911–85)   On TV (1951–54), Kirby Grant starred as Sky King. Musically trained, Grant had performed as a band vocalist and as an actor in outdoor action films. Interest in flying made him a natural for the role of Sky King. He commuted by air from his Chicago home to California for filming. Watching *Sky King* influenced some young people toward aviation careers. As a role model, Kirby was invited to witness a space shuttle launch from Cape Canaveral. An auto accident en route ended his life.

GLORIA WINTERS (1932–)   Gloria Winters entered films as a child. While still in her teens, she made several films, including *Stagecoach Driver* with Whip Wilson. She was a guest on TV Westerns and played Babs on TV's *The Life of Riley*. On *Sky King*, she was Sky's niece Penny. She received a Golden Boot Award.

"Sky King and Penny" on the Rodeo Trail

The *Sky King* cast took to the rodeo circuit in addition to other personal appearances. Gloria Winters was 1959 Rodeo Queen at Riverside, California. In the fall of 1960, Grant and Winters headlined the St. Louis Fireman's Rodeo. At the San Antonio Livestock Exposition Rodeo early in 1963, they joined a multi-star lineup. Reports stated that they "ended their act with the audience in the palm of their hands." Grant and Winters each sang solos and then joined in a duet. There might also be some pistol-shooting. Winters instructed and led gentlemen from the audience in a dance, the name of which varied by locality. In

The cast of TV's *Sky King* (left to right): Kirby Grant (Sky King), Gloria Winters (Penny) and Ron Haggerty (Clipper).

San Antonio, it was the "Texas Wig Walk." Audience applause determined the winner, who was presented a Sky King pistol, as well as a picture and a kiss from Winters. She and Grant then mounted horses for a ride around the arena perimeter to greet fans. Winters said of her rodeo days, "We had a lot of fun and laughs."

"26 Men" Cast

TRISTRAM COFFIN (c. 1910–90) Born and raised on the outskirts of Salt Lake City, Tristram Coffin toured the Northwest in stock theater and earned a speech degree from

Kelo Henderson (left) and Tris Coffin of TV's *26 Men*.

the University of Washington. In films from 1939, including many Westerns, he usually played a dress villain. He played historical Capt. Tom Rynning on *26 Men*, a series based on Arizona Ranger files.

KELO HENDERSON (1923–)   Colorado-born Paul Henderson learned gun-handling skills at an early age and became an actor. For *26 Men*, producer Russell Hayden gave him the new first name Kelo and cast him as Clint Travis, young Arizona Ranger. Kelo did his own riding and stunts.

"26 Men" on the Rodeo Trail

In 1958, Tristram Coffin and Kelo Henderson appeared at the rodeo in West Monroe, Louisiana. Kelo made solo appearances at the 1959 Imperial Valley Cattle Call Rodeo in Brawley, California, and at the 1962 Wyoming State Fair and Rodeo in Douglas. Kelo's rodeo act relied heavily on fast-draw, trick handling and firing of his brace of six-shooters.

"The Virginian" Cast

JAMES DRURY (1935–)   From his birthplace in New York, where his father was on the faculty of New York University, James Child Drury, Jr., frequently traveled to Oregon, where his mother's family operated a ranch. He later noted, "I always tell people I left New York when I was six weeks old, and I've been on the road ever since." The ranch provided Jim grounding in the cowboy way of life, while New York gave him his start as an actor. He played in children's theater and, by age 12, made his professional debut in a touring company of *Life with Father*. He attended NYU and chose acting as a career. In Los Angeles, he gained a contract with MGM, appearing in seven films in a year's time. His

Fort Madison (Iowa) rodeo pins for appearances of Doug McClure and Clu Gulager.

Westerns included *The Last Wagon* (1956), *Love Me Tender* (1956), *Good Day for a Hanging* (1959) and *Ten Who Dared* (1960).

In 1962, Jim was in the classic MGM Western *Ride the High Country*. He was a guest on many Western TV series, several more than once. A number of his film and TV roles were in non–Westerns. On *The Virginian* (1962–71), he played the no-name title character, foreman of the Shiloh Ranch, through about 250 90-minute color episodes. In the final season, the show was renamed *The Men from Shiloh*. Following the long run of *The Virginian*, Jim appeared on *Firehouse* (1974), but mostly remained true to his Western image doing guest spots on TV Western series. Jim has been active in various aspects of horsemanship, applying his skills at celebrity rodeos for charity. He received a Golden Boot Award and has been inducted into the Hall of Great Western Performers at the National Cowboy Hall of Fame.

"The Virginian" on the Rodeo Trail

In late 1963, James Drury appeared at the Imperial Valley Cattle Call Rodeo at Brawley, California. He and co-star Lee J. Cobb were booked for the Fort Worth Stock Show Rodeo, but Cobb's health precluded him from appearing. Jim rode his Appaloosa, Shamrock. The Sons of the Pioneers (with Pat Brady), John Mitchum and Jon Locke provided music and comedy. At a performance of the 1966 New Mexico State Fair Rodeo, a Texas horse breeder presented Jim an Appaloosa gelding to recognize *The Virginian*'s promotion of

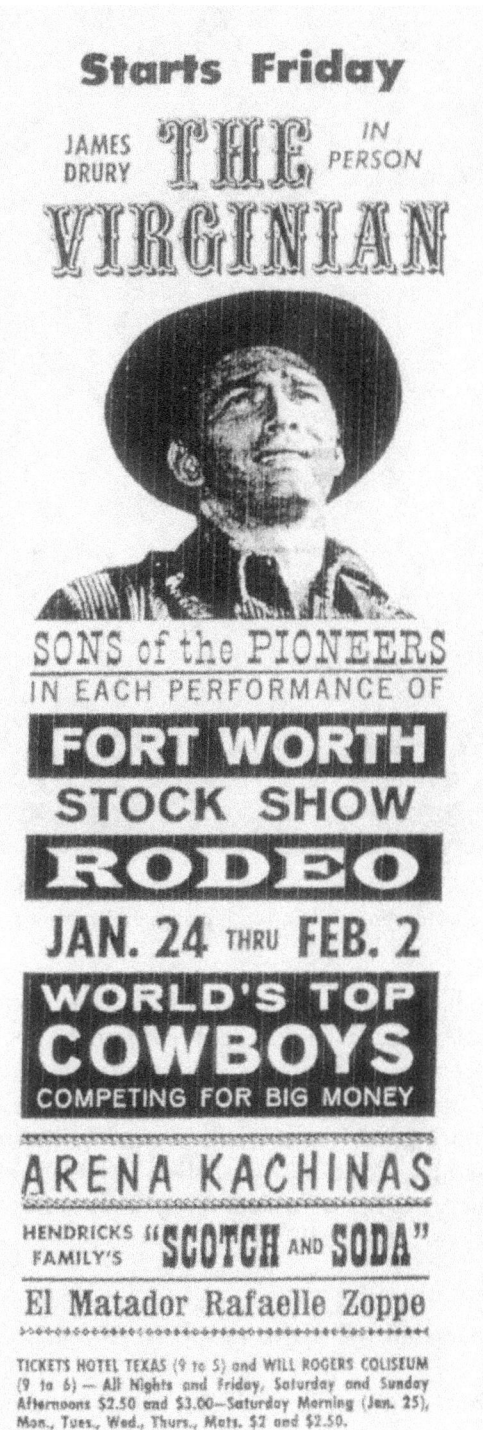

Advertisement for James Drury's appearance as "The Virginian" at the 1964 Fort Worth Stock Show Rodeo.

James Drury, "The Virginian," signs autographs during his 1964 appearance at the Fort Worth Stock Show Rodeo (courtesy *Fort Worth Star-Telegram* Photograph Collection [George Smith photo], University of Texas at Arlington Libraries, Arlington. FWST #4840).

the breed. In 1968, Jim and co-star Doug McClure (Trampas) headlined the Southwest District Livestock Show and Rodeo at Lake Charles, Louisiana. Jim told reporters he appreciated the community's commitment to projects such as the rodeo. He credited the success of *The Virginian* to the show's large behind-the-scenes contingent. When the two visited the local newspaper plant, Jim conducted a mock interview of Doug. Receiving the Buffalo Bill Award at North Platte, he served as rodeo parade grand marshal. In 1992, he was co-grand marshal (with Doug McClure) at Clebourne, Texas,' rodeo. As a parade grand marshal at Cheyenne Frontier Days in 1996, Jim revived a tradition of years past.

DOUG MCCLURE (1935–95)

Born in Glendale, California, and raised in Pacific Palisades, Doug McClure enjoyed the outdoors and was active in sports. As the lead in a school drama production, he won a "best actor" award and began to think of acting as a possible career. He was an accomplished swimmer and surfer. A rider at age eight, he honed his riding and roping skills by working summers as a wrangler on a Nevada ranch. He entered junior rodeos, and then competed in RCA bareback riding, steer wrestling and roping. In his words, he spent his youth "with a saddle under one arm and a surfboard under the other."

At Santa Monica City College and UCLA, Doug studied drama. He worked his way through college by modeling for magazine advertisements. As a junior, he made his TV debut in a soap commercial. At 6'2" and 185 pounds, the boyishly handsome, blue-eyed, blond-haired actor remained before the camera. His role as a midshipman on the syndicated TV series *Men of Annapolis* led to his first movie role as an ensign in *The Enemy Below* (1957). He was in *The Unforgiven* (1960) and episodes of TV Westerns. As co-star of TV's *The Overland Trail* (1960), he gained additional Western experience. From playing a detective on *Checkmate* (1960–62), he was cast as Trampas on *The Virginian*. His happy-go-lucky character (revised from Owen Wister's novel) supported and provided contrast to the stern title character. He did most of his own riding on *The Virginian* and kept horses of his own.

Doug entertained friends with celebrity imitations. Like many Western stars, he developed singing talent for his rodeo act. Following *The Virginian*, Doug's on-screen visibility continued through additional TV series, TV guest spots and TV movies. His big-screen films were mostly of the science fiction or horror type. He had roles in the TV mini-series *Roots* and *North and South*. He reprised his Trampas character for *The Fall Guy*, *The Gambler IV: The Luck of the Draw* and Mel Gibson's *Maverick*. On the celebrity rodeo circuit, he was 1986 team-roping champion. He was awarded a Golden Boot, was honored with a saddle plaque on the Newhall (California) Western Walk of Fame and received a Buffalo Bill Award. His star was placed in the Hollywood Walk of Fame. Doug succumbed to cancer.

"Trampas" on the Rodeo Trail

Doug McClure was grand marshal of the 1963 Palm Springs rodeo parade. He headlined the 1964 Phoenix rodeo. In 1965, he joined co-star Clu Gulager at rodeos in Lake Charles, Louisiana, and Camdenton, Missouri. At some early rodeos, supporting cast member–musician Randy Boone joined the troupe. As the star of Brawley, California's, 1967 Imperial Valley Cattle Call Rodeo, Doug led the rodeo parade. Early in 1968, he returned to Lake Charles with James Drury. That summer, he headlined the rodeo at Alexandria, Louisiana. The following year, he was the star rodeo attraction at the Kentucky State Fair, Fort Madison and Memphis' Mid-South Fair. Doug's rodeo act included humor as well as then-popular vocal selections such as "Little Green Apples," "Gentle on My Mind" and "Raindrops Keep Falling on My Head." He would also include a spiritual number such as "Just a Closer Walk with Thee" and do star imitations.

Doug appeared at the 1970 rodeo in Mercedes, Texas. For *The Men from Shiloh* in the fall of 1970, Doug grew longer hair and a mustache to reflect Trampas' greater maturity in a later time period. Arriving by air 24 hours in advance of his first performance at the Heart O'Texas Rodeo in Waco, Doug was greeted by a large airport crowd. He participated in a press conference, shared dinner with about 100 students and visited the city's newspaper office. In the arena, The Frontiersman and Joanie supported musically. He added "Hurray for Texas" to his musical repertoire. His songs met with applause; however, the majority of fans wanted him to shave his mustache. Early in 1971, Doug headlined the Dixie National Rodeo. That year, he returned for a third appearance at Lake Charles, Louisiana. Shortly, he shared billing with the Sons of the Pioneers at Montgomery, Alabama's, rodeo. That fall, he was featured at the Arkansas State Fair Rodeo in Little Rock.

CLU GULAGER (1929–)

Clu Gulager was born in Muskogee, Oklahoma. Following U.S. Marine service, he pursued drama at Baylor University and in summer plays. His dramatic training and experience included Paris as well as London's Old Vic Theater. He was associated with Dallas theater, and was a drama instructor at Baylor. In Hollywood, Clu was in an episode of *Have Gun, Will Travel* and other TV shows. He gained notice for two unusual roles, one as a drug addict, the other as a mad killer. He was selected to play Billy the Kid on TV's *The Tall Man*. His six-foot, blue-eyed handsomeness contrasted with the appearance of the historical Kid. His character was toned down from history. After two seasons as Billy the Kid, he joined *The Virginian* in its third season, remaining for four seasons as Deputy Sheriff Emmett Ryker. He operated actor's workshops in Hollywood, including one for child actors. He also worked in summer theater, and prepared himself to write and direct for the screen. His credits included *The Last Picture Show* (1971), TV's *The Gambler* and the TV mini-series *North and South*.

"Billy the Kid" and "Emmett Ryker" on the Rodeo Trail

Clu Gulager entertained at several rodeos as Billy the Kid. At Waco's 1961 Heart O'Texas Fair Rodeo, he was welcomed for his connection with Baylor University. He was interviewed on radio and TV, toured newspaper offices and visited the Children's Hospital. He joined about 50 students at a luncheon, which he kicked off with a staged shootout. The occasion soon became a photo and autograph opportunity. Throughout his visit, reporters made note of his charm, personality and dedication. He starred at the Texas Prison Rodeo. In the fall of 1962, Clu's performance at Elk City, Oklahoma, was rated as "especially pleasing to the kids," who enjoyed a close-up view and touch as he rode around the arena. At Fort Madison, Iowa, he visited Sacred Heart Hospital accompanied by rodeo performers. His 25-minute arena performance was described as including "bright Western humor and Western songs." He rode his horse next to the arena fence and shook the hands of most of the youthful audience. He signed hundreds of autographs. That fall, he appeared at the Imperial Valley Cattle Call Rodeo at Brawley, California.

Early in 1965, Clu and Doug McClure paired for the first time at the Southwest District Livestock Show and Rodeo at Lake Charles, Louisiana. The actors, lanky, blue-eyed and long-haired, made a favorable impression as they comfortably signed autographs and joked with fans. They joined again for the summer J Bar H Rodeo in Camdenton, Missouri. Clu appeared solo that fall at the Southeast Arkansas Livestock Show and Rodeo at Pine Bluff. With several singers, dancers and musicians, he broke in a new act. He described it as, "We sing a lot, shoot a lot and tell jokes, with a few surprises." The troupe borrowed songs from friend Randy Sparks of The New Christy Minstrels. Son John, dressed in a Western outfit, responded to his dad's questions. Asked what his favorite town was, the boy replied, "Pine Bluff," to the crowd's delight. Asked what his favorite TV Western was, the seven-year-old generated laughter by responding, *Rawhide*. When Clu sang one number with a beat, two of his vocalists who had been dressed as cowgirls traded their skirts for more abbreviated costumes and gyrated through moves of then-popular dances. A reporter called it "rodeo disco a-go-go."

In the summer of 1966, Clu headlined the Independence (Missouri) Civic Rodeo. Visiting the Municipal Building, he signed autographs on the person of female employees, drew his pistol for mock hold-ups and made the mayor honorary mayor of Medicine Bow, as he received a key to the city. In his free time, he jogged several miles. Young fans enjoyed his arena handshakes. Early in 1967, Clu and Richard Long of *The Big Valley*, backed by the Frontiersmen and Joanie, entertained at the Dixie National Rodeo in Jackson, Mississippi. That spring, at Ardmore, Oklahoma's, Shrine Club Rodeo, he shared billing with George "Goober" Lindsey.

"Wagon Train" Cast

ROBERT HORTON (1924–) Meade Howard Horton, Jr., was born in Los Angeles to a professional family. As a youngster he endured medical problems and surgeries, but learned to ride horses. During World War II, he served in the Coast Guard. He studied theater arts at the University of Miami and UCLA. In New York, he pursued drama at the American Theater Wing and with Lee Strasberg, and acted with stock companies. His films included some Westerns. He was featured in TV's *King's Row* (1955–56). Appearing on TV dramatic shows, he earned notice for a 1957 role on *Alfred Hitchcock Presents*. That year, he won the role of scout Flint McCullough on NBC-TV's *Wagon Train* and a five-year Universal contract. To prepare, he studied the history of Old West scouts and acquired a sense of the man. He traced a wagon train route from St. Joseph, Missouri, the historical "jumping-off" point, to California, visiting key landmarks. Horseback riding was a means of keeping in shape. Robert gained greater expertise riding his Appaloosa while on *Wagon Train*.

Wagon Train enjoyed high ratings and was nominated for awards, making Robert a well-known star. Each episode was the story of a character played by a guest star, allowing regular cast to perform with top Hollywood talent. Robert provided a large measure of the show's action and romantic appeal. Not compatible personally, he and Ward Bond had on-screen chemistry that provided much of the show's spark. In 1959, he performed as a vocalist at London's Palladium. His airport greeting and on-stage reception left no doubt

Robert Horton of *Wagon Train*.

as to his popularity. The next year he returned for a Command Performance before the Royal Family. Upon Ward Bond's sudden death in November 1960, other cast members, especially Robert, shouldered additional responsibility. In spring 1961, John McIntire became the new wagonmaster. Robert declined a generous contract renewal, preferring to explore other aspects of show business. He departed the series in May 1962.

Neither casting officials nor Horton, quick to point out his diverse résumé, considered him a Western actor. Yet viewers agreed that the ruggedly handsome actor cut a fine Western image in buckskin, on horseback or afoot. His athletic presence engendered passion or commanded respect, depending on the script. Trained and performing as a vocalist, he starred in the musical *101 Degrees in the Shade*. He recorded a cast album and an album of popular songs. He returned to the saddle in 1965 for MGM's Western TV series *A Man Called Shenandoah*, as a man without memory who drifts about searching for clues to his identity and past. He sang the show's theme song and recorded an album, also called "A Man from Shenandoah." Seen in the TV movie *The Dangerous Days of Kiowa Jones* (1966), Robert returned to the theater, performing mostly in musicals with his wife Marilynn. He sang in nightclubs and made films overseas. He acted on the CBS-TV soap opera *As the World Turns*, from 1982 to 1984. Semi-retirement was interrupted by occasional TV roles. A welcome guest at film festivals, he received a Golden Boot Award.

"Flint McCullough" on the Rodeo Trail

Robert Horton led Houston's 1960 rodeo parade through cold temperatures, piercing winds and rain. Smiling and

Robert Horton, *Wagon Train*'s Flint McCullough, addresses the crowd at a 1958 Texas Prison Rodeo, Huntsville (courtesy Texas Department of Criminal Justice).

Robert Horton (left) and donor Joe Kirshenbaum (right) of Wolf Brothers' Western Store present a saddle to Gay Lynn Robinson at the 1961 Ak-Sar-Ben Rodeo (courtesy Ak-Sar-Ben/River City Rodeo, Omaha, NE).

Fort Madison (IA) rodeo pin for the 1961 appearance of Robert Horton.

waving, he greeted fans from horseback. On his arena perimeter ride to shake hands with youngsters, he reached a spot where disabled kids couldn't crowd and climb the rail like their contemporaries. He dismounted, jumped on the railing and greeted his special fans one by one with the same smile, handshake and conversation he granted all youngsters. At a Little Rock orphanage, he taught more than 100 students Western history, answered *Wagon Train* questions and visited very young fans in the nursery. At the children's hospital, he greeted patients and signed casts. Driving to the arena via the prescribed route, at a time of school integration and civil rights unrest, his vehicle was stopped at gunpoint. Scout Flint McCullough had to be at his most diplomatic. In Omaha for the 1961

Ak-Sar-Ben Rodeo, Robert visited the stockyards, flew over wagon train landmarks and met with the historical society. Rodeo contestants noted his riding skill, and the star expressed his admiration for the courage with which rodeo cowboys face danger. Horton once sat astride a Brahma bull in the chutes for the film *Arena* (1953). He played another rodeo cowboy on a 1958 *General Electric Theater* episode, "The Last Rodeo."

Upon introduction, Robert rode into the arena dressed in a simple Western outfit tailored to flatter his trim physique. Following remarks about *Wagon Train*, he sang a half-dozen Western songs and popular ballads such as "Wagon Wheels," "Don't Fence Me In," "Tom Dooley," "The Wayward Wind," "Jingle, Jangle, Jingle" and, when in Texas, "The Eyes of Texas." Crowds found his singing quite polished and pleasing. In Albuquerque, Jimmy Wakely's trio provided back-up music. In Houston, he shared the musical spotlight with Brenda Lee. He sometimes flew his airplane to rodeos. For the New Mexico State Fair Rodeo, he flew his Comanche aircraft into town, to Santa Fe for a day and on his return to Hollywood. He headlined some of the country's most prestigious rodeos: Phoenix, Houston, Omaha and San Francisco. He appeared at the Texas Prison Rodeo and twice each at the Caldwell (Idaho) Night Rodeo and the New Mexico State Fair Rodeo. Fans who caught his rodeo act witnessed a quality performance.

FRANK MCGRATH (1903–67) AND TERRY WILSON (1923–99) Frank McGrath, born in Mound City, Missouri, and Terry Wilson, a native of Huntington Park, California, began a long friendship and working relationship as Hollywood stuntmen. Frank in his earlier years had experienced small-time rodeos, and had been a jockey at Midwest bush racetracks. He began his career as a movie stuntman-double in 1919. At approximately 5'8", he performed stunts for female stars. He doubled for Pedro Armendariz in *3 Godfathers* and Gene Kelly in *The Three Musketeers*. Terry played college football, and then served with the U.S. Marines during World War II. In 1946, he was among a group of athletes Warner Brothers chose for stunt training. His initial specialties were fistfights and stunts with horses.

Frank and Terry's partnership began in 1947 as they filmed *Devil's Doorway* for MGM. Terry, doubling for a hero, rescued Frank, dressed as a lady. Both worked on John Wayne films, with Terry sometimes doubling "The Duke" or Ward Bond. Adventures which the pair shared on location are documented in Chuck Roberson's book *The Fall Guy*. Stunting, Frank broke just about every bone in his body, including his back. Terry's nose was broken when an actor failed to miss in a fight scene. Still hurting from a horsefall injury, Terry missed a leap onto a running stagecoach team and fell beneath the horses. Luckily, he only wrenched his shoulder. When these stars visited hospitals and autographed casts, they could identify with the injured youths.

Ward Bond brought his two friends with him to *Wagon Train*. Terry had been a stuntman for ten years. Frank, one of the oldest stuntmen in movies, was ready for retirement. As Ward's double, Terry needed convincing that there would be sufficient planning time to execute stunts safely. Early on, he became the character Bill Hawks, and saw his part expanded over time to assistant wagonmaster. Despite long association with filmmaking, Frank was a stranger to dialogue. Ward gave him opportunity and some coaching. He let Frank ad-lib instead of adhering strictly to the script. Frank's choppy speech was ideal for the comic relief role of Charlie Wooster, cook, handyman and lead driver. Frank and Terry made the transition from stuntmen to actors, staying with *Wagon Train* for its eight-year duration. On the set, Terry earned extra respect by bulldogging a runaway horse that threatened cast and crew, and by instructing newcomers in stunt fighting. After *Wagon Train*,

Frank McGrath (left) as Charlie Wooster, cook, and Terry Wilson as Bill Hawks, assistant wagonmaster, of TV's *Wagon Train*.

there were more John Wayne films and new TV series. Terry supervised a construction company and managed a working movie location ranch.

"Charlie Wooster and Bill Hawks" on the Rodeo Trail

In the early to mid–1960s, Frank McGrath and Terry Wilson made personal appearances at rodeos across the country. Their act varied from one performance to another. An arena skit might include Charlie Wooster cooking one of his "chef's specials." The two circled the arena on horseback to shake hands with youngsters. They rode in parades, visited hospitals and signed autographs. In 1961, at Kansas' Old Santa Fe Trail Rodeo and the Colorado State Fair Rodeo, Stan Jones and the Wagonmaster quartet provided music. At the latter rodeo, Ward Bond's widow was their guest. Performing at an Arkansas rodeo in 1963, Terry visited his uncle and grandmother, who lived in the area. In 1963, Terry appeared solo at the Heart of the North Rodeo and at the Texas Prison Rodeo. A rodeo fan, he arranged for rodeo world champions Dean Oliver and Jim Bynum to appear on a *Wagon Train* episode. In 1964, he accepted the "TV Award" for *Wagon Train* from the California Rodeo at Salinas. Frank's solo appearances included Odessa, Texas,' rodeo. He stated that he was used to being confused with the *Rawhide* character Wishbone. Terry added that he was sometimes called Ben Cartwright.

"(THE ADVENTURES OF) WILD BILL HICKOK" CAST

GUY MADISON (1922–96)   California-born Robert Moseley debuted on film while still in World War II military service. His part as a sailor in *Since You Went Away* (1944)

Guy Madison (right) and Andy Devine as Wild Bill Hickok and Jingles in *Trouble on the Trail* (1954), a "feature" made by combining TV episodes.

led to a name change and roles as a romantic lead. Supported by Andy Devine and riding his Appaloosa mount Buckshot, he starred in TV's popular Western series *The Adventures of Wild Bill Hickok* (1951–58) and a concurrent radio show. Some TV episodes were combined to create feature films. Guy starred in the first 3-D Western, *The Charge at Feather River* (1953) and other oaters. Later, he made a number of European Westerns and adventure films. He received a Golden Boot Award.

"Wild Bill Hickok" on the Rodeo Trail

Guy Madison was featured at the 1952 Palm Springs rodeo. In 1953 at Cheyenne Frontier Days, he and Andy Devine rode on parade and made appearances with their TV show's contest winners. In 1957, Guy and his wife Sheila Connelly performed at the Texas Prison Rodeo on their wedding anniversary. Accordingly, inmates presented them with a gift. Guy joined Chill Wills as a special guest at Fort Worth's 1971 rodeo.

ANDY DEVINE (1905–77) Raised in Kingman, Arizona, Andy had a rambunctious and accident-prone boyhood. One incident damaged his vocal cords and changed his voice. About 1926, he was awarded a bit part in a Universal silent film. After the advent of sound, his unique voice helped him land a studio contract that lasted into the 1940s. Over six decades, he performed in films, on radio and TV shows, and on stage. His Western roles included sidekick to Roy Rogers in nine Republic color features in 1947 and '48. He was Jingles on TV's *The Adventures of Wild Bill Hickok*.

"Jingles" on the Rodeo Trail

Andy appeared with Guy Madison at Cheyenne Frontier Days in 1953 to recognize winners of Kellogg's "Name Jingles' Ranch" contest. In 1969, in connection with the rodeo, he received the Buffalo Bill Award at North Platte, Nebraska. In 1970, Kingman inaugurated an annual Andy Devine Days celebration, adding in 1985 the Andy Devine Days Rodeo, one of few named for Western stars.

WESTERN STAR CLUSTERS AT RODEOS

In 1924, Famous Players Lasky filmed *North of 36*, the first large-scale movie made in Texas. A Fort Bend County ranch was chosen for its 3,000 head of longhorns. Jack Holt, Ernest Torrence, Lois Wilson and Noah Beery starred. Each performance of a North of 36 Rodeo, staged for the cast, featured a movie scene. Texas theaters showed film of the rodeo.

In 1941, film producer Harry Sherman led a group of Western stars to the Reno (Nevada) Rodeo. Celebrities included Russell Hayden, Tim Holt, Jennifer Holt, Jean Phillips, June (Jan) Clayton, Preston Foster, Martha O'Driscoll, Bill Elliott, Brad King and Dorothy Gulliver.

In October 1946, *Red River*, wrapped up location filming near Elgin, Arizona. The town housed cast and crew (and became Abilene for the film, with locals as costumed extras). In gratitude, producer-director Howard Hawks hosted a community barbeque held in conjunction with the Sonoita Rodeo. John Wayne and Joanne Dru led the rodeo's grand entry, and cast members mingled with the crowd.

At Oklahoma City's Taft Stadium in June of 1947, four weekend performances of the

Top: Joanne Dru and John Wayne, stars of *Red River* (United Artists, 1948), led the grand entry of the Sonoita (Arizona) Rodeo in 1946. *Bottom*: Gene Autry and Champion at the 1947 Woodward Relief Rodeo, Oklahoma City, Oklahoma (Orren Mixer photograph, used with permission, obtained from Imogene Veach Beals, © 2004. Photograph © Autry Qualified Interest Trust and The Autry Foundation, provided courtesy Gene Autry Entertainment).

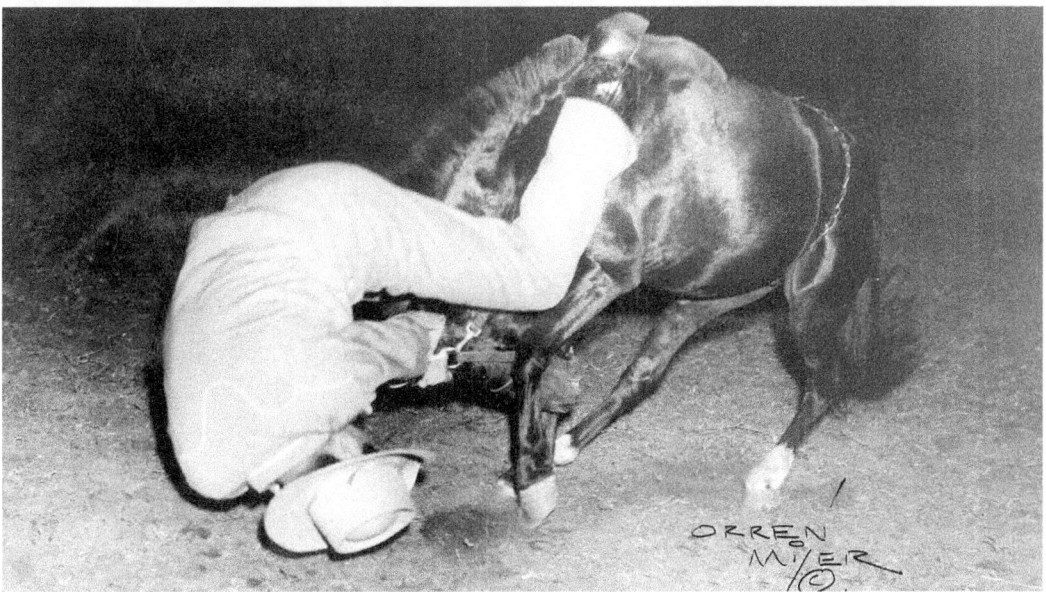

Top: Western star Rod Cameron attempts to ride a bucking pony at the 1947 Woodward Relief Rodeo (Orren Mixer photograph, obtained from Imogene Veach Beals, used with permission of Orren Mixer). *Bottom*: Rod Cameron's ride ends in a spill, reportedly injuring his shoulder (Orren Mixer photograph, obtained from Imogene Veach Beals, used with permission of Orren Mixer).

Woodward Relief Rodeo raised $100,000 for tornado victims. An American Airlines–donated "Oklahoma Tornado Relief Flagship" brought in stars Roscoe Ates, Johnny Bond, Rod Cameron, The Cass County Boys, Kay Christopher, Jimmie Davis, Eddie Dean, Nancy Gates, Connie Haines, Jennifer Holt, The Kettle Sisters, Nan Leslie, Adele Mara, Alan Massey and the Westerners, Bob Nolan and the Sons of the Pioneers and Ruth Upham. Bill Elliott was master of ceremonies. Gene Autry sang and Champion did his tricks. Among skits and songs, Kirby Grant sang "Empty Saddles" to honor Will Rogers while a spotlight followed a riderless horse.

Cessation of location shooting for Eagle-Lion's *Tulsa*, on Oklahoma Governor Roy J. Turner's ranch, east of Sulpher, coincided with the second annual (1948) Hereford Heaven Stampede. Susan Hayward headed movie dignitaries introduced at the rodeo. An announcement that the actress would rope a calf fooled the audience momentarily. Miss Hayward's riding double, in costume, did the roping.

IV

Rodeo-Related Films

FEATURE FILMS

Adventures of Gallant Bess (Eagle Lion, 1948) Contestant Ted (Cameron Mitchell), capturing wild horses for Bud's rodeo, keeps a red mare Bess though it means quitting the rodeo. Teaching her high-school tricks costs him his ranch job. When Bud's man oils the horns of his bulldogging steer, Ted's leg fractures require a long recovery. Evading restraint, Bess incurs damage claims. Sold at auction, she becomes "Bess the Wonder Horse" at Bud's rodeo. Seeing Bud mistreat her at the rodeo, Ted tries to return her to the wild and confronts Bud in pursuit. Bess returns to Ted's corral.

Arena (MGM, 1953) This film recorded action in 3D ("Look Out! He's Coming At You!") at Tucson's La Fiesta de los Vaqueros. Harry Morgan is Lew, former competitor working as a clown. Gig Young is Hob, rodeo rider whose estranged wife wants him to quit before he is injured. His girlfriend is thrilled by his rodeoing. Western TV stars Robert Horton and Lee Aaker support. To impress his son and prove that he is not washed up, Lew substitutes for a disabled saddle bronc rider, injuring his knee. Distracting bulls while injured, he suffers a broken neck. Hob and wife attempt reconciliation, leaving the girlfriend to a rival. Rodeo competitors and clowns doubled.

The Arizona Cowboy (Republic, 1950) After three years out of the country teaching rodeo, Rex Allen stars in the Mammoth Rodeo. Announced as a Willcox, Arizona, cowboy, he rides a saddle bronc. He is implicated in an irrigation company robbery, for which his missing father is falsely accused. Working undercover, he suspects collusion between the chief engineer and a banker. He eludes plots to eliminate him and discovers that the crooks' motive is oil. At a ghost town hotel, he finds his hostage dad. Justice prevails.

Back in the Saddle (Republic, 1941) In a Madison Square Garden dressing room, Gene Autry sings while rodeo hands go about their chores at the rodeo's closing. Instead of following the rodeo to Boston, prize money winner Gene returns to duties as ranch foreman. Mostly he deals with the ranch's wild young heir, greedy copper miners killing cattle with pollution and his relationship with a singer. Smiley Burnette and Mary Lee assist.

Bells of Capistrano (Republic, 1942) Worldwide Rodeo suffers in competition with Johnson Brothers. A Johnson courts Worldwide's owner Jennifer to obtain control of her rodeo. Managers Ma and Pa McCraken hire Gene Autry, "the singing bronco buster," and business improves. The rival crew inflicts a damaging raid on Worldwide. When Jennifer transfers ownership to her workers, Johnson reveals his true intent. Gene rounds up the lawbreakers and secures a specialist for Pa, injured in an arson fire. Gene leads a patriotic rodeo finale. Hit with such lines as "Rodeo calls for mostly fancy riding, very little fancy singing" and "I don't know why a rodeo crowd should want a singer," Gene faces real-life criticism.

Big Boy Rides Again (RKO, 1935) Big Boy Williams plays a rodeo cowboy estranged from his father and trying to earn enough prize money to be a suitable suitor for his girlfriend. His father's letter interrupts a saloon celebration of his bronc-riding win. Accepting an invitation to return home, he learns that his father has been shot dead. He must find his hidden inheritance before a black-caped villain, eliminating ranch employees one by one, stops him.

In RKO's *Big Boy Rides Again*, Guinn Williams (center) enjoys a happy rodeo moment with a group of unidentified cowboys before becoming embroiled in the mysery of his father's murder (courtesy Jerry Ohlinger's).

The Big Show (Republic, 1936)   No rodeo, but Gene Autry riding on parade, mobbed by fans, making radio broadcasts, starring in production numbers and being awarded a Texas Ranger commission, foreshadows future rodeo appearances. Gene plays dual roles: arrogant Western film star and likable stuntman. The singing stuntman's Texas Centennial appearance in place of the star confuses respective girlfriends and gangsters out to collect a debt.

Born Reckless (Warner Brothers, 1958)   Good-hearted rider Kelly (Jeff Richards) rodeos to buy a ranch he shares with a family. Trick rider Jackie (Mamie Van Doren) sings that she is a "good, sweet home-type girl," while Jeff fights off the men who make advances toward her. Involved with the wrong kind of woman, he comes to his senses, puts his rodeo winnings toward the ranch and sees Jackie in a new light. Tex Williams performs in a club scene. May Boss tutored Miss Van Doren in trick riding. Wag Blessing and Gerald Roberts doubled riding scenes.

The Boss Rider of Gun Creek (Universal, 1936)   Buck Jones plays two roles: Larry Day and Gary Elliot. Arrested at a rodeo, Larry is convicted of a murder committed by lookalike Gary. He escapes to seek the real killer. The sheriff, misled by Elliot's resemblance to Day, kills him. Feigning amnesia, Larry finds that Gary, with a crooked sheriff and banker, has been stealing cattle and plotting foreclosure on a young woman's ranch valued as a dam

Gene Autry bulldogs a steer in a scene from *The Big Show* (Republic, 1936) (obtained from Eddie Brandt's, © 2004 Autry Qualified Interest Trust and The Autry Foundation, provided courtesy Gene Autry Entertainment).

Advertisement for Universal's *The Boss Rider of Gun Creek*, starring Buck Jones (courtesy Jerry Ohlinger's).

site. As suspicion about Larry mounts, a confession brings the guilty to justice, and Larry wins the woman's heart.

Bronco Buster (Universal-International, 1952) Actual rodeo footage and personalities add realism. Stars and crew filmed for five days at Cheyenne's 1951 Frontier Days. All stars appeared in parades. Lead doubles Dan Poore and Bill Williams were Cheyenne contestants. For some scenes, Budd Boetticher directed from a wooden beam balanced above the chutes. Technicolor cameras, including two in a specially constructed eight-foot-square pit-type abutment dug into the arena floor, covered arena action. Tom (John Lund) is a veteran rodeo champion, Bart (Scott Brady) the arrogant rookie sensation. Judy (Joyce Holden), daughter of rodeo clown Dan (Chill Wills), is attracted to both men. The rival riders' relationship sours as they compete in the arena and for Judy, reaching a climax in Cheyenne. Showing off, Bart causes a bull to injure Dan. In a $1,000 showdown, Tom and Bart simultaneously ride penned bulls.

Bus Stop (20th Century–Fox, 1956) Naïve young ranch-bound cowboy Beau (Don Murray) travels to the Phoenix rodeo vowing to find his "angel." He meets lounge chanteuse and drink hustler Cherie (Marilyn Monroe). Declaring her his angel, he proposes. They watch the rodeo parade, and she witnesses his arena exploits. Actual bronc riders are introduced. Beau forces Cherie on his return bus to Montana. When snow requires an overnight stay at a diner bus stop, Cherie is impressed with his sincere apology.

The Calgary Stampede (Universal-Jewel, 1925) In this silent film with music, rodeo rider Dan (Hoot Gibson) loves Marie. The murder of her father, who had objected

Amidst this rodeo crowd can be seen Marilyn Monroe (standing) and Don Murray (center, in white shirt and hat), stars of 20th Century–Fox's ***Bus Stop*** (courtesy Eddie Brandt's).

to their relationship, casts suspicion on Dan. Feeling that Marie believes him guilty, Dan drifts to a distant ranch. A year later, a Mountie officer, still on the case, suspects the new hand. Marie, brought to the ranch, declares her belief in Dan. At the Calgary Stampede, Dan substitutes as a contestant to save the wagered ranch. A scorned witness identifies the killer, who attempts escape by wagon. Dan pursues and is cleared.

Carolina Moon (Republic, 1940) Gene Autry's calf-roping and steer-wrestling win $2,000 in rodeo prize money. Smitten by lively Southern girl June Storey, he settles her grandfather's wager loss in exchange for the family's horse. Failing to tell his granddaughter, the colonel returns home, leaving Gene without money or horse. Following him to the family plantation, Gene and Frog encounter younger sister Mary Lee, a foxhunt and a duel challenge. When unscrupulous land dealers try to take over plantations, Gene rides in a steeplechase.

Cheyenne (First National, 1928) In summer 1928, Ken Maynard's unit arrived at Cheyenne Frontier Days to record this film, dedicated "to those men who have lost their lives in contest riding that the old West may still exist in the minds of the American people." Ken gave daily trick and fancy riding exhibitions, participated in a Roman riding race and rode a bucking horse to obtain close-up footage. Director Al Rogell had about 20,000 crowd extras cheer Ken's rides and react in horror to a staged arena "accident." In early August, cast and crew returned to Hollywood to complete the film. Ben Corbett appears. Leonard Stroud doubled Ken.

The Cowboy and the Blonde (20th Century–Fox, 1941) In this romantic comedy, George Montgomery is rodeo champion Lank Garrett. Brought to Hollywood by a studio owner-rodeo fan, he fails a series of screen tests. Falling for him, temperamental star Crystal (Mary Beth Hughes) becomes more cooperative. The studio plans to give Lank a contract just to keep Crystal in line. An outdoor test with Crystal shows Lank's true potential and the couple's charisma. Misunderstanding sends Lank back to his ranch, but sidekick Skeeter (Fuzzy Knight) concocts a ruse that brings the "palomino" and the "beautiful dope" together.

The Cowboy and the Lady (Samuel Goldwyn, 1938) Mary (Merle Oberon), the high-society daughter of a potential presidential candidate, leaves New York for the family's Palm Beach home. On a blind date with rodeo cowboy Stretch Willoughby (Gary Cooper), she deceives him into believing that she is a "work horse," a dressing maid with family responsibilities. They are married aboard a ship bound for Galveston, the next rodeo site. From the rodeo camp, Mary is called to a politically important Palm Beach dinner. When she fails to return on time, Stretch follows and learns her true status. He confronts her falsehoods and returns to Montana. At the ranch, Mary's father accepts responsibility. Stretch and Mary are reconciled. Hank Worden, Walter Brennan and Fuzzy Knight appear.

Cowboy Up (Neverland, 2002) The lives of two contentious brothers revolve around bull riding. Once a rider, Hank (Kiefer Sutherland) conducts bull-riding schools and works rodeos as a bullfighter-clown, hoping to contract bulls to rodeos. Ely (Marcus Thomas), medically disqualified, cannot stop riding bulls. At the bull-riding finals, Ely draws his brother's bull. The result is unexpected and tragic. Bo Hopkins is a rodeo promoter. Bullfighters Joe Baumgartner and Flint Rasmussen contribute. Gary Leffew was technical coordinator. Mike McGaughy coordinated stunts.

The Cowboy Way (Universal, 1994) In this action-comedy film, New Mexico team ropers Pepper (Woody Harrelson) and Sonny (Kiefer Sutherland) have been estranged since Pepper was a no-show at the National Finals Rodeo that might have won them the world's

Gary Cooper carries Merle Oberon through the rodeo tent camp in this scene from the Samuel Goldwyn–United Artists production *The Cowboy and the Lady* (courtesy Eddie Brandt's).

championship. They combine to investigate the disappearance in New York City of their friend and his daughter. Sam, a mounted policeman inspired by Bill Pickett, aids their efforts to foil murderous sweatshop operators. The mounted ropers chase a subway train.

***Desert Trail* (Monogram, 1935)** Rodeo contestant John Wayne insists on collecting his full prize money although hard-pressed rodeo management is paying only a fraction of amounts won. When the rodeo pay agent is robbed and murdered, John must elude the posse and prove his innocence. Meanwhile, he woos a pretty general store operator, sister to the villain's reluctant helper.

Down Laredo Way (Republic, 1953)   Rex Allen, as star of a Western Rodeo Circus, rides a saddle bronc. An aerial artist fights over his fiancée's diamond smuggling. He hides the diamonds in his daughter's doll before falling to his death. A crooked judge joins the fiancée's search for the diamonds, making the daughter his legal ward. Sidekick Slim Pickens and a gypsy woman help Rex, who rejoins his rodeo once justice is done.

8 Seconds (New Line Cinema, 1994)   Luke Perry plays real-life bull rider Lane Frost, whose philosophy was to do his best and to help others to do *their* best. He won the 1987 world bull-riding championship. A Challenge of the Champions matched Lane against Red Rock, a bull unridden in 309 attempts. The film depicts three of Lane's seven attempts. At Cheyenne's 1989 Frontier Days, Lane was fatally gored after making a qualified bull ride. Actors play Lane's parents, wife and companions, who all had input into the film. Stephen Baldwin supports. An epilogue shows pictures of Lane's life.

The Electric Horseman (Columbia, 1979)   No rodeo scenes after the opening credits. Robert Redford is former five-time world champion all-around cowboy Sonny Steele, a drinker reduced to appearing in a lit-up Western suit to promote a breakfast cereal. Feeling that his company horse is being mistreated, he escapes Las Vegas to set the horse free. Corporate villains pursue. Willie Nelson, as Sonny's manager, contributes songs. Jane Fonda is a reporter following the story.

Feud of the West (Diversion, 1936)   Hoot Gibson is Whitey, rodeo steer-wrestling winner, who defeats Six-Bits (Buzz Barton) in the bronc riding finals. Walters, leader of

Luke Perry as real-life champion bull rider Lane Frost in New Line Cinema's *8 Seconds* (courtesy Eddie Brandt's).

one cowboy crew, offers Whitey a ranch of his own to infiltrate rival Hawk's crew of wild horse hunters and identify his son's murderer. Former ranch owner "Wild Horse" feels cheated by both feuding factions. Six-Bits helps Whitey bring the bad men to justice. Whitey earns his ranch and a lady's heart.

Frontier Town (Grand National, 1938) Tex Ritter opposes villain Charles King. Tex bests the organizer's handpicked favorites in each rodeo event, but is framed for murder to prevent him from winning the prize money.

Harley Davidson and the Marlboro Man (MGM, 1991) Mickey Rourke is biker Harley and Don Johnson is Robert, a third-generation rodeo cowboy wanting to return to the National Finals. This action-buddy film concerns struggle for possession of a deadly exotic drug. Only a brief rodeo scene at the conclusion.

Heart of the Rockies (Republic, 1951) Highway engineer Roy Rogers encounters opposition to his road project, a ranch foreman substituting scrub cattle for purebreds, and a first-offender work camp youth accused of robbery. The tense story includes murder of the work camp warden. A guest ranch rodeo features the Valkyries and music by Roy and the Riders of the Purple Sage. Rand Brooks and Buzz Henry appear.

Heldorado (Republic, 1946) Amidst Las Vegas' Helldorado Days Rodeo, Roy Rogers

Lobby card for Republic's *Heldorado*, set at Las Vegas' Helldorado Days (courtesy Eddie Brandt's).

is a rodeo star and ranger captain investigating a black market scheme that involves passing money in casinos. Helldorado Queen Dale Evans, as honorary deputy sheriff, hampers and aids Roy. Announcer Gabby Hayes introduces Roy, who charges into the arena on Trigger to be joined in song by The Sons of the Pioneers. Dale takes advantage of Roy's performing to investigate a murder. The Helldorado treasure hunt leads to a railroad station fistfight. The stars ride in the rodeo parade. Tex Cooper, Clayton Moore and Doye O'Dell contribute. Polly Mills Burson doubles Dale.

Home in Wyomin' (Republic, 1942) Radio singer Gene Autry, with Frog and Tadpole, travels to aid Pop Harrison's Wyoming rodeo. Pop was Gene's early mentor, but his son Tex, the rodeo star, tends to drink and gamble. A magazine photographer and a reporter arrive at the rodeo ranch. The reporter insults and fights Tex, and then spots Chicago gangsters. During Tex's shot-filled act, the reporter is shot dead. The sheriff arrests Tex, and Gene suspects the gangsters. The killer is revealed in a suspenseful mine tunnel climax. The rodeo gets a bid for the big time.

James Coburn as saddle bronc rider Lew Lathrop in United Artists' *The Honkers*.

The Honkers (United Artists, 1972) James Coburn is Lew, a quick-tempered, selfish saddle bronc rider who sacrifices family and friends. His rodeo clown partner (Slim Pickens) sings his composition "I'm a Rodeo Cowboy." Harry Vold provided stock and plays a stock contractor. Son Doug Vold doubled for the star's bronc riding. Real-life announcer Chuck Parkison is at the mike. Larry Mahan plays himself. Rodeo clowns Chuck Henson, Larry McKinney and Wiley McCray also contribute. Jerry Gatlin, wrangler and stuntman, plays Shorty and Ross Dollarhide is Travis. Some filming took place at Carlsbad, New Mexico.

J.W. Coop (Columbia, 1972) Cliff Robertson wrote, produced, directed and starred. After ten years in prison, J.W. resumes pro rodeo competition. He finds changes in people, society and rodeo. At the rodeo grounds, he and a pal, real-life bull rider Myrtis Dightman, fight bigots in a bar rest room. Making some concessions to modern ways, J.W. mostly relies on traditional integrity to avoid depending on a "dead end" job. He moves up in the standings against defending world champion, Hot Pistol Billy (rodeo cowboy Dennis Reiners), to qualify for Oklahoma City's National Finals Rodeo. With his leg in a cast, J.W. is hung up on a tough bull, tossed on the horns and bloodied in the dirt, ending his dream. RCA personnel, including Gary Leffew, appear.

Bull rider Myrtis Dightman, of Crockett, Texas,

IV. Rodeo-Related Films 321

Cliff Robertson, producer, director and star of *J.W. Coop*, released by Columbia.

was a key figure in the history of black rodeo cowboys. In the tradition of Bill Pickett, George Fletcher, Jesse Stahl, Willie Thomas, Buck Wyatt, Felix Cooper, Marvel Rogers and others, Myrtis was the first black rodeo contestant to compete at the National Finals Rodeo, qualifying seven times between 1964 and 1972. Following in his footsteps was 1982 world champion bull rider Charles Sampson. Fred Whitfield, multiple world champion calf roper and 1999 champion all-around cowboy, is active as of this writing.

Junior Bonner (ABC Pictures Corp., 1972) Steve McQueen filmed *Junior Bonner* at the 1971 Prescott Frontier Days Rodeo. The only one of his films not to make money, *Junior Bonner*, directed by Sam Peckinpah, was reportedly Steve's favorite role. The supporting cast includes Robert

Bull rider Myrtis Dightman in a scene from *J.W. Coop* (courtesy Jerry Ohlinger's).

Steve McQueen in the Cinerama Releasing Corp. film *Junior Bonner*.

Preston, Ida Lupino and Ben Johnson. The story tells of progress outpacing a rodeo contestant's values. Filming at an established rodeo lends a feel of authenticity. Rodeo competitor J.C. Trujillo rode for Steve.

Kid from Gower Gulch (Friedgen, 1950) Western film star Spade Cooley arrives with Walt his stuntman, to perform at the Wells Valley Stampede. Others do Spade's film riding, fighting and singing. The Bar W Ranch owner, needing cattle to pay his mortgage, bets 500 head that a rider representing the Bar W will win top rodeo honors. Walt agrees to ride, but reneges on the eve of the rodeo. Overcoming fear and inexperience, Spade rides a "killer" bronc to save the ranch. Richard Farnsworth doubled for Spade in his riding scenes and won prize money at the actual Ridgecrest Rodeo. Boyd Stockman also did stunts.

King of the Cowboys (Republic, 1943) The governor calls rodeo headliner Roy Rogers from a parade to serve as special investigator of saboteurs causing explosions or fires along a carnival's itinerary. Working undercover, Roy learns how coded messages are being passed. After the saboteurs begin to suspect him, Roy has several narrow escapes. Wounded, Roy climbs a railroad trestle bridge to defuse a bomb set to destroy a supply train. The governor's award, presented at the rodeo, calls Roy "King of the Cowboys." Smiley Burnette and the Sons of the Pioneers support.

King of the Rodeo (Universal-Jewel, 1929) His dad wants him to return to college, but the rebellious Montana Kid (Hoot Gibson) rides his horse to Tex Austin's 1928 Chicago rodeo and wins several events. A thief steals one of the Kid's two trademark white shirts to divert suspicion when he robs the cashier's office. The Kid pursues the robber by taxi and police motorcycle just to retrieve his shirt. Justice and romance are served. Lanky Slim Summerville and diminutive Jack Knapp provide comedy.

Lobby card for Universal's *King of the Rodeo*, starring Hoot Gibson (courtesy Eddie Brandt's).

A Lady Takes a Chance, a.k.a. The Cowboy and the Girl (RKO, 1943) This romantic comedy has New York City girl Molly (Jean Arthur) on a bus tour of "the wonders of the West." After rodeo bronc rider Duke Hudkins (John Wayne) is bucked into the stands on top of her, their evening together causes Molly to miss her bus. In the morning, she tries to hitchhike to Gold City, his next rodeo site and her bus stop. Eventually she joins Duke and his sidekick Waco, camping out on the plains between towns. Duke's concern for his ill horse convinces Molly that he can love a girl. When Molly relays news of the horse's recovery to Duke at the rodeo, she senses a receptive mood, but Duke withdraws in fear of being "hooked." Following Molly home, he brings her back to the West.

Let 'Er Buck (Universal, 1925) Texas cowboy Bob (Hoot Gibson) is in love with a rancher's daughter. When it appears that he has killed her cousin Jim in a gunfight, he flees. Another ranch enlists him to ride a bronc at the Pendleton RoundUp. His old Texas outfit, including Jim (alive), arrives, wanting him to ride for them. Bob is torn between two ranches and two ranchers' daughters. He escapes from a kidnapping to win the rodeo's chariot race versus Ben Corbett. Actual rodeo footage adds authenticity. Additional scenes were filmed at a grandstand reproduction on Universal's lot. Stars Marian Nixon and Josie Sedgwick were both, in time, rodeo queens. Fred Humes is the sheriff.

Lights of Old Santa Fe (Republic, 1944) Gabby Hayes, manager of Brooks International Rodeo, keeps its troubles from owner Dale Evans. A rival rodeo owner uses marriage proposals and sabotage to eliminate Brooks as a competitor. Roy Rogers saves Gabby from death, defeats the villains and wins Dale's approval for a rodeo performance leading to Madison Square Garden. When Roy and Gabby enter in four-horse chariots, Dale joins Roy singing the title song. Riding double, the two exemplify their movie magic. Gabby's lines include:

> "Singers ain't got no place in rodeo."
>
> "A good rider gets throwed, he don't sit, he gets up. Yes he does, boss gal. He gets up, dusts off the seat of his pants and climbs back into the saddle. That's what a top hand does."
>
> "Yes siree boy, this is the life, Roy, wagons rollin,' ready to play, camping for a meal and, then, the crowds — the crowds fillin' the bleachers."

The Long, Long Trail (Universal, 1929) In Hoot Gibson's first talking picture, The Ramblin' Kid (Hoot) captures a wild palomino to race in the rodeo. Just prior to the race, Mike, saloonkeeper and rival racehorse owner, has drugged coffee delivered to the Kid. Groggy and barely able to stay on his horse, the Kid comes from behind to win, saving his girl's dad's ranch. Despondent that his girl and her dad think he is drunk, the teetotaler Kid visits the saloon, where he overhears Mike quarreling over splitting the race purse. The Kid overcomes the villains, restoring his girl's trust. Walter Brennan, Sally Eilers and Abe Lefton appear.

The Lusty Men (RKO, 1952) Posters read, "A fast buck... A fast bronc... A fast thrill! They ride ... play ... and love hard ... in the brawling camps of Big-Time Rodeo." Robert Mitchum is Jeff, broke former champion forced out by injury. For a percentage, he manages up-and-comer Wes (Arthur Kennedy), who leaves a ranch to rodeo full-time, to the disapproval of his wife Louise (Susan Hayward). Tension between Wes and Jeff leads to a fatal saddle bronc ride. Glenn Strange, Sheb Wooley and announcer Chuck Parkison appear. Casey Tibbs and Eddy Akridge double.

Advertisement for RKO's *The Lusty Men* (courtesy Eddie Brandt's).

Mackintosh and TJ (Penland Productions, 1976) Roy Rogers, leaving movie retirement to make this values-laden film, is Mackintosh, a past-his-prime top hand. Waylon Jennings' background songs "All-Around Cowboy" and "Ride Me Down Easy" suggest a rodeo background. A drifter himself, he mentors youthful TJ, played by future PRCA world champion team roper Clay O'Brien. Mackintosh tells and shows TJ that "a man without pride ain't worth beans." Larry Mahan and Dean Smith contribute.

The Man from Rainbow Valley (Republic, 1946) Monte Hale is a cowboy cartoonist who draws the comic strip "Outlaw, King of the Wild Stallions." The inspiration for the strip runs free with his herd on Monte's Rainbow Valley Ranch. Unscrupulous horse dealers capture the stallion, hoping to make a profit. When the disguised horse becomes a rodeo bronc, Monte wins back his horse by riding him in rodeo competition. His charm wins over Adrian Booth.

The Man from Utah (Monogram, 1934) Marshal George Hayes enlists the aid of John Wayne, who arrives playing a guitar and singing, to help him solve a crooked rodeo scheme. Yakima Canutt appears. This film was remade by Monogram in 1944 as *The Utah Kid*, starring Hoot Gibson and Bob Steele (see below).

Monte Hale and Adrian Booth in Republic's *The Man from Rainbow Valley* (courtesy Eddie Brandt's).

John Wayne mounts a rodeo bronc in the Lone Star–Monogram film, *The Man from Utah* (courtesy Jerry Ohlinger's).

Melody Trail (Republic, 1935)   At a rodeo, Gene Autry is both contestant and singer. In footage shot at Saugus and Gilroy, California, Abe Lefton announces. Gene reportedly asked a rodeo clown to tutor Smiley Burnette, mainly in arena safety, for his role as a rodeo clown. After besting villain Al Bridge in saddle bronc riding, Gene is robbed of his $1,000 prize money. This light film features romantic interest, a dog that steals objects (and a baby), and cattle rustling from a ranch staffed by young women. Frog ropes and wrestles a calf. Gene and Frog work as ranch cooks, and they chase a wrongly suspected "kidnapper."

Mesquite Buckaroo (Metropolitan, 1939)   On the eve of a rodeo, the home ranch depends on Bob Steele, who rejects a bribery attempt. Arena footage identifies real rodeo personalities. After scoring well at the first performance, Bob is held at a cabin under guard. When he fails to appear for the rodeo's second day, judges postpone disqualifying him and rearrange the order of events. Impatient to collect his money, the guard unties Bob's feet so he can ride. Bob subdues his captor and arrives at the rodeo in time to repeat as champion. He captures the villains and recovers money bet on the rodeo.

The Misfits (UA, 1961)   Arthur Miller wrote the screenplay for his then-wife, Marilyn Monroe. Clark Gable, a mustanger, and Montgomery Clift, a rodeo rider, are the male leads. It was the last film for each of the stars and was filmed on location in Nevada. Dramatic tension revolves around a rodeo and a round-up of wild mustangs.

In *Melody Trail* (Republic, 1935), rodeo rider Gene Autry (right) confronts villain Al Bridge (center) at the chutes. Smiley Burnette (left), dressed as a rodeo clown, is eager to help, and other cowboys look on (obtained from Eddie Brandt's, © 2004 Autry Qualified Interest Trust and The Autry Foundation, provided courtesy Gene Autry Entertainment).

My Heroes Have Always Been Cowboys (Samuel Goldwyn, 1991) Scott Glenn is a hard-luck, nearly over-the-hill bull rider. To save the family ranch and keep his father (Ben Johnson) from a retirement home, he must win a $100,000 bull-riding prize. Filming was done at Guthrie, Oklahoma. Two world champions, Tuff Hedeman and Jim Sharp, served as bull-riding doubles. Special camera set-ups captured the action. An Oklahoma City premiere benefited the Justin Cowboy Crisis Fund.

My Pal the King (Universal, 1932) A boy king (Mickey Rooney) rules Albonia. Tom Mix headlines a world-touring Wild West Show, performing feats typical of Western stars at rodeos. Tom rides on parade, charges into the arena waving his hat, trick-rides, makes a four-horse catch with his lariat, rides a bucking horse, displays his gun-spinning and target shooting skills, leads Tony through a trick routine and rescues a stagecoach from attack. The young king, fascinated with the cowboy's prowess, invites him to his castle. Tom's advice regarding more democratic rule ("life, liberty and the pursuit of happiness") conflicts with the schemes of a wicked count. Tom saves the king from danger, and the two part as friends.

Northwest Stampede (Eagle Lion, 1948) Former rodeo contestant Chris (Joan Leslie) is a ranch foreperson. Absentee owner-rodeo rider Dan (James Craig) returns to the ranch

Left to right: Scott Glenn, Kate Capshaw and Ben Johnson star in the Samuel Goldwyn film *My Heroes Have Always Been Cowboys* (courtesy Jerry Ohlinger's).

Advertisement for Universal's *My Pal the King*, starring Tom Mix and Mickey Rooney.

when he learns of his father's passing. Posing as an ordinary hand, he wants to capture a wild white stallion he had known as a colt. Chris recognizes Dan from a photo, and they clash over the ranch's future. Dan hopes to sell the ranch; Chris wants to save it. They compete in Calgary's bronc riding and chuckwagon race. Harry Cheshire is a rodeo announcer. "Miss Polly Mills Burson" is the announced wild cow milking winner. Chris spends Dan's prize money on horses. Dan captures his stallion, and then frees it. Chris has the stallion follow a mare into the ranch corral. Jack Oakie and Chill Wills provide comedy. Location filming was done in Alberta, Canada.

Painted Hero (Cabin Fever, 1995)   This unscreened independent film stars Dwight Yoakam as Virgil and Bo Hopkins as Brownie. The film won the gold award as Best Dramatic Feature Film at the 1995 Houston International Film Festival.

Rhythm on the Range (Paramount, 1936)   In this romantic comedy, Jeff (Bing Crosby) competes in all events, including a singing contest, at the Madison Square Garden rodeo. His prize money buys Cuddles, a bull. Returning with Cuddles in a railroad stock car, Jeff meets Doris, a socialite escaping from her impending marriage. Her Aunt Penny owns the ranch where Jeff works. At the ranch, Jeff is cleared of blame for Doris' disappearance. He and Doris remain together. The Sons of the Pioneers appear. The reworked script became *Pardners* (1956), starring Dean Martin and Jerry Lewis.

Owner of the Spring Creek Ranch near Elko, Nevada, Bing Crosby was associated with the Silver State Stampede from 1948 until he sold the ranch in 1958. A donated Bing Crosby

Bing Crosby in the rodeo chute in *Rhythm on the Range* (courtesy Eddie Brandt's).

Trophy, engraved with the names of champion all-around cowboys, was to be retired if a cowboy won three times. Winners kept a Bing-donated belt buckle.

Rhythm of the Saddle (Republic, 1938)   Pomeroy, crooked owner of a Nevada gambling house, wants to win the contract for the ongoing rodeo from the Silver Saddle Ranch, for which Gene Autry is foreman. Pomeroy's contestant wins the bucking horse event when Silver Saddle entry Dixie is injured in the chute. Gene learns that Dixie's rope was deliberately severed by acid and finds evidence of Pomeroy's bronc-riding bet. The committee decides the rodeo contract will go to the stagecoach race winner. A telephone and an audio recorder help Gene and Frog foil the villains. Escaping from jail, Gene drives a coach in the race.

Ride Him Cowboy (Warner Bros., 1932)   John Wayne is a harmonica-playing Texas rodeo cowboy, whose riding of a "killer" horse on trial spares the animal's life. John volunteers to track down Hawk, the leader of murderous raiders. Respected citizen Mr. Simms, acting as guide across the desert, reveals that he is the Hawk and leaves John tied to a tree. Duke, the horse he saved, helps John escape, but the Hawk makes John a suspect in his next raid. At a trial, Hawk's men are tricked into giving away their boss. Hawk kidnaps a young woman before all is resolved. Ben Corbett appears.

Rodeo (Monogram, 1952)   Unsuccessful in collecting her dad's feed store bill from a cash-strapped rodeo, Nancy (Jane Nigh) assumes control of the rodeo as a cooperative business. Tex (John Archer), rodeo ramrod and contestant, is attracted to her. After Nancy tells aging Barbecue that he is washed up, his bronc ride ends in injury. Personnel quit, dissolving the rodeo. Learning that Nancy paid Barbecue's hospital bill, Tex decides she's not so bad. He invites Nancy to a Bonelli Ranch performance that leads to the rodeo's sale. Nancy pays the store debt, Tex buys his ranch and the couple plan their future.

Rodeo Girl (CBS-TV, 1980)   Katharine Ross stars as Sue Pirtle, who served the film as technical advisor and double for rodeo riding. Sue was an all-around champion of the Girl's Rodeo Association (now Women's Professional Rodeo Association). Some filming took place at the Randall Ranch in Newhall. H.P. Evetts rides a bull for Bo Hopkins. Wilford Brimley appears. R.L. Tolbert coordinates the action.

Rodeo King and the Senorita (Republic, 1951)   Wild West Show co-owner Pablo Morales (Buff Brady, Jr.) is killed exhibiting a Roman ride over an automobile, leaving his young daughter Juanita as the show's half-owner. Rex Allen, new rodeo star, rides a bronc and ropes a calf. Rex learns that acid caused his harness to fail in a cross-country chariot race. He traces Pablo's harness and Roman-jumping team to another outfit. Rex's Roman jump earns a pony for the ailing Juanita. He wins a combined stagecoach–saddle horse relay race, gaining full ownership of Koko. Apprehending the villains, he becomes manager of the Allen-Morales rodeo.

Rodeo Rhythm (PRC, 1942)   In this low-budget film, Aunt Tillie's home for orphans plans an excursion to her brother Buck's ranch. When a bitter mortgage holder takes the children's travel money as payment, friends help with the trip. At the ranch, the children plan a fund-raising rodeo. They help extricate the visiting mortgage holder from a vehicle accident and later visit him at the hospital. In gratitude, he releases attached horses and

Katharine Ross ties her calf in the CBS-TV film *Rodeo Girl* (courtesy Jerry Ohlinger's).

Rex Allen in calf-roping scene from Republic's *Rodeo King and the Senorita* (courtesy Eddie Brandt's).

equipment, allowing the rodeo to proceed. Buck (Fred Scott) leads the entry with a song, and the children ride. The mortgage holder lets the children keep their rodeo earnings and promises an improved home.

Rovin' Tumbleweeds (Republic, 1939) When Gene Autry's radio singing aids flood refugees, shady political interests help elect him to Congress, where he has difficulty advancing his flood control bill. To gain publicity and funds, he enters a rodeo, winning the ear of an influential committee chairman-rodeo fan. However, the man is killed in an auto accident. When Congress adjourns, Gene returns home empty-handed. Battling renewed flooding, he gets ranchers, migrants and politicians to cooperate on the sandbag crew. His adversary changes his heart, vowing to back the flood control bill and help create jobs.

Ruby Jean and Joe (Showtime, 1995) Tom Selleck is Joe Wade, an over-the-hill rodeo cowboy. The film, shot in Cochise County, Arizona, deals with how Joe and young black runaway Ruby Jean (Rebekah Johnson) help each other know themselves better. Tucson's Fiesta de los Vaqueros is the setting for some rodeo scenes. Ben Johnson appears. Walter Scott and Jerry Gatlin coordinated stunts. PRCA saddle bronc riders (chosen for their height) double Tom Selleck. Bob Tallman announces.

The Saddle Buster (RKO Pathe, 1932) At rodeo training quarters, Montana (Tom Keene) encounters Rance, a jealous, bragging bronc-riding champion. Monty is thrown and trampled when Rance goads him into a ride on Wild Fury. Evidence suggests that Rance cut the cinch. Recovered physically, Monty, now in fear of horses, leaves for a cabin in wild horse country. A wild horse inspires Monty with his spirit. Newly confident, Monty arrives at a rodeo seeking to get even with Rance. He learns that Wild Fury has put Rance, who admits his guilt, in a wheelchair. Monty donates his $1,000 prize for riding Wild Fury toward Rance's treatment and plans his next rodeo. Ben Corbett and Skeeter Bill Robbins appear.

Sky Full of Moon (MGM, 1952) In this romantic comedy, Harley (Carleton Carpenter), an innocent cowboy, enters a Las Vegas rodeo. He falls in love with change girl Dixie Delmar (Jan Sterling). Sheb Wooley appears.

Smoky (20th Century–Fox, 1946) This is one of three film versions of Will James' story of the relationship between a man and a horse. Fred MacMurray, as loner cowboy Clint, patiently makes a cow horse of the steel brown wild stallion Smoky. His underhanded brother Frank beats Smoky and is trampled to death. Smoky escapes, becoming a rodeo bucking horse. Clint searches in vain for the horse. As years pass, Smoky is hurt in an arena fall and sold to a riding academy. Later, seeing a junk wagon horse join a Cheyenne Frontier Days parade, Clint buys Smoky and puts him out to pasture. Burl Ives adds songs. Ben Johnson doubles for Fred.

Somewhere in Sonora (Warner Bros., 1933) When sabotage injures a competing rodeo stagecoach race driver, John (John Wayne) is accused and jailed. Bob aids John's escape, relating that his son Bart, wrongly accused of a crime, fled to Mexico. The father believes his son is unwillingly part of Sonora's Monte Black gang. In gratitude, John seeks Bart. Cleared of blame for the arena accident, John is taken into the gang and foils a raid of a silver mine office. Attempting escape with Bart, he is about to be rushed by the gang. He sends his horse Duke for help. Bart and Mexican forces save him from execution.

Fred MacMurray (right) and Burl Ives in a scene from 20th Century–Fox's *Smoky*.

***Song of Texas* (Republic, 1943)**   Rodeo star Roy Rogers entertains hospitalized children. At the rodeo, he competes in a chuckwagon race against aging rodeo great Sam Bennett. Sam in his prime had endowed the visited children's ward, but now is reduced to begging for work. Roy provides Sam, injured when his wagon overturns, with medical aid and recovery on his ranch. Learning that poor maintenance caused Sam's wagon to lose a wheel, Roy quits the rodeo. To help Sam appear more prosperous during his daughter's visit, Roy loans his ranch. Sam's daughter sells his "interest" in the ranch to the rodeo owner. A rodeo chuckwagon race settles the dispute.

***Song of the Trail* (Ambassador, 1936)**   Jim (Kermit Maynard) practices for the upcoming rodeo, including trick riding and roping a horse and rider in motion. Target shooting, he re-meets Betty. Losing a mine quitclaim in a crooked poker game, her father Dan (George Hayes) vows revenge, making him a suspect when outlaws are killed during shooting competition. A wild saloon fight ensues. In time, the villain tips his hand.

***Spirit of the West* (Allied, 1932)**   When rancher Moore threatens to report livestock brokers selling stolen cattle, the villains kill him, keeping his money and his note. They trample temporary foreman Bud Ringo to take possession of Moore's ranch. Bud's champion rodeo-riding brother Johnny (Hoot Gibson) poses as a dishwasher at the ranch where disabled Bud is bedridden and Mr. Moore's visiting daughter is a "guest." To improve the odds, Johnny captures a few bad men each night. With the gang locked in a storehouse and the sheriff called, the leaders plan a getaway. Arguing over their gain, they are subdued.

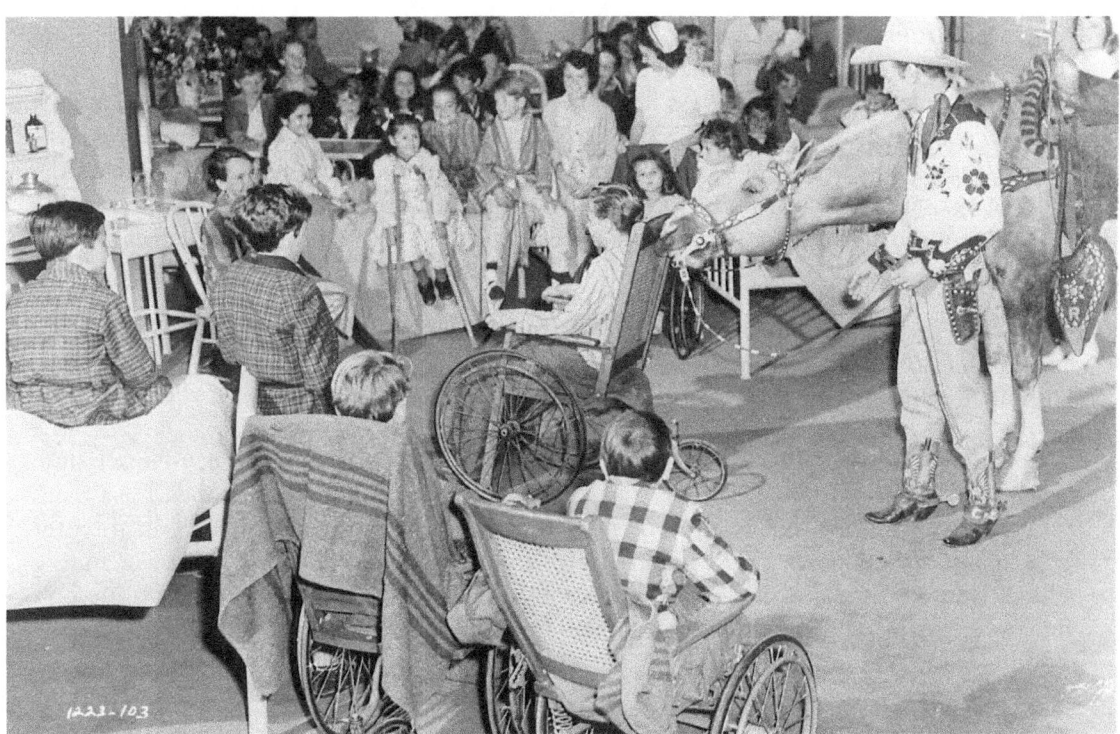

Rodeo star Roy Rogers entertains hospitalized children in Republic's *Song of Texas* (courtesy Jerry Ohlinger's).

Roy Rogers' ranch is on the line at the start of a rodeo cross-country chuckwagon race in Republic's *Song of Texas* (courtesy Jerry Ohlinger's).

Spurs (Universal-Jewel, 1930) This Hoot Gibson production features an elaborate rock-cave villain hideout with secret entrance and a machine-gun trained on the approach. Lone Pine scenery and a fatherless boy add to the film's appeal. Hoot binds some of the crooked gang in a shack, allowing sidekick Shorty to join him in rodeo competition. Following Shorty's rodeo ride, the crooks take him and the boy prisoner. Hoot breaches the hideout again to save his friends, sharing with them the $5,000 reward. With the gang captured, Hoot wins the rodeo's prize spurs, cash and the girl. Rodeo scenes were filmed at Hoot's Ranch Rodeo.

Still Holding On: The Legend of Cadillac Jack (TV, 1998) Starring Clint Black and Lisa Hartman, this drama is based on the true story of rodeo contestant Jack Favor. His wife struggles to clear Jack of an unjust murder conviction.

Stir Crazy (Columbia, 1980) This R-rated comedy directed by Sidney Poitier stars Gene Wilder and Richard Pryor as two ne'er-do-wells wrongfully imprisoned for a bank robbery. Wilder's prowess on a mechanical bull prompts warden Barry Corbin to enter him in a prison rodeo, during which inmates seek to escape. Rodeo personnel, including Chuck Henson, contributed. Action was shot at the Texas Prison Rodeo and at Tucson's rodeo. Jimmy Medearis, assisted by John Miller, served as wrangler.

Richard Pryor (left) and Gene Wilder (top, right) take advantage of a prison rodeo to attempt escape in Columbia's *Stir Crazy* (courtesy Jerry Ohlinger's).

Rodeo star Rex Allen serenades Tomboy and her steer Champie in *Tomboy and the Champ*.

Tomboy and the Champ (Universal-International, 1961) Eleven-year-old orphan girl Tommie Jo is being raised by her uncle Jim (Ben Johnson) and wife on a ranch that has fallen on hard times. The girl (called Tomboy) nabs a black Angus in the boy's calf scramble and is determined to raise it to be a show champion. The narrator, Parson Dan, reminds all of what faith can do. At the Houston Fat Stock Show, Tommie Jo meets Casey Tibbs and Rex Allen. Rex, in rodeo dress, raises the girl's spirits, singing "Who Says That Animals Don't Cry." Overcoming medical problems, the tomboy's tale has a happy ending.

Trouble in Texas (Grand National, 1937) Tex Ritter and Carmen (Rita Cansino, a.k.a. Hayworth) are on separate undercover investigations into rodeo crooks and murderers, he avenging his rodeo cowboy brother and she as a federal agent. Tex's success in rodeo competition makes him a target. He fights the villain aboard a runaway explosive-filled wagon. Rodeo footage includes real rodeo notables. Yakima Canutt plays a villain and doubles for Tex. Glenn Strange and Hank Worden appear.

Under Fiesta Stars (Republic, 1941) On rodeo parade and riding a saddle bronc, star Gene Autry gets bad news and departs. His foster father has died, leaving a mine to Gene and a niece. Aided by Frog and Tadpole, Gene convinces his co-owner to keep the mine operating to support the workers.

The Unknown Cavalier (First National, 1926) This Ken Maynard film included Fred Burns in a supporting role. The story was re-made as a 1932 John Wayne Western, *Ride Him Cowboy* (see above).

The Utah Kid (Monogram, 1944) In this Trail Blazer film, Marshal Hoot Gibson enlists rodeo rider Bob Steele to go after a gang whose contestant wins rodeo prize money when rivals fall victim to "snake bite." Bob enters the rodeo while Hoot, posing as a salesman, seeks information. The gang plans to win the rodeo prizes and rob the town's rodeo week treasury. After winning the first day events, Bob is tied up in a cabin under guard. Hoot aids his escape. The gang boss urges Bob to slack off and earn more money betting on a less-favored rider. When Bob shows winning form, the villains tamper with his bronc saddle. Bob's pre-ride examination uncovers a needle with snake venom. Bob foils the bank-robbing gang's getaway. Earle Hodgins announces the rodeo.

When the Legends Die (20th Century–Fox, 1972) This film is based on Hal Borland's novel. At age 19, Ute Indian orphan Tom Blackbull escapes the demands of the reservation by becoming the ward of broken, drunken ex–rodeo rider Red Dillon (Richard Widmark). Red's harsh tutelage refines Tom's bronc riding skills. Avoiding Red's dissolute lifestyle, Tom develops self-respect from his newfound expertise, but Red is motivated by greed. His bets on Tom's rides degrade into a scam whereby Tom takes dives to build up

Mentor Red (Richard Widmark, left) profits from Indian Tom Blackbull's (Frederick Forrest) rodeo rides in 20th Century–Fox's *When the Legends Die* (courtesy Eddie Brandt's).

Jack Lord as TV's *Stoney Burke* (courtesy Jerry Ohlinger's).

Andrew Prine (left) and Earl Holliman, stars of TV's *Wide Country*.

the odds. Ashamed, Tom leaves Red to win money rodeoing on his own. He returns a year later to Red's place, and closes out the past. Tom has learned that it is good for people to change but not to forget.

Wild Horse (Allied, 1931) Hoot Gibson and Skeeter Bill compete with champion rider Gil to capture Devil, a wild killer palomino, for the colonel's rodeo. Prior to the partners' arrival, a bank robber stashes his loot at a cabin. Hoot ropes Devil and corrals him at the cabin. With Hoot chasing the pair's mounts, Gil kills Skeeter in the cabin and takes the palomino. The bank robber is a witness, but goes on the run. Hoot, arrested for the murder, escapes. He learns that Gil plans to ride Devil at the rodeo. When Devil injures a man at the rodeo, Gil leaves before his ride. With no volunteers, Hoot rides though it means arrest. He escapes from jail to pursue Gil, who has taken the bank loot. The robber's testimony clears Hoot.

Wild Horse Rodeo (Republic, 1937) The Three Mesquiteers (Bob Livingston, Crash Corrigan and Max Terhune) star. Stoney Brooke rides broncs at Col. Nye's rodeo. From the 3M Ranch, pal Tucson telegrams that he needs $1,000. Noting a magazine article on the wild horse Cyclone, Stoney has the colonel advance him money to capture the horse as a rodeo attraction. He sends the money to Tucson. At the ranch, the colonel learns that Tucson has spent the money and objects to removing the horse from the wild. Eventually, Cyclone is taken on the rodeo circuit. Riding him, the boys take the horse instead of prize money. When Cyclone escapes, the colonel tries to direct his capture from an airplane, while the Mesquiteers try to keep him free. Dick Weston, a.k.a. Roy Rogers, sings.

Rodeo-Themed TV Shows

Of the many Western TV series, two had rodeo settings. Both were scheduled for the same season.

Stoney Burke (1962–63) *Stoney Burke* was an hour-long, black-and-white ABC-TV series. Beutler Brothers provided livestock for the show. Casey Tibbs was technical advisor and stunt double, aided by rodeo cowboys Harley May and Lex Connelly. Daystar Productions filmed action scenes at the 1962 Sidney, Iowa, rodeo. Stoney (Jack Lord), reportedly inspired by Casey, was a Dakota saddle bronc rider. A loner, he applied integrity to life's challenges as he sought the world championship. Bruce Dern and Warren Oates supported. Many stations later carried the show in syndication.

Wide Country (1962–63) NBC telecast this hour-long, black-and-white production. Earl Holliman, Sundance on TV's *Hotel de Paree*, played champion bronc rider Mitch Guthrie. Versatile actor Andrew Prine played younger brother Andy, determined to follow in his brother's footsteps. Prine later starred in the Western series *The Road West*, and Holliman on *Police Woman*.

Appendix A — Golden Age Rodeo Personalities

The 1940s and '50s were an era of national interest in things Western. Coinciding with greater involvement of Western stars at rodeos, several extraordinary rodeo champions emerged to create a "golden age" within the sport. In addition to contestants, stock contractors (some of whom were partners with Western stars), women trick riders and rodeo clowns, all added to the colorful impact of rodeos. Some with Hollywood connections have been mentioned elsewhere in this volume. Years have passed since they thrilled rodeo audiences, but their contributions are remembered.

EDDY AKRIDGE (1929–)   Eddy Akridge, born near Pampa, Texas, left $30-per-month working cowboy wages to win three consecutive world bareback bronc riding championships (1953–55). Eddy's hobby of playing guitar and singing led to a contract with Western star Rex Allen, recordings and TV's *Ozark Jubilee*. Re-injury to his knee in 1957 forced his exit from competition. In late 1959, he discarded the heavy metal brace he had worn for two years and painfully regained his rodeo conditioning. Winning his fourth world bareback championship in 1961, he retired. He performed at Las Vegas hotel-casinos in the 1980s and '90s. Eddy is inducted at the National Cowboy and ProRodeo Halls of Fame.

NANCY BRAGG (WITMER) (1926–)   Born at Fort Smith, Arkansas, Nancy Bragg moved to Tulsa, Oklahoma. About age 16, her acrobatic ability and showmanship, paired with her palomino Texas Clipper, created a distinctive trick riding partnership. With her horse running at full speed, Nancy, from a standing position, executed a full back bend and grasped the cantle. She then pointed one toe in the air before returning to a standing position in her trademark maneuver "The Falling Tower." Her rodeos included Madison Square Garden and Boston Garden for seven consecutive years, as well as Denver, Fort Worth, Houston, Cheyenne and the Oklahoma State Prison Rodeo. She won Girl's Rodeo Association cutting championships in 1954 and '55. She is an inductee of the National Cowgirl and National Cowboy Halls of Fame.

FRECKLES BROWN (1921–87)   The youngest of ten children, Warren Brown was born in Wheatland, Wyoming. He roomed as a boy in a chilly tarpaper shack, but was inspired by Will James' books. A farm boss dubbed him "Freckles." His rodeo years were interrupted by World War II Army service. Against younger competition, he continued to improve. In fall 1962, a bull crushed vertebrae in his neck. Doctors advised that he would not ride again. Following surgery, he was in a cast from the top of his head to his hips, forcing him to miss the remaining season. His solid lead in the standings made him world bull riding champion, the oldest man ever to win a riding event. Exercising his way back into rodeo shape, he placed among 1966's top five bull riders. At the 1967 Oklahoma City National Finals Rodeo, Freckles, age 46, rode Jim Shoulders' bull Tornado, unridden in more than 200 attempts over seven years. Gaining rodeo immortality, Freckles is inducted at the Oklahoma Sports, Ak-Sar-Ben, ProRodeo and National Cowboy Halls of Fame.

JACK BUSCHBOM (1927–) Born in Iowa, Jack Buschbom grew up at Cassville, Wisconsin. Instead of school sports, he helped his father break and train colts. By age 14, he rode try-out horses. Still a teen, he teamed with Casey Tibbs to cowboy and break horses in South Dakota before turning professional in 1946. In 1949, he was world champion bareback bronc rider. Exhibiting timing and a wild spurring style, Jack was averse to asking other riders about a strange horse. Consistent over 13 years, he never finished lower than fourth in the bareback standings. He was world champion two more times (1959 and '60). Three times he won his event at the National Finals Rodeo. He finished among top ten all-around cowboys seven times. He was inducted into the Ak-Sar-Ben, ProRodeo and National Cowboy Halls of Fame.

EVERETT COLBORN (1892–1972) A native of western Idaho, young Everett Colborn was a rancher, calf roper and pick-up man. A northwest rodeo stock contractor, he escorted leased stock to New York and Boston rodeos, and rose to the position of arena director. Following the 1936 contestant walkout at Boston Garden, he purchased the World's Championship Rodeo with several partners, becoming managing director. Near Dublin, Texas, he established the world's largest ranch exclusively devoted to rodeo. In 1942, he formed a partnership with Gene Autry. For more than 20 years, he produced World's Championship Rodeos at Madison Square Garden and Boston Garden, as well as rodeos across the country. Daughter Carolyn's act featured her horse Omar, descendant of a Gene Autry Champion and a 16th birthday gift from Gene and her dad. In 1957, Everett sold his rodeo to Gene Autry and Harry Knight, remaining as director into 1960. He was inducted into the ProRodeo and National Cowboy Halls of Fame. The Dublin (Texas) Rodeo Heritage Museum honors his rodeo years.

The Rodeo Train That Spawned Two Rodeos

In 1937, Everett Colborn established his Lightning C Ranch headquarters close to the Dublin, Texas, railhead. Each fall, an exclusive rodeo train, about 18 cars long, departed for two months in New York City and Boston. Baggage cars held feed, tack and equipment. Stock, including about 200 horses, was transported in fully enclosed express cars. After watching the train loading, Dublin townspeople asked for their own rodeo. A park with borrowed facilities accommodated Dublin's first rodeo in 1940. The Colborn Bowl later hosted the rodeo just prior to the train's departure. Gene Autry and other stars entertained during 20 years of Dublin's rodeo. As the train pushed on from Dublin, regulations required that stock be let out every 36 hours for food, water and exercise. En route to Chicago, where the Santa Fe line gave way to the New York Central, the stop was Fort Madison, Iowa. For ten years, onlookers watched the unloading. Reasoning that stock was already on site, townspeople in 1948 organized for their rodeo.

Appendix A — Golden Age Rodeo Personalities

Left to right: Everett Colborn, Gene Autry and announcer Abe Lefton at Soldier Field, Chicago, Illinois, circa 1942 (obtained from Doubleday Collection, Wyoming Division of Cultural Resources, Cheyenne, Neg. #420, © 2004 Autry Qualified Interest Trust and The Autry Foundation, provided courtesy Gene Autry Entertainment).

Gene Autry led many Western headliners during the initial 20 or so years of a rodeo still held as of this writing. The Colborn rodeo train temporarily linked West and East, leaving lasting rodeo traditions in two towns.

COL. JIM ESKEW (1888–1965) Born in Wilson City, Tennessee, young Jim Eskew found that his health improved on his uncle's Texas ranch. He became a roper, bronc rider and Wild West performer. With Tom Mix on Oklahoma's 101 Ranch, he shared chores, early moviemaking and rodeos. About 1939, his railroad-accessible headquarters at Waverly, New York, became the "Rodeo Capital of the East." Each spring into the 1950s, the JE Ranch Rodeo left for indoor and outdoor arenas. Son Junior Eskew was World Champion Trick Roper. Tom Mix Eskew helped his father run the rodeo. Jim, who presented Gene Autry in spring 1940 and Roy Rogers in 1941, produced "The Roy Rogers Rodeo" from 1946 to 1948 in several cities. He was inducted into the National Cowboy Hall of Fame.

Rodeo promoter Col. Jim Eskew (from a 1944 JE Ranch Rodeo program).

Plymouth Cordage Company advertisement from the 1948 Boston Garden rodeo program.

Plymouth Cordage Company Lariats

In 1824 at Plymouth, Massachusetts, landing place of the Pilgrims, Yankee entrepreneurs founded Plymouth Cordage Company. The small rope-making company served an expanding maritime market, including America's Cup sailing race entries, and filled military uses during World War II. The "Plymouth Silk Finish Lariat Rope," specifically made in the late 19th century from high-grade Manila fiber, earned respect on the range and in rodeo arenas. Impressed with a coil in 1916, Jim Eskew recommended a demonstration to rodeo cowboys at New York's Sheepshead Bay. Harry Taylor, Plymouth's western and southern district sales manager (1930s–'50s), served into his retirement as a rodeo timer at Houston, Tucson and Cheyenne. In the 1930s and '40s, the company presented lariats, belt buckles and watches to calf-roping winners, earning thanks for their sponsorship. The National Cowboy and Western Heritage Museum's Rodeo Hall displays five Plymouth ropes.

HARRY KNIGHT (1907–89) Canadian Harry Knight won bareback and saddle bronc titles at the 1926 Calgary Stampede and Cheyenne's amateur riding title in 1928. Nicknamed "Stormy," he was bronc-riding champion three times in four years at Ellensburg, Washington, and twice was Canadian saddle bronc champion. He quit riding broncs in 1941, but kept involved with rodeos. In 1953, Gene Autry made Harry a partner and manager of the 20,000-acre Flying A rodeo ranch at Fowler, Colorado, which supported the former Cremer rodeo circuit and supplemented the Lightning C Ranch in Texas. Later, Harry managed the combined Cremer/World's Championship rodeos and stock. He sold his rodeo company in 1967; in 1975, the Flying A Ranch was sold. Harry was inducted into the Ak-Sar-Ben, ProRodeo, Canadian and National Cowboy Halls of Fame.

BILL LINDERMAN (1920–65) Montana-raised Bill Linderman was a good student talented at gentling horses. He gained upper body strength swinging a pickaxe in coal and chrome mines, and acquired rodeo skills through hard practice. He was world champion riding bareback broncs in 1943 and saddle broncs in 1945. In 1950, he won world championships in steer wrestling, saddle bronc riding and as all-around cowboy. At Calgary, he was champion saddle bronc rider three times and all-around cowboy six times. In 1953, he was world champion all-around cowboy and the "Cream of Wheat" cowboy. He endorsed Wrangler jeans. Formerly unsalaried president, Bill was traveling as RCA secretary-treasurer in 1965 when his commercial airliner crashed. The PRCA presents the Bill Linderman Memorial Award buckle to a deserving cowboy winning the most money in three events, including a roughstock event and a timed event. Bill was inducted into the Ak-Sar-Ben, ProRodeo and National Cowboy Halls of Fame.

Bill Linderman competing in bareback bronc riding, 1945 (courtesy Doubleday Collection, Wyoming Division of Cultural Resources, Cheyenne. Neg. 381).

TOOTS MANSFIELD (1914–98) Toots Mansfield was born at Bandera, Texas. After high school, he apprenticed to ropers Juan and Tony Salinas. Seeing his potential, they provided him with instruction, loaned him a horse and paid his rodeo entry fees in exchange for a percentage of his prize winnings. The four-year arrangement proved profitable for both parties. On his own in the 12-year span beginning 1939, Toots was world champion calf roper seven times. He was calf-roping champion seven times at Madison Square Garden, three times at Boston Garden, and at other major rodeos. He endorsed Wrangler jeans. At Cheyenne, Toots won all-around cowboy honors in 1947 and steer roping in 1948. In 1945, he became the first Rodeo Cowboy Association president. Retired from rodeo for two years, at age 41 he returned to rank third in calf roping, earning needed funds to counteract a drought affecting his ranch. The first world champion to conduct a rodeo school, he was inducted into the ProRodeo, National Cowboy and Texas Sports Halls of Fame.

GEORGE MILLS (1912–80) Born at Palisade, Colorado, George Mills grew up on ranches. His mother's family exploits are chronicled in a manuscript, written c. 1892, parts of which were incorporated into the film *The Sons of Katie Elder* (1965). His father trained race horses. A *Saturday Evening Post* article stated that young George and brother Hank rode everything from hogs to milk cows. When weight gain disqualified them as jockeys, they turned to rodeo. Younger sister Anna Lee (the nation's first licensed woman jockey, winner of relay races at Pendleton and Cheyenne, and a rodeo trick rider) is an inductee of the National Cowgirl Hall of Fame. World champion bareback rider in 1941, George

Rodeo clown George Mills in arena action at the 1942 Phoenix, Arizona, rodeo (courtesy Doubleday Collection, Wyoming Division of Cultural Resources, Cheyenne. Neg. #423).

wrestled steers at rodeos from 1937 into the mid–1950s. After clowning at small rodeos, he understudied a master bullfighter. As a substitute clown, he impressed fans and promoters, becoming the clown of choice at major arenas. For more than 20 years, through numerous injuries, George delivered thrills and comedy of the highest order. He cited two primary credentials to good clowning: guts and respect for bulls. George was inducted into the Ak-Sar-Ben, ProRodeo and National Cowboy Halls of Fame.

HOMER PETTIGREW (1914–97) Homer Pettigrew was born on a ranch at Grady, New Mexico. Scouted as an athlete for play at higher levels, he set his mind on rodeo. From 1940 through 1950, he was world champion seven times, including six steer wrestling titles and one all-around cowboy honor. He was runner-up to world champions five times. In 1941, he was Montgomery Ward's Circle M-W cowboy, featured in their advertisements and sponsored for a year. Homer won more money than any other rodeo cowboy in the decade of the 1940s. He shared credit with such equine partners as Sadie, a streak-faced sorrel mare that carried him to many championships and that he once kept in his motel room during a sleet storm. He was inducted into the ProRodeo and National Cowboy Halls of Fame.

GENE RAMBO (1920–88) Gene Rambo was born at San Miguel, California, learning early from his ranch foreman father. He left school sports at age 17 and soon was competing in rodeos. At major individual rodeos, he won championships riding bareback and saddle broncs, wrestling steers, roping calves and as all-around cowboy. He placed in these events, bull riding and team roping. His record of winning in varied events is unequalled. He was IRA all-around cowboy champion in 1946, 1948, 1949 and 1950. In the same years, the RCA ranked him in its top five. After years of retirement, he returned as a team roper, helping Jim Rodriguez, Jr., win three world championships. He won his first trophy saddle in the 1930s and his last at a senior roping in 1986. Gene was inducted into the Pendleton Round Up, National Cowboy and ProRodeo Halls of Fame.

MITZI LUCAS RILEY (1928–) Born prematurely at Fort Worth, Texas, to top 1920s cowgirl Tad Lucas, Mitzi was carried in a hat in Fort Worth's grand entry. At nine months, she was at Madison Square Garden. As Tad adjusted to limitations of a serious arm injury, Mitzi practiced trick riding. For a contract waiting at the 1934 Colorado State Fair rodeo, rodeo officials accepted a mother-daughter act. At age six, Mitzi took on professional responsibilities, winning audience approval at many rodeos with Tad. Two years later, she began working independently. In 1943 and 1944, she was a ranch sponsor girl for the New York and Boston rodeos. She declined an MGM movie contract in favor of rodeo stardom, trick riding at New York, Boston, Cheyenne and elsewhere. During World War II, she and Tad performed for military personnel. In 1947, Mitzi married calf roper Lanham Riley. Inducted at the National Cowboy and National Cowgirl Halls of Fame, she advocates for the preservation and promotion of her cowgirl heritage.

BUCK RUTHERFORD (1929–88) Born near Nowata, Oklahoma, Buck Rutherford rode bareback broncs, saddle broncs and bulls with either hand, and wrestled steers. He won bull-riding championships and placed in saddle bronc riding at individual rodeos. In 1951, he won all-around at Elko, Nevada, and bull riding at the Los Angeles Sheriff's Rodeo.

Buck Rutherford competes in bull riding at the 1957 Pikes Peak or Bust Rodeo (courtesy Pikes Peak Library District Local History Collection, Colorado Springs, CO. Stewarts #1937).

In 1952, a serious automobile accident knocked him out of action. He finished the season second in the RCA's all-around cowboy standings and was IRA all-around champion. Returning to competition in late May 1953, he wore a safety cap beneath his hat. By 1954, he was world champion all-around cowboy. Struck by a bull in January 1955, he healed slowly. He returned to rodeo in August with a steer wrestling win. Buck, wearing a helmet, was bull-riding champion at Pendleton in 1956 and bareback bronc-riding champion at Denver in 1957. He was inducted into the Ak-Sar-Ben and National Cowboy Halls of Fame.

JIMMY SCHUMACHER (1920–) Arizona-born Jimmy Schumacher was interested as a boy in horses and racing events at Prescott's Frontier Days. With Clyde Miller's Wild West Show in the late 1930s, he tried quadrille riding, all five competitive events and support duties. Beginning in 1941, he was a bull and bareback bronc rider for ten years. Dismissing his roughstock riding days, he said, "I've been a rodeo clown all my life but I've just been paid for it the last 15 years." He won individual rodeo championships and endured his share of injuries. In 1949, George Mills pressed Jimmy into service as his barrelman partner. The pair assured fans of the very best in arena tomfoolery. Jimmy stated that the key to out-maneuvering a bull was the animal "telegraphing" its intended move, giving the clown a split-second of reaction time. In the 1960s, Jimmy was a National Finals Rodeo clown for nine years. He is inducted at the National Cowboy Museum and at the ProRodeo Hall of Fame, which displays his walking barrel.

Barrel clown Jimmy Schumacher, in makeup, competes in bareback riding at the 1955 Pikes Peak or Bust Rodeo (courtesy Pikes Peak Library District Local History Collection, Colorado Springs, CO. Stewarts #1225).

Jim Shoulders rides a bareback bronc at the 1955 Pikes Peak or Bust Rodeo (courtesy Pikes Peak Library District Local History Collection, Colorado Springs, CO. Stewarts #1230).

Appendix A — Golden Age Rodeo Personalities

Trick rider-roper Nancy Kelley Sheppard dressed for spectacular action (Nancy Kelley Sheppard personal publicity photo, used with permission. Obtained from PRCA–Media, Colorado Springs, CO).

NANCY KELLEY SHEPPARD (1929–) Texan Nancy Kelley grew up in a rodeo environment. Schooling in acrobatics and dance supplemented practice in riding and roping. By age 11, she had performed at the Pendleton Round Up. In 1945 and 1946, she publicized the Madison Square Garden rodeo and rode in the grand entry. Returning to New York in 1947, she performed as a trick rider and quadrille rider and at public schools. Working at rodeos with Gene Autry, Roy Rogers and Rex Allen, she appreciated their wardrobes, horses and friendliness. Designing and tailoring her costumes, she trick-rode on a mount she trained herself. She executed a Hippodrome stand at a run while spinning a lariat loop in each hand. She visited hospitals. In 1948, Nancy married calf roper-steer wrestler Lynn Sheppard. She appeared on national TV shows, endorsed Tony Lama boots and selected Lee Riders' jean colors. She declined Republic's offer of a movie role as Rex Allen's leading lady, choosing live rodeo audiences and her family. She is an inductee of the National Cowgirl, National Cowboy and ProRodeo Halls of Fame.

JIM SHOULDERS (1928–) Born at Tulsa, Oklahoma, Jim Shoulders was raised at the edge of town, where he had limited experience with livestock. Encouraged in rodeo by his older brother, Jim joined the Cowboys' Turtle Association while still in high school. He developed riding skills in rodeo contests. At Madison Square Garden, he was bull-riding, bareback bronc-riding and all-around cowboy champion. At age 21, he was world champion all-around cowboy. Over a period of about a decade, Jim won five all-around, four bareback bronc-riding and seven bull-riding world championships. His record of 16 total world championships stood until 2003. Jim found a way to win money at most rodeos he entered. Lean and lanky, he withstood multiple injuries (*Life* magazine tagged him

"Mr. Broken Bones") with minimum downtime. To his advantage, he could ride with either hand. Appearing in TV and print advertisements for various products, Jim's association with Wrangler jeans began in 1948. He conducted rodeo schools and operates a ranch in Henryetta, Oklahoma. He was an early partner on Neal Gay's TV Mesquite (Texas) Rodeo. Jim's Tornado was five-time Bucking Bull of the Year. Jim is honored at the Ak-Sar-Ben, National Cowboy, ProRodeo, Oklahoma and Oklahoma Sports Halls of Fame.

TOMMY STEINER (1926–99) Tommy Steiner was born in Austin, Texas, learning his rodeo skills on a ranch. He competed on broncs and bulls. At age 24, he took over the family rodeo producing business and formed a partnership with Western star Bill Elliott. Their combined resources produced two full seasons of fast-moving, colorful rodeos. At the close of 1952, when he bought Bill's interest, Tommy had become the youngest big-time rodeo

Advertisement for Elliott-Steiner rodeo as it appeared in *Hoofs and Horns* magazine.

producer in the country, putting on rodeos in more and bigger cities. During the height of TV Westerns, Tommy probably headlined more Western stars than any other rodeo promoter. He was inducted into the Texas Cowboy, National Cowboy and ProRodeo Halls of Fame.

HARRY TOMPKINS (1927–) Born in Furnace Woods, New York, Harry Tompkins grew up in Peekskill, showing exceptional natural balance. As a Cimarron Guest Ranch wrangler, he rode hundreds of horses and as many as 40 steers a day. Invited as a dude ranch entry to the 1946 Madison Square Garden rodeo. Harry, a veteran of three bull rides, insisted on riding bulls, as well as bareback broncs, winning $316. After Army service, he returned to rodeo. From 1948 through 1960, he won world championships as a bull rider five times, as a bareback bronc rider once and as all-around cowboy twice. In addition to eight world championships and a Triple Crown year (1952), he finished among the top five of bull riders seven times, of bareback riders six times and of all-around cowboys seven times. He placed at many individual rodeos. Of him, Jim Shoulders said, "He could sure ride" and "For my money, he's the toughest and with the most natural ability [of] anyone I've ever seen." Harry has been inducted into the ProRodeo and National Cowboy Halls of Fame.

SHOAT WEBSTER (1925–) Named for the town of Choteau, Oklahoma, Shoat Webster was born near Lenapah. He aspired to be like champion ropers who were local heroes. In 1949 and '50, he was IRA and RCA world champion steer roper. In 1951, he set a new world steer-roping record. At Pendleton, he was champion all-around cowboy for three consecutive years, retiring the Sam Jackson Trophy. He won again in 1952. He shared credit for his success with his horses, preferring to train his own smaller roping horses. He was world champion steer roper in 1954 and '55. Although he curtailed competition to manage his ranch, Shoat won steer roping at Clovis, New Mexico, five times and at Cheyenne three

Shoat Webster, three-time all-around champion at the Pendleton Round-Up, holds the Sam Jackson Trophy he retired. Bus Howdyshell photo, used with permission of Matt Johnson (obtained from the ProRodeo Hall of Fame, Colorado Springs, CO).

times. He has been inducted into the Pendleton Round Up, ProRodeo and National Cowboy Halls of Fame.

TODD WHATLEY (1920–66) Born near Rufe, Oklahoma, Todd Whatley entered his first rodeo at age 17. He rode bareback and saddle broncs, and wrestled steers. In 1945, he won bull-riding championships at Houston and Cheyenne. In 1947 at Madison Square Garden, he set a 29-year record for money won at an individual rodeo. That year, he was world champion steer wrestler and placed second in bull riding. The RCA recognized him as the first new-era all-around champion. He endorsed Wrangler jeans. In 1948, he finished the season in the top five of world rankings for steer wrestling, bull riding and all-around cowboy. Todd was 1953's world champion bull rider and ranked among the top ten all-around cowboys. He is tied for the all-time fastest time in steer wrestling (with barrier) at 2.4 seconds. For several years, his bulldogging and hazing horses represented a sizable percentage of those on the steer wrestling circuit. Todd was inducted into the National Cowboy and ProRodeo Halls of Fame.

Appendix B — 25 Rodeos Presenting Western Stars

These rodeos were selected for presenting the greatest number and variety of Western stars over several years. Years not addressed either had no star or a non–Western star. Rodeos are listed alphabetically by state-city. *Note:* Rodeo names changed over time.

Southeastern Livestock Exposition Rodeo Montgomery, Alabama

1958	Tod Andrews
1959	Gail Davis
1960	Amanda Blake, Dennis Weaver and Milburn Stone
1961	Dale Robertson
1962, 1963	Rex Allen
1964	Clint Eastwood and Paul Brinegar
1965	Frank McGrath and Terry Wilson
1967	Fess Parker
1968, 1969	Ken Curtis
1970	Ken Curtis and Milburn Stone
1971	Doug McClure and The Sons of the Pioneers
1972	Roy Rogers, Dale Evans and The Sons of the Pioneers
1973	Ken Curtis
1976	Lorne Greene
1977	Ken Curtis
1981	The Sons of the Pioneers
1983	Rex Allen, Jr.

Phoenix, Arizona, Rodeos

1956	Rex Allen
1957	Jimmy Wakely
1959	Robert Horton
1960	Dale Robertson
1961	Rex Allen
1962	Lorne Greene and Dan Blocker
1963	Clint Walker
1964	Doug McClure
1965	Michael Landon
1966	*F Troop* cast
1967	Ed Ames
1968	Rex Allen
1969	Michael Landon
1970	David Canary
1971	Walter Brennan, Tex Williams and Montie Montana

Old Fort Days/ Arkansas-Oklahoma Rodeo, Fort Smith, Arkansas

1958	Michael Ansara
1959	Guy Williams
1960	Dale Robertson
1961	Clint Walker
1962	Ty Hardin
1963	Frank McGrath and Terry Wilson
1964	Milburn Stone
1965	Paul Brinegar and Jeannine Riley
1967	Ken Curtis
1968	Fess Parker
1969	Richard Long and Peter Breck
1970	David Canary

Arkansas State Fair, Livestock Show and Rodeo, Little Rock, Arkansas

Note: In the late 1940s, Wayne Morris and Roy Rogers, separately, visited the rodeo as special guests.

1950	Monte Hale/Bob Wills and the Texas Playboys
1951	Tim Holt
1952	Noah Beery, Jr.
1953	Leo Carrillo
1954	Jock Mahoney
1955	Tex Williams
1956	Jimmy Wakely
1957	Gene Autry and Gail Davis
1958, 1959	Rex Allen
1960	Robert Horton
1961	Amanda Blake, Dennis Weaver and Milburn Stone
1962	Lorne Greene and Dan Blocker; Sheb Wooley
1964	(split) Ken Curtis and Milburn Stone; Jeannine Riley
1965	Fess Parker and The Sons of the Pioneers
1966	Michael Landon
1967	Roy Rogers and Dale Evans
1969	Ken Curtis
1970	Roy Rogers and Dale Evans
1971	Doug McClure

Pikes Peak or Bust Rodeo, Colorado Springs, Colorado

1941	Wallace Beery
1947	Russell Hayden and his Rio Grande Serenaders, with Dub "Cannonball" Taylor at a local nightclub
1951	Gene Autry's Champion and Little Champ
1952	Gene Autry
1953	The Sons of the Pioneers
1954	Casey Tibbs and Midnight
1956, 1957	Montie Montana
1958	Rex Allen
1959	Dale Robertson
1961, 1962	Rex Allen
1963	Lorne Greene and Dan Blocker; Jimmy Dodd in parade
1966, 1967	Ken Curtis and Milburn Stone
1968	The Sons of the Pioneers
1969	Richard Long and Peter Breck
1970	Ken Curtis and Milburn Stone
1971	Rex Allen
1973	Ken Curtis; Joel McCrea in parade
1974	Rex Allen
1975	Rex Allen, Jr., and The Sons of the Pioneers
1978	Ken Curtis
1979	Ben Johnson parade marshal
1980	The Sons of the Pioneers
1982	Yakima Canutt parade marshal
1983	Rex Allen, Jr.; Rex Allen, Sr. (parade and first night)

Colorado State Fair Rodeo, Pueblo, Colorado

1948–1951	Fred Harman "Red Ryder"
1952	The Sons of the Pioneers
1953	The Sons of the Pioneers
1954	Gene Autry
1955	Rex Allen
1956	Gene Autry and Gail Davis
1957	Rex Allen
1958	Guy Mitchell
1959	Rex Allen
1960	Don Durant
1961	(split) Frank McGrath and Terry Wilson with Stan Jones; Jimmy Wakely
1962	Pedro Gonzales-Gonzales
1963	Rex Allen
1964	Ken Curtis and Milburn Stone
1966	The Sons of the Pioneers
1967	Rex Allen
1968	Ken Curtis
1969	Roy Rogers, Dale Evans and The Sons of the Pioneers
1972	(split) Ken Curtis; Rex Allen
1973	Montie Montana

Snake River Stampede, Nampa, Idaho

1947	Eddie Dean
1950	Gene Autry
1951	The Sons of the Pioneers
1952	Gene Autry
1953	Rex Allen
1954	Jimmy Wakely
1955	Rex Allen
1956	Gail Davis; The Sons of the Pioneers
1958	Duncan Renaldo
1959	Rex Allen
1961	Dale Robertson
1962	Clint Walker
1964	Jack Lord
1966	Ken Curtis and Milburn Stone
1967	Michael Landon

1968	Ken Curtis and Milburn Stone	1951	Ray Whitley
1969	Fess Parker	1954	Jock Mahoney and Dick Jones
1970	Ken Curtis and Milburn Stone	1955	Rin Tin Tin
1971	Lorne Greene	1956	Johnny Mack Brown
1975	Roy Rogers, Dale Evans and Roy "Dusty" Rogers, Jr.	1957	Gene Autry and Gail Davis
1977	Rex Allen	1958	Rex Allen
1978	Ken Curtis	1959	Dale Robertson
1985	Rex Allen, Jr.	1960	Rex Allen
1986	Roy "Dusty" Rogers, Jr.	1961	Robert Horton
		1962	Clu Gulager
		1963	Chuck Connors
		1964	Michael Landon
		1965	Ken Curtis and Milburn Stone
		1966	Fess Parker
		1967	Robert Conrad
		1968	Ken Curtis
		1969	Doug McClure
		1970	Ken Curtis (sub for Jimmy Dean)

Chicago, Illinois, Rodeos

Chicago's rodeo tradition dates at least to the Shankin Rodeo of 1916, which featured William F. "Buffalo Bill" Cody. Tex Austin and, later, Col. W.T. Johnson produced rodeos in Chicago. Will Rogers endorsed the 1933 "Century of Progress" World's Fair rodeo as "the Olympic Games of Western Sports." Some Western stars who appeared at Chicago rodeos over the years included:

1928	Hoot Gibson
1941	Ken Maynard
1942	Gene Autry
1946	Roy Rogers, Dale Evans and The Sons of the Pioneers
July 1947	Jimmy Wakely and his Saddle Pals, with Wesley Tuttle
October 1947	Roy Rogers, Dale Evans and The Sons of the Pioneers (George "Gabby" Hayes introduced); Tex Williams and band at a theater
1948	Roy Rogers, Dale Evans and The Riders of the Purple Sage; Smiley Burnette and Lulu Belle of Lulu Belle and Scotty (guests). A *Station West* premiere, with Roy and Dale, Ellen Drew, "Big Boy" Williams, Jane Greer and others, benefited hospitalized veterans.
1950	Brace Beemer (radio's Lone Ranger)
1951	Duncan Renaldo and Leo Carrillo
1953	Rex Allen
1954	Duncan Renaldo and Leo Carrillo
1955, 1956	Gene Autry, Gail Davis and The Cass County Boys
1957	Rex Allen

Tri-State Rodeo, Fort Madison, Iowa

1948	Gene Autry
1949	Gene Autry; Rex Allen in parade
1950	Leo Carrillo

Kentucky State Fair Rodeo, Louisville, Kentucky

1956	Gene Autry and Gail Davis
1957	Dick Jones
1959	Gail Davis
1960	Dale Robertson
1962	Lorne Greene and Dan Blocker
1964	Ken Curtis and Jeannine Riley
1965	Michael Landon
1966	Fess Parker
1967	Dale Robertson
1968	Michael Landon
1969	Doug McClure

Southwest Louisiana District Livestock Show and Rodeo, Lake Charles, Louisiana

1952	"Wild Bill" Elliott
1953	Tim Holt
1954	Light Crust Doughboys
1955	Smiley Burnette
1956	Eddie Dean
1957	Jimmy Wakely
1958	Gail Davis
1959	Dale Robertson
1960	Rex Allen
1961	Dale Robertson
1962	John Smith
1963	(split) Lorne Greene and Clint Walker; Michael Landon
1964	Jack Lord
1965	(split) Doug McClure and Clu Gulager; Frank McGrath and Terry Wilson

1966	Michael Landon
1967	Ken Curtis
1968	James Drury and Doug McClure
1969	Ken Curtis
1970	David Canary
1971	Doug McClure
1972	Ken Curtis

Shreveport, Louisiana, Rodeo

1956	Eddie Dean
1957	Gene Autry and Gail Davis
1958	Dale Robertson
1959	Gail Davis
1960	Dale Robertson
1961	Allen Case
1962	Lorne Greene and Dan Blocker
1964	Jack Lord
1965	Michael Landon
1966	Peter Brown, Phil Carey and William Smith
1967, 1968	Ken Curtis
1969	Linda Cristal and Mark Slade
1970	Fess Parker

J Bar H Rodeo, Camdenton, Missouri

1953, 1954	Casey Tibbs
1955	Casey Tibbs; Slim Pickens
1956	Slim Pickens
1957, 1958	Rex Allen
1959	Tex "Smokey" Williams; Casey Tibbs; Slim Pickens
1960	(split) Amanda Blake, Dennis Weaver and Milburn Stone; Dale Robertson
1961	(split) Clint Walker; Lorne Greene and Dan Blocker
1964	(split) Michael Landon; Rex Allen
1965	Doug McClure and Clu Gulager
1966	Fess Parker
1967	Ken Curtis and Milburn Stone

Fireman's Rodeo, St. Louis, Missouri

1946, 1947	Roy Rogers, Dale Evans and The Sons of the Pioneers
1952	Duncan Renaldo and Leo Carrillo
1953	Duncan Renaldo
1955	Smiley Burnette
1956	Dick Jones
1957	Gene Autry and Gail Davis
1958	Dale Robertson
1959	Steve McQueen

1960	Kirby Grant and Gloria Winters
1962	John Smith
1963	Lorne Greene
1964	Michael Landon
1965	Ken Curtis and Milburn Stone
1966	Ed Ames replaced ill Fess Parker
1967	Michael Landon
1968	Ken Curtis
1971	Doug McClure

Jaycee Bootheel Rodeo, Sikeston, Missouri

1957	Smiley Burnette
1958	James Arness
1959	Amanda Blake, Dennis Weaver and Milburn Stone
1960	(split) Don Durant; Hugh O'Brian
1961	Clint Eastwood, Paul Brinegar and Sheb Wooley
1962	Rex Allen
1963	Lorne Greene and Dan Blocker
1967	Robert Conrad
1968	Ken Curtis
1969	Fess Parker
1970	Michael Landon
1971	Ken Curtis
1973	Roy Rogers, Dale Evans, Roy "Dusty" Rogers, Jr., and The Sons of the Pioneers

Ak-Sar-Ben Rodeo, Omaha, Nebraska

1956	Gail Davis and The Cass County Boys
1959	Chuck Connors and Johnny Crawford
1960	Smiley Burnette
1961	Robert Horton
1962	Tex Ritter (partial dates)
1964	(split) Rex Allen; Jimmy Wakely
1967	(split) Marty Robbins; Ken Curtis
1968	Rex Allen
1969	Fess Parker
1974	The Sons of the Pioneers
1977	Roy Rogers, Dale Evans, Roy "Dusty" Rogers and The Sons of the Pioneers

New Mexico State Fair Rodeo, Albuquerque, New Mexico

1957	Roy Rogers, Dale Evans, Pat Brady, The Sons of the Pioneers and Carl "Alfalfa" Switzer
1958	Jimmy Wakely, M.C.
1959	(split) Robert Horton; Dale Robertson; Steve McQueen; Amanda Blake, Dennis Weaver and Milburn Stone; Jimmy Wakely; Flicka

1960 (split) Peter Brown and Peggie Castle; Robert Horton; Rex Allen
1961 Jimmy Wakely (M.C.); Lorne Greene and Dan Blocker
1962 (split) Paul Brinegar and Sheb Wooley; Don Collier and Slim Pickens
1963 (split) Dale Robertson; Rex Allen; Jimmy Wakely
1964 (split) Paul Brinegar and Clint Eastwood; Jack Lord
1965 (split) Ken Curtis and Milburn Stone; Buddy Ebsen; Lorne Greene and Dan Blocker
1966 (split) The Sons of the Pioneers; Michael Landon; Rex Allen; James Drury (accepting an Appaloosa)
1967 Dale Robertson (partial dates)
1968 Fess Parker (partial dates)
1970 Ken Curtis (partial dates)
1972 Rex Allen (partial dates)

Shrine Rodeo, Ardmore, Oklahoma

1942, 1949 Gene Autry
1955 Ken Maynard
1956 Merle Travis
1962 Lorne Greene and Dan Blocker
1963 Michael Landon; Johnny Crawford
1964 Rex Allen
1965 Frank McGrath
1966 Rex Allen
1967 Clu Gulager
1968 Rex Allen
1969 Rex Allen and Pedro Gonzalez-Gonzalez

Emerald Empire Rodeo, Eugene, Oregon

1954 Rex Allen and Slim Pickens
1955 *Rin Tin Tin* cast, Slim Pickens (clown) and Bob Wills (dance)
1956 Duncan Renaldo and Tex Williams (dance)
1958 *Rin Tin Tin* cast and Slim Pickens (clown)
1960 Robert Horton (Frank McGrath and Terry Wilson substituted when Mr. Horton was detained.)
1961 Michael Landon and Pernell Roberts
1962 Chuck Connors and Joe Higgens (fast-draw artist)
1963 Dale Robertson
1964 Rex Allen

Mid-South Fair and Rodeo, Memphis, Tennessee

1951 Tim Holt
1952 "Wild Bill" Elliott
1955 Casey Tibbs
1956 Duncan Renaldo; Smiley Burnette on the midway
1957 (split) Clayton Moore and Jay Silverheels; Dick Jones
1958 Duncan Renaldo
1959 (split) Gene Barry; Roy Rogers, Dale Evans, Pat Brady and The Sons of the Pioneers
1960 Dale Robertson
1962 Chuck Connors
1963 Clint Walker (partial dates)
1964 Lorne Greene and Dan Blocker
1965 Michael Landon
1966 Fess Parker
1967 (split) Ken Curtis and Milburn Stone; Roy Rogers, Dale Evans and The Sons of the Pioneers
1968 Ken Curtis
1969 Doug McClure

Southwest Exposition and Livestock Show Rodeo, Fort Worth, Texas

1934 Tom Mix at opening performance
1941 Ken Maynard; Rufe Davis (night show); Errol Flynn and Bruce Cabot (guests)
1946 Gene Autry
1947 Light Crust Doughboys (pre-rodeo music)
1948 "Wild Bill" Elliott (week-long observer); Tex Ritter and Arkansas Slim Andrews (theater); "Albuquerque" premiere brought Russell Hayden, Gabby Hayes, Catherine Craig and others.
1949 Don Reynolds; Audie Murphy and Wanda Hendrix (guests)
1950 Stuart and Dorrell McGowan scouted for a rodeo movie; Roy Rogers and Dale Evans special guests at a performance.
1951, 1952 "Wild Bill" Elliott (cutting event)
1954 Football and Western stars Sammy Baugh and John Kimbrough (spectators); *Red Garters* movie premiere with Guy Mitchell, Gene Barry, Buddy Ebsen and others
1957 Fred MacMurray and June Haver visited
1958 Gail Davis; Roy Rogers, Dale Evans, Gabby Hayes and The Sons of the Pioneers (*TV Chevy Show* on the rodeo's final night); Clint Walker (theater)

1959	Dale Robertson		1959, 1961	Dale Robertson
1960	Rex Allen		1962	Rex Allen
1962	Lorne Greene and Dan Blocker		1963	Kirby Grant and Gloria Winters
1964	James Drury and The Sons of the Pioneers, with Jon Locke and John Mitchum		1964, 1966, 1968	Rex Allen
1967	Ken Curtis		1973	Ken Curtis
1968	Rex Allen		1976, 1980	Rex Allen
1969	Fess Parker		1986	Rex Allen and Rex Allen, Jr.
1970	David Canary			
1971	Guy Madison and Chill Wills (special guests)			

Houston Fat Stock Show Rodeo, Texas

1942, 1943, 1944	Gene Autry
1946	Tex Ritter and Brace Beemer (radio Lone Ranger); Roy Rogers (guest)
1947, 1948	Gene Autry
1950	Roy Rogers and Dale Evans
1951	William "Hopalong Cassidy" Boyd
1952	Roy Rogers and Dale Evans
1953	Jock Mahoney and Dick Jones
1954	Duncan Renaldo and Leo Carrillo
1955	Gene Autry and Gail Davis
1956	Roy Rogers and Dale Evans
1957	Roy Rogers, Dale Evans, Pat Brady and The Sons of the Pioneers
1958	Hugh O'Brian; Hoot Gibson (special guest)
1959	James Arness
1960	(split) Michael Ansara; Robert Horton; Roy Rogers and Dale Evans
1961	Rex Allen
1962	Rex Allen; Chill Wills (special guest)
1963	Chuck Connors and Johnny Crawford
1964	Michael Landon
1965	Dale Robertson
1966	(split) Ken Curtis and Milburn Stone; Lorne Greene and Dan Blocker
1968, 1969, 1972	Roy Rogers and Dale Evans

San Antonio, Texas, Rodeos

1950	Foy Willing and The Riders of the Purple Sage
1952	Tito Guizar
1953–1956	Rex Allen
1958	Gene Autry and Gail Davis

Heart O'Texas Fair and Rodeo, Waco, Texas

1955	Duncan Renaldo
1956	(split) Eddie Dean; Preston Foster
1957	Eddie Dean
1958	Roy Rogers, Dale Evans, Pat Brady and The Sons of the Pioneers
1959	Dale Robertson
1960	Eric Fleming
1961	Clu Gulager
1962	Rex Allen
1963	Clint Walker
1965	Rex Allen
1966	Ken Curtis
1968	Fess Parker
1969	Robert Conrad
1970	Doug McClure
1973	Michael Landon
1975	Ken Curtis
1980	Rex Allen, Jr.

Days of '47 Rodeo, Salt Lake City, Utah

1949	Gene Autry
1950	Riders of the Purple Sage
1951	Slim Pickens (clown)
1953	Don Kay Reynolds (contract act)
1955	Gene Autry and Gail Davis
1956	Rex Allen
1957	Tex Williams
1958	Rex Allen
1959	Roy Rogers, Dale Evans, Pat Brady and The Sons of the Pioneers
1960	Chuck Connors and Johnny Crawford
1961	Rex Allen
1962	Dale Robertson
1963	Frank McGrath and Terry Wilson
1964	Rex Allen
1966	Fess Parker
1967	Rex Allen

Appendix C — 11 Special Rodeos

Rodeos are listed alphabetically by state-city.

U.S. Marine Rodeo, Camp Pendleton, California

For about 20 years, Hollywood personalities, most known for Western roles, attended the Camp Pendleton Rodeo, held annually for U.S. Marines and their dependents. Guests of the commanding general, stars typically rode in the grand entry and viewed the rodeo from the stands. A few (with asterisk) entertained.

1951	*Roy Rogers, Dale Evans and Trigger
1952	Whip Wilson
1953	*Montie Montana
1956	Leo Carrillo
1957	*Montie Montana; Leo Carrillo, James Arness, Dennis Weaver, Milburn Stone, Amanda Blake and Michael O'Shea
1958	*Montie and Louise Montana; Leo Carrillo, Will Hutchins, Johnny Washbrook, Amanda Blake and Milburn Stone
1959	*Montie Montana
1960	Lorne Greene, Pernell Roberts, Dan Blocker, Michael Landon, Steve Raines, Clint Eastwood, Paul Brinegar, Abby Dalton, Rocky Shahan, Kathy Nolan, John Newland and James Murdock
1961	Glenn Ford, Bob Denver, James Murdock, Lorne Greene, Pernell Roberts, Dan Blocker, Michael Landon, Kathy Nolan, Eric Fleming, Clint Eastwood, Rocky Shahan, Sheb Wooley, Paul Brinegar, Steve Raines, Frank McGrath, Terry Wilson and others
1962	*Montie Montana; Michael Landon, Don Collier and Nick Adams
1963	*Montie Montana; John Russell
1964	John Russell, Judy Canova, John Agar and others
1965–70	*Montie Montana

Sheriff's Rodeo, Los Angeles, California

The Los Angeles Sheriff's Rodeo was the largest one-day rodeo. Held annually from 1945 through 1962 at the Los Angeles Coliseum, it annually drew from 50,000 to 100,000 spectators. They were led by Sheriffs Eugene W. Biscailuz (1945–58) and Peter J. Pitchess (1959–62), and proceeds benefited the Los Angeles County Sheriff's Relief Association, aiding sheriff's department orphans and widows. Attracting top contestants, many contract performers with Hollywood connections and a galaxy of Hollywood stars, Western and non–Western, the event was noted for its spectacular grand entry. Montie Montana directed activities and frequently performed with his family troupe. Andy Jauregui provided livestock and directed the arena. California's governor, Los Angeles' mayor and other dignitaries commonly attended.

1945 (two days) Esther Williams (queen) and John Carroll (grand marshal)
1946 Yvonne DeCarlo (queen); Roy Rogers, Dale Evans and The Sons of The Pioneers; Leo Carrillo
1947 Janis Paige (queen) and "Wild Bill" Elliott (grand marshal); Gene Autry
1948 Ann Sheridan (queen) and Dennis Morgan and Jack Carson (grand marshals); Roy Rogers and Dale Evans; Preston Foster and Michael O'Shea; Phyllis Coates (pre-rodeo publicity)
1949 Jane Russell (queen) and John Wayne (grand marshal); Gene Autry
1950 June Haver (queen) and Joel McCrea (grand marshal); Roy Rogers; Leo Carrillo (acting host)
1951 Lucille Norman (queen) and Randolph Scott (grand marshal); Gene Autry and Pat Buttram
1952 Patrice Wymore (queen) and Will Rogers, Jr. (grand marshal); Rex Allen and The Sons of the Pioneers; Carolina Cotton, Leo Carrillo and Monte Hale
1953 Debbie Reynolds (queen) and William Boyd (grand marshal); Tex Ritter, Andy Parker and The Plainsmen; Carolina Cotton, Laurie Anders, Bill Williams and Roscoe Ates; Ann Robinson (pre-rodeo publicity)
1954 Ann Blyth (queen) and Howard Keel (grand marshal); Gene Autry and The Sons of the Pioneers; Carolina Cotton and Gail Davis; Will Rogers, Jr. judged pre-rodeo youth roping.
1955 Piper Laurie (queen) and Clayton Moore (grand marshal); Roy Rogers, Dale Evans, Pat Brady and The Sons of the Pioneers; Rory Calhoun and Jay Silverheels
1956 Natalie Wood (queen) and Clint Walker (grand marshal); Rex Allen; Don "Red" Barry
1957 Audie Murphy (grand marshal); Frankie Laine; John Bromfield, Jimmy Hawkins and Johnny Washbrook
1958 Barbara Stanwyck (queen) and Will Hutchins (grand marshal); Johnny Cash and his Tennessee Two
1959 James Arness (grand marshal)
1960 Jayne Mansfield (queen) and Art Linkletter (grand marshal); Dale Robertson
1961 Shirley MacLaine (queen) and Richard Boone (grand marshal)
1962 Lucille Ball (queen) and Fred MacMurray (grand marshal); stars of *Rawhide*

Mounted Police Rodeo of the Stars, Palm Springs, California

Andy Jauregui and Montie Montana, frequent participants in this rodeo, are not mentioned below unless designated for a special role.

1940 Roy Rogers (grand marshal); Tom Mix and Leo Carrillo
1941 This "War Relief Show" had four marshals: Roy Rogers, Leo Carrillo, Dick Foran and Tex Ritter
1942 Tom Keene and Anne Gwynne
1947 Leo Carrillo (grand marshal)
1949 "Wild Bill" Elliott (grand marshal and announcer), Shirley Lucas (queen) and Carolina Cotton
1950 Monte Hale and Allan "Rocky" Lane (parade), Slim Pickens (clown)
1951 Leo Carrillo and Slim Pickens (rodeo clown)
1952 Reno Browne (queen), Johnny Mack Brown, Whip Wilson, Guy Madison, Andy Devine and Rex Allen
1953 Leo Carrillo (grand marshal), Carolina Cotton and Hoot Gibson
1954 Dale Robertson (grand marshal)
1955 Jock Mahoney (grand marshal), Doye O'Dell and Eddie Dean (marshals)
1956 Piper Laurie (queen), Jock Mahoney
1958 Audie Murphy (grand marshal)
1959 Robert Horton (grand marshal) and Barbara Stanwyck (hostess)
1960 Dennis Weaver (grand marshal) and Jayne Mansfield (queen)
1961 Jack Kelly (grand marshal) and Barbara Nichols (queen)
1962 Jackie Cooper (grand marshal) and Abby Dalton (queen)
1963 Doug McClure (grand marshal), Rita Hayworth (queen), Lorne Greene (Mr. Rodeo), Scott Brady, Richard Coogan and Skip Ward (rodeo sheriffs)
1964 Gene Autry (grand marshal, in gold Cadillac convertible) and Connie Stevens (queen)
1965 Walter Brennan (grand marshal) and Carroll Baker (queen)
1967 Richard Long (grand marshal), Mara Corday, Slim and Daryle Ann Pickens, Andrew Prine and Glenn Corbett
1968 Mike Connors (grand marshal), Lana Turner (queen), Chuck Connors (Mr. Rodeo) and Gerald Edwards; Andrew Prine (marshal)
1969 Gene Autry (grand marshal), Sue Ane Langdon (queen), Peter Breck (Mr. Rodeo) and Andrew Prine (high sheriff)

1971	Johnny Grant (grand marshal), Gisele MacKenzie (queen) and Jackie Coogan (high sheriff)
1972	Ruta Lee (queen), Johnny Grant (Mr. Rodeo) and Montie Montana (high sheriff)
1973	George Montgomery (honorary captain)
1974	Jack Kelly (high sheriff)
1977	Leo Carrillo and James Caan
1978	Don "Red" Barry (marshal)
1979	John Hart (grand marshal)
1980	Gene Autry (grand marshal and man of the year) and Stuart Hamblen
1987	Cliffie Stone's Hometown Jamboree, with Pat Buttram, Eddie Dean and others

California Rodeo, Salinas, California

Begun in 1911 as a Wild West Show adjunct to racing meets, the California Rodeo grew in stature until ranked as one of North America's biggest rodeos. The rodeo attracted competitors and contract performers with Hollywood connections, and hosted celebrities as special guests. In 1958, the rodeo began, on an irregular basis, to honor Western TV stars for "keeping alive the spirit of the Old West."

1921	Actress Viola Dana ("California Rodeo Girl")
1925	Western film star William Desmond and other movie cowboys arrived from location near Boulder Creek to shoot scenes at the rodeo. Hippy Burmeister, Ben Corbett and Andy Jauregui contested. Andy took the award for "best-dressed cow horse."
1927	Abe Lefton clowned. Mabel Strickland won the cowgirl relay race. Alice Van won the women's trick and fancy riding competition; Paris Williams was second. Babe DeFreest raced.
1928	Abe Lefton gave up clowning to become a rodeo announcer. Vera McGinnis was a trick rider.
1929	Abe Lefton announced. Jack Knapp clowned, and placed in the trick and fancy roping contest. Hoot Gibson's crew filmed parade and rodeo scenes. Wallace Beery flew in on his own plane. Western film star George O'Brien met his father, San Francisco Police Chief Dan O'Brien.
1930	Will Rogers, refusing a box seat, viewed the rodeo from fence-top near the chutes. Mrs. Jack Holt and her daughter Jennifer Holt were on hand.
1931	Will Rogers observed from the chute area. Andy Jauregui won single steer and calf roping.
1932	Will Rogers declared Salinas "the best dangedest rodeo in the whole country." He received a city key cut from a plug of chewing tobacco. He "perched all afternoon atop Chute #2, chewed chicle, and wisecracked with the cowboys." Wallace Beery returned.
1933	Will Rogers flew in for the rodeo. Kermit Maynard, second in 1931, was this year's champion trick rider, defeating Hollywood stunt double, Marco Borello. Andy Jauregui roped calves and team-roped. Fox Film Company filmed for *Smoky*.
1937	Young actress Jane Withers was on hand.
1938	Jane Withers returned.
1939–1940	Leo Carrillo was on hand.
1941	Montie Montana and family performed. Western star Tom Keene and actress Nancy Kelly were guests.
1947	Montie Montana and family again performed. Michael O'Shea was in a parade. Slim Pickens and George Mills clowned. Jerry Ambler, Don Happy, Andy Jauregui, Walt LaRue, Casey Tibbs and Alice Van competed. Jane Withers, honorary rodeo director, donated the Jane Withers Trophy for award to the best kiddie parade float.
1948	Montie Montana and troupe again performed. Slim Pickens and George Mills clowned. Jerry Ambler, Don Happy and Andy Jauregui contested.
1949	Hoot Gibson was special guest all four days. Slim Pickens and Andy Womack clowned. The Montie Montana family and Buff Brady, Jr., performed. Ross Dollarhide and Casey Tibbs contested.
1951	Slim Pickens clowned.
1952	Ken Maynard trick-rode and performed his shooting act. Pete Logan announced. Andy Jauregui provided livestock and team-roped. Pete Crump, Ross Dollarhide, Ben Johnson and Dan Poore competed. Casey Tibbs appeared two days at the Lee Riders dealer. Faye Blessing, Buff Brady, Jr., and the Lucas Sisters trick-rode.
1953	Chill Wills was on parade. Jerry Ambler contested. Ross Dollarhide was all-around champion; Casey Tibbs was second. Faye Blessing was a trick rider. Mel Lambert, bareback rider in 1936 and trick roper in 1938–39, announced.

Montie Montana spins a lariat loop in Palm Springs' 1949 rodeo parade (courtesy Palm Springs Historical Society, Palm Springs, CA).

1954	Ross Dollarhide was again all-around champion. Faye Blessing, Buff Brady, Jr., and Donna Hall trick rode. Bill Elliott judged cutting.
1955	Ross Dollarhide competed. May Boss, Donna Hall, Edith Happy and Shirley Lucas were trick riders.
1956	Buff Brady, Jr., Edith Happy and Nancy Sheppard trick rode.
1958	Ross Dollarhide competed. Edith Happy, Pat North Ommert and Nancy Sheppard trick-rode. Robert Culp of *Trackdown*, first TV award winner, led the parade and rode in the grand entry.
1959	Richard Boone, Paladin of *Have Gun, Will Travel*, received the TV belt buckle award, was parade grand marshal and awarded a saddle to a track event winner. Edith Happy, Pat North Ommert and Nancy Sheppard were trick riders.
1960	Eric Fleming and Clint Eastwood of *Rawhide* received the TV award. Montie Montana and family performed. Edith Happy, Pat North Ommert, Rex Rossi and JW Stoker were trick riders.
1962	Don Collier and Slim Pickens received the TV award for *The Outlaws* and were co–grand marshals of the parade. They awarded a saddle in a stock event and appeared at the rodeo.
1964	Terry Wilson accepted the TV award for *Wagon Train*. He rode horseback as parade marshal, made a stock award and appeared at the rodeo. Donna Hall was a trick rider. Casey Tibbs competed and provided stock.
1965	Andy Jauregui provided rodeo livestock. Chuck Henson clowned. Sammy Thurman won women's barrel racing.
1966	Andy Jauregui provided rodeo stock.
1967	Andy Jauregui provided rodeo stock. Mel Lambert announced for the fifteenth time. Rodeo clown Wilbur Plaugher appeared at a theater showing his film *Run, Appaloosa, Run*. Larry Mahan competed.
1968	Amanda Blake, Miss Kitty of *Gunsmoke*, became the first female recipient of the TV award. She was at the rodeo all four days, entered the arena in a stagecoach and was parade grand marshal. Her award was a silver tray. Gene McLaughlin trick roped. At age 65, Andy Jauregui was still providing stock.

Note: In a later year, movie stuntmen Richard Farnsworth and Loren Janes demonstrated horse falls and other stunts.

World's Championship Rodeo, Boston Garden, Massachusetts

1935, 1936	Ray Whitley and the Rodeo Range Ramblers
1937, 1939	Ray Whitley and the Bar-Six Cowboys
1940, 1941	Gene Autry, Jimmy Wakely and the Melody Ranch Boys
1942, 1943	Roy Rogers and The Sons of the Pioneers
1944	Roy Rogers
1945	Roy Rogers and Ray Whitley and his Oklahoma Wranglers
1946	Gene Autry
1947, 1948	Gene Autry, Cass County Boys, Johnny Bond and Ray Whitley
1949, 1950	Gene Autry, Cass County Boys and Johnny Bond
1951	Gene Autry
1952	Duncan Renaldo and Leo Carrillo; Glenn Randall horse acts, including Roy Rogers Liberty Eight, Trigger, Jr., and The Red Pony
1953, 1954	Jock Mahoney and Dick Jones
1955	Roy Rogers, The Sons of the Pioneers, Ray Whitley, Pat Brady and Nellybelle
1956	*Rin Tin Tin* cast; The Collins Kids and Eddy Akridge
1957	Gene Autry, Gail Davis and The Riders of the Purple Sage
1958	John Bromfield and Joe Bodrie

Cowgirl Races at Rockingham Park

From 1941 through 1953, a sideline to the Boston Garden rodeo was the annual rodeo cowgirl race inserted in the regular program at Rockingham Park in Salem, New Hampshire. Purses were in the $500–$600 range. Race format details changed over the years. Polly Mills Burson, second in 1941's "Gene Autry Special," received her victory prize from Roy Rogers in 1942. In 1944, Mitzi Lucas edged out her mom, Tad, for first place. Roy Rogers awarded 1945's first place prize to young sponsor girl Jerry Ann Portwood. Edith Happy, trick rider and Hollywood stuntwoman, was third in 1951. The Range Rider and Dick West, rodeo stars, appeared as Pat North won and May Boss placed third in 1953. Soon a fire temporarily halted racing at Rockingham, and cowgirl races were not resumed. The fire destroyed much of the record of the cowgirl races.

At Rockingham Park, Salem, New Hampshire, Roy Rogers (right), track officials and cowgirl racers recognize Polly Mills Burson as 1942 cowgirl race winner (provided by Polly Burson and Marge Earlywine. Used with permission of Rockingham Park, Salem, NH).

Year	Win	Place	Show
1941	Tad Lucas	Polly Mills Burson	Marge Greenough
1942	Polly Mills Burson	Billie Burks Osborne	Mary Parks
1943	Bernice Taylor	Mary Iler	Polly Mills Burson
1944	Mitzi Lucas	Tad Lucas	Bernice Taylor
1945	Jerry Ann Portwood	Tad Lucas	Fay Kirkwood
1946	Tad Lucas	Sis Mills	Mitzi Lucas
1947	Sis Mills	unknown	unknown
1948	Sis Mills	Faye Blessing	Tad Lucas
1949	Fay Kirkwood	Norma Shoulders	Tad Lucas
1950	Norma Shoulders	Virginia Clemons	Sis Mills
1951	Ann Miller	Mitzi Riley	Edith Happy
1952	Tad Lucas	Guy Weeks	Shirley Robinson
1953	Pat North	Pat Torrance	May Boss

Other participants over the years included June Bull, Joan Chambers, JoAnn Coyle, Bobbie Dorman, Marianne Estes, Jeanne Godshall, Alice Greenough, Mildred Mix Horner, Berneta Kersher, Marianne Rich, Berva Dawn Sorenson, Vivian White and Wanda Wharton.

Nebraskaland Days Buffalo Bill Rodeo, North Platte, Nebraska

North Platte, Nebraska, is one of several claimants to the distinction of "first" rodeo. In 1882, William F. Cody staged a Fourth of July celebration that awarded prize money for bronc riding and other events. Cody made North Platte his home and headquarters of his Wild West Show. The Buffalo Bill Rodeo, begun in 1947, contracted Western stars in the years 1959–61. From 1965 to this writing, the Buffalo Bill Award, a statue by Nebraska artist Ted Long, has been presented annually in conjunction with the rodeo to a Western star. In 1969, the rodeo name was changed to Nebraskaland Days Buffalo Bill Rodeo.

Contract Western Stars:

1959 Rex Allen
1960 Smiley Burnette
1961 Allen Case

Buffalo Bill Award Winners:

1965 Dale Robertson
1966 Charlton Heston
1967 Chuck Connors; (Tim McCoy with Tommy Scott's country caravan at a junior high school)
1968 Leif Erickson
1969 Andy Devine
1970 Robert Fuller; (Milburn Stone, *Gunsmoke*, and Elizabeth Bauer, *Lancer*, at the Western Writers of America Spur Awards Banquet)
1971 Slim Pickens
1972 Amanda Blake
1973 Ken Curtis
1974 Harry Carey, Jr.
1975 Henry Fonda
1976 Ben Johnson
1977 Tim McCoy
1978 Iron Eyes Cody
1979 Buck Taylor
1980 Sam Elliott
1981 Louis L'Amour
1982 Monte Hale
1983 Gene Autry
1984 Denver Pyle
1985 Rex Allen
1986 James Drury
1987 Wilford Brimley
1988 Bruce Boxleitner
1989 Doug McClure
1990 Richard Farnsworth
1991 Alex Cord
1992 Barry Corbin
1993 G.W. Bailey
1994 Peter Sherako

Hide autographed by more than 20 years of Buffalo Bill Award winners at NEBRASKAland Days/Buffalo Bill Rodeo, North Platte, NE (photograph by the author).

Year	Celebrity
1995	Frank Stallone
1996	Rodney Grant
1997	Pierce Lyden
1998	Peter Breck
1999	Will Hutchins
2000	Burt Kennedy
2001	Dick Jones
2004	Michael Martin Murphey

Helldorado Days Rodeo, Las Vegas, Nevada

Las Vegas' Helldorado Days celebration began in 1935. Rodeo became a part, as did parades with celebrity marshals. In the early years, Western star Rex Bell drew some of his Hollywood comrades and was a recurring participant. His name is not repeated below. The celebration became a magnet for Western personalities. Tex Ritter and Roy Rogers came to make movies. Following is a partial celebrity listing, including some in later years whose entertainment bookings coincided with the celebration.

Year	Celebrity
1935	Maxie Rosenbloom
1936	Marian Nixon
1937	Tex Ritter and film crew
1938	Dick Foran and Curley Fletcher (writer of *The Strawberry Roan*)
1939	Dick Foran, Curley Fletcher and Tex Ritter
1940	Dick Foran, Curley Fletcher, Tex Ritter and Buck Jones
1941	Dick Foran, Curley Fletcher and Buff Brady, Jr.
1942	Montie Montana
1943	Roy Rogers and Trigger, Montie Montana and Tex Ritter
1945	Roy Rogers, Dale Evans, George "Gabby" Hayes, The Sons of the Pioneers (filming for *Heldorado*); Dick Foran, Tex Ritter, Rex Bell, "Big Boy" Williams and Don "Brown Jug" Reynolds
1946	Hoot Gibson, Rex Bell and Clara Bow, Dick Foran and Jimmy Wakely
1947	Gene Autry, Dick Foran, Reno Browne and Leo Carrillo
1948	Dick Foran, Reno Browne, Victor Jory (dedicated the rodeo arena), Barbara Hale, Bill Williams and Bob Hope

Left to right: **Dick Foran, Buck Jones and Curley Fletcher autograph at Las Vegas' Heldorado Days, circa 1940 (courtesy Logan Collection, UNLV Library Special Collections, Las Vegas, NV. Neg. #0019–0067).**

1949 Johnny Mack Brown, Eddie Arnold, Casey Tibbs and The Cass County Boys
1950 Glenn Randall horse acts, including Trigger, Jr.
1952 Rex Allen
1953 Rex Allen and Carolina Cotton; Slim Pickens (rodeo clown)
1954 Carolina Cotton
1955 Ray "Crash" Corrigan, Elaine DuPont, Casey Tibbs and Roy Rogers Liberty Horses
1956 William "Hopalong Cassidy" Boyd
1957 Hank Penny and Sue Thompson at the Golden Nugget
1958 John Bromfield; Hank Penny, Sue Thompson and Wade Ray at the Golden Nugget
1959 Tex Ritter, Casey Tibbs and Montie Montana; Eddie Akridge at the Saddle Club; Hank Penny, Sue Thompson and Wade Ray at the Golden Nugget; Pinky Lee at the Dunes; Dale Robertson at the Thunderbird immediately following the rodeo
1960 Britt Wood and The Ray Whitley Trio at the El Cortez Hotel
1961 Hank Thompson and The Brazos Valley Boys at the Golden Nugget
1962 Rex Bell (Rex passed away before the next rodeo.)

Reno Rodeo, Reno, Nevada

The Reno Rodeo attracted Hollywood celebrities almost since its inception in 1919. Rex Bell was a frequent participant. In 1949, the Reno Chamber of Commerce initiated the Silver Spurs Award. Early presentations were made to the star and director of a film of the past year, selected by film critics as best keeping alive the Western spirit. A parade and the award presentation occurred in the weeks preceding the Reno Rodeo, which (through 1959) was held around the Fourth of July. Awardees Alan Ladd (1954) and Spencer Tracy (1955) did not appear. In the years 1956 through 1959, awards were presented at a rodeo performance. Fred MacMurray was recognized in 1959 for his several Western films. Beginning in 1960, Silver Spurs Awards were made to TV Western stars just prior to the rodeo, held in mid–June. In 1966, John Wayne was presented with gold spurs, and the award lapsed. In subsequent years, the Silver Spurs Award was presented periodically to Western stars.

1921 Star Viola Dana was rodeo queen; Mabel Strickland trick-rode.
1932 Rex Bell and Bob Steele were on hand.
1935 Abe Lefton announced, and Homer Holcomb clowned. Contestants included Andy Jauregui and Turk Greenough, bucking horse champion. The Avalon Boys, an instrumental quartette, "provided comedy, novelty, singing and talking." This group launched member Chill Wills on a long film career.
1937 Alice Van performed trick and fancy riding. Andy Jauregui competed. Turk Greenough was all-around cowboy champion.
1939 The Montie Montana troupe performed. Andy Jauregui was champion all-around cowboy.
1940 Montie Montana trick-roped, and Polly Mills Burson trick rode. Andy Jauregui competed.
1941 Western film producer Harry Sherman led a delegation of Western stars who were in the rodeo parade and the grand entry. Brad King edged Russell Hayden to win a novelty race, requiring donning (mostly feminine) clothing, and opening an umbrella before mounting horses for the race. Andy Jauregui contested. Abe Lefton announced. Homer Holcomb, scheduled for post-rodeo movie work, clowned.
1942 Clowns Wilbur Plaugher and Slim Pickens competed in rodeo events.
1944 Clown Jimmy Schumacher competed in bareback riding.
1945 Reno Browne was rodeo queen; Slim Pickens clowned; Wag Blessing, Wayne Burson, Larry Finley and Andy Jauregui contested; and Polly Mills Burson trick-rode.
1947 Reno Browne was awarded "best parade horse." Bob Steele was on hand. Slim Pickens clowned. Larry Finley and Andy Jauregui competed.
1948 John Jordan announced.
1949 Pete Logan announced, and Faye Blessing trick-rode. George Mills clowned. Clown Wilbur Plaugher earned a first in saddle bronc riding. Black Jack O'Shea spoke at a theater playing *The Last Bandit* and promoted the soapbox derby. Just prior to the rodeo, Rufe Davis played the CAL-NEVA casino.
1950 This inaugural year, John Wayne and director John Ford won Silver Spurs Awards for the film *She Wore a Yellow Ribbon* (1949). Ben Johnson and Harry Carey, Jr., rode in a wagon on parade. Former queen Reno Browne rode in the rodeo parade, as did Sandy Sanders. Contestants included Wilbur Plaugher and Andy Jauregui.

1951 Gregory Peck and director Henry King received Silver Spurs Awards in May for *The Gunfighter*. Ernest Palmer was honored as director of photography for *Broken Arrow*. Wag Blessing, Ross Dollarhide, Larry Finley, Ben Johnson, Dan Poore, Gerald Roberts (third time all-around champion), Casey Tibbs and Bill Williams contested. Andy Womack clowned. The Lucas Sisters were trick riders.

1952 James Stewart and director Anthony Mann were awarded Silver Spurs in May for *Winchester '73*. William C. Mellor won as director of photography for *Across the Wide Missouri*. Jay C. Flippen was master of ceremonies. Chuck Parkison announced the rodeo. Casey Tibbs was all-around champion cowboy. The Lucas Sisters were trick riders. Carolina Cotton played the Terrace Room.

1953 Gary Cooper and director Fred Zimmerman were Silver Spurs recipients in May for *High Noon*. Filming in Europe, Cooper had Montgomery Clift accept his award. Ronald Reagan was master of ceremonies, and Ann Robinson attended. "Brown Jug" Reynolds performed his riding act. May Boss, Edith Happy and The Lucas Sisters were trick riders.

1954 Alan Ladd and director George Stevens, selected for Silver Spurs Awards for *Shane*, were not present. Rex Bell was in the grand entry. Don Reynolds performed. Pat North trick-rode.

1955 Spencer Tracy and director Edward Dmytryk were named as Silver Spur Award winners for *Broken Lance*, but were not present. Rex Bell headed the rodeo parade, participated in the rodeo queen's coronation and was guest of honor.

1956 At the rodeo, James Stewart and director Anthony Mann received second Silver Spur Awards for *The Man From Laramie*. Also honored, with a white Stetson hat, was producer William Goetz. Stewart was pictured on rodeo posters. Rex Bell, parade grand marshal, presented the awards. Reno Browne appeared with former rodeo queens. Sammy Fancher competed in team roping with her father and contested in calf roping. Casey Tibbs was champion all-around cowboy. Frank Sinatra donated two silver belt buckles as prizes.

1957 Glenn Ford and director Russell Rouse were named as Silver Spur Award winners for *The Fastest Gun Alive*. Rouse received his award at the rodeo's opening performance. Film commitments kept Ford from appearing. Anne Francis, a recent co-star of Ford's, accepted. She was presented with a white Stetson hat, a key to the city and a Reno Wrangler scroll. On hand also was Western star Rod Cameron, of TV's *State Trooper*, which offered stories from files of the Nevada Peace Officer's Association. Rod was guest of honor at a dinner and appeared at a theater matinee. He was presented a silver Nevada State Trooper's badge at the rodeo. Rex Bell crowned the rodeo queen and was co–grand parade marshal.

1958 Glenn Ford personally accepted the Silver Spurs Award for his film *Cowboy*. Julian Blaustein was presented a producer's hat on the opening parade day. Jack Lemmon (not present) also received an award. In the parade, Ford rode with the Boy Scouts. Rex Bell was parade grand marshal and crowned the rodeo queen. Harry Tompkins was champion all-around cowboy. Pat North Ommert was a trick rider. The Sons of the Pioneers played Harrah's shortly after the rodeo ended.

1959 The Silver Spurs Award went to Fred MacMurray for the many Western films in his career. Fred, his wife June Haver and their son rode a stagecoach in the rodeo parade. Award presentation was made at the final rodeo performance. Rex Bell, on Beau Gold, was parade grand marshal and crowned the rodeo queen. Pete Logan announced.

1960 James Arness, Matt Dillon of *Gunsmoke*, was the recipient of the Silver Spurs Award, presented in May by Rex Bell, who was again parade grand marshal. Eddy Akridge and Casey Tibbs competed. Women's barrel racing was added, and Sammy Fancher won.

1961 Richard Boone, Paladin of *Have Gun, Will Travel*, was honored with the Silver Spurs Award in June. He distributed calling cards along the parade route. John Wayne and Mrs. Ward Bond were on hand as a Silver Spurs Award was presented posthumously to Ward Bond of *Wagon Train*. Rex Bell led the parade, and Tony Young of TV's *Gunslinger* was an honorary grand marshal.

1962 Dan Blocker of *Bonanza* received the Silver Spurs Award in May. Rex Bell was parade grand marshal and crowned the queen. Rex passed away before the next rodeo. Casey Tibbs co-produced the rodeo. Eddy Akridge won bareback bronc riding for the second consecutive year.

1963 Dan Blocker attended as the Silver Spurs Award was presented to Lorne Greene of *Bonanza* in May. John Smith of *Laramie* was parade grand marshal and crowned the rodeo queen.

1964 Michael Landon of *Bonanza* was awarded Silver Spurs in May. Montie Montana, Jr., served as rodeo clown.

1965 Dan Blocker of *Bonanza* received his second Silver Spurs Award. Wilbur Plaugher was rodeo clown.

1966 John Wayne was awarded a second Silver Spurs award. Jane Russell promoted the film *Waco*.

1970 Celebrities appearing for a rodeo street dance included Slim Pickens, Chill Wills, Jim Mitchum, Dean Stockwell and Dennis Hopper.

1971 Slim Pickens and Pat Wayne were co–grand parade marshals. During the rodeo, Slim presented Nevada Governor Mike O'Callaghan with a Winchester N.R.A. Centennial rifle. Sammy Fancher Thurman took her third barrel-racing title.

1972 Michael Landon was parade grand marshal. Chill Wills was also in the parade. Cliff Robertson crowned the queen.

1973 Montie Montana was parade grand marshal and trick-roped.

1979 James Whitmore was parade grand marshal.

1981 Katharine Ross was parade grand marshal and the first female recipient of the reinstated Silver Spurs Award.

1983 Russ Solberg was steer wrestling champion.

1984 Jim Shoulders was parade grand marshal.

1988 Wilford Brimley was parade grand marshal and received the Silver Spurs Award. He demonstrated his team-roping skills.

1994 Sam Elliott was parade grand marshal and received the Silver Spurs Award.

World Series/ World's Championship Rodeo Madison Square Garden, New York, New York

1934 Hoot Gibson introduced, Bobby Benson one day
1935 Ray Whitley and the Rodeo Range Ramblers; Bobby Benson
1936 Ray Whitley and The Rodeo Range Ramblers
1937–1939 Ray Whitley and The Bar-6 Cowboys
1940, 1941 Gene Autry, Jimmy Wakely and The Melody Ranch Boys
1942, 1943 Roy Rogers and The Sons of the Pioneers
1944 Roy Rogers
1945 Roy Rogers, Ray Whitley and The Oklahoma Wranglers
1946 Gene Autry
1947, 1948 Gene Autry, Cass County Boys, Johnny Bond, Ray Whitley
1949, 1950 Gene Autry, Cass County Boys, Johnny Bond
1951 (split) The Lone Ranger (Brace Beemer)/Vaughn Monroe
1952 Roy Rogers, Dale Evans and Pat Brady
1953 Gene Autry; Jock Mahoney and Dick Jones
1954 Roy Rogers, Dale Evans and The Sons of the Pioneers
1955 Roy Rogers, The Sons of the Pioneers and Pat Brady
1956 *Rin Tin Tin* cast
1957 (split) Clayton Moore and Jay Silverheels; Lassie
1958 Roy Rogers, Dale Evans, Pat Brady and The Sons of the Pioneers
1959 Gail Davis and the *Rin Tin Tin* cast

Texas Prison Rodeo, Huntsville, Texas

Barely 100 spectators viewed the first Texas Prison Rodeo in a vacant field in 1931. Expanding audiences were accommodated first by wooden stands and, after World War II, by a brick and steel stadium seating 22,500. Supporting inmate education and recreation, the rodeo became the biggest penal sporting event in the country, a national attraction, presented each Sunday in October. Inmates rounded up prison-owned stock, sewed uniforms, made saddles and chaps, produced the program and entertained musically. Special contests included Brahma bull-drawn chariot races and "Hard Money," snatched from a bull's horns. Entrants received $5 a day and kept prize money won. Western stars were succeeded, as "on the outside," by country music singers. Up to 100,000 persons attended annually. In 1986, the rodeo was discontinued.

1934 Tom Mix
1957 Fess Parker
1958 Richard Boone/Dale Robertson/Robert Horton/Robert Culp
1959 James Arness and Johnny Cash/Dale Robertson/Steve McQueen/Guy Madison

Top: Tom Mix at the 1934 Texas Prison Rodeo (courtesy Texas Department of Criminal Justice). *Bottom:* Dale Robertson greets young fans upon his arrival for the Texas Prison Rodeo, at which he performed in 1958 and 1959 (courtesy Texas Department of Criminal Justice).

Top: Robert Horton of *Wagon Train* performs at a 1958 Texas Prison Rodeo in lieu of co-star Ward Bond (courtesy Texas Department of Criminal Justice). *Bottom:* Robert Culp of TV's *Trackdown* gets to know his mount prior to a 1958 Texas Prison Rodeo. Inmates made the "Texas Ranger" honorary president of the "Crime Doesn't Pay Club" and sang an inmate-composed "Trackdown Ballad" (courtesy Texas Department of Criminal Justice).

Guy Madison, TV's *Wild Bill Hickok*, receives a gift from an inmate at a 1959 Texas Prison Rodeo. He and his wife Sheila Connelly appeared on their wedding anniversary (courtesy Texas Department of Criminal Justice).

1960 Ricky Nelson/Allen Case/John Wayne and Frankie Avalon
1961 Rex Allen/Clu Gulager/Chuck Connors
1962 Rex Allen/Dan Blocker
1963 Terry Wilson

Cheyenne Frontier Days, Wyoming

To increase ridership, the Union Pacific Railroad in the late 1800s assigned distinctive celebrations to cities along its front range of the Rockies line. A special train went from Denver to the event. Cheyenne's theme, "rodeo days," began, in 1897, Cheyenne Frontier Days, dominated by one of the oldest, biggest and most famous of rodeos, "The Daddy of 'Em All." Contract performers (1966–71) were only a few of the Western personalities who appeared over the years.

1898 Buffalo Bill's Wild West Show.
1903 Special cowboy contests were presented for President Theodore Roosevelt's May visit.
1904 Bill Pickett bulldogged.
1910 A former president, "Col." Teddy Roosevelt, shared the VIP stand with artist Frederick Remington.
1913 Art Acord won the Roman standing race. Tom Grimes competed in Roman racing and in bulldogging.
1917 Douglas Fairbanks, filming nearby, presented a trophy saddle.
1919 Filming in Cheyenne, Fred Stone was in a parade, entered rodeo contests and awarded a trophy revolver to the steer-roping champion.
1920 Tim McCoy served on a Frontier Days committee.
1922 William S. Hart sent a check for contest prizes, to include 1,000 feet of whale line for lariats.
1925 Ike Rude, calf roping winner, received a Douglas Fairbanks saddle. Tim McCoy was on hand.

Top: Film star Wallace Beery participates in a Cheyenne Frontier Days parade, circa 1930s (courtesy Brammar Collection, Wyoming Division of Cultural Resources, Cheyenne. Neg. #304). *Bottom:* Young fans assist William "Wild Bill" Elliott in scoring rodeo events at 1947's Frontier Days (courtesy Brammar Collection, Wyoming Division of Cultural Resources, Cheyenne. Neg. 1535).

Top: At a Cheyenne ceremony in June 1948, radio's "Masked Man" Brace Beemer cuts a cake with a saber to celebrate 15 years of *The Lone Ranger* on radio. Looking on are Lady-in-Waiting Norma Jean Bell and Miss Frontier Susan Murray (courtesy Brammar Collection, Wyoming Division of Cultural Resources, Cheyenne. Neg. #1894). *Bottom:* Western star Tim Holt sits between Miss Frontier Joy Vandehei (left) and Lady-in-Waiting Laura Bailey (right) at 1950s Frontier Days coronation ceremony. Bandleader-singer Tex Beneke is in background, left (courtesy Wyoming Division of Cultural Resources, Cheyenne. Neg. #26387/H56–28).

1926 "Wild Bill" Elliott competed, c. 1926, at Cheyenne. The Bill Hart trophy, a $1,500 bronze statue, was awarded to Bill Wilkerson, champion bronc rider. Pete Morrison made an exhibition ride, and Buck Jones was a spectator.

1928 Will Rogers flew in unexpectedly. Contestants included Turk Greenough and Cliff Lyons. "Baby Peggy" and her dad, movie stuntman Jack Montgomery, were on hand. The First National Pictures Ken Maynard unit arrived on July 19 to film *The Glorious Trail* at Fort Russell. This set was closed to the public lest the camera photograph onlookers. A second film, *Cheyenne*, incorporated Frontier Days' crowds.

1937 Wallace Beery participated in the Frontier Cavalcade pageant and crowned its queen.

1938 Andy Jauregui was the champion steer roper and Montie Montana made the first of many trick-roping demonstrations.

1939 Tim McCoy was a spectator. Polly Mills Burson tied for the championship in the women's relay race, and Neal Hart was in attendance.

1940 Monte Blue began a 20-year stint as announcer for ancillary events and as resident celebrity.

1941 Tim McCoy rode in a parade. With Sioux Chief Charles Red Cloud, he demonstrated Indian sign language. Competing cowboys drew stock from the hat of rodeo judge Turk Greenough. Young radio and Western film singer Mary Lee visited.

1942 U.S. Army Private Turk Greenough took time from his service at Fort Riley, Kansas, to serve again as rodeo judge. His wife, fan dancer Sally Rand, appeared with him on parade and at the rodeo. Private Robert "Rocky" Shahan, later a movie stuntman, competed. Tim McCoy, candidate for U.S. Senator, was a spectator.

1943 Tim McCoy was again on hand. Tech Sgt. Gene Autry and rodeo partner Everett Colborn watched from the judges' stand. Slim Pickens was a bronc rider and wild horse race contestant. Wayne Burson and Richard (Dick) Farnsworth rode bareback broncs.

1945 Filming took place for *Smoky*, starring Fred MacMurray. Montie Montana performed.

1946 With only film executives and the horse on hand, *Smoky* premiered on the Denver-Cheyenne train.

1947 "Wild Bill" Elliott, Vera Ralston, Republic Studios head Herbert J. Yates, Bob Nolan and The Sons of the Pioneers arrived to pro-

Charles "Durango Kid" Starrett (left) waves from the special Union Pacific Denver-Cheyenne train. At center is former presidential candidate Alf Landon. A.J. Seitz, executive vice president of the Union Pacific Railroad, is on the right. Starrett crowned Miss Frontier to open the 1949 Frontier Days (Cloyd Teter photograph for *The Denver Post*, July 26, 1949, courtesy Robert Hanesworth collection, Neg. #29726, American Heritage Center, Laramie, WY. Used with permission of *The Denver Post*. Best available picture).

mote the Cheyenne premiere of Republic's film *Wyoming*. The stars participated in the rodeo's grand entry and a parade, made appearances at two theaters and were inducted into the Ogallala Sioux Indian tribe. They attended a children's party in the park, made a radio broadcast and were guests at an official reception. They joined fans in the stands. Montie Montana performed his roping act.

1948 Bruce Cabot and Tim McCoy were on hand. Opening day honored radio's Lone Ranger, Brace Beemer, and the General Mills "Frontier Town" contest winner, who won an all-

At the airport, film star Fred MacMurray is welcomed by Miss Frontier Laura Bailey upon his arrival for Frontier Days, 1951 (courtesy Brammar Collection, Wyoming Division of Cultural Resources, Cheyenne, WY. Neg. 1876A).

expense paid trip to Cheyenne Frontier Days.

1949 Charles Starrett, "The Durango Kid," arrived on the Union Pacific train from Denver. In an all-black outfit, complete with gun belt and white hat, he placed the crown and a kiss on Miss Frontier in ceremonies opening Frontier Days. His film *South of Death Valley* played downtown.

1950 Western star Tim Holt was greeted by officials and a fan club delegation at Denver's airport. He flew to Cheyenne to crown Miss Frontier and boarded the special train. At Cheyenne, he rode in parades and the rodeo's grand entry for two days before returning to California. Montie Montana performed trick roping.

1951 John Lund, Scott Brady, Joyce Holden and Chill Wills led 45 actors and crew of the rodeo-themed Universal-International film *Bronco Buster*. Fred MacMurray was welcomed by thousands of spectators and received gifts at Denver's and Cheyenne's airports. His latest film, *A Millionaire for Christy*, was shown in the senate chamber of Cheyenne's state capitol, followed by a chuck wagon meal in the rotunda. Fred's crowning of Miss Frontier opened Frontier Days. He appeared on parade and in the opening day grand entry.

1952 Dennis Morgan, star of several Western films, crowned Miss Frontier. He rode the special train and appeared on parade.

1953 Guy Madison, TV's Wild Bill Hickok, and Andy Devine, who played Madison's sidekick Jingles, were at Frontier Days to entertain as their guests young winners of the nationwide "Name Jingles' Ranch" contest sponsored by Kellogg's cereals. The TV heroes were photographed with the winners in the mayor's office, rode horseback on parade and joined spectators in the stands.

1954 Robert Taylor, narrator-host of *Death Valley Days*, with his new bride Ursula Thiess, viewed the rodeo. They met the governor at the capitol and viewed a parade from their hotel. Hank Thompson and the Brazos Valley Boys entertained at the pavilion.

1956 The 60th Annual Cheyenne Frontier Days featured a three-day visit by Dick Jones,

Top: Bronco Buster stars Scott Brady (in checkered shirt), John Lund and Joyce Holden can be spotted among state governors and rodeo royalty aboard the Union Pacific's Denver Post Special at 1951 Frontier Days (courtesy Brammar Collection, Wyoming Division of Cultural Resources, Cheyenne. Neg. 1599). *Bottom:* Star Dennis Morgan plants a kiss on Miss Frontier Jane Henderson riding the carousel at the 1952 Frontier Days. The Lady-in-Waiting is Carol Rees (courtesy Brammar Collection, Wyoming Division of Cultural Resources, Cheyenne. Neg. #4437).

Top: Andy Devine ("Jingles"), left, and Guy Madison ("Wild Bill Hickok") ride in a 1953 Frontier Days parade (obtained from Cheyenne Frontier Days Old West Museum, used courtesy, and with permission of, the U.S. Air Force). *Bottom:* At the governor's reception, *Buffalo Bill, Jr.* stars Nancy Gilbert and Dick Jones (center) pose with their gifts among 1956 Frontier Days royalty: Miss Frontier Marilyn Ryan, Wyoming governor Simpson, Gilbert, Jones, Miss Indian America and Lady-in-Waiting Lynne Mabee (courtesy Brammar Collection, Wyoming Division of Cultural Resources, Cheyenne. Neg. #1895).

Buffalo Bill, Jr., and Nancy Gilbert, Calamity of TV's *Buffalo Bill, Jr.* Greeted at the airport by the mayor, they rode in the opening day grand entry, rode on parade and appeared at the night show. Representing Las Vegas' Flamingo Hotel, Abe Schiller rode on parade aboard a silver saddle once owned by William S. Hart, sporting hundreds of small silver hearts. Kids visiting the Lee Rider "branding chutes" picked up a Casey Tibbs bandana.

1957 Guests were movie Tarzan Gordon Scott and Willard Parker, who played Ranger Jace Pearson on TV's *Tales of the Texas Rangers*. Willard visited a hospital children's ward.

1958 Colorado-born and Wyoming-educated Western star Wayde Preston, Christopher Colt of the TV series *Colt .45*, crowned Miss Frontier. On behalf of the Colt Firearms Company, Preston presented special Colt .45 six-guns to the governors of Colorado and Wyoming, who engaged in a pre-rodeo quick draw contest. He appeared on parade and in the stands. Smiley Burnette was the midway's "Kid's Day" entertainer.

Willard Parker (right), pictured with partner Harry Lauter of TV's ***Tales of the Texas Rangers***, was a special guest at 1957's Frontier Days.

1960 Rex Allen presented a Western hat to vice presidential candidate Lyndon B. Johnson.

1964 Tim McCoy, age 73, performed with Tommy Scott's Medicine Show at a junior high school. About TV Western stars, he quipped, "[W]e were cowboys trying to be actors. And they are actors trying to be cowboys." Leon McAuliffe and the Cimarron Boys played nightly at the Frontier pavilion.

1965 Robert Preston narrated an ABC-TV documentary. Leon McAuliffe returned.

1966 Milburn Stone and Ken Curtis, *Gunsmoke*'s Doc and Festus, were contract entertainers for the night show, and received keys to the city. Interviewing newspaper carriers gave them medallions. Glenn Randall raced the Ben-Hur chariots. At the rodeo's opening, Slim Pickens presented Wyoming's governor with a custom engraved Winchester Centennial 1966 carbine commemorating the one-hundredth anniversary of "the gun that won the West." Slim noted that on this trip he had met the governor and the mayor, whereas 20 years ago as a contestant, he didn't even meet the pick-up man.

1967 Michael Landon of *Bonanza* was the night show headliner, along with The Sons of the Pioneers with Pat Brady. Landon visited the local Air Force base and hospital, and received a sword as an "Honorary U.S. Air Force Recruiter." Newspaper carriers interviewed him.

1968 Fess Parker, TV's Davy Crockett and Daniel Boone, took the night show stage. He was awarded a plaque as an "Honorary Recruiter for the U.S. Army" in recognition of his visits to troops in Vietnam.

1969 Robert Conrad of *The Wild Wild West* combined action and singing in his night show act. Festus and Doc returned, crowning and enjoying the first dance with Miss Frontier and her Lady-in-Waiting. The Laramie

Wayde Preston of TV's *Colt .45* presents a Colt revolver to Wyoming governor Simpson (center) as George Kauffman Observes at Cheyenne Frontier Days, 1958 (courtesy of Brammar Collection, Wyoming Division of Cultural Resources, Cheyenne. Neg. #3904).

County Medical Society honored Doc and Festus.
1970 Lorne Greene of *Bonanza* was the night show star. He presented roses to, and danced with, Frontier Days royalty. Greene visited the pediatric ward at Memorial Hospital. Tim McCoy was on hand, and The Sons of the Pioneers performed for rodeo fans at the Hitching Post Inn.
1971 For Cheyenne's 75th Anniversary, Chill Wills met the governor and rode a stagecoach on parade. Ken Curtis (Festus) did the coronation honors. For the night show, he was joined by *Gunsmoke* co-stars Buck Taylor and Glenn Strange. All participated in the parade. Roy Rogers, Dale Evans and The Sons of the Pioneers performed at night shows. Montie Montana roped, and Johnny Western entertained rodeo fans at Little America.
1996 James Drury, star of TV's *The Virginian*, was a parade grand marshal.

References

Books

Aaker, Everett. *Television Western Players of the Fifties.* Jefferson, NC: McFarland, 1997.

Allen, Michael. *Rodeo Cowboys in the North American Imagination.* Las Vegas: University of Nevada Press, 1998.

Allen, Rex. *My Life from Sunrise to Sunset.* Scottsdale, AZ: RexGarRus Press, 1989.

Arness, James, with James E. Wise, Jr. *James Arness: An Autobiography.* Jefferson, NC: McFarland, 2001.

Autry, Gene, with Mickey Hershkowitz. *Back in the Saddle Again.* Garden City, NY: Doubleday, 1978.

Barabas, SuzAnne, and Gabor Barabas. *Gunsmoke: A Complete History and Analysis.* Jefferson, NC: McFarland, 1990.

Birchard, Robert S. *King Cowboy: Tom Mix and the Movies.* Burbank, CA: Riverwood Press, 1993.

Bond, Johnny. *Gene Autry, Champion, or the First Hand Report of My 30 Years with Gene Autry.* Burbank, CA: 1973 (unpublished manuscript).

_____. *Reflections: The Autobiography of Johnny Bond.* Los Angeles: The John Edwards Memorial Foundation, 1976.

_____. *The Tex Ritter Story.* New York: Chappell, 1976.

California Rodeo Salinas. *California Rodeo Salinas: One Hundred Years of History.* Pacific Grove, CA: Park Place, 2002.

Campbell, Rosemae Wells. *From Trappers to Tourists.* Colorado Springs: Century One Press, 1972.

Canutt, Yakima. *Stunt Man.* New York: Walker, 1979.

Carey, Harry Jr. *Company of Heroes.* Metuchen, NJ: Scarecrow Press, 1994.

Carman, Bob, and Dan Scapperotti. *Red Ryder in the Movies.* Lindenhurst, NY: self-published, 1982.

_____. *Rex Allen, The Arizona Cowboy.* Lindenhurst, NY: self-published, 1982.

_____. *The Western Films of Monte Hall.* Lindenhurst, NY: self-published, 1984.

Carr, Patrick, ed. *The Illustrated History of Country Music.* Garden City, NY: Doubleday, 1980.

Chesnar, Lynn. *February Fever: Historical Highlights of the First 60 Years of the Houston Livestock Show and Rodeo 1932–1992.* Houston: Gulf, 1991.

Clancy, Foghorn. *My Fifty Years in Rodeo.* San Antonio: Naylor, 1952.

Clifton, Guy. *Reno Rodeo, A History— The First 80 Years.* Reno, NV: Reno Rodeo Foundation, 2000.

Copeland, Bobby. *Bill Elliott, The Peaceable Man.* Madison, NC: Empire, 2000.

_____. *The Bob Baker Story.* Oak Ridge, TN: BoJo Enterprises, 1998.

_____. *The Whip Wilson Story.* Madison, NC: Empire, 1998.

Corneau, Ernest N. *The Hall of Fame of Western Film Stars.* North Quincy, MA: Christopher, 1969.

Croy, Homer. *Our Will Rogers.* New York: Duell, Sloan and Pearce, 1953.

Daly, Marsha. *Michael Landon: A Biography.* New York: St. Martin's Press, 1987.

Dary, Davis. *Cowboy Culture: A Saga of Five Centuries.* Lawrence: University Press of Kansas, 1989.

Davis, Elise Miller. *The Answer Is God.* Old Tappan, NJ: Fleming H. Revell, 1955.

Dawson, Patrick. *Mr. Rodeo: The Big Bronc Years of Leo Cremer.* Livingston, MT: Cayuse Press, 1986.

Day, Donald, ed. *The Autobiography of Will Rogers.* Boston: Houghton Mifflin, 1949.

Diran, Edward. *Cow Palace Great Moments, Cow Palace Tales.* San Mateo, CA: Western Book/Journal Press, 1991.

Drake, Oliver. *Written Produced & Directed by Oliver Drake.* Baldwyn, MS: Outlaw Press, 1990.

Ehringer, Gavin. *Rodeo Legends— 20 Extraordinary Athletes of America's Sport.* Colorado Springs, CO: Western Horseman, 2001.

Emmens, Carol A. *Stunt Work and Stunt People.* New York: Franklin Watts, 1982.

Emrich, David. *Hollywood Colorado.* Lakewood, CO: Post Modern, 1997.

Fagen, Herb. *White Hats and Silver Spurs: Interviews with 24 Stars of Film and Television Westerns of *the Thirties through the Fifties.* Jefferson, NC: McFarland, 1996.

Fields, Armond. *Fred Stone: Circus Performer and Musical Comedy Star.* Jefferson, NC: McFarland, 2002.

Fleckenstein, Mary Ann. *Fort Madison Rodeo, The First 40 Years.* Manchester, MO: G. Bradley, 1988.

Fleming, Steve, and Judi Lakin, eds. *Pikes Peak or Bust Rodeo: The First Fifty Years.* Colorado Springs, CO: ProRodeo Hall of Fame and Museum of the American Cowboy, 1990.

Flynn, Shirley E. *Let's Go! Let's Show! Let's Rodeo! The History of Cheyenne Frontier Days.* Cheyenne: Wigwam, 1996.

Ford, Dan. *Pappy: The Life of John Ford.* Englewood Cliffs, NJ: Prentice-Hall, 1979.

Fredricksson, Kristine. *American Rodeo, From Buffalo Bill to Big Business.* College Station, TX: Texas A&M University Press, 1985.

Freeman, Danny. *World's Oldest Rodeo: 100-Year History, 1888–1988.* Prescott Frontier Days, 1988.

Freese, Gene Scott. *Hollywood Stunt Performers: A Dictionary and Filmography of Over 600 Men and Women, 1922–1996.* Jefferson, NC: McFarland, 1998.

Froome, George, and Marie Froome. *50 Years of Rodeo: A Pictorial History of the Red Bluff Round-Up.* Red Bluff, CA: Walker Lithograph, 1972.

Fury, David. *Chuck Connors, "The Man Behind the Rifle."* Minneapolis: Artist's Press, 1997.

Goldrup, Tom, and Jim Goldrup. *Feature Players— The Stories Behind the Faces, Vol. I.* Ben Lomand, CA: self-published, 1986.

Gray, James H. *A Brand of Its Own: The 100 Year History of the Calgary Exhibition and Stampede.* Saskatoon, Saskatchewan: Western Producer Prairie Books, 1985.

Gray, Robert N. *Mr. Rodeo Himself— Cecil Cornish, His Life and Treasures.* Waukomis, OK: Rodeo Press, 1990.

Green, Douglas B. *Country Roots— The Origins of Country Music.* New York: Hawthorne Books, 1976.

_____. *Singing in the Saddle: The History of the Singing Cowboy.* Nashville: The Country Music Foundation Press and Vanderbilt University Press, 2002.

Griffis, Ken. *Hear My Song: The Story of the Celebrated Sons of the Pioneers* (revised edition). Camarillo, CA: Norken, 1994.

Hagner, John G. *Falling for Stars.* Los Angeles: John G. Hagner, 1964.

Hamann, G.D., ed. *Gene Autry in the 1930's* and *Gene Autry in the 1940's,* with supplements. Hollywood, CA: Filming Today Press, 2000.

_____. *Roy Rogers in the 1940's,* with supplements. Hollywood, CA: Filming Today Press, 2000.

Hanes, Col. Bailey C. *Bill Pickett, Bulldogger.* Norman: University of Oklahoma Press, 1977.

Hanesworth, Robert "Bob." *Daddy of 'Em All: The Story of Cheyenne Frontier Days.* Cheyenne: Flintrock, 1967.

Hart, William S. *My Life: East and West.* Cambridge, MA: Riverside Press, 1986 (New York: Benjamin Bloom, 1929).

Hartnagle-Taylor, Jeanne Joy. *Greasepaint Matadors: The Unsung Heroes of Rodeo.* Loveland, CO: Alpine, 1993.

Heinz, W.C. *Once They Heard the Cheers.* Garden City, NY: Doubleday, 1979.

Hennessey, Paul. *"Tin Horn Hank" Keenan and the World's Youngest Cowboy.* Pierre, SD: State, 1993.

Holland, Ted. *B Western Actors Encyclopedia.* Jefferson, NC: McFarland, 1989.

Huey, William R. *In Search of Hollywood, Wyoming 1894— The Silent Years—1929.* Self-published, 1985.

Ingram, Wayne, and Jane Pattie. *Jasbo.* San Antonio: Naylor, 1959.

Ireland, Karin. *Hollywood Stuntpeople.* New York: Julian Messner, 1980.

Jackson, Ronald. *Classic TV Westerns.* New York: Citadel Press Book, Carol, 1994.

Johnson, Cecil. *Guts.* Fort Worth: Summit, 1994.

Jordan, Bob. *Rodeo History and Legends.* Montrose, CO: Rodeo Stuff, 1994.

Jordan, Teresa. *Cowgirls— Women of the American West.* Lincoln: University of Nebraska Press (updated Bison Book ed.), 1992.

Katchmer, George A. *Eighty Silent Film Stars: Biographies and Filmographies of the Obscure to the Well Known.* Jefferson, NC: McFarland, 1991.

Kennedy, Fred. *Calgary Stampede: The Authentic Story of the Calgary Exhibition and Stampede, "The Greatest Outdoor Show on Earth" 1912–1964.* Vancouver, British Columbia: West Vancouver Enterprises, 1965.

Knowles, Thomas W., and Joe R. Lansdale, eds. *Wild West Show!* New York: Random House, 1994.

Knucky, Ted. *Recollections of a Rodeo Cowboy.* New York: Carlton Press, 1996.

Lahue, Kalton C. *Riders of the Range: The Sagebrush Heroes of the Sound Screen.* New York: A.S. Barnes, 1973.

_____. *Winners of the West.* Secaucus, NJ: Castle Books, 1972.

Lamb, Gene. *R-O-D-E-O: Back of the Chutes.* Denver: Bell Press, 1956.

LeCompte, Mary Lou. *Cowgirls of the Rodeo.* Urbana: University of Illinois Press, 1993.

Leiby, Bruce R., and Linda Leiby. *A Reference Guide to Television's* Bonanza. Jefferson, NC: McFarland, 2001.

Leonard, John W. *Wild Bill Elliott,* N.p.: self-published, 1976.

Logsdon, Guy. *"The Whorehouse Bells Were Ringing" and Other Songs Cowboys Sing.* Urbana: University of Illinois Press, 1989.

_____, Mary Rogers and William Jacobson. *Saddle Serenaders*. Salt Lake City: Gibbs-Smith, 1995.

Ludtka, John. *The Tradition Lives, A 75-Year History of the Ellensburg Rodeo*. Ellensburg, WA: Ellensburg Rodeo Association, 1997.

Magers, Boyd, and Michael Fitzgerald. *Westerns Women: Interviews with 50 Leading ladies of Movie and Television Westerns from the 1930s to the 1960s*. Jefferson, NC: McFarland, 1996.

Mann, Al. *My Home was the Open Range of Wyoming*. Dodgeville, WI: The Dodgeville Chronicle, 1993.

Marschall, Rick. *The Encyclopedia of Country and Western Music*. New York: Exeter Books, 1985.

Maturi, Richard J., and Mary Buckingham Maturi. *Will Rogers, Performer: An Illustrated Biography with a Filmography*. Jefferson, NC: McFarland, 1999.

McClure, Arthur F., and Ken D. Jones. *Western Films — Heroes, Heavies and Sagebrush*. New York: A.S. Barnes, 1972.

McCoy, Tim. *Tim McCoy Remembers the West*. Lincoln: University of Nebraska Press, 1978.

McKinney, Grange B. *Art Acord and the Movies*. Raleigh, NC: Wyatt Classics, 2000.

Meyers, Monica. *Crashing Thru — My Life With Whip Wilson*. St. Louis: Robert T. Shockey, 1981.

Miller, Lee O. *The Great Cowboy Stars of Movies and Television*. Westport, CT: Arlington House, 1979.

Mix, Paul E. *Tom Mix: A Heavily Illustrated Biography of the Western Star, with a Filmography*. Jefferson, NC: McFarland, 1995.

Montana, Montie. *Not Without My Horse*. Agua Dulce, CA: Double M, 1993.

Moore, Clayton. *I Was That Masked Man*. Dallas: Taylor, 1996.

Morison, Samuel Eliot. *The Ropemakers of Plymouth: A History of the Plymouth Cordage Company 1824–1949*. Boston: Houghton-Mifflin, 1950.

Morris, Georgia, and Mark Pollard, ed. *Roy Rogers: King of the Cowboys*. San Francisco: Collins, 1994.

Murphy, Audie. *To Hell and Back*. New York: MJF Books, 1949.

Nareau, Bob. *Kid Kowboys, Juveniles in Western Films*. Madison, NC: Empire, 2003.

Nevins, Francis M. *The Films of Hopalong Cassidy*. Waynesville, NC: World of Yesterday, 1988.

_____. *The Films of the Cisco Kid*. Waynesville, NC: World of Yesterday, 1998.

Nicholas, John H. *Tom Mix Riding Up to Glory*. Oklahoma City: National Cowboy Hall of Fame and Western Heritage Center, 1980.

Norris, M.G. "Bud." *The Tom Mix Book*. Waynesville, NC: World of Yesterday, 1989.

O'Brien, P.J. *Will Rogers, Ambassador of Good Will, Prince of Wit and Wisdom*. Chicago, IL: John C. Winston, 1935.

Ohrlin, Glenn. *The Hellbound Train, Cowboy Songbook*. Urbana: University of Illinois Press, 1973.

O'Neal, Bill. *Tex Ritter, America's Most Beloved Cowboy*. Austin: Eakin Press, 1998.

O'Neal, Bill, and Fred Goodwin. *The Sons of the Pioneers*. Austin: Eakin Press, 2001.

Peel, John. *The Gunsmoke Years*. Las Vegas: Pioneer Books, 1989.

Phillips, Robert W. *Roy Rogers: A Biography, Radio History, Television Career Chronicle, Discography, Filmography, Comicography, Merchandising and Advertising History, Collectibles Description, Bibliography and Index*. Jefferson, NC: McFarland, 1995.

_____. *Singing Cowboy Stars*. Salt Lake City: Gibbs-Smith, 1994.

Porter, Willard H. *Who's Who in Rodeo*. Oklahoma City: Powder River Book, 1983.

PRCA Media Guides.

Professional Rodeo Cowboys Association. *The Finals, A Complete History of the National Finals Rodeo*. Colorado Springs, CO: Professional Rodeo Cowboys Association, 1998.

Rainey, Buck. *The Fabulous Holts*. Nashville: Western Film Collectors Press, 1976.

_____. *The Reel Cowboy: Essays on the Myth in Movies and Literature*. Jefferson, NC: McFarland, 1996.

_____. *Saddle Aces of the Cinema*. New York: A.S. Barnes, 1980.

_____. *The Strong, Silent Type: Over 100 Screen Cowboys, 1903–1930*. Jefferson, NC: McFarland, 2004.

_____. *Sweethearts of the Sage: Biographies and Filmographies of 258 Actresses Appearing in Western Movies*. Jefferson, NC: McFarland, 1992.

Rathmell, William. *The Life of the Marlows: A True Story of Frontier Life of Early Days as Related by Themselves (George and Charles Marlow)*. Ouray, CO: Ouray Herald Print, c. 1892.

Reynolds, Clay. *A Hundred Years of Heroes — A History of the Southwestern Exposition and Livestock Show*. Fort Worth: Texas Christian University Press, 1995.

Riske, Milt, and Joy Riske. *Cheyenne Frontier Days: A Marker from Which to Reckon All Events*. Cheyenne: Cheyenne Corral of Westerners, 1984.

Roach, Joyce Gibson. *The Cowgirls*. Denton: University of North Texas Press (updated and revised edition), 1990.

Roberson, Chuck, with Bodie Thorne. *The Fall Guy*. N. Vancouver, British Columbia, Canada: Hancock House, 1980.

Robinson, Ray. *American Original: A Life of Will Rogers*. New York: Oxford University Press, 1996.

Rogers, Roy, and Dale Evans, with Jane and Michael Stern. *Happy Trails: Our Life Story*. New York: Simon and Schuster, 1994.

Rogers, Roy, with Carlton Stowers. *Happy Trails: The Story of Roy Rogers and Dale Evans*. Waco: Word, 1979.

Rogers, Roy, Jr., with Karen Ann Wojahn. *Growing Up with Roy and Dale*. Ventura, CA: Regal Books, 1986.

Rogers-Barnett, Cheryl, and Frank Thompson. *Cowboy Princess*. Lanham, MD: Taylor Trade, 2003.
Rothel, David. *The Gene Autry Book* (revised ed.). Madison, NC: Empire, 1988.
_____. *The Roy Rogers Book*. Madison, NC: Empire, 1987.
_____. *The Singing Cowboys*. Cranbury, NJ: A.S. Barnes, 1978.
_____. *Those Great Cowboy Sidekicks*. Waynesville, NC: World of Yesterday, 1984.
_____. *Those Great Show Business Animals*. La Jolla, CA: A.S. Barnes, 1980.
_____. *Tim Holt*. Madison, NC: Empire, 1994.
_____. *Who Was That Masked Man?* La Jolla, CA: A.S. Barnes, 1981.
Rupp, Virgil. *Let 'er Buck — A History of the Pendleton Round-Up*. Pendleton, OR: Pendleton Round-Up Association, 1985.
Russell, Don. *The Wild West: A History of the Wild West Shows* Fort Worth: Amon Carter Museum of Western Art, 1970.
Russell, William C. *Legends of the Silent West*. Altamonte Springs, FL: A Western Revue Publication, 1998.
Rutherford, John A. *From Pigskin to Saddle Leather: The Films of Johnny Mack Brown*. Waynesville, NC: World of Yesterday, 1996.
Scar, Ethel. *The Great American — A John Wayne Biography*. Winterset, IA: John Wayne Birthplace Society, n.d.
Shapiro, Melany. *Bonanza — The Unofficial Story of the Ponderosa*. Las Vegas: Pioneer Books, 1993.
Simpson, Harold B. *Audie Murphy, American Soldier*. Hillsboro, TX: The Hill Junior College Press, 1975.
Smith, Fran Devereux. *Team Roping with Jake and Clay*. Colorado Springs: Western Horseman, 1998.
Stern, Jane, and Michael Stern. *Way Out West*. New York: HarperCollins, 1993.
Stone, Fred. *Rolling Stone*. New York: McGraw-Hill, 1945.
Summers, Neil. *The First Official TV Western Book*. Vienna, WV: The Old West Shop, 1987; and Vol. #2, 1989; Vol. #3, 1991; and Vol. #4, 1992.
Terrill, Marshall. *Steve McQueen: Portrait of an American Rebel*. New York: Primus, Donald I. Fine, 1994.
Tibbets, John C., and James Michael Welsh. *His Majesty the American: The Cinema of Douglas Fairbanks, Sr.* New York: A.S. Barnes, 1977.
Tinsley, Jim Bob. *For a Cowboy Has to Sing*. Orlando: University of Central Florida Press, 1991.
_____. *He Was Singin' This Song*. Orlando: University Press of Florida, 1981.
Toffel, Neile McQueen. *My Husband, My Friend*. New York: Atheneum Books, 1986.
Tuska, Jon. *The Filming of the West*. Garden City, NY: Doubleday, 1976.
Vaughn, Gerald F. *Ray Whitley: Country-Western Musicmaker and Film Star*. Newark, DE: Shamrock Printing, 1973.
Wakely, Linda Lee. *See Ya' Up There, Baby — The Jimmy Wakely Story*. Canoga Park, CA: Shasta Records, 1992.
Weiland, Victoria. *100 Years of Rodeo Stock Contracting*. Reno: Professional Rodeo Stock Contractors Association, 1997.
West, Richard. *Television Westerns: Major and Minor Series, 1946–1978*. Jefferson, NC: McFarland, 1998.
Westermeier, Clifford P. *Man, Beast, Dust, The Story of Rodeo*. Lincoln: University of Nebraska Press, 1947.
Williams-Jobe-Gibson Post No. 128, Inc., American Legion, Sidney, IA. *50 Years of Rodeo with Williams-Jobe-Gibson American Legion Post No. 128 Sidney, Iowa Rodeo*. Shenandoah, IA: Rodeo Printers, 1973.
Wills, Rosetta. *The King of Western Swing — Bob Wills Remembered*. New York: Billboard Books, 1998.
Wilson, Cheryl Landon. *I Promised My Dad*. New York: Simon and Schuster, 1992.
Witney, William. *Trigger Remembered*. Toney, AL: Earl Blair Enterprises, 1989.
Woerner, Gail Hughbanks. *A Belly Full of Bedsprings: The History of Bronc Riding*. Austin: Eakin Press, 1998.
_____. *Cowboy Up: The History of Bull Riding*. Austin: Eakin Press, 2001.
_____. *Fearless Funnymen: The History of the Rodeo Clown*. Austin: Eakin Press, 1993.
Yenne, Bill. *The Legend of Zorro*. New York: Mallard Press, 1991.
Yoggy, Gary A., ed. *Back in the Saddle: Essays on Western Film and Television Actors*. Jefferson, NC: McFarland, 1998.
Zmijewsky, Steve, Boris Zmijewsky, and Mark Ricci. *The Complete Films of John Wayne*. New York: Citadel Press, 1993.

Newspapers and Periodicals

Abilene (TX) Reporter-News
Acreage, Western Edition
Albuquerque (NM) Journal
Albuquerque (NM) Tribune
Alexandria (LA) Daily Town Talk
Amarillo (TX) Globe
Amarillo (TX) News
Amarillo (TX) Sunday News Globe
American Cowboy
The American Horseman
Ardmore (OK) Daily Ardmorite
Arizona Highways

Arizona (Phoenix) Republic
Arizona (Globe) Silver Belt
Arkansas (Little Rock) Gazette
Austin (TX) American Statesman
Bakersfield Californian
Baton Rouge (LA) Advocate Times
The Big Reel
The Big Trail
Black Hills (SD) Press
Blazing West
Boston (MA) Globe
Boston (MA) Pilot
Boston (MA) Record
Bristol Virginia Tennessean
Brockton (MA) Daily Enterprise
Brookhaven (MS) Leader-Times
The Buckboard
Buffalo (NY) Courier-Express
Burnet (TX) Bulletin
Burt County (NE) Plain Dealer
Caldwell (ID) News-Tribune
Calgary (Alberta) Herald
Camdenton (MO) Reveille
Canon City (CO) Daily Record
Casper (WY) Morning Star
Casper (WY) Star Tribune
Casper (WY) Tribune Herald
The Cattleman, Fort Worth, TX
Central Missouri Leader (Camdenton)
Channel Islands (CA) Gazette
Charlotte (NC) Observer
Chicago (IL) Daily News
Chicago (IL) Herald American
Chicago (IL) Sun
Chicago (IL) Tribune
Chiro Page, Windsor, Ontario
Claremore (OK) Daily Progress
Classic Images
Clear Lake (SD) Courier
Cleveland (OH) Plain Dealer
Cliffhanger
Clovis (CA) Independent
Cody (WY) Enterprise
Coffeyville (KS) Daily Journal
Colliers
Colorado Springs Free Press
Colorado Springs Gazette-Telegraph
Colorado Springs Sun
The Columbian (MO) Progress
Country and Western Variety
Cowboy
Cowboys and Country
Cowboys and Indians
Daily Oklahoman (Okla. City, OK)
Dallas (TX) Morning News
Denver (CO) Post
Des Moines (IA) Register
Deseret News (Salt Lake City, UT)
The Desert Sun (Palm Springs, CA)
Double R Bar Ranch News
Dubuque (IA) Telegraph Herald
Duncan (OK) Eagle
East Oregonian (Pendleton)
Edmonton (Alberta) Journal
Elk City (OK) Daily News
Eugene (OR) Register-Guard
Favorite Westerns
Films in Review
Fort Madison (IA) Evening Democrat
Fort Smith (AR) Times Record
Fort Worth (TX) Press
Fort Worth (TX) Star Telegram
Fowler (CO) Tribune
Fresno (CA) Bee
Gainesville (TX) Daily Register
Gene Autry's Friends
Gering (NE) Courier
Glenrock (WY) Independent
Golden West
Golden West Airlines Magazine
Graham (TX) Leader
Grant County (WI) (Herald) Independent
Great Bend (KS) Tribune
The Gringo, publication of The Tex Ritter Fan Club
Guns of the Old West
Guthrie (OK) Daily Leader
The Hereford Brand
Hockley County (Levelland, TX) Herald
Hoofs and Horns
Houston (TX) Post
Houston (TX) Press
Humboldt Times (Eureka, CA)
Huntsville (TX) Item
Idaho Free Press (Nampa)
Imperial Valley (Brawley, CA) News Press
Independence (MO) Examiner
Jackson (MS) Clarion Ledger
Jackson (MS) Daily News
Jasper (TX) News Boy
Journal of the American Academy for the Preservation of Old Time Country Music
Journal of Western Music
Kansas City (MO) Star
Kerrville (TX) Mountain Sun
The Ketchpen
Klamath Falls (OR) Herald (and News)
Lafayette (LA) Daily Advertiser
Lake Charles (LA) American Press
Las Vegas (NV) Review Journal
Las Vegas (NV) Sun
Lawton (OK) Constitution
Levelland(TX) Sun-News
Lewiston (ID) Morning Tribune
Life
Lodi (CA) News Sentinel
Los Angeles Examiner
Los Angeles Herald and Express
Los Angeles Mirror
Los Angeles Times
Louisville (KY) Courier-Journal
Lubbock (TX) Morning Avalanche
Lufkin (TX) News
McCook (NE) Daily Gazette
Mandan (ND) Daily Pioneer
Mangum (OK) Daily Star
Memphis (TN) Commercial Appeal
Miami (FL) Herald
Miles City (MT) Daily Standard
Milwaukee (WI) Journal
Minneapolis (MN) Times Tribune
Mohave County (Kingman, AZ) Miner
Montgomery (AL) Advertiser
Nevada State Journal (Reno)
The Nevadan
New York Post
New York Times
New York World Telegram
Newport (RI) News
Nogales (AZ) International
North Platte (NE) Telegraph
Nugget
Oakland (CA) Tribune
Odessa (TX) American
Oklahoma City Journal
Oklahoma City Times
The Oklahoma Roundup
Old Cowboy Picture Show
Omaha (NE) World-Herald
Orange (TX) Leader
Parade magazine
Pendleton (OR) Evening Tribune
Performance Horse
Persimmon Hill
Pine Bluff (AR) Commercial
Pittsburgh (PA) Post-Gazette
Plainview (TX) Herald
Pomona (CA) Progress-Bulletin
Ponca City (OK) News

Prescott (AZ) Courier
Prescott (AZ) Journal-Miner
ProRodeo Sports News, including Annuals and "Insight"
Providence (RI) Evening Bulletin
Providence (RI) Journal
Pueblo (CO) Chieftain
The Pueblo Lore
Pueblo (CO) Star Journal
The Quarter Horse
Raleigh (NC) News and Observer
The Ranchman
Rapid City (SD) Daily Journal
Rawlins (WY) Daily Tribune
Redding (CA) Record-Searchlight
Redwood City (CA) Tribune
Reno (NV) Gazette Journal
Riverside (CA) Daily Press
Rochester (NY) Democrat and Chronicle
Rocky Mountain News (Denver, CO)
Rodeo News
Rodeo Sports News
Sacramento (CA) Bee
Salinas Californian
Salt Lake (UT) Tribune
San Angelo (TX) Standard
San Antonio (TX) Light
San Diego (CA) Union
San Francisco Chronicle

San Francisco Examiner
San Saba (TX) News
Santa Clarita Valley Magazine
Santa Clarita Valley (CA) Signal
Santa Ynez (CA) Valley News
The Saturday Evening Post
Scott's Bluff County (Minatare, NE)
Seattle (WA) Times
Shawnee (OK) News-Star
Shreveport (LA) Times
Sidesaddle
Sidney (IA) Argus-Herald
Sikeston (MO) Standard
Silver State Post (Deer Lodge, MT)
Song of the West
Southwest Times-Record (Fort Smith, AR)
Spokane (WA) Spokesman Review
Spooner (WI) Advocate
Sports Illustrated
Springfield (MA) Republican
Stephenville (TX) Empire-Tribune
Steppin' Out, Lincoln, NM
Stockton (CA) Record
St. Joseph (MO) Post-Dispatch
Sulpher (OK) Times-Democrat
Taunton (MA) Gazette
This Week magazine

Time
Toledo (OH) Blade
Toppenish (WA) Daily Republic
Toronto (Ontario) Globe and Mail
Trail Dust
Tucson (AZ) Daily Citizen
Tucumcari (NM) Daily News
Tulsa (OK) Daily World
Tulsa (OK) Tribune
TV and Movie Western
Under Western Skies
Waco (TX) News-Tribune
Walters (OK) Herald
Washington D.C. Evening Star
Western Clippings
The Western Horse
The Western Horseman
Western Stars
Westerner
Wewoka (OK) Times-Democrat
Wichita Falls (TX) Daily News
Wildest Westerns
Winston-Salem (NC) Journal
World of Rodeo and Western Heritage
Wyoming Eagle (Cheyenne)
Wyoming State Tribune (Cheyenne)
Yesterday
Yippi Yi Yea Western Lifestyles
Yuma (AZ) Sun

Index

Aaker, Lee 290–293, 311
Acord, Art 7, 8, 35–36, 376
Adams, Nick 101
Adventures of Gallant Bess 311
The Adventures of Rin Tin Tin 290–293
The Adventures of Wild Bill Hickok 306–307
Agar, John 48
Akridge, Eddy 324, 343, 367
Ak-Sar-Ben Rodeo, Omaha, NE 250, 360
Albuquerque, NM, rodeos 360–361
Allen, Prairie Lily 8
Allen, Rex 53, 73, 76, 92, 101–110, 206, 250, 311, 318, 331, 332, 337, 364, 369, 371, 376, 383,
Allen, Rex, Jr. 75, 109
Alsace, Gene 178
Ambler, Jerry 8–9
Ames, Ed 248, 250
Anders, Laurie 364
Andrews, Arkansas Slim 17, 188
Andrews, Tod 110
Ansara, Michael 110–112
Archer, Pamela 183
Ardmore, OK, rodeos 361
Arena 311
The Arizona Cowboy 311
Arkansas-Oklahoma Rodeo, Fort Smith, AR 187, 357
Arkansas State Fair Livestock Show and Rodeo, Little Rock, AR 187, 358
Arness, James 252–254, 364, 372, 373
Arnold, Eddie 112, 129
Ates, Roscoe 310, 364
Austin, Tex 37, 51, 62, 96, 161, 322
Autry, Gene 2, 34, 35, 53, 54, 56, 60, 67, 77, 84, 112–123, 127, 134, 143, 146–148, 195, 210, 211, 213, 218, 308–310, 311, 312, 313, 316, 320, 326, 327, 331, 333, 337, 344, 345, 346, 364, 369, 379
Avalon, Frankie 88, 217–218, 376
Avalon Boys 224, 371

Back in the Saddle 311
Bailey, G.W. 369

Baker, Bob 9
Baker, Carroll 364
Baldwin, Tillie 9
Bannon, Jim 81–82, 187
Barnes, Frank 290, 291, 292–293
Barnes, Jake 28
Barry, Don "Red" 186, 364, 365
Barry, Gene 123
Barton, Buzz 10, 47
Bascom, Texas Rose 10, 11, 155
Basquette, Lina 155
Bauer, Elizabeth 369
Baugh, Sammy 10–11, 12, 361
Baze, Floyd 11
Bee, Molly 192
Beemer, Brace 268, 270, 378, 379–380
Beery, Noah, Jr. 123
Beery, Wallace 124, 365, 377, 379
Bell, Rex 39, 98, 124–125, 370, 371
Bells of Capistrano 312
"Ben-Hur chariot race" (arena act) 80
"Benson, Bobby" 125–126, 161
Berry, Ken 251
Big Boy Rides Again 312
The Big Show 313
The Big Valley 227–229
Biscailuz, Eugene 363
Blake, Amanda 255–256, 258–259, 367, 369
Blake, Bobby (Robert) 154, 187
Blancett, Bertha 11–12
Blaustein, Julian 372
Blessing, Faye (Johnson) 12–14, 37, 53, 198
Blessing, Wag 9, 313
Blocker, Dan 230, 231, 234, 372, 373, 376
Blue, Monte 379
Blyth, Ann 364
Bodrie, Joe 131
Bohlin, Edward 37
Bonanza 229–239
Bond, Johnny 116, 123, 126–127, 210
Bond, Ward 218, 304, 372
Boone, Richard 127–128, 364, 367, 372, 373
Booth, Adrian 163, 325
Born Reckless 14, 83, 313

Born to Buck 80, 92–93, 94
Boss, May 14, 313, 367–368
The Boss Rider of Gun Creek 313–314
Boston (MA) Garden rodeos 2, 161, 367
Bow, Clara 124
Bowman, Tillie and Ed 14
Boxleitner, Bruce 369
Boyd, William 97, 128–129, 206, 364, 371
Brady, Buff, Jr. 14–15, 117, 118, 188, 196, 198, 331
Brady, Pat 194, 195, 199, 201, 204, 205, 206, 383
Brady, Scott 314, 364, 380, 381
Bragg (Witmer), Nancy 223, 343
Brand, Neville 134
Brands, X 15
Branham, Craig 15
Breck, Peter 228–229, 370
Brennan, Walter 316, 324, 364
Brimley, Wilford 33, 129–130, 331, 369, 373
Brinegar, Paul 282, 283–284
Bromfield, John 130–131, 364, 371
The Bronc Stomper 27
Bronco Buster 72, 92, 96, 98, 314
Brooks, Doyle 291, 293
Brooks, Rand 291, 293, 319
Brown, Freckles 343–344
Brown, James 291–293
Brown, Joe E. 198
Brown, Johnny Mack Brown 34, 89, 131–132, 245, 371
Brown, Peter 132–134
Brown, Troy 15
Browne, Reno 15–17, 364, 370, 371
Buffalo Bill *see* Cody, William F. "Buffalo Bill"
Buffalo Bill Award 369–370
Buffalo Bill Rodeo, N. Platte, NE 369–370
The Bull-Dogger 75–76
Burmeister, A.H. "Hippy" 17, 365
Burnette, Smiley 60, 113, 134–135, 322, 326, 327, 369, 380
Burns, Bob 18
Burns, Forrest 18
Burns, Fred 17–18
Burson, Polly Mills 18–20, 30, 37,

393

40, 53, 54, 61, 117, 119, 196, 198, 330, 367–368, 379
Burson, Wayne 20, 32, 379
Burton, Bill 20
Burton, Hal 20
Bus Stop 44, 99, 314, 315
Buschbom, Jack 344
Busse, Hi 104, 105
Buttram, Pat 115, 134, 145, 364, 365

Caan, James 135–136, 365
Cabot, Bruce 379
Caldwell, Lee 22, 28
The Calgary Stampede 314–315
Calhoun, Rory 364
California Rodeo, Salinas, CA 365–367
Call, Kenny 20–21
Camdenton, MO, rodeos 360
Cameron, Rod 309–310, 372
Camp Pendleton Marine Rodeo, CA 363
Canary, David 238–239
Cangy, Dick 140
Canova, Judy 363
Canutt, Yakima 21–26, 28, 56, 74, 78, 160–161, 337, 358
Carey, Harry 36, 37, 43, 48, 56, 136–138, 218
Carey, Harry, Jr. 48, 53, 369, 371
Carey, Philip 134
Carolina Moon 316
Carrillo, Leo 34, 84, 88, 198, 240–246, 364
Carroll, John 364
Carson, Jack 364
Carson, Sunset 138
Case, Allen 139, 369, 376
Cash, Johnny 364, 373
Cass County Boys 119, 121, 146–147, 371
Castle, Peggie 132–134
Catching, Bill 244, 245
Cheetham, Everett 188
Cheshire, Harry 274, 280, 330
Cheyenne 316
Cheyenne Frontier Days, WY 160, 376–385
Chicago, IL, rodeos 165, 359
The Cisco Kid 239–247
Clift, Montgomery 32, 326, 372
Coates, Phyllis 35, 364
Coats, Tommy 26
Cody, Iron Eyes 369
Cody, William F. "Buffalo Bill" 1, 4, 5, 26
Cody, Wyoming 26
Coffin, Tristram 295–296
Colborn, Everett 15, 54, 117, 118, 119, 344, 345, 379
Coleman, Lloyd "Don" 26–27
Collier, Don 75, 267, 367
The Collins Kids 367
Colorado Springs, CO, rodeos 358
Colorado State Fair Rodeo, Pueblo, CO 358
Connelly, Edith Happy *see* Happy (Connelly), Edith

Connelly, Lex 43, 341
Connors, Chuck 285, 286, 287–290, 369, 376
Connors, Mike 364
Conrad, Robert 139–140, 383
Conrad, William 252
Coogan, Jackie 365
Coogan, Richard 364
Cooper, Clay O'Brien 27–28, 325
Cooper, Gary 48, 316, 317, 372
Cooper, Tex 28, 37, 118, 155, 320
Corbett, Ben 23, 28–29, 36, 323, 331, 333, 365
Corbett, Glenn 364
Corbin, Barry 336, 369
Cord, Alex 29–30, 369
Corday, Mara 364
Corrigan, Ray "Crash" 34, 341, 371
Cotton, Carolina 140–142, 364, 371
Courtney, Chuck 267
The Cowboy and the Blonde 316
The Cowboy and the Lady 316, 317
Cowboy Up 316
The Cowboy Way 316–317
Cowgirl races, Rockingham Park 367–368
Cox, Jimmy Don 50
Crabbe, Buster 142
Crawford, Johnny 64, 285–290
Creach, Everett 30
Cremer, Leo J. 119, 121, 122, 165, 348 153,
Cristal, Linda 265–267
Cronin, Joe 120
Crosby, Bing 330–331
Crouch, Worth 30
Crump, Pete 129
Culp, Robert 142–143, 367, 373, 375
Curtis, Ken 98, 187, 204, 259–263, 265, 369, 385
Cury, Ivan 126

Dalton, Abby 364
Dana, Viola 365, 371
Daniel Boone 247–250
Daniels, Charlie 93
Darrow, Henry 266–267
Davis, Gail 42, 96, 122, 143–148, 208, 364
Davis, Jimmie 268
Davis, Rufe 120
Days of '47 Rodeo, Salt Lake City, UT 362
Dean, Eddie 39, 118, 148–151, 190, 365
DeCarlo, Yvonne 364
DeFreest, Thelma "Babe" 20, 30, 365
Dent, Danny 30
Desert Trail 317
Desmond, William 365
Devine, Andy 195, 306–307, 369, 380, 382
Dightman, Myrtis 320–321
Dmytryk, Edward 372
Doc and Festus 256–263, 383, 385
Dodd, Jimmy 358

Dodds, John 30
Dollarhide, Ross 30, 320, 365, 367
Dortort, David 266–267
Dossey, Carl 51
Douglas, Mildred 30–31
Douthitt, Buff 31
Down Laredo Way 318
Drayer, Polly *see* Burson, Polly Mills
Dru, Joanne 218, 307–308
Drury, James 296–298, 369, 385
Dublin, TX, rodeos 344–346
Duncan, Lee 290, 291, 293
Dunstan, Dorothy 37
Durant, Don 151–153

Eastwood, Clint 43, 53, 282, 283, 367
Ebsen, Buddy 102, 247, 250
Edwards, Gerald 364
Edwards, Penny 163, 195
8 Seconds 62, 318
Eilers, Sally 37
The Electric Horseman 318
Ellerman, Troy 31
Elliott, Sam 95, 369, 373
Elliott, William "Wild Bill" 84, 120, 153–160, 187, 197, 198, 307, 310, 354–355, 364, 377, 379
Emerald Empire Rodeo, Eugene, OR 361
Erickson, Leif 265, 369
Eskew, Col. Jim 29, 37, 84, 155, 161, 196, 198, 246, 346, 347
Eskew, Junior 64, 346
Estes, Bob 60
Eugene, OR, rodeos 361
Evans, Dale 20, 53, 78, 96, 102, 194, 195, 196, 197, 198, 200, 201, 202, 203, 320, 324, 364, 385
Evetts, H.P. 31, 331

"F Troop" 251
Fairbanks, Douglas 82, 160–161, 376
Fancher, Sammy 31, 372, 373
Farnsworth, Diamond 33
Farnsworth, Richard 31–33, 155, 176–177, 322, 367, 369, 379
Favor, Jack 336
Feud of the West 318–319
Finley, Evelyn 33–34, 118
Finley, Larry 34–35, 118
Fireman's Rodeo, St. Louis, MO 360
Fisher, Orville 188
Fleming, Eric 281–283, 367
Fletcher, Curley 370
Fletcher, Tex 161
Flippen, Jay C. 372
Flying A Ranch Stampede/ Rodeo 117–118
Flynn, Errol 361
Fonda, Henry 56, 92, 139, 369
Foran, Dick 161–162, 370
Ford, Glenn 43, 162, 372
Ford, John 36, 43, 48, 50, 168, 218, 259, 371
Fort Madison, IA, rodeos 250, 359

Index

Fort Smith, AR, rodeos 250, 357
Fort Worth, TX, rodeos 166, 361
Foster, Preston 162, 362, 383
Fox (horse) 22
Francis, Anne 372
Frontier Town 188, 319
The Frontiersmen 104, 105, 228
Fuller, Robert 267, 269, 369

Garner, James 87
Garrett, Sam 35
Gatlin, Jerry 35, 320, 333
Gibson, Hoot 35–39, 46, 51, 53, 60, 65, 67, 82, 84, 88, 96, 98, 197, 198, 222, 322–323, 324, 334, 336, 338, 341, 365
Gilbert, Mickey 39
Gilbert, Nancy 274, 275, 279, 280, 380, 382, 383
Goetz, William 372
Gonzalez-Gonzalez, Pedro 106, 162
Grant, Johnny 365
Grant, Kirby 294–295, 310
Grant, Rodney 369
The Great American Cowboy 53, 58
The Great Bar 20 55–56
Greene, Lorne 47, 217, 230–231, 232–234, 373, 385
Greenman, Lsyle 60, 155
Greenough, Alice 39, 223
Greenough, Marge 39, 222, 223
Greenough, Thurkel "Turk" 39–40, 379
Greer, Joe 116
Griffin, Audrey O'Brien 95–96
Grimes, Tom 376
Guizar, Tito 162–163
Gulagher, Clu 56, 228, 299–300, 376
Gunsmoke 187, 252–265
Gwynne, Anne 364

Hale, Barbara 370
Hale, Monte 155, 163–164, 325, 364, 369
Hall, Donna 40–42
Hall, Sydney 95
Hamblen, Stuart 155, 164, 365
Happy, Don 42, 365
Happy (Connelly), Edith 42–43, 367–368
Hardin, Ty 164
Harley Davidson and the Marlboro Man 319
Harman, Fred 186–187, 208
Hart, Bill 43
Hart, John 365
Hart, Neal 43, 379
Hart, William S. 48, 165, 376, 379
Haver, June 364, 372
Hawkins, Jimmy 143, 364
Hawks, Howard 307
Hayden, Russell 222, 358, 371
Hayes, Edd 93
Hayes, George "Gabby" 154, 165–167, 194, 197, 198, 201, 319–320, 324, 325, 334, 370
Hayward, Chuck 43–44

Hayward, Susan 310, 324
Hayworth, Rita (Cansino) 337, 364
Heart of the Rockies 96, 319
Heart O'Texas Fair and Rodeo, Waco, TX 362
Heaton, Buddy 44
Heldorado 165, 195, 319–320
Helldorado Days Rodeo, Las Vegas, NV 162, 165, 319–320, 370–371
Henderson, Kelo 295–296
The Hendricks Family 44
Hendrix, Wanda 183
Henry, Buzz 44, 45, 319
Henry, Carol 32, 44
Henson, Chuck 44, 320, 336
Heston, Charlton 369
The High Chaparral 265–267
Hinkle, Robert 44
Holcomb, Homer 37, 44, 53, 72
Holden, Joyce 380, 381
Holliman, Earl 35, 340, 341
Holt, Jack 168, 307
Holt, Jennifer 167, 168, 310, 365
Holt, Nat 190
Holt, Tim 167–172, 218, 378, 380
Home in Wyomin' 320
The Honkers 58, 72, 74, 320
Hope, Bob 370
Horton, Robert 301–304, 311, 364, 373, 375
Houston Fat Stock Show Rodeo, Houston, TX 362
Howell, Chris 44
Hoxie, Jack 28, 46
Hudkins, Art and Ace 78, 83
Hughes, Howard 48
Hughes, Whitey 151
Humes, Fred 46, 47, 323
Huntsville, TX, prison rodeos 373–376
Hutchins, Will 56, 172–173, 364, 370

Ives, Burl 172, 333, 334

J Bar H Rodeo, Camdenton, MO 250, 360
Janes, Loren 367
Jauregui, Andy 10, 37, 42, 47–48, 363, 365, 367
Jauregui, Ed 47
Jaycee Bootheel Rodeo, Sikeston, MO 258, 360
JE Ranch Rodeo 116, 346
Johnson, Ben "Son" 21, 32, 33, 48–51, 76, 176, 322, 327, 328, 333, 337, 369, 371
Johnson, Ben, Sr. 48, 50
Johnson, Brad 51
Johnson, C.L. 51
Johnson, Col. W.T. 37, 219
Jones, Buck 58, 67, 370
Jones, Clarence "Fat" 40, 47, 48
Jones, Dick 122, 274–280, 370, 380, 382, 383
Jones, Stan 173, 206, 306
Jordan, John 51, 222
Jory, Victor 370

Junior Bonner 11, 50, 54, 178, 321–322
J.W. Coop 58, 80, 320–321

Keehn-Dashnaw, Tracy 51
Keel, Howard 364
Keene, Tom 333, 364, 365
Kell, Jess 69
Keller, Allan 51
Kelly, Jack 268, 364, 365
Kelly, Nancy 365
Kennedy, Burt 370
Kennedy, Douglas 173
Kentucky State Fair Rodeo, Louisville, KY 187, 359
Kid from Gower Gulch 322
King, Brad *see* Watt, Jack O.
King, Henry 372
King of the Cowboys 322
King of the Rodeo 37, 322–323
Kirby, Jay 52
Knapp, Jack 37, 52, 196, 322, 365
Knight, Harry 122, 344, 347–348
Krone, Fred 280

Ladd, Alan 372
A Lady Takes a Chance 323
Laine, Frankie 364
Lake Charles, LA, rodeos 359
Lambert, Mel 52–53, 194
L'Amour, Louis 51, 369
Landon, Michael 20, 234–238, 373, 383
Lane, Allan "Rocky" 196, 364
Langdon, Sue Ane 364
Laramie 267–268, 269
Laredo 132, 134
LaRue, Walt 32, 53
Las Vegas, NV, Helldorado Days 142, 370–371
Laswell, Frank 192
Laurie, Piper 364
Lee, Mary 379
Lee, Pinky 371
Lee, Ruta 365
LeFevour, Rick 53
Leffew, Gary 53, 316, 320
Lefton, Abe 37, 53, 168, 324, 326, 345
The LeGarde Twins 192
Leonard, Terry 54
Lerner, Fred 54
Let 'Er Buck 36, 323
The Light Crust Dough Boys 359, 361
Lights of Old Santa Fe 324
Linderman, Bill 348
Linkletter, Art 364
Little Rock, AR, rodeos 250, 357–358
Locke, Jon 297
Logan, Pete 54
The Lone Ranger 188, 197, 268, 270–273
Long, Richard 228, 229, 364
The Long, Long Trail 324
Lord, Jack 173–175, 339, 341
Los Angeles (CA) Sheriff's Rodeos 188–189, 363–364

Louisville, KY, rodeos 250, 359
Lucas, Sharon 54
Lucas, Shirley 54
Lucas, Tad 53
Lulu Belle and Scotty 102
Lund, John 98, 314, 380, 381
The Lusty Men 72, 324
Lybbert, Chris 55–56
Lyden, Pierce 154, 370
Lynn, Judy (Voiten) 121
Lyons, Cliff 56, 379

Mack, Cactus 101
Mackintosh and TJ 58, 195, 325
MacLaine, Shirley 364
MacMurray, Fred 175–176, 333, 334, 364, 372, 380
Madison, Guy 32, 306–307, 373, 376, 380, 382
Madison Square Garden, New York City, rodeos 161, 188, 373
Madsen, Harry 57
Mahan, Larry 57–58, 320, 325
Mahoney, Jock 122, 273–274, 275–280
Maloney, Leo 27
The Man from Rainbow Valley 325
The Man from Utah 325–326
Mann, Al 58
Mann, Anthony 372
Mansfield, Jayne 364
Mansfield, Toots 349
Marciano, Rocky 245
Markley, William "Bill" 58
Martin, Dude 141, 178
Martin, Richard "Chito" 168, 172
Martin, Ross 139
Maynard, Ken 37, 38, 58–60, 134, 149, 316, 338, 365
Maynard, Kermit 60–61, 334, 365
Mayo, O.W. 222
Mayo, Virginia 184–185
McAdams, Roy 61
McAuliffe, Leon 222, 383
McCarroll, Frank 61–62
McClure, Doug 296, 298–299, 369
McCoy, Tim 29, 78, 175, 369, 376, 379, 383
McCray, Wiley 62, 135, 320
McCrea, Joel 48, 358, 364
McDonough, Tom 192
McGaughy, Mike 62, 316
McGinnis, Vera 62
McGrath, Frank 304–306
McKay, Wanda 213
McLaglen, Victor 198
McLaughlin, Don 63–64
McLaughlin, Gene 63–64, 119
McQueen, Steve 32, 43, 176–178, 190, 321–322, 373
Medearis, Jimmy 64, 336
Mellor, William C. 372
Melody Trail 326, 327
Melton, Troy 244, 245
Memphis, TN, rodeos 361
Merlin, Jan 178
Merrill, Keith 58
Mesquite Buckaroo 326

Mid-South Fair Rodeo, Memphis, TN 250, 361
Miles, Betty 37, 178
Miller, John 50, 336
Mills (Aldred), Anna Lee 349
Mills, George 18, 37, 349–350
Mills, Hank 245, 349
Mills, Polly *see* Burson, Polly Mills
The Misfits 54, 326
Mitchell, Guy 178–180
Mitchum, John 297
Mix, Ruth 116, 125
Mix, Tom 23, 28, 31, 36, 51, 56, 64–67, 75, 84, 204, 327, 329, 346, 373, 374
Monroe, Vaughn 373
Montana, Linda 69
Montana, Louise 67, 69
Montana, Montie 37, 67–70, 198, 218, 363, 366, 385
Montana, Montie, Jr. 373
Montgomery, Baby Peggy 379
Montgomery, George 316, 365
Montgomery, Jack 379
Montgomery, AL, rodeos 357
Moore, Bennie 70
Moore, Clayton 268, 271, 273, 320, 364
More Than a Champion 76
Morgan, Dennis 364, 380, 381
Morrell, Dorothy 82
Morris, Wayne 357
Morrison, Pete 379
Motes, Dennis 71
Mounted Police Rodeo of the Stars, Palm Springs, CA 364–365, 366
Murdock, James 285
Murphy, Audie 159, 180–183, 364
Murphy, Hardy 116
Murphey, Michael Martin 370
My Heroes Have Always Been Cowboys 50, 327, 328
My Pal the King 327, 329

Nampa, ID, rodeos 358–359
Nebraskaland Days/Buffalo Bill Rodeo, N. Platte, NE 369–370
Nelson, Ricky 376
New Mexico State Fair Rodeo, Albuquerque, NM 250, 360–361
Newland, John 363
Nichols, Barbara 364
Nixon, Marion 323, 370
Nolan, Bob 204–205
Nolan, Kathy 178, 363
Norman, Lucille 364
North of 36 307
North Platte, NE, rodeos 369–370
Northwest Stampede 61, 327, 330
Nudie of Hollywood 145, 220

O'Brian, Hugh 38, 183–184
O'Brien, Clay *see* Cooper, Clay O'Brien
O'Brien, George 50, 218, 365
O'Dell, Doye 155, 184, 320, 365
O'Donnell, Doug 245
Old Fort Days Rodeo, Fort Smith, AR 357

Omaha, NE, rodeos 360
Ommert, Pat North 71, 367–368
Orrison, George 72
O'Shea, Black Jack 371
O'Shea, Michael 184–185, 364, 365

Paige, Janis 364
Painted Hero 330
Palm Springs, CA, rodeos 142, 162, 364–365, 366
Parker, Andy and the Plainsmen 364
Parker, Fess 247–250, 373, 383
Parker, Willard 383
Parkison, Chuck 72, 320, 324
Paul, Pat 72, 188
Peck, Gregory 74, 372
Peckinpah, Sam 51, 321
Penny, Hank 371
Pettigrew, Homer 350
Phelps brothers 218
Phoenix, AZ, rodeos 218, 250
Pickens, Slim 32, 37, 51, 53, 58, 62, 69, 72–75, 102, 176, 291, 318, 320, 367, 369, 373, 379, 383
Pickett, Bill 64, 75–76, 317, 321, 376
Pickwick Arena 54, 83
Pickwick Café 9
Pikes Peak or Bust Rodeo, Colorado Springs, CO 358
Pitchess, Peter 363
Plaugher, Wilbur 76, 367
Plymouth Cordage Company lariats 347
Poore, Dan 76, 102, 313
Portwood (Taylor), Jerry Ann 76–77, 188, 367–368
Power, Tyrone 56
Pratt, Jim 77
Preston, Robert 11, 321–322, 383
Preston, Wayde 383, 384
Prine, Andrew 340, 341, 364
Pruett, Gene 169
Pueblo, CO, rodeos 358
Pyle, Denver 369

Raines, Steve 77–78, 285
Ralston, Vera 155, 379
Rambo, Gene 350
Rand, Sally 379
Randall, Corky 78
Randall, Glenn 34, 78–80, 95, 102, 198, 203, 371, 383
Randall, Glenn, Jr. 80
Randles, Larry 80
Randolph, Florence Hughes 80
The Range Rider 273–280
Rawhide 187, 281–285
Ray, Wade 371
Reagan, Ronald 372
Red River 77, 307
"Red Ryder" 186–187
Reiners, Dennis 80, 320
Renaldo, Duncan 84, 239–240, 242–247
Reno, NV, Rodeo 371–373
Reynolds, Debbie 364
Reynolds, Don Kay "Little Brown Jug" 37, 81–82, 155, 187, 370

Reynolds, Fess 81
Reynolds, Max 82
Rhythm of the Saddle 331
Rhythm on the Range 330
Richards, Rusty 206, 207
Ride Him Cowboy 331
The Rifleman 285–290
Riley, Jeannine 187
Riley, Mitzi Lucas 350
Rin Tin Tin *see The Adventures of Rin Tin Tin*
Ritter, Tex 17, 34, 40, 77, 99, 149, 154, 187–190, 198, 337, 364, 370, 371
Riverside, CA, rodeos 142
Robbins, Skeeter Bill 37, 82, 333, 341
Roberts, Gerald 83, 118, 313
Roberts, Pernell 229–230
Robertson, Cliff 320–321, 373
Robertson, Dale 53, 88, 131, 148, 190–194, 364, 369, 371, 373, 374
Robinson, Ann 364, 372
Rockingham Park, Salem, NH 367–368
Rodeo 331
Rodeo Girl 95, 331, 332
Rodeo King and the Senorita 44, 331, 332
Rodeo Rhythm 331, 333
Rodeo train 344, 346
Rogers, Roy 37, 53, 77, 78, 81, 84, 96, 98, 119, 134, 143, 148, 165, 166, 194–203, 319–320, 322, 324, 325, 334, 335, 341, 346, 364, 370, 385
Rogers, Roy, Jr. "Dusty" 195, 202, 203
Rogers, Will 47, 64, 69, 76, 112, 190, 203–204, 209, 365, 379
Rogers, Will, Jr. 69, 364
Rooney, Lonnie 116
Rose, Fred 218
Ross, Katharine 331, 332, 373
Rossi, Rex 29, 37, 84–85, 198, 246
Rossi, Wanda 84
Rouse, Russell 372
Rovin Tumbleweeds 333
Ruby Jean and Joe 333
Run Appaloosa Run 54, 76
Russell, Jane 364, 373
Russell, John 132, 363
Rutherford, Buck 350–351

The Saddle Buster 333
St. Louis, MO, rodeos 250, 360
Salinas, Juan 349
Salinas, Tony 349
Salinas, CA, rodeos 365, 367
Salt Lake City, UT, rodeos 250, 362
San Antonio, TX, rodeos 362
San Bernardino, CA, rodeos 142, 293
Sanders, Sandy 85, 371
Sawyer, Joe 291, 293
Schumacher, Jimmy 76, 135, 202, 351–352
Scott, Gordon 383
Scott, Randolph 98, 273, 364

Scott, Walter 85, 333
Shahan, Rocky 32, 85–86, 285, 379
Shannon, Billy 86
Sheppard, Jim 86–87
Sheppard, Nancy Kelly 119, 353
Sherako, Peter 369
Sheridan, Ann 364
Sheriff's Rodeo, Los Angeles, CA 363–364
Sherman, Harry 128, 307, 371
Shoulders, Jim 352, 353–354, 355, 373
Shreveport, LA, rodeo 250, 360
Sikeston, MO, rodeos 360
Silver Spur Awards 371–373
Silverheels, Jay 20, 270, 272, 273
Six Bar Cowboys 218, 219
Sky Full of Moon 333
Sky King 293–295
Slade, Mark 266
Smith, Dean 87–88, 325
Smith, John 217, 267–268, 269, 373
Smith, Jute 60
Smith, Richard 279
Smith, William 134
"Smoky" (1946) 333, 334, 379
Snake River Stampede, Nampa, ID 250, 358–359
Somewhere in Sonora 333
Song of Texas 334, 335
Song of the Trail 334
The Sons of the Pioneers 102, 129, 155, 194, 195, 196, 197, 198, 200, 201, 203, 204–209, 250, 297, 310, 320, 322, 330, 357, 364, 379, 383, 385
Southeastern Livestock Exposition, Montgomery, AL 357
Southwest Exposition and Livestock Show Rodeo, Fort Worth, TX 361–362
Southwest Louisiana District Livestock Show and Rodeo, Lake Charles, LA 359–360
Spellman, Cardinal 119
Spirit of the West 334
Springsteen, R.G. "Bud" 96
Spurs 336
Stahl, Jesse 47, 321
Stallone, Frank 369
Stanwyck, Barbara 227, 364
Starrett, Charles 134, 204, 379, 380
Steele, Bob 38, 39, 84, 98, 326, 338, 371
Steiner, Tommy 123, 150, 155–159, 354–355
Stevens, George 372
Stewart, Don 37, 88, 155, 223
Stewart, James 372
Still Holding On: The Legend of Cadillac Jack 336
Stir Crazy 64
Stockman, Boyd 32, 89, 245, 322
Stoker, J.W. 89–90
Stone, Cliffie 365
Stone, Fred 204, 209, 376
Stone, Milburn 256–259, 261–262, 369

Stoney Burke TV series 43, 72, 339, 341
Storch, Larry 251
Strange, Glenn 37, 101, 149, 263–265, 324, 337, 385
Strickland, Mabel 37, 89, 98, 365
Stroud, Leonard 91, 316
Sundown, Jackson 22
Sweet, Tom 151
Switzer, Carl "Alfalfa" 201

Taillon, Cy 54
Take Willy with Ya 39
Tatum, John 91
Taylor, Buck 264–265, 369, 385
Taylor, Dub 154, 188, 264–265, 358
Taylor, Harry 347
Taylor, Robert 190, 380
"Texas" arena show 15, 72, 77, 188
Texas Prison Rodeo, Huntsville, TX 250, 373–376
Thompson, Hank 371, 380
Thompson, Sue 371
Thorpe, Jim 155
Thurman, Sammy *see* Fancher, Sammy
Tibbs, Casey 35, 48, 72, 91–94, 104, 130, 324, 337, 341
Tipperary (horse) 23
Tolbert, R.L. 95, 331
The Tomboy and the Champ 337
Tompkins, Harry 104, 355
Tracy, Spencer 372
Travis, Merle 123, 210
Tri-State Rodeo, Fort Madison, IA 359
Trouble in Texas 337
Truth or Consequences, NM, rodeos 142
Tryon, Tom 178
Tucker, Forrest 251
Tucson, AZ, rodeos 142
Tulsa 310
Turner, Lana 364
Tuttle, Wesley 188, 211
26 Men 295–296

Ugland, Rudy 95
Under Fiesta Stars 337
The Unknown Cavalier 338
U.S. Marine Rodeo, Camp Pendleton, CA 363
The Utah Kid 338

The Valkyries 95–96, 319
Van, Alice 37, 96, 198, 365
Vaughn, Gerald F. vii
The Virginian 296–300

Waco, TX, rodeos 250, 362
Wagon Train 301–306
Wakely, Jimmy 116, 149, 177, 210–215, 370
Walker, Clint 215–217, 234, 364
Warren, Charles Marquis 252
Warren, Dale 206, 209
Washbrook, Johnny 364
Watt, Jack O. 96–97, 371
Watts, Black Jack 247

Wayne, John 48, 50, 56, 217–218, 253, 307, 308, 317, 323, 325–326, 331, 333, 364, 371, 372, 373, 376
Wayne, Pat 35, 373
Weadick, Guy 65
Weaver, Dennis 254–255, 258–259
Webster, Shoat 355–356
Wells, Ted 97
Western, Johnny 72, 122, 385
Whatley, Todd 356
When the Legends Die 338, 341
The Whipporwills 199
Whitecloud, Tony and the Jemez Pueblo Indian dancers 115, 121
Whitley, Ray 119, 168, 198, 218–219, 280, 371
Whitmore, James 373
Wide Country TV series 72, 340, 341
Wilbur, George P. 97
Wild Bill Hickok see *The Adventures of Wild Bill Hickok*
Wild Horse 341
Wild Horse Rodeo 341
Williams, Bill (stuntman) 97–98, 314

Williams, Bill "Kit Carson" 364, 370
Williams, Esther 364
Williams, Guinn "Big Boy" 39, 98, 312, 370
Williams, Guy 32, 220
Williams, Paris 37, 98, 365
Williams, Tex 220, 221, 313
Willing, Foy and the Riders of the Purple Sage 69, 122, 148, 166, 195, 197, 198, 199, 319
Wills, Bob 163, 221–223
Wills, Chill 44, 58, 222, 223–224, 314, 330, 365, 380, 385
Wills, Johnnie Lee 172, 221–223
Wilsey, Jay 98–99
Wilson, Ben 23, 25
Wilson, Terry 304–306, 367, 376
Wilson, Whip 211, 224–225, 364
Winters, Gloria 294–295
Withers, Jane 365
Womack, Andy 99
Wood, Britt 371
Wood, Natalie 364
Woods, Ray 182, 183

Woodward Relief Rodeo, Okla. City, OK 307–310
Wooley, Sheb 284–285, 324, 333
Worden, Hank 99, 88, 316, 337
World's Championship Rodeo, Boston Garden, MA 367
World's Championship Rodeo, Madison Square Garden, New YorkCity, NY 293, 373
Wright, Wen 100
Wyatt, Al 254
Wyatt, Walter 100
Wymore, Patrice 364

Yates, Herbert J. 117, 154, 155, 239, 379
Young, Tony 372

Zimmerman, Fred 372
"Zorro" *see* Williams, Guy

www.ingramcontent.com/pod-product-compliance
Lightning Source LLC
Chambersburg PA
CBHW081533300426
44116CB00015B/2617